Fodor's

HONG KONG

WELCOME TO HONG KONG

Hong Kong's gravity-defying skyline is breathtaking, especially when the sun goes down and the glittering glass towers are reflected in Victoria Harbour. Take it all in from a vintage ferry, or ride the rumbling tram up lofty Victoria Peak. At street level, spot British colonial landmarks in Central or explore the maze-like alleys of Kowloon. Cramped antiques shops and sprawling malls packed with designer boutiques lure shoppers. A million shades of neon point the hungry masses to storefront noodle shops and penthouse-level restaurants with wraparound views.

TOP REASONS TO GO

★ **Amazing eats:** Dim sum reigns supreme, and celebrity chefs reinvent classic dishes.

★ **Marvelous markets:** Whether you want goldfish or gold earrings, you'll find them here.

★ **Sacred spaces:** The Tian Tan Buddha beckons, as do many other spots to find enlightenment.

★ **After dark:** Everyone from hipsters to high-rollers can indulge in serious barhopping.

★ **Artsy vibe:** Traditional treasures and cutting-edge modern works draw art lovers.

★ **Great outdoors:** Amazing hikes, verdant parks, and far-flung beaches provide some R&R.

Fodor's HONG KONG

Publisher: Amanda D'Acierno, *Senior Vice President*

Editorial: Arabella Bowen, *Editor in Chief*; Linda Cabasin, *Editorial Director*

Design: Tina Malaney, *Associate Art Director*; Chie Ushio, *Senior Designer*; Randy Glance, *Production Designer*

Photography: Jennifer Arnow, *Senior Photo Editor*; Mary Robnett, *Photo Researcher*

Production: Linda Schmidt, *Managing Editor*; Evangelos Vasilakis, *Associate Managing Editor*; Angela L. McLean, *Senior Production Manager*

Maps: Rebecca Baer, *Senior Map Editor*; David Lindroth, *Cartographers*

Sales: Jacqueline Lebow, *Sales Director*

Marketing & Publicity: Heather Dalton, *Marketing Director*; Katherine Punia, *Publicity Director*

Business & Operations: Susan Livingston, *Vice President, Strategic Business Planning*; Sue Daulton, *Vice President, Operations*

Fodors.com: Megan Bell, *Executive Director, Revenue & Business Development*; Yasmin Marinaro, *Senior Director, Marketing & Partnerships*

Copyright © 2015 by Fodor's Travel, a division of Random House LLC

Writers: Charley Lanyon, Maloy Luakian, Dorothy So, Kate Springer

Editors: Mark Sullivan, Susan MacCallum-Whitcomb

Production Editor: Carolyn Roth

24th Edition   *5 6 6 / 7 9 9 5*

ISBN 978-1-101-87819-4

ISSN 1070-6887   *6 / 15*

SPECIAL SALES

This book is available at special discounts for bulk purchases for sales promotions or premiums. For more information, e-mail specialmarkets@penguinrandomhouse.com

PRINTED IN THE UNITED STATES OF AMERICA

10 9 8 7 6 5 4 3 2 1

CONTENTS

CONTENTS

ABOUT
THIS GUIDE

Fodor's Recommendations

Everything in this guide is worth doing—we don't cover what isn't—but exceptional sights, hotels, and restaurants are recognized with additional accolades. **Fodor's Choice★** indicates our top recommendations; and **Best Bets** call attention to notable hotels and restaurants in various categories. Care to nominate a new place? Visit Fodors.com/contact-us.

Trip Costs

We list prices wherever possible to help you budget well. Hotel and restaurant price categories from $ to $$$$ are noted alongside each recommendation. For hotels, we include the lowest cost of a standard double room in high season. For restaurants, we cite the average price of a main course at dinner or, if dinner isn't served, at lunch. For attractions, we always list adult admission fees; discounts are usually available for children, students, and senior citizens.

Hotels

Our local writers vet every hotel to recommend the best overnights in each price category, from budget to expensive. Unless otherwise specified, you can expect private bath, phone, and TV in your room. For expanded hotel reviews, facilities, and deals visit Fodors.com.

Top Picks	Hotels &
★ **Fodor's**Choice	**Restaurants**
	🏨 Hotel
Listings	⤵ Number of
✉ Address	rooms
✉ Branch address	⧖ Meal plans
☎ Telephone	✖ Restaurant
🖷 Fax	⚑ Reservations
⊕ Website	🏛 Dress code
✍ E-mail	▭ No credit cards
🎟 Admission fee	$ Price
⊙ Open/closed	
times	**Other**
Ⓜ Subway	⇨ See also
⊹ Directions or	☞ Take note
Map coordinates	🏌 Golf facilities

Restaurants

Unless we state otherwise, restaurants are open for lunch and dinner daily. We mention dress code only when there's a specific requirement and reservations only when they're essential or not accepted. To make restaurant reservations, visit Fodors.com.

Credit Cards

The hotels and restaurants in this guide typically accept credit cards. If not, we'll say so.

EUGENE FODOR

Hungarian-born Eugene Fodor (1905–91) began his travel career as an interpreter on a French cruise ship. The experience inspired him to write *On the Continent* (1936), the first guidebook to receive annual updates and discuss a country's way of life as well as its sights. Fodor later joined the U.S. Army and worked for the OSS in World War II. After the war, he kept up his intelligence work while expanding his guidebook series. During the Cold War, many guides were written by fellow agents who understood the value of insider information. Today's guides continue Fodor's legacy by providing travelers with timely coverage, insider tips, and cultural context.

EXPERIENCE HONG KONG

HONG KONG TODAY

Hong Kong's skyline of gleaming glass towers, streets plastered with neon signs, and alleys crammed with street vendors have long served as the backdrop for local and international films, but this multifaceted city's charms go beyond its photogenic qualities. Steeped in a hot pot of cultural influences, Hong Kong is full of surprises for everyone from first-timers to those who've visited year after year.

Cosmopolitan city. Living up to the title of Asia's World City, Hong Kong is a buzzing stage that attracts millions of visitors from all over the globe. Business travelers pass through frequently because it's so close to China, and Hong Kong's soaring market development makes it one of the world's leading financial hubs. And just as many people come here for leisure travel. Navigation is easy within the city center, since road signs, maps, and directions on public transportation are spelled out in Chinese and English. Most major tourist attractions—including museums, parks, and performance venues—also have bilingual directories and information centers. While the city has a distinct tradition of its own, you'll also find foreign influences embedded in its culture, language, food, and lifestyle.

Shopper's paradise. You can score great bargains here on everything from electronics to clothing—on top of heavily discounted prices on many items, there's no sales tax. You'll find all the world-renowned brands at modern shopping malls and boutiques in the main shopping hubs of Central, Causeway Bay, and Tsim Sha Tsui, but it's worth visiting the loud and crowded local markets, where you can haggle for cheap trinkets. At the larger markets, like the one on Temple Street in Yau Ma Tei and Tung Choi Street in Mong Kok, most of the vendors are used to tourists and can speak basic phrases of English. Fashion and design connoisseurs might want to look into the independent boutiques hidden away in complexes such as Island Beverly mall in Causeway Bay or in trendy areas like Tai Ping Shan Street, Star Street, and Tin Hau. These shops offer unique items from local and international designers, but be warned that they don't usually open before noon.

Food lovers' delight. There is no reason not to eat well in Hong Kong, regardless of your budget. While Hong Kong's Michelin-starred Asian and European restaurants continue to add names to their wait lists, it's also not unusual to

WHAT'S NEW

Although its reputation as a world-class shopping and dining destination is well known, Hong Kong has also been making a real effort to showcase its many cultural attractions. Historic sites—known here as heritage buildings—are being rejuvenated into cultural hubs, the latest being the Former Hollywood Road Police Married Quarters in Central, now more commonly known to locals as the PMQ. Visitors will find shops and markets featuring local designers, as well as regular arts events at a location whose historical significance dates back to 1889.

The arts scene in Hong Kong is growing every year. The upscale galleries might give you sticker shock, however. Affordable Art Fair Hong Kong recently appeared on the art

see queues outside humble-looking local eateries and *dai pai dongs*—the open-air food stalls that line Temple Street and other major arteries. Immigrants from other parts of Asia also marked out their territories on the city's culinary map, with Kowloon City known for its Thai food, Tsim Sha Tsui for Indian and Korean, and Causeway Bay for Japanese. In the hip neighborhoods of Hong Kong many trendy restaurants have opened their doors to an eager clientele. Private kitchens were once the rage, and small restaurants serving artisanal cuisine continue to flourish. Waves of food trends in Hong Kong also mean that every other year or so there's a boom in restaurants serving a particular dish or cuisine, with ramen being the most recent craze.

Getting greener. Despite its expansive rural landscape, Hong Kong has always been identified more as a concrete jungle plagued by urban development and inner-city pollution than as an eco-destination. But the times they are a-changin', and residents have really stepped up their efforts to turn their home into an eco-friendly city. The most notable change is the increase of interest in farming and a back-to-basics lifestyle, especially from the younger community. Weekend trips to farms out in the New Territories are gaining popularity as a way to relieve stress from the hustle and bustle of city life. And while Hong Kong's size makes it difficult to find arable land, some enterprising farmers are looking up and building rooftop gardens right in the heart of the city. Restaurants are also doing their part, with more chefs designing menus based on sustainable seafood and locally grown produce.

Focused on Health. In recent years traditional Chinese medicine has received a lot of holistic hype in the West. Around here, though, it's been going strong for a while—more than 2,000 years, to be precise. Although modern Hong Kongers may see western doctors for serious illnesses, for minor complaints and everyday pick-me-ups they still turn to traditional remedies. To get to the root of your body's disequilibrium, a traditional Chinese medicine practitioner takes your pulse in different places, examines your tongue, eyes, and ears, and talks to you. Your prescription could include herbal tonics, teas, massage, dietary recommendations, and acupuncture.

scene, providing collectors a less expensive alternative to Art Basel Hong Kong.

This developing focus on the arts has permeated all other aspects of Hong Kong life, as seen by the much-heralded appearance of Duddell's, a new bar and restaurant in Central's posh Shanghai Tang Mansion. Designed to look like the luxurious interior of an art-collector's residence, Duddell's also functions as a gallery, performance space, and hub for creative minds.

The gay community comes out louder and prouder every year.

The annual Pride Parade saw a record turnout with legislative councilors and notable celebs—including Tat Ming Pair's vocalist Anthony Wong and Cantopop songstress Denise Ho—banding together to speak up for gay rights and same-sex marriage.

WHAT'S WHERE

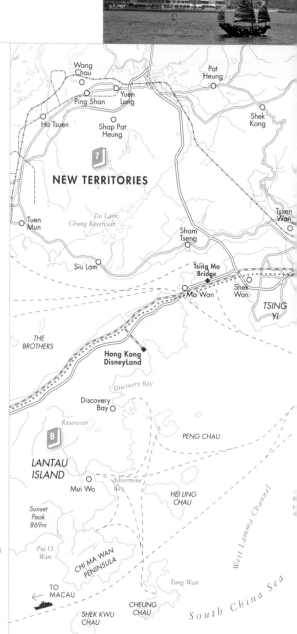

1 Western. Just west of the skyscrapers, this older and quieter neighborhood of Hong Kong Island has long been known for its Chinese medicine and antiques shops, temples, and the tram. Nowadays it's becoming a hip area where visitors can find quirky restaurants, cafés, and shops.

2 Central. Hong Kong's world-famous finance hub extends through Admiralty and boasts skyline high-rises, including the city's tallest office building. Head up the Mid-Levels Escalator to enjoy drinks in trendy SoHo or take the funicular to Victoria Peak for postcard views of the city and harbor.

3 Wan Chai, Causeway Bay, and Eastern. Wan Chai still has its strip of harmless red-light venues, though not so far away are furniture and home-accessories shops and wine bars. Shoppers flock to Causeway Bay's Times Square, Hysan Place, Sogo, and Lee Gardens, as well as the many boutique shops that pepper the area. Happy Valley has the racecourse, where for a small entrance fee you can cheer on your favorite horse.

4 Southside. Stanley, with its colonial remnants, outdoor market, waterfront restaurants, and annual Dragon Boat

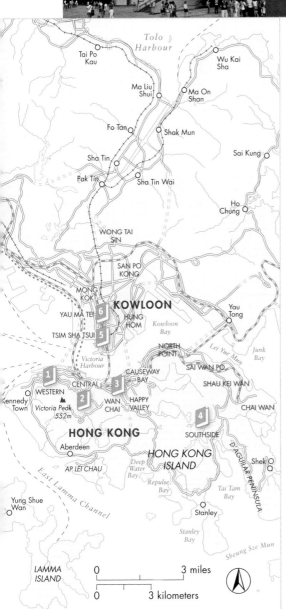

races, may be Southside's obvious destination. But don't let it stop you from visiting beaches, from Repulse Bay to Shek O, at the start (or finish) of the Dragon's Back scenic hiking trail. Or play with the pandas at Ocean Park.

5 Tsim Sha Tsui. Moving across the harbor to Kowloon, Tsim Sha Tsui begins at the 50-year-old Star Ferry Terminal followed by the eastward promenade along the Avenue of Stars, which offers front-row views of the famous Hong Kong Island skyline.

6 Yau Ma Tei, Mong Kok, and Northern Kowloon. Yau Ma Tei and Mong Kok are the epicenters of night and day markets, where you can score souvenirs and knickknacks on the cheap. North of here are residential areas and attractions, including the famed Kowloon Walled City Park.

7 New Territories. Hong Kong's least developed areas are the sites of still-inhabited historic villages and relatively unspoiled natural beauty, in addition to the Ten Thousand Buddhas Monastery and Hong Kong Heritage Museum in the new town of Sha Tin.

8 Lantau Island. Of the Hong Kong archipelago of 260 islands, Lantau is by far the largest. It's home to the Big Buddha and Disneyland.

HONG KONG PLANNER

Looks Deceive

On the surface, Hong Kong is a big, chaotic jumble of bustling alleys and streets punctuated by imposing skyscrapers and shopping malls. A closer look reveals the marks of a century of colonialism and several thousand years of Chinese ancestry. Then, notice that rural mountains, forests, and outlying islands comprise more than 70% of Hong Kong's land mass.

Visitor Information

Swing by the Hong Kong Tourist Board (HKTB) visitor center before even leaving the airport. It publishes stacks of helpful, free exploring booklets and maps, offers free classes and workshops on local culture, runs a plethora of tours, and operates a multilingual helpline. Its detailed, comprehensive website is a fabulous resource. If you're planning on visiting several museums in a week, pick up a Museum Weekly Pass, which gets you into seven museums for HK$30. Buy it at participating museums or at the visitor center at the Tsim Sha Tsui Star Ferry Concourse.

Hong Kong Tourist Board (*HKTB*). ☎ *2508–1234* ⊕ *www. discoverhongkong.com.*

Wording It Right

Learn to recognize a few basic Cantonese expressions such as "*lei-ho?*" ("hello, how are you?") and "*mm-goi*" ("excuse me" or "thank you"). Hong Kong's official languages are Chinese and English, but the native dialect is Cantonese. Mandarin Chinese has gained popularity here and in Macau.

In hotels, large stores, international restaurants, and clubs, most people speak English. Many taxi and bus drivers and staffers in small shops, cafés, and market stalls do not.

Ask MTR (Mass Transit Railway) employees or English-speaking policemen, identifiable by their red-striped epaulets, for directions. Get your concierge to write down your destination in Chinese if you're headed off the main trail.

Open Hours

Business hours for most shopping malls and boutiques are from 11 am until 8 or 9 pm, though hours may be extended during weekends and festive seasons. Small family-owned businesses might close for big public holidays—especially Chinese New Year—but major operations, supermarkets, and chain stores usually stay open year-round.

Hong Kong will keep you well fed through the day and deep into the night. Breakfast can start as early as 6 am with options such as congee, dim sum, or scrambled eggs on toast with a glass of milk tea. In between lunch and dinner, most cha chaan tengs (Hong Kong–style cafés) offer an afternoon tea menu, which is basically the regular menu at a discounted price. Typical closing time for restaurants is 10:30 or 11 pm, but you'll find plenty of late-night dining establishments, including street snack stalls that sell local delicacies, including fish balls on a stick, until well past midnight.

After dinner, take advantage of Hong Kong's buzzing nightlife scene. Bars and clubs stay open until the wee hours of the morning. Or you can rent a private room and sing the whole night away at one of the many karaoke lounges in town.

Getting Around

Hong Kong's streets may seem utterly chaotic, but the public transport system is not. Be sure to purchase a rechargeable Octopus card, which can be used on all buses, trains, and trams, the ferry, and even to make purchases at vending machines, convenience stores, supermarkets, fast-food restaurants, some shops, and the racetrack.

The quickest and perhaps safest way to travel is with the ever-reliable MTR (underground railway), which links to most of the areas you'll want to visit. There's no timetable because trains run so frequently. Signs and announcements are in both Chinese and English, and posted maps help visitors navigate outside the stations, too.

Although you can cross the harbor on the MTR, the Star Ferry is a cheaper ride, with the added bonus of letting you enjoy the fantastic harbor views during the 10-minute journey between Hong Kong Island and Tsim Sha Tsui. Fast and regular ferries are also available for the outlying islands, although you can take a sampan or hire an air-conditioned junk for the day.

If you prefer street-level travel, the city's air-conditioned double-decker buses can take you anywhere, provided you know which number and route to take. On the northern side of Hong Kong Island you can also take the tram (listen for the distinctive "ding-ding"), a fun and inexpensive way to get from one side of the island to the other—and it's the same route that the MTR follows, so you should be able to walk to an MTR station from any tram stop between Sheung Wan and Shau Kei Wan.

If you do get lost, you can always hail a cab. Prices are reasonable if you're not traveling too far, and tipping is not required. Not all drivers are willing to cross the harbor, though, so be sure to ask before getting in. Unless it's a designated cross-harbor vehicle, expect to be charged for the return-trip toll as well.

Perhaps best of all, Hong Kong is a city that's easy to explore on foot. In Central, a covered walkway connects major buildings in the business district, and Mid-Levels is easily accessed by an outdoor escalator, thus avoiding stoplights, exhaust fumes, and weather conditions (but not crowds). The same can apply to the pedestrian overpasses all around the city.

When to Go

High season, from September through late December, sees sunny, dry days and cool, comfortable nights. January and February are mostly cool and damp, with periods of overcast skies. March and April are pleasant, and by May the temperature is consistently warm and comfortable.

June through August are the cheapest months for one reason: they coincide with the hot, sticky, and very rainy typhoon (hurricane) season. Hong Kong is prepared for blustery assaults; if a big storm approaches, your hotel will post the appropriate signals (a No. 10 signal indicates the worst winds; a black warning means a rainstorm is brewing). This is serious business—bamboo scaffolding and metal signs can hurtle through the streets, trees can break or fall, and large areas of the territory can flood. Museums, shops, restaurants, and transport shut down at signal No. 8, but supermarkets, convenience stores, and cinemas typically stay open.

Hong Kong Temperatures

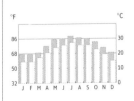

HONG KONG TOP ATTRACTIONS

Mid-Levels Escalator
(A) The longest outdoor covered escalator system in the world covers half a mile of moving stairs, walkways, and passageways from the business hub of Central to the residential heights of Mid-Levels. Step off a few flights up from Central in SoHo or on Hollywood Road for gallery hopping, eating out, or pub crawling.

Victoria Peak
(B) At 1,810 feet above sea level, the peak is Hong Kong Island's highest hill above the harbor. Buy a ticket for the 125-year-old Peak Tram, take in the postcard views, pop into the Police Museum, then take a scenic nature walk or bus ride back down to Central.

Mong Kok Markets
(C) Flowers, birds, goldfish, turtles, and jade by day; clothes, sneakers, toys, and knickknacks by night. And there's always food around Temple Street. Visit the stronghold of the Triads (secret-society gangs) on Nathan Road, or wander down Sai Yeung Street, which is full of snacks, buskers, and touts.

Kowloon Walled City Park
(D) Exempted from British rule and abandoned by the Chinese following their treaty in 1842, the Walled City grew into a lawless, labyrinthine slum occupied by Triads, gambling houses, brothels, and disease. In 1995 it was resurrected as a peaceful and expansive Qing Dynasty–style garden. The documentary photos and restored South Gate remnants exhibit how far the park has come.

Tian Tan Buddha
(E) The Ngong Ping 360 cable-car ride can take you only so far. The true path to divine ascension is by way of 268 steps leading up to the 275-ton Tian Tan Buddha (the Big Buddha), which sits on a hill next to the Po Lin Buddhist Monastery. Nearby is the Wisdom Path, a beautiful walk that offers splendid views.

1

Dragon's Back Trail

(F) This hiking trail across the southeast end of Hong Kong Island will give you a whole new perspective of Hong Kong, though you don't need to be an athlete to walk the undulating ridge.

Victoria Harbour

(G) There's no better way to see the city than from the water, so taking a cruise on Victoria Harbour is on every first-timer's itinerary. The city skyline looks incredibly modern, especially when surrounded by the more distant mountains. For the full treatment, take a ride in a traditional junk.

Ocean Park

(H) This popular theme park has exciting rides as well as up-close access to some of the world's most fascinating animals. The park is best known for its marine-life exhibits, the grand aquarium, and spectacular dolphin shows. Make sure to pay a visit to the giant panda habitat, too.

Wong Tai Sin Temple

(I) One of the busiest religious shrines in the city, Wong Tai Sin Temple is perpetually packed with dedicated worshippers looking to have their prayers answered or their fortunes read. The complex itself is a stunning structure that houses the teachings of Taoism, Buddhism, and Confucianism. The temple can get crazily crowded during major Chinese festivities, so check the lunar calendar before you go if you want to avoid the madness.

Chi Lin Nunnery

A tranquil oasis in the middle of residential Diamond Hill, the nunnery and surrounding garden are built in the Tang Dynasty style and feature Buddhist treasures and relics. Every object in the garden—from the stones to the plants—has been placed according to specific traditional rules. A well-regarded vegetarian restaurant and teahouse is also located in the park.

TOP EXPERIENCES

Yum Cha
No trip to Hong Kong is complete without a *yum cha* (translates into "drink tea") experience. Along with their tea, guests nibble on small plates of delicacies and bamboo steamers of designed-to-share dim sum. Traditionally, yum cha is available for breakfast and lunch, but there are many dedicated restaurants that serve made-to-order dim sum all through the day.

Ride the Star Ferry
The iconic Star Ferry has been shuttling passengers across Victoria Harbour for more than a century. Today's green-and-white boats are relics of the '50s and '60s. Take one from either Wan Chai or Central to Tsim Sha Tsui, then turn around and admire that famous Hong Kong skyline. At night, catch the eye-popping Symphony of Lights show.

Take the Tram
These rattling cars have become giant rolling advertisements, carrying everyone from schoolboys to grannies through all the main street action straight across Hong Kong Island. Climb aboard at off-peak hours on an early weekday afternoon for a leisurely ride from the busy Western Market terminus to Happy Valley or Victoria Park.

Nightlife in Lan Kwai Fong
Hong Kong has no shortage of after-hours hangouts, but for the most concentrated stretch of clubs and bars, head to Lan Kwai Fong. Options here range from casual beer joints to happening dance clubs, and everything is concentrated in a small area, so it's easy to hop from one venue to the next.

Mid-Levels Escalator
The longest outdoor covered escalator system in the world covers half a mile of moving stairs, walkways, and passageways from the business hub of Central to the residential heights of Mid-Levels. Step off a few flights up from Central in SoHo or on Hollywood Road to check out the galleries, restaurants, and bars. Note that the escalators go in only one direction during rush hour, so be prepared to take the stairs if you're heading in the opposite direction.

Go to the Races
Even if you're not a gambler, it's worth heading to Hong Kong's tracks in Happy Valley and Sha Tin. It's a multimillion-dollar-a-year business, and the season runs from September through June and draws serious crowds. In the public stands the vibe is electric and loud, thanks to the gamblers shouting and waving their newspapers madly. Out of money? You can still grab a beer and a slice of pizza from the food stands and enjoy live music as the horses thunder past.

Take a Walk
In town you can take in colonial architecture during an hour-long stroll through Western between the University of Hong Kong and Western Market. Or try walking across Central through buildings linked by covered pedestrian passages. You can also head for the hills and hike along the Dragon's Back or up to Lion Rock.

FREE AND ALMOST FREE

It's easy to spend money in the big city: shopping, entrance fees, food, shows, late-night cocktails. But if you'd like to put your wallet away for a while, here are some of our favorite options.

Art

Visitors are free to browse antiques and art works by Asian prodigies at private galleries in Central, SoHo, Sheung Wan, Chai Wan, and Aberdeen. Kowloon Park's winding Sculpture Walk features 20 works—including an Eduardo Paolozzi—against a leafy backdrop. And be sure to keep your eyes open at the malls, most notably Harbour City and Times Square, where you'll see pop-up art exhibitions.

Bird-Watching

See our feathered friends up close and personal without leaving town—either at the Yuen Po Street Bird Garden in Kowloon or at the Edward Youde Aviary in the heart of Hong Kong Park.

Bright Lights

Victoria Harbour's Symphony of Lights is performed every evening at 8 to a crowd of mesmerized visitors and proud residents. Music and narration blast through low-fi outdoor speakers as 44 skyscrapers are synchronized to light up on cue. Watch from the waterfront promenade in Tsim Sha Tsui, Golden Bauhinia Square in Wan Chai, or the InterContinental Hotel's lobby lounge.

Culture Classes

The Hong Kong Tourist Board runs free classes on feng shui, kung fu, Cantonese opera, and Chinese tea appreciation. If you prefer a more immersive experience, a tai chi master will guide you through the moves at the Sculpture Court, just outside the Hong Kong Museum of Art, every Monday, Wednesday, and Friday morning at 8.

Enlightenment

Inner peace is priceless, and though it's customary to make a small donation, all of Hong Kong's temples are free. Don't miss out on Man Mo Temple in Sheung Wan, dedicated to Man, the god of literature, and Mo, the god of war. Built in the 19th century, the temple is still visited regularly by locals, especially students looking to pass exams.

Heritage

Visit the Hong Kong Heritage Museum in Sha Tin on a Wednesday, when admission is free of charge for the whole family. This expertly curated museum chronicles Hong Kong's changing face, from scattered fishing and farming communities to booming towns. The Hong Kong Museum of Art, Museum of History, Museum of Coastal Defence, Science Museum, Space Museum, and Dr. Sun Yat-sen Museum also offer free admission on Wednesday.

Views

It doesn't cost a cent to ride up to the Bank of China's 43rd-floor observation deck, or to visit the Hong Kong Monetary Authority on the 55th floor of the International Finance Centre, for fabulous harbor views over to Kowloon. Get the reverse vista from the Tsim Sha Tsui waterfront promenade. For a glorious panoramic bay view of Victoria Park, visit the fifth and sixth floors of the main library in Causeway Bay.

BEST FESTS AND FÊTES

Traditional Festivals

Cheung Chau Bun Festival. Thousands make the yearly trip to Cheung Chau Island for the exuberant Cheung Chau Bun Festival, a four-day-long Taoist thanksgiving feast. A procession of children dressed as gods winds its way toward Pak Tai Temple, where 60-foot towers covered in sweet buns quiver outside—the idea is that people climb the towers to collect the buns; the higher the bun the better the fortune bestowed on the person. It's held on the eighth day of the fourth moon, usually in May.

Chinese New Year. The loudest and proudest traditional festival, Chinese New Year brings Hong Kong to a standstill each year. Shops shut down, and everywhere you look there are red and gold signs, kumquat trees, and pots of yellow chrysanthemums, all considered auspicious. On the lunar new year's eve the crowds climax at the flower markets and fairs; on the first night there's a colorfully noisy parade; on the second night the crowds ooh and ahh at the no-costs-spared fireworks display over the harbor. It's usually in late January or early February.

Dragon Boat Festival. The Dragon Boat Festival pits long, dragon-head boats against one another in races to the shore; the biggest event is held at Victoria Harbour. The festival commemorates the hero Qu Yuan, a poet and scholar who drowned himself in the 3rd century BC to protest government corruption. These days it's one big beach party. It's usually held in June.

Hong Kong Arts Festival. Held each year in February and March, the Hong Kong Arts Festival has hosted Mikhail Baryshnikov, Pina Bausch, and José Carreras in the past. The focus is on performing arts. ⊕ *www.hk.artsfestival.org.*

Lantern Festival. The Chinese New Year festivities end with the overwhelmingly red Lantern Festival. Hong Kong's parks—especially Victoria Park—become a sea of light as people, mostly children, gather with beautifully shaped paper or cellophane lanterns. It's also a traditional day for playful matchmaking, so it's particularly auspicious for single people. It's held on the 15th day of the first moon, usually in February.

Mid-Autumn Festival. Families and friends gather to admire the full moon while munching on moon cakes, which are traditionally stuffed with lotus-seed paste, though many other varieties—from chocolate to black truffle—are also popular. Colorful paper lanterns fill Hong Kong's parks, and a 220-foot-long "fire dragon" dances through the streets of Tai Hang near Victoria Park. Look for it in September or October.

Nontraditional Events

Clockenflap. Hong Kong's answer to Coachella, Clockenflap has brought major musical acts to the city, including Primal Scream, Santigold, and the Cribs. Concertgoers can sit on grassy patches surrounding the stages or can check out the multimedia art exhibitions and film tent. Expect it in November or December. ⊕ *www.clockenflap.com.*

Wine and Dine Festival. Every year the Hong Kong Tourism Board throws a month-long culinary extravaganza packed with restaurant deals, tours, and food-themed street carnivals. The highlight event is the four-day Wine and Dine Festival at the New Central Harbourfront, which has colorful booths offering tasty snacks and tipples, as well as live music and entertainment. It's usually held in late October or early November.

TOURING
HONG KONG

With so many things to see and do in bustling Hong Kong, it can be daunting to tackle it all by yourself. If you want to leave the planning to someone else, there are some excellent guided tours catering to all sorts of interests.

General Tours

Big Bus Tour. These double-decker tourist buses cover three routes—Hong Kong Island, Kowloon, and Stanley—with recorded commentary in ten languages. Tourists can hop on or off at any stop along the way to take in the neighborhood sights. There's also a night-time bus tour that takes visitors through the neon-lit streets of Tsim Sha Tsui, Mong Kok, and Yau Ma Tei. ☎ 2723–2108 ⊕ *www.bigbustours.com*.

Gray Line Heritage Tour. Perfect for history buffs, the Gray Line Heritage Tour takes visitors to the sites of Hong Kong's five great clans in the New Territories. The route stops at several well-preserved monuments, including Tai Fu Tai—the home of a Man clan scholar in the late 1800s. There's also a chance to visit a historic walled village as well as a traditional ancestral hall. Before you leave, don't forget to make a wish under the Lam Tsuen Banyan Trees. Tours are scheduled on Monday, Wednesday, Friday, and Saturday. ⊠ *Cheong Hing Building, 72 Nathan Rd., 5th fl., Tsim Sha Tsui* ☎ 2368–7111 ⊕ *www.grayline.com.hk*.

Kowloon Market Walk. With its mazelike detours and dizzying neon signs, Kowloon can be a bit chaotic for the first-time visitor, but a guided Kowloon Market Walk will take you through the nooks and crannies of Yau Ma Tei and Mong Kok. You'll shop at famed street markets that sell everything from fine jade to cheap clothing and brightly colored goldfish in small plastic bags. ☎ 9187–8641 ⊕ *www.walkhongkong.com*.

Nature Walks

Tai Po Kau Nature Walk. This company hosts guided trails through the Tai Po Kau forest in the New Territories. The forest is known for its wide variety of flora and fauna and is popular for bird-watching. Guests have a chance to visit a butterfly garden during the half-day tour. ☎ 9187–8641 ⊕ *www.walkhongkong.com*.

Offbeat Tours

Fodor's Choice ★ | **Dialogue in the Dark Exhibition.** A truly unique way to experience Hong Kong, the Dialogue in the Dark Exhibition is a simulated tour of the city from the perspective of the visually impaired. The walk covers five iconic scenes of the city, including a ride on the Star Ferry and a trip to the market. The whole tour is conducted in pitch-black darkness, allowing visitors to experience their surroundings through their other senses. ⊠ *The Household Centre, 8 King Lai Path, 2nd fl., Mei Foo* ☎ 2310–0833 ⊕ *www.dialogue-in-the-dark.hk* ⊘ *Closed Mon*.

Foodie Tasting Tour. Celebrating the vibrant flavors of Hong Kong, the Foodie Tasting Tour takes visitors to six restaurants either in Central and Shueng Wan or Sham Shui Po, with a certified foodie guide who will help you decipher menus and will talk you through the traditional eating customs at each stop. All meals are included in the ticket price. Arrive hungry, because you'll be feasting on everything from wonton noodles to freshly steamed dim sum. ☎ 2850–5006 ⊕ *www.hongkongfoodietours.com* ⊘ *Closed Sun*.

HIKING

Although most visitors to Hong Kong don't come for the lush lowlands, bamboo and pine forests, rugged mountains with panoramas of the sea, or secluded beaches, nature is never very far from all the city's towering skyscrapers. About 40% of Hong Kong's territory is protected in 23 parks, including four marine parks and one marine reserve.

Don't expect unspoiled wilderness, however. Few upland areas escape Hong Kong's plague of hill fires for more than a few years at a time. Partly because of these fires, most of Hong Kong's forests, except for a few spots in the New Territories, have no obvious wildlife other than birds—and mosquitoes. Still, you can enjoy magnificent views along many of the hiking trails, most of which are easily accessible by public transportation.

Getting Ready

Necessities include sunglasses, hat, bottled water, bug repellent, day pack, and sturdy hiking boots. Weather tends to be warm during the day and cool toward nightfall. Check the weather before you set off: Hong Kong Observatory (⊕ *www. hko.gov.hk*) has special forecasts for hiking and mountaineering.

Remember to familiarize yourself with your trail to avoid getting lost. Pick up a guide like *Hong Kong Hikes* from any bookstore.

Trails

★ **Fodor's Choice** **Dragon's Back.** One of the most popular trails crosses the "rooftop" of Hong Kong Island. Take the Peak Tram from Central up to Victoria Peak, and tackle as much or as little of the range as you feel like—there are numerous exits downhill to public transport networks. The surprisingly wild countryside feels a world away from the urban bustle

below, and the panoramas—of Victoria Harbour on one side, and Southside and outlying islands on the other—are spectacular. You can follow the trail all the way to the delightful seaside village of Shek O, where you can relax over a casual dinner before returning to the city by bus or taxi. The most popular route, and shorter, is from Shek O Country Park, which has three hiking trails. To get here, take the MTR from Central to Shau Kei Wan, then Bus 9, and alight after the first roundabout.

Lion Rock. The easiest way to access the trail to Lion Rock, a spectacular summit, is from Kowloon. The hike passes through dense bamboo groves along the Eagle's Nest Nature Trail and up open slopes to Beacon Hill for 360-degree views over hills and the city. The contrasting vistas of green hills and the cityscape are extraordinary. There's a climb up the steep, rough track to the top of Lion Rock, a superb vantage point for appreciating Kowloon's setting between hills and sea. The trail ends at Wong Tai Sin Taoist Temple, where you can have your fortune told. To start, catch the MTR to Choi Hung (25 minutes from Tsim Sha Tsui) and a 10-minute taxi ride up Lion Rock to Gilwell Campsite. At the end of the road you'll see a sign indicating the start of the trail. From Wong Tai Sin, return by MTR.

★ **Fodor's Choice** **MacLehose Trail.** Named after a former Hong Kong governor, the 97-km (60-mile) MacLehose Trail is the grueling course for the annual MacLehose Trailwalker charity event. Top teams finish the hike in an astonishing 15 hours. Mere mortals should allow three to four days or simply tackle one section on a day hike.

This isolated trail starts at Tsak Yue Wu, beyond Sai Kung, and circles High Island Reservoir before breaking north. A portion takes you through the Sai Kung Country Park and up a mountain called Ma On Shan. Turn south for a high-ridge view, then walk through Ma On Shan Country Park. From here, walk west along the ridges of the mountains known as the Eight Dragons, which gave Kowloon its name.

After crossing Tai Po Road, the path follows a ridge to the summit of Tai Mo Shan (Big Hat Mountain), which, at 3,140 feet, is Hong Kong's tallest mountain. Continuing west, the trail drops to Tai Lam Reservoir and Tuen Mun, where you can catch public transport back to the city. To reach Tsak Yue Wu, take the MTR to Diamond Hill, then Bus 92 to Sai Kung Town. From Sai Kung Town, take Bus 94 to the country park.

An easier way to access Tai Mo Shan is via an old military road. En route you'll see the old British barracks, now occupied by the People's Liberation Army. Take the MTR to Tsuen Wan and exit the station at Shiu Wo Street, then catch Minibus 82.

Wilson Trail. The 78-km (48-mile) trail runs from Stanley Gap on the south end of Hong Kong Island, through rugged peaks that have a panoramic view of Repulse Bay and the nearby islands, and to Nam Chung in the northeastern New Territories. You have to cross the harbor by MTR at Quarry Bay to complete the entire walk. The trail is smoothed by steps paved with stone, and footbridges aid with steep sections and streams. Clearly marked with signs and information boards, this popular walk is divided into 10 sections, and you can easily take just one or two (figure on three to four hours per section); traversing the whole trail takes about 31 hours.

Section 1, which starts at Stanley Gap Road, is only for the very fit. Much of it requires walking up steep mountain grades. For an easier walk, try Section 7, which begins at Sing Mun Reservoir and takes you along a greenery-filled, fairly level path that winds past the eastern shore of the reservoir in the New Territories and then descends to Tai Po, where there's a sweeping view of Tolo Harbour. Other sections will take you through the monkey forest at the Kowloon Hill Fitness Trail, over mountains, and past charming villages. To reach Section 7, take the MTR to Tsuen Wan, then catch Minibus 82. Get off at the bus terminus and walk for 15 minutes toward the main eastern dam. Turn left where the dam ends and you'll find the start of the trail.

HONG KONG WITH KIDS

One child's buzz is another child's bore, so plan a variety of amusements to keep everyone entertained. Hong Kong has two major amusement parks, but so many more opportunities to laugh and learn at museums, parks, and wildlife reserves.

Hong Kong Disneyland

Hong Kong's version of the Magic Kingdom, on Lantau Island, is as polished as all the other Disneys but much smaller. You can easily go on every ride at least once and see all the attractions in a day. If your kids are theme-park savvy, the tame rides here won't win their respect, but there is lots to entertain littler kids. Space Mountain is the most thrilling ride, though the U-shaped RC Racer at Toy Story Land also gets a few screams. Otherwise, watch the Festival of the Lion King, or just wait for the fireworks.

Hong Kong Park

This large public park has stunning architecture against a backdrop of lush greenery. The highlight is the Edward Youde Aviary, home to about 600 birds of 90 species indigenous to the endangered rain forests around Southeast Asia. Plant lovers should pay the Forsgate Conservatory a visit.

Hong Kong Zoological and Botanical Gardens

Hong Kong has grown around these gardens, which opened in 1864, and although they're now watched over by skyscrapers, a visit here is still a delightful escape. Burmese pythons, Chinese alligators, Bali mynahs, Bornean orangutans, ring-tailed lemurs, and lion-tailed macaques are among its 400 birds, 70 mammals, and 50 reptiles in the zoo enclosures.

Ocean Park

This homegrown marine theme park offers a balance of toned-down thrills and high-octane rides suitable for toddlers to teenagers, as well as a giant aquarium and the popular giant-panda enclosure. The park stretches out over 200 hilly acres, which you can gaze down upon from the cabins of the mile-long cable car that connects the tamer Lowlands area to the action-packed Headland.

Science Museum

Kids can spend a full day bouncing from one exhibition zone to another at this science-themed museum. Take the fitness challenge or learn about light, sound, and motion through interactive presentations and activities. The museum is closed on Thursday; Wednesday is free admission.

CENTRAL HONG KONG AND KOWLOON

Updated by
Kate Springer

The Hong Kong Island skyline, with its ever-growing number of skyscrapers, speaks to ambition and money. Paris, London, and even New York were already centuries in the making when Hong Kong's gleaming glass towers landed it on the map as one of the world's leading financial centers.

Commerce is concentrated in the glittering high-rises of Central, tucked between Victoria Harbour and the forested peaks on Hong Kong Island's north shore. While it's easy to think all the bright lights are the sum of today's Hong Kong, you need only walk or board a tram for the short jaunt west into the Western neighborhood to discover a slower-paced side of Hong Kong that is more traditionally Chinese. You'll discover the real Hong Kong to the east of Central, too, in Wan Chai, Causeway Bay, and beyond. Amid the residential towers are restaurants, shopping malls, bars, convention centers, a nice smattering of museums, and—depending on fate and the horse you wager on—one of Hong Kong's most fortuitous spots, the Happy Valley Racecourse.

Across Victoria Harbour, Kowloon sprawls across a generous swath of the Chinese mainland. Tsim Sha Tsui, at the tip of Kowloon peninsula, is packed with glitzy shops, first-rate museums, and eye-popping views of the skyline across the water. Just to the north are the teeming market streets of Mong Kok, and two of Hong Kong's most enchanting spiritual sights, Wong Tai Sin Temple and Chi Lin Nunnery, in the dense residential neighborhoods beyond.

As you navigate this huge metropolis (easy to do on the excellent transportation network), keep in mind that streets are usually numbered odd on one side, even on the other. There's no baseline for street numbers and no block-based numbering system, but street signs indicate building numbers for any given block.

WESTERN

Sightseeing
☆★★★
Dining
☆☆★★
Lodging
☆☆★★
Shopping
☆☆★★

2

Despite its name, the Western district is the part of Hong Kong that has been least affected by western influence. Many of the narrow, jammed streets that climb the slopes of Victoria Peak seem to be light-years from the dazzle of Central, just a 15-minute walk down the road. Though developers are making short work of the traditional architecture, Western's colonial buildings, rattling trams, old-world medicine shops, and lively markets still recall bygone times. Western is a foodie's idea of heaven, as you'll soon discover when you step into Sheung Wan Wet Market on Queen's Road Central or browse the dried delicacies—abalone, bird's nests, sea cucumbers, mushrooms—in shops around Wing Lok Street and Des Voeux Road.

TOP ATTRACTIONS

Hong Kong Museum of Medical Sciences. You can find out all about medical breakthroughs at this private museum, which is housed in an Edwardian-style building at the top of Ladder Street. The 11 exhibition galleries cover 10,000 square feet, and present information on both western and Chinese medical practices. ⊠ *2 Caine La., Western* ☏ *2549–5123* ⊕ *www.hkmms.org.hk* ⌂ *HK$20* ⊘ *Tues.–Sat. 10–5, Sun. and holidays 1–5* Ⓜ *Sheung Wan, Exit A2.*

Man Mo Temple. No one knows exactly when Hong Kong Island's oldest temple was built—but the consensus is sometime between 1847 and 1862. The temple is dedicated to the Taoist gods of literature and of war: Man, who wears green, and Mo, dressed in red. The temple bell, cast in Canton in 1847, and the drum next to it are sounded to attract the gods' attention when a prayer is being offered. ⊠ *124–126 Hollywood Rd., Sheung Wan, Western* ⊘ *Daily 8–6* Ⓜ *Sheung Wan, Exit A2.*

Fodor's Choice
★

University Museum and Art Gallery. Chinese harp music and a faint smell of incense float through peaceful rooms filled with a small but excellent collection of Chinese antiquities. On view are ceramics and bronzes, some dating from 3,000 BC, as well as paintings, lacquerware, and carvings in jade, stone, and wood. Some superb ancient pieces include ritual vessels, decorative mirrors, and painted pottery. The museum has the world's largest collection of Nestorian crosses, dating from the Mongol Period (1280–1368). There are usually two or three well-curated temporary exhibitions on view; contemporary artists who work in traditional mediums are often featured. The collection is spread between the T.T.

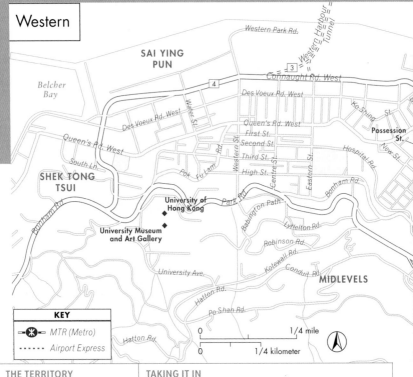

Western

SAI YING PUN

Belcher Bay

Western Park Rd.

Western Harbour Tunnel

Connaught Rd. West

Des Voeux Rd. West

Ko Shing St.

Des Voeux Rd. West

Water St.

Queen's Rd. West

First St.

Possession St.

Second St.

Western St.

New St.

Queen's Rd. West

Third St.

Hospital Rd.

South Ln.

Pok Fu Lam Rd.

High St.

Eastern St.

SHEK TONG TSUI

Bonham Rd.

Bonham Rd.

Centre St.

University of Hong Kong

Park Rd.

Babington Path

Lyttelton Rd.

University Museum and Art Gallery

Robinson Rd.

Kotewall Rd.

University Ave.

Conduit Rd.

MIDLEVELS

Hatton Rd.

Po Shan Rd.

KEY

Hatton Rd.

━●✕━ MTR (Metro)

· · · · · Airport Express

0   1/4 mile

0   1/4 kilometer

THE TERRITORY

Several main thoroughfares run through Western parallel to the shore: Des Voeux Road (where the trams run), Queen's Road, Hollywood Road, and Caine Road.

Western technically reaches all the way to Kennedy Town, where the tram lines end, but there's not much of interest for a sightseer beyond Sheung Wan and Sai Ying Pun.

TAKING IT IN

Colonial Architecture. You can see Western's colonial buildings on an hour-long stroll from the University of Hong Kong (take a cab or bus out). Heading east along Bonham Road, which becomes Caine Road, are Victorian apartments. The Museum of Medical Sciences is at Caine Lane. Head down the staircase, then left onto Hollywood Road to Possession Street. Follow this downhill, doglegging right and left through Bonham Strand, onto Morrison, and to the Western Market.

Traditional Goods. An hour is enough time to wander Sheung Wan's traditional shops. In the morning, when trade's brisk, take the tram to Wilmer Street. Walk a block south and turn left onto Queen's Road West (herbal remedies, temple goods). Walk left for a block at Possession, then loop left through Bonham Strand West (ginseng), right for a block at Des Voeux, then back along Wing Lok (dried seafood). Continue on Bonham Strand (bird's nests), dipping left onto Hillier (snakes) and beyond to Man Wa Lane (chops).

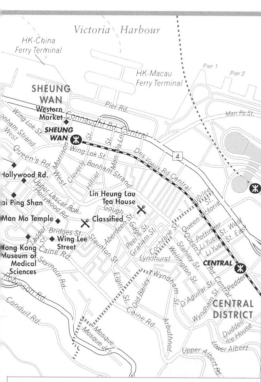

GETTING AROUND

The most scenic way to cross Western is on a tram along Des Voeux Road; the route runs all the way from Central to Sheung Wan. From Central this is probably the quickest route into Western: no traffic, no subway lines, no endless underground walks. There are stops every two or three blocks. The Sheung Wan MTR station brings you within spitting distance of Western Market. Alternatively, Bus 3B runs between Jardine House in Central and the university, as does green Minibus 8. Buses 40 and 40M also run through Central to the university.

QUICK BITES

Gage Street's *dai pai dongs* (street-stall restaurants) are great for Hong Kong fast food, like a bowl of steaming wonton noodles.

Classified. Sit on weathered wooden benches at Classified and sample cheeses from a vast selection. Or have a coffee, a glass of wine, or a hearty plate of pasta. ⊠ *108 Hollywood Rd., Sheung Wan, Western* ☎ *2525–3454* ⊕ *www. classifiedfood.com.*

Lin Heung Lau Tea House. Cracked Formica tabletops, cranky waiters, and old men reading the newspapers: there's nothing fancy about Lin Heung Lau Tea House, but it's been doing great dim sum for years. Stop by any time after 6 am and fill up on such dishes as *har gow* (steamed shrimp dumplings) and *char siu bao* (barbecue pork buns), washed down with lots of tea. ⊠ *160–164 Wellington St., Sheung Wan, Western* ☎ *2544–4556.*

Tsui Building, where there is a Tea Gallery, and the Fung Ping Shan Building, which you access via a first-floor footbridge. The museum is a bit out of the way—20 minutes from Central via Buses 3B, 23, 40, 40M, or 103, or a 15-minute uphill walk from Sheung Wan MTR—but it's a must for the true Chinese art lover. ⊠ *University of Hong Kong, 90 Bonham Rd., Western* ☎ *2241–5500* ⊕ *www.hkumag.hku.hk* ⊡ *Free* ⊙ *Mon.–Sat. 9:30–6, Sun. 1–6* Ⓜ *Sheung Wan.*

WORTH NOTING

Hollywood Road. Hong Kong's best antiques shops and classical-art galleries are on this street, named for the holly trees that once grew here. The western end of this historic street has sprouted dozens of small, independent art galleries that serve complimentary wine to browsers. On nearby Upper Lascar Row, a flea market commonly known as Cat Street, vendors sell curios, porcelain, and not-very-old trinkets masquerading as artifacts. They might not be authentic, but they do make for great souvenirs and less expensive gifts. ⊠ *Hollywood Rd., between Arbuthnot Rd. and Queen's Rd., Western* Ⓜ *Sheung Wan, Exit A2.*

Tai Ping Shan. The maze of streets west of Man Mo Temple is known as Tai Ping Shan (the Chinese name for Victoria Peak, which towers above it). It's a sleepy area that's filled with small local shops, local design outposts, and cozy cafés. One of the city's oldest residential districts, it has undergone major gentrification in recent years. ⊠ *Tai Ping Shan St., between Upper Station St. and Square St., Western* Ⓜ *Sheung Wan, Exit A2.*

The University of Hong Kong. It's worth a trip out to the western end of the Mid-Levels to see these imposing Edwardian-era buildings. The institution opened in 1912 with the Faculty of Medicine, which had been known as the Hong Kong College of Medicine since 1887. Today the exteriors of University Hall, the Hung Hing Ying Building, and the Tang Chi Ngong Building are on the government's Declared Monument List. ⊠ *Bonham Rd. at Pok Fu Lan Rd., Pok Fu Lam, Western* ☎ *2859–2111* ⊕ *www.hku.hk.*

Western Market. The Sheung Wan district's iconic market, a hulking Edwardian-era brick structure, is a good place to get your bearings. Built in 1906, it functioned as a produce market for 83 years. Today it's a shopping center selling trinkets and fabrics—the architecture is what's worth the visit. Nearby you'll find herbal medicine on Ko Shing Street and Queen's Road West, dried seafood on Wing Lok Street and Des Voeux Road West, and ginseng and bird's nest on Bonham Strand West. ⊠ *323 Des Voeux Rd. Central, Sheung Wan, Western* ☎ *6029–2675* ⊕ *www.westernmarket.com.hk* ⊙ *Daily 10–7* Ⓜ *Sheung Wan, Exit B or C.*

Wing Lee Street. Just minutes away from Man Mo Temple, Wing Lee Street is one of the city's last thoroughfares where every building features 1950s-era "tong lau" architecture. In 2010 the tenement buildings on this tucked-away street were saved from demolition following a series of protests from preservationists. ⊠ *Wing Lee St., between Ladder and Shing Wong Sts., Sheung Wan, Western* Ⓜ *Sheung Wan, Exit A2.*

2

CENTRAL

Sightseeing
★★★★
Dining
★★★★
Lodging
☆★★★
Shopping
★★★★

Hong Kong's historic heart has been a world center of trade and commerce since the mid-19th-century British-colonial era. Streets and squares are lined with architectural landmarks that these days are overshadowed by soaring masterpieces of contemporary architecture. Somehow the mishmash works. Central is still the city center, packed with businesspeople, shoppers, and tourists. Bankers and diplomats rub elbows with *tai-tais*—the local term for ladies who lunch, but the term can certainly apply to men as well—who can work off a meal shopping at designer-packed malls or luxury emporiums selling made-to-measure Chinese-style suits. With the harbor on one side and Victoria Peak on the other, Central also provides unrivaled views—once you get high enough to see them, whether from a skyscraper or the hillsides towering behind the district.

TOP ATTRACTIONS

Central Star Ferry Pier. Take in the view of the Kowloon skyline from this pier, from which sturdy green-and-white Star Ferry vessels cross the harbor. Naturally, the views are even better from the open water. ⊠ *Pier 7, Central Ferry Pier, Man Kwong St., Central* ☏ *2367–7065* ⊕ *www.starferry.com.hk* Ⓜ *Hong Kong Station, Exit A2.*

Fodor's Choice
★

Flagstaff House Museum of Tea Ware. All that's good about British colonial architecture is exemplified in the Flagstaff House Museum of Tea Ware's simple white facade, wooden monsoon shutters, and colonnaded verandas. Look for hundreds of delicate antique tea sets from the Tang

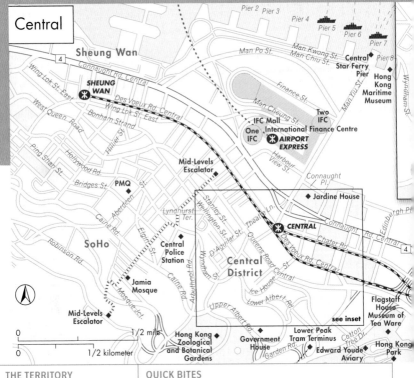

THE TERRITORY

The Mid-Levels Escalator runs through SoHo, the heart of Central's dining and nightlife scene. Just a few blocks east, past Aberdeen Street, and you're in Sheung Wan. The streets between Queen's Road Central and the harbor are laid out more or less geometrically. To the south of Queen's Road, lanes climbing the slopes of Victoria Peak are steep and don't appear to follow any sort of pattern. Overhead walkways connect Central's major buildings, an all-weather alternative to the chaotic streets below.

QUICK BITES

At lunchtime people flood the cul-de-sac that is affectionately known as Rat Alley (Wing Wah Lane off D'Aguilar Street). Choose from Thai, Malay, Indian, Chinese, or American open-air eateries.

Genki Sushi. Need an instant sushi fix? Pull up a stool at the conveyor belt at Genki Sushi. ⊠ *Far East Finance Centre, 16 Harcourt Rd., Admiralty, Central* ☎ 2865–2933 ⊕ *www.genkisushi.com.hk.*

Tsui Wah. No visit to Central is complete without a bowl of noodles at Tsui Wah, open around the clock. ⊠ *15–19 Wellington St., Central* ☎ 2525–6338 ⊕ *www.tsuiwahrestaurant.com.*

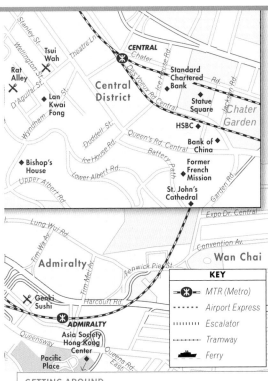

The Urban Runway. Cross Central without touching street level. Start in the IFC Mall; leave by Pret A Manger on the southeast side, turn right into the walkway, pass the General Post Office and Jardine House, and enter on the Armani floor of the Chater Building. Follow the signs to Alexandra House; take the stairs to the right of Dolce & Gabbana up into the Landmark. Go straight ahead toward Harvey Nichols, then turn right at Anya Hindmarch, and walk into the Central Building. Turn left, go up the stairs past Clarins Skin Spa, and into Central Tower. Turn right in the elevator lobby and take the bridge into the Entertainment Building, which drops you in Lan Kwai Fong. Time your 20-minute walk to finish at 6 pm—just in time for happy hour.

GETTING AROUND

Central MTR station is a mammoth underground warren with a host of far-flung exits. A series of "travelators" join it with Hong Kong Station, under the IFC Mall, where Tung Chung Line and Airport Express trains arrive and depart. Rattling old trams along Des Voeux Road reliably get you into Western, or as far east as Wan Chai, with views along the way. Star Ferry vessels to Kowloon leave Pier 7 every 6 to 12 minutes.

Discovery Bay Transportation Services. High-speed boats head for the northeastern coast of Lantau Island every 20 to 30 minutes during peak periods from Pier 3. Trips take 25–30 minutes and cost HK$40 to HK$57, depending on time of day. ⊕ www.td.gov.hk.

New World First Ferry. Headed to Cheung Chau, these ferries take 35 to 55 minutes and cost HK$13.20 to HK$37.20. ☎ 2131–8181 ⊕ www.nwff.com.hk.

(618–907) through the Qing (1644–1911) dynasties filling the rooms that once housed the commander of the British forces. ■ TIP→ Skip the lengthy, confusing tea-ceremony descriptions and concentrate on the porcelain pieces themselves. Look out for the unadorned brownish-purple clay of the Yixing pots, whose beauty hinges on perfect form. A room on the ground floor has interactive computer stations on the history of tea. ⊠ *Hong Kong Park, 10 Cotton Tree Dr., Central* ☎ *2869–0690* ⊕ *www.lcsd.gov.hk* ✆ *Free* ⊗ *Wed.–Mon. 10–6* Ⓜ *Admiralty, Exit C1.*

FAMILY
Fodor's Choice
★

Hong Kong Park. One of the prettiest parks in the city proper, Hong Kong Park is a sprawling mix of rock gardens and leafy pathways. It's not uncommon to stumble upon locals practicing tai chi or reading in a secluded spot. This welcome respite from the surrounding skyscrapers occupies the site of a garrison called the Victoria Barracks, and some buildings from 1842 and 1910 are still standing. The park is home to the Flagstaff House Museum of Tea Ware and the Edward Youde Aviary. ⊠ *19 Cotton Tree Dr., Central* ☎ *2521–5041* ⊕ *www.lcsd.gov.hk* ✆ *Free* ⊗ *Daily 6 am–11 pm* Ⓜ *Admiralty, Exit C1.*

Mid-Levels Escalator. The unimaginatively named Mid-Levels district is halfway up the hill between the Western and Central districts and Victoria Peak. Running through it is the world's longest covered outdoor escalator, which connects to several main residential streets and walkways. Free of charge and protected from the elements, this series of moving walkways makes the uphill journey a cinch. Before 10 am the escalators only move downward, carrying an endless stream of workers and their cups of coffee. ⊠ *Next to 100 Queen's Rd. Central, Central* ⊗ *6–midnight* Ⓜ *Central, Exit D1.*

SoHo. The area south of Hollywood Road—hence the name—is the epicenter of Hong Kong's latest gastro revolution. The bars here are a chiller alternative to the crowded drinking spots in Lan Kwai Fong, Central's nightlife mecca. Trendy boutiques are tucked in between, some featuring local designers and one-of-a kind goods. ⊠ *South of Hollywood Rd. and north of Caine Rd., just off Mid-Levels Escalator, SoHo, Central* ⊕ *www.ilovesoho.hk* Ⓜ *Central, Exit D1.*

Fodor's Choice
★

Star Ferry. Since 1898 the Star Ferry pier has been the gateway to Hong Kong Island. If it's your first time in the city, taking the Star Ferry across Victoria Harbour is a must. It's a beautiful and relaxing 10-minute trip on roughly 50-year-old vessels. An evening ride is the most spectacular, especially if you can time your ride to coincide with the 8 pm Symphony of Lights show.

The Central Star Ferry Terminal is at Piers 7 and 8. On ferries between Central and Tsim Sha Tsui there are two classes: first (HK$2.50 to HK$3.40) and second (HK$2 to HK$2.80). Since second-class seats on the lower deck tend to be stuffier, opt for a first-class seat on the roomier upper deck. ■ TIP→ For trips from Central to Tsim Sha Tsui, seats on the eastern side have the better views. Across the way, the pier is a convenient starting point for any tour of Kowloon. As you face the bus station, Ocean Terminal, where luxury cruise ships berth, is on your left. Inside this terminal and in the adjacent Harbour City complex are miles of air-conditioned shopping arcades. Across the street, the Peninsula hotel is the classic destination for afternoon tea. Or simply stroll eastward along the Avenue of Stars for an extended waterfront view of the famous Hong Kong skyline. ☎ *2367–7065* ⊕ *www.starferry. com.hk* ⊙ *Daily 6:30 am–11:30 pm.*

Fodor's Choice ★ **Victoria Peak and the Victoria Peak Tram.** As you step off the Victoria Peak Tram, you might be surprised to encounter two shopping arcades crowning Hong Kong's most prized mountaintop. But venture up the escalators to the free viewing platforms—yep, through the Peak Galleria mall—and the view will astound you. Whatever the time, whatever the weather, be it your first visit or your 50th, this is Hong Kong's one unmissable sight. Spread below you is a glittering forest of skyscrapers; beyond them the harbor and—on a clear day—Kowloon's eight mountains. On rainy days wisps of clouds catch on the buildings' pointy tops, and at night both sides of the harbor burst into color. Consider having dinner at one of the restaurants near the Upper Terminus. ■ **TIP→** Skip the Peak Tower's observation deck, which is pricey. The free sights from atop the Galleria are just as good.

Soaring just over 1,805 feet above sea level, Victoria Peak looks over Central and beyond. The steep funicular tracks up to the peak start at the **Peak Tram Terminus,** near St. John's Cathedral on Garden Road. Hong Kong is proud that its funicular railway is the world's steepest. Before it opened in 1888, the only way to get up to Victoria Peak was to walk or take a bumpy ride in a sedan chair on steep steps. At the Lower Terminus, the Peak Tram Historical Gallery displays a replica of the first-generation Peak Tram carriage. On the way up, grab a seat on the right-hand side for the best views of the harbor and mountains. The trams, which look like old-fashioned trolley cars, are hauled the whole way in seven minutes by cables attached to electric motors. En route to the Upper Terminus, 1,300 feet above sea level, the cars pass four intermediate stations, with track gradients varying from 4 to 27 degrees.

There are well-signed nature walks around Victoria Peak, which make for wonderful respites from the commercialism. Before buying a return ticket on the tram or on a bus, consider taking one of the beautiful low-impact trails back to Central. You'll be treated to spectacular views in all directions on the **Hong Kong Trail,** an easygoing 40- to 60-minute paved path that begins and ends at the Peak Tram Upper Terminus. Start by heading north along fern-encroached Lugard Road. There's another stunning view of Central from the lookout, 20 minutes along, after which the road snakes west to an intersection with Hatton and Harlech roads. From here Lantau, Lamma, and—on incredibly clear days—Macau come into view. The longer option from here is to wind your way down Hatton to the University of Hong Kong campus in Western District.

Bus 15C, sometimes a red double-decker with an open top, shuttles you between the Peak Tram Lower Terminal and Central Bus Terminal near the Star Ferry Pier every 15 to 20 minutes for HK$4.20. ✉ *Between Garden Rd. and Cotton Tree Dr., Central* ☎ *2522–0922* ⊕ *www.*

From Victoria Peak, Hong Kong Island's multiple levels of skyscrapers stretch out below.

thepeak.com.hk 🎫 *HK$28 one way, HK$40 round-trip* ⊙ *Tram daily every 10–15 mins, 7 am–midnight.*

WORTH NOTING

Asia Society Hong Kong Center. A former explosives magazine compound built by the British Army in the 19th century, the Asia Society Hong Kong Center's Chantal Miller Gallery is a pleasant setting for exhibitions pertaining to Asian countries and cultures. Views from the lush roof garden are spectacular; a walk on the grounds is a must. The Center's AMMO (Asia, Modern, Museum, Original) restaurant and bar is a lovely spot for lunch or a drink. ⊠ *9 Justice Dr., Admiralty, Central* ☎ *2103–9511* ⊕ *www.asiasociety.org/hong-kong* 🎫 *HK$30 to enter Chantal Miller Gallery* ⊙ *Tues.–Sun. 11–6* Ⓜ *Admiralty, Exit C1.*

Bank of China Building. The art-deco building at the southern end of Statue Square is the former headquarters of the Bank of China, which was built in the 1950s. The building now houses offices, as well as the members-only China Club restaurant. Don't confuse it with the newer Bank of China Tower, one of the most iconic skyscrapers in the city, just down the street on Garden Road. Designed by I.M. Pei, this imposing structure is said to resemble bamboo—a symbol of the city's strength, growth, and enterprising nature. ⊠ *2A Des Voeux Rd., Central* Ⓜ *Central, Exit K.*

Bishop's House. Formerly the campus of St. Paul's College, the Bishop's House dates back to 1843. This historic Victorian building, which is a pretty shade of yellow, has been the official residence of the Anglican bishop since 1851. ⊠ *1 Lower Albert Rd., Central* Ⓜ *Central, Exit D1.*

Central Ferry Pier. The pier juts out into the harbor in front of the International Finance Centre. Ferries regularly leave from here for Lantau, Lamma, and Cheung Chau islands. The Star Ferry Pier is just steps away. ⊠ *Man Kwong St., between Rumsey and Man Yiu Sts., Central* Ⓜ *Hong Kong Station, Exit A2.*

Central Police Station. This colonial building is a must-have location for any self-respecting Hong Kong cop movie. It was the neighborhood headquarters from 1864—when part of it was built—to 2004. Closed for renovations, it's slated to reopen as an arts and culture center. ⊠ *10 Hollywood Rd., Central* ⊕ *www.centralpolicestation.org.hk* Ⓜ *Central, Exit D1.*

Cheung Chau. This 2½-km-long (1½-mile-long) island southwest of Hong Kong is best known as the home of windsurfing Olympic gold medalist Lee Lai-shan. Residents live mostly on the sandbar connecting the two hilly tips of this dumbbell-shaped island. The town harbor is lined with seafood restaurants and shops. A 35-minute fast ferry departs from Central's Pier 5 outside Two IFC.

On sunny weekends Cheung Chau's Tung Wan beach is so crowded that its sweep of golden sand is barely visible. At one end of the beach is the Warwick Hotel, and plenty of nearby restaurants offer food, refreshments, and shade. Apart from emergency vehicles, no private cars are allowed on this island. Among the tourist attractions, find the striking Pak Tai Temple, one of the oldest in Hong Kong, as well as a cave that allegedly housed the hidden treasures of pirate Cheung Po Tsai.

Edward Youde Aviary. This pleasant attraction in the southern corner of Hong Kong Park boasts hundreds of birds in a tropical environment. There are dozens of types of birds, including kid favorites like the great pied hornbill. ⊠ *Hong Kong Park, 10 Cotton Tree Dr., Central* ☎ *2521–5041* ⊕ *www.lcsd.gov.hk* ⊠ *Free* ☉ *Daily 9–5* Ⓜ *Admiralty, Exit C1.*

Former French Mission Building. A tree-lined lane called Battery Path was built by the British in 1841 to move their cannons uphill—hence the name. At the top of Battery Path sits the elegant Former French Mission Building, a neoclassical redbrick building with white columns and green shutters. Finished in 1917, the historic monument is now home to the Court of Final Appeal. ⊠ *1 Battery Path, Central* Ⓜ *Central, Exit D1.*

Government House. This handsome white Victorian was constructed in 1855 as the official residence of British governors, and is now home to Hong Kong's chief executive. During the Japanese occupation the house was significantly rebuilt, so it exhibits a strong Japanese influence, particularly in the roof eaves. The gardens are usually open to the public in March when the azaleas bloom. ⊠ *Upper Albert Rd., Mid-Levels, Central* ☎ *2878–3300* ⊕ *www.ceo.gov.hk/gh* Ⓜ *Central, Exit D1.*

Hong Kong Maritime Museum. Originally located in Stanley, this museum relocated to the old Hung Hom Star Ferry Pier in 2013. The rich collections explore Hong Kong's 2,000-year maritime history, one of the gems being a 59-foot-long scroll painting called *Pacifying the South China Sea,* which chronicles the nine-day Battle of Lantau against Hong Kong's most famous pirate, Cheung Po Tsai, in the early 1800s. The scroll has been digitized and transformed into a 360-degree animation experience. ⊠ *Central Pier No. 8, Central* ☎ *2813–1723* ⊕ *www. hkmaritimemuseum.org* 🎫 *HK$30* 🕙 *Weekdays 9:30–5:30, weekends and holidays 10–7.*

FAMILY   **Hong Kong Zoological and Botanical Gardens.** This welcoming green space includes a children's playground and gorgeous gardens with more than 1,000 plant species, but the real attractions are the dozens of mammals housed in the zoo. If you're a fan of primates, look for rare sightings like the golden lion tamarin and the black-and-white ruffed lemur. Buses 3B, 12, and 13 run from various other stops in Central; the walk from the Central MTR stop is long and uphill. ⊠ *Albany Rd., between Robinson and Upper Albert Rds., Central* ☎ *2530–0154* 🎫 *Free* 🕙 *Daily 6 am–7 pm* Ⓜ *Central.*

HSBC Main Building. The spectacular strut-and-ladder facade of this Lord Norman Foster building makes it one of the most important structures in 20th-century architecture. Look up into the atrium through the curved glass floor, or duck inside for a view of the building's mechanics. ⊠ *1 Queen's Rd., across from Statue Square, Central* 🎫 *Free* 🕙 *Weekdays 9–5:30, Sat. 9–12:30* Ⓜ *Central, Exit K.*

International Finance Centre. One building towers above the Central skyline: Two IFC. The slender second tower of the International Finance Centre has been compared to at least one—unprintable—thing, and is topped with a clawlike structure. Designed by Argentine architect Cesar Pelli, its 88 floors top a whopping 1,352 feet. Opposite stands its dinky little brother, the 38-floor One IFC. The massive IFC Mall stretches between the two, and Hong Kong Station is underneath. If you wish to see the breathtaking views from Two IFC, visit the 55th-floor Hong Kong Monetary Authority. While there, take a quick look at exhibits tracing the history of banking in Hong Kong. Upon arrival, you may need to register your passport with the concierge. ⊠ *8 Finance St., Central* ⊕ *www.ifc.com.hk* 🎫 *Free* 🕙 *Hong Kong Monetary Authority weekdays 10–6, Sat. 10–1* Ⓜ *Hong Kong Station, Exit A2.*

Jamia Mosque. The Mid-Levels Escalator zooms by the first mosque in Hong Kong. Commonly known as the Lascar Temple, the original 1840s structure was rebuilt in 1915 and shows its Indian heritage in the perforated arches and decorative facade work. The mosque isn't open to non-Muslims, but it occupies a small, verdant enclosure that's a welcome retreat. ⊠ *30 Shelley St., above Caine Rd., Central* ☎ *2523–7743* ⊕ *www.amo.gov.hk* Ⓜ *Central, Exit D1.*

Jardine House. Just behind the IFC is a notable '60s skyscraper recognizable by its many round windows. The 52-level building is home to Jardine, Matheson & Co., the greatest of the old British *hongs* (trading companies) that dominated trade with imperial China. Once linked to opium trafficking, the firm is now a respected investment bank. ⊠ *1 Connaught Place, Central* ☎ *2500–0555* Ⓜ *Hong Kong Station, Exit A2.*

Lan Kwai Fong. In Hong Kong the word "nightlife" is synonymous with LKF, a few narrow lanes filled with bars and clubs uphill from the intersection of Queen's Road Central and Pedder Street. Wyndham Street has a series of high-caliber antiques shops, as well as more drinking spots.

Spend a few minutes, an hour, or a day people-watching in Hong Kong Park.

✉ *Lan Kwai Fong and D'Aguilar St. between Wyndham and Wellington Sts., Central* ⊕ *www.lankwaifong.com* Ⓜ *Central, Exit D1.*

PMQ. This hip and happening area has a long history: back in the 1880s this was the campus of the Central School, where Dr. Sun Yat-sen studied. After suffering severe damage in World War II, the area became the city's first Police Married Quarters. After standing empty for more than a decade, it reopened in 2014 as a design hub where locals could showcase their art, host workshops, arrange pop-up shops—there's even an atmospheric night market and a handful of excellent restaurants and cozy cafés. ■ TIP→ Take advantage of one of the free guided tours of the underground foundations and historic architecture. ✉ *35 Aberdeen St., SoHo, Central* ☎ *2870–2335* ⊕ *www.pmq.org.hk* ☉ *Daily 7 am–11 pm.*

Queen's Road. Hong Kong's answer to New York's 5th Avenue and London's King's Road are the first few blocks of Chater Road, Des Voeux Road Central, and Queen's Road Central (the thoroughfares that stretch west from Statue Square). Most high-end designers have boutiques in über-posh shopping centers like the Landmark or Alexandra House. A stone's throw away, but at the other end of the income scale, are Li Yuen Street East and Li Yuen Street. Known as the Lanes, they're packed with stalls selling cheap *cheongsams* (sexy silk dresses with Mandarin collars), phone cases, backpacks, and Hello Kitty merchandise. On the south side of Queen's Road is steep Pottinger Street, a haberdasher's dream. ✉ *Queen's Rd. Central, Chater Rd., and Des Voeux Rd. Central, between Peel and Bank Sts., Central* Ⓜ *Central, Exit D1.*

St. John's Cathedral. A peaceful gap in the skyscrapers accommodates the graceful Gothic form of this Anglican church. Completed in 1849, the cathedral is made of Canton bricks in the shape of a cross. The doors are constructed from timber salvaged from the World War II–era British warship HMS *Tamar.* ⊠ *4–8 Garden Rd., Central* ☎ *2523–4157* ⊕ *www.stjohnscathedral.org.hk* ▧ *Free* ☉ *Daily 7–6* Ⓜ *Central, Exit K.*

Standard Chartered Bank Building. This wedgelike building includes a pair of stained-glass windows by Remo Riva that represent visions of "Hong Kong Today" and "Hong Kong Tomorrow." ⊠ *4 Des Voeux Rd. Central, Central* Ⓜ *Central, Exit K.*

Statue Square. The land was gifted to the public by HSBC, whose headquarters dominate the southern end, with the proviso that nothing built on it could block the bank's view of the water. The Victorian–Chinese hybrid building on Statue Square's east side was built for the Supreme Court in 1912 and now houses the Court of Final Appeal. In front of the council building is the Cenotaph, a monument to all who lost their lives in the two World Wars. ⊠ *Between Chater Rd. and Des Voeux Rd. Central, Central* Ⓜ *Central, Exit K.*

DID YOU KNOW?

Statue Square took its name from bronze figures of British royalty that stood here before the Japanese occupation, when they were removed and melted down. The only figure exempt was stern Sir Thomas Jackson (1841–1915), who looks over the square toward HSBC—he was the chief manager for more than 30 years.

WAN CHAI, CAUSEWAY BAY, AND EASTERN

Sightseeing
☆★★★

Dining
★★★★

Lodging
☆☆★★

Shopping
☆☆★★

Explore beyond Western and Central and you'll discover that Wan Chai, Causeway Bay, Happy Valley, and the neighborhoods of the Eastern District are equally as vibrant—revealing another facet of Hong Kong. Though Wan Chai is known primarily for its nightlife (think raunchy entertainment and rowdy expats), it is also home to the Convention Centre, beautiful colonial buildings, and a handful of arts institutions. Causeway Bay, one of the city's liveliest areas, is a shopping and dining mecca, and the Happy Valley horse races, a big part of Hong Kong life, are just a short walk away.

WAN CHAI

All in all, Hong Kong's notorious center of lowlife is fairly tame these days, with a bustling mix of hotels, shops, and convention facilities. This doesn't mean that the old neighborhood has lost all its character. A few blocks back from Wan Chai's new office blocks are crowded alleys where you can still experience old Hong Kong and stumble across a wet market, a tiny furniture-maker's shop, an age-old temple, and yes, the strip joints, dive bars, and gambling dens that have long made the quarter popular with denizens of the night. Like all of Hong Kong, Wan Chai is quite safe after dark, but single women strolling the streets in the wee hours might get unwanted attention from groups of drunken tourists.

TOP ATTRACTIONS

Hong Kong Arts Centre. The 19-story Hong Kong Arts Centre houses a branch of the Hong Kong Art School, several contemporary art galleries, interactive workshops, multimedia installations, art studios, a cinema, and performing arts venues. There are also a handful of eateries. The art hub has long been a champion of up-and-coming artists, and its latest project is Comix Home Base on nearby Mallory Street. There are free guided tours every Wednesday and Saturday at 3 pm, lasting about 45 minutes. ✉ *2 Harbour Rd., Wan Chai* ☎ *2582–0200* ⊕ *www.hkac.org.hk* 🎟 *Free* ☉ *Daily 8 am–11 pm* Ⓜ *Wan Chai, Exit C.*

WORTH NOTING

Central Plaza. Clad in reflective gold, silver, and copper-colored glass, this triangular building is glitzy to the point of tastelessness. In 1992 it was briefly the city's tallest building, but Two IFC soon beat it by 130 feet. Note the colorful fluorescent lights atop the building; they actually are a clock so complicated that no one knows how to tell time using it. ✉ *18 Harbour Rd., Wan Chai* ☎ *2586–8111* ⊕ *www.centralplaza.com.hk.*

Comix Home Base. Devoted to the creative and quirky world of comics and animation, this center celebrates local artists by offering up ample space to create, exhibit, and sell their work. The complex is also a great example of Hong Kong's historic East-meets-West architecture, as it's housed in a cluster of revitalized prewar tenement-style buildings with cantilevered balconies, high ceilings, and staircases made of China fir wood. ✉ *7 Mallory St., Wan Chai* ☎ *2824–5303* ⊕ *www. comixhomebase.com.hk* ☉ *Daily 10–8.*

Hong Kong Convention and Exhibition Centre. Land is so scarce in Hong Kong that developers usually only build skyward, but the HKCEC juts into the harbor instead. Curved-glass walls and a swooping roof make it look like a tortoise lumbering into the sea or a gull taking flight, depending on who you ask. Of all the international trade fairs, regional conferences, and other events held here, by far the most famous was the 1997 Handover Ceremony. An obelisk commemorates it on the waterfront promenade, which also affords great views of Kowloon.

Outside the center stands the *Golden Bauhinia*. This gleaming sculpture of the bauhinia flower, Hong Kong's symbol, was a gift from China. The police hoist the flag daily at 7:50 am; on the first of every month, there is an enhanced flag-raising ceremony with musical accompaniment at 7:45 am. ✉ *1 Expo Dr., Wan Chai* ☎ *2582–8888* ⊕ *www.hkcec.com. hk* Ⓜ *Wan Chai, Exit A.*

Johnston Road. Trams clatter along this busy road, which is choked with traffic day and night. It's also packed with shops selling food, cell phones, herbal tonics, and bargain-basement clothes. Rattan furniture, picture frames, paper lanterns, and Chinese calligraphic materials make up the more traditional assortment at Queen's Road East, which runs parallel to Johnston Road. The lanes that stretch between the two roads are also lined with stalls, forming a mini-market of clothing and accessories. ✉ *Johnston Rd., between Heard and Gresson Sts., Wan Chai* Ⓜ *Wan Chai, Exit A3.*

Lovers' Rock. High above Wan Chai sits the suggestively shaped monolith known as Lovers' Rock, or Yan Yuen Shek. It's a frequent destination among local single women, who burn joss sticks and make offerings in hope of finding a husband. Not in the market? The walk along Bowen Road offers excellent views over the city, particularly at dusk. The

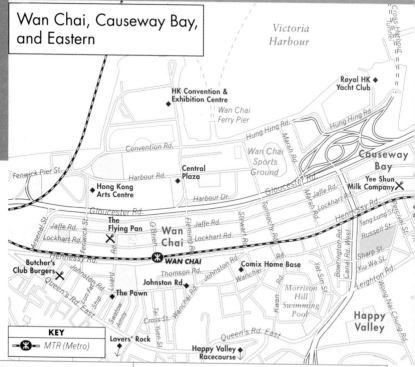

Wan Chai, Causeway Bay, and Eastern

Victoria Harbour

HK Convention & Exhibition Centre

Wan Chai Ferry Pier

Royal HK Yacht Club

Hung Hing Rd.

Marsh Rd.

Hung Hing Rd.

Convention Rd.

Wan Chai Sports Ground

Causeway Bay

Fenwick Pier St.

Harbour Rd.

Central Plaza

Gloucester Rd.

Yee Shun Milk Company

Hong Kong Arts Centre

Harbour Dr.

Jaffe Rd.

Lockhart Rd.

Hennessy Rd.

Gloucester Rd.

The Flying Pan

Jaffe Rd.

Jaffe Rd.

Stewart Rd.

Tonnochy Rd.

Marsh Rd.

Tang Lung St.

Russell St.

Percival St.

Jaffe Rd.

Lockhart Rd.

O'Brien Rd.

Wan Chai

Lockhart Rd.

Fleming Rd.

Sharp St.

Bowrington Rd.

Canal Rd. West

Hennessy Rd.

WAN CHAI

Rd.

Yiu Wa St.

Leighton Rd.

Butcher's Club Burgers

Johnston Rd.

Luard Rd.

Ship St.

Thomson Rd.

Johnston Rd.

Wanchai

Comix Home Base

Yat Sin St.

Wong Nai Chung Rd.

Johnston Rd.

The Pawn

Swatow

Amoy

Tai Yuen St.

Wanchai Rd.

Kwan

Morrison Hill Swimming Pool

Happy Valley

KEY

Cross St.

Queen's Rd. East

MTR (Metro)

Lovers' Rock

Happy Valley Racecourse

Cross Harbour Tunnel

THE TERRITORY

Wan Chai's trams run mostly along Hennessy Road, with a detour along Johnston Road at the neighborhood's western end. Queen's Road East runs parallel to these two streets to the south, and a maze of lanes connects it with Hennessy.

The thoroughfares north of Hennessy—Lockhart, Jaffe, and Gloucester, which is a freeway—are laid out in a grid. Causeway Bay's diagonal roads make the neighborhood hard to navigate, but it's small; wander around and before long you'll hit something familiar.

TAKING IT IN

Once Upon a Time in the East. There were settlements here long before the British arrived, and the area was strategically important after colonization. Find out about it all from local historian Jason Wordie (⊕ www.jasonswalks.com), who runs tours through Wan Chai, Causeway Bay, Shau Kei Wan, Central, and beyond.

A Wan Chai Wander. Rattle to Wan Chai by tram along roads dense with jutting signs. Get off at Southorn Playground, and wander the lanes south of Johnston Road before heading up Luard Road and over walkways to the Hong Kong Academy for Performing Arts and Hong Kong Arts Centre, in adjacent buildings. The Hong Kong Convention and Exhibition Centre is a few minutes away—wander its harborside promenade. If you're here at dusk, Wan Chai's drinking holes will be lighting up as you walk back to the MTR along Fleming Road. Look up at Central Plaza on your right.

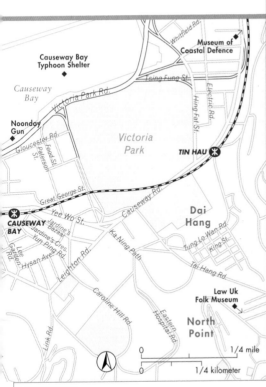

Causeway Bay Typhoon Shelter

Causeway Bay

Museum of Coastal Defence

Tsing Fung St.

Victoria Park Rd.

Whitfield Rd.

Hing Fat St.

Electric Rd.

Noonday Gun

Gloucester Rd.

Food St.

Paterson St.

Victoria Park

TIN HAU

Great George St.

Yee Wo St.

Causeway Rd.

CAUSEWAY BAY

Jardine's Bazaar

Jardine's Cres.

Yun Ping Rd.

Lee Garden Rd.

Hysan Ave.

Leighton Rd.

Caroline Hill Rd.

Link Rd.

Ka Ning Path

Tung Lo Wan Rd.

King St.

Tai Hang Rd.

Eastern Hospital Rd.

Dai Hang

Law Uk Folk Museum

North Point

0   1/4 mile
0   1/4 kilometer

GETTING AROUND

Both Wan Chai and Causeway Bay have their own MTR stops, but a pleasant way to arrive from Central is on the tram along Hennessy Road. If you're going beyond Wan Chai, check the sign at the front: some continue to North Point and Shau Kei Wan, via Causeway Bay, while others go south to Happy Valley.

The underground MTR stations are small labyrinths, so read the signs carefully to find the best exit. Traffic begins to take its toll on journey times to places beyond Causeway Bay, and the MTR is often the quickest way to travel.

QUICK BITES

Butchers Club Burgers. With hands-down the best burgers in Hong Kong, Butchers Club Burgers is run by an affable bunch who are serious about their minced-to-order bacon cheeseburgers and duck-fat fries. ⊠ *Ground fl., Rialto Bldg., 2 Landale St., Wan Chai* ☎ *2528–2083* ⊕ *www.butchersclub. com.hk.*

The Flying Pan. In a nightspot-packed district, a café serving breakfast round-the-clock is bound to be a hit. The Flying Pan's Wan Chai branch has 19 different types of omelets, waffles, blintzes, grilled sandwiches—the list goes on. This is the perfect spot to hit after barhopping. ⊠ *3rd fl., 81–85 Lockhart Rd., Wan Chai* ☎ *2528–9997* ⊕ *www.the-flying-pan.com.*

Yee Shun Milk Company. Yee Shun Milk Company sounds kooky, but you can't leave Causeway Bay without dessert at this crowded little diner. The signature dish is steamed milk pudding with ginger juice. ⊠ *506 Lockhart Rd., Causeway Bay* ☎ *2591–1837.*

easiest way up is on Minibus 24A from the Admiralty MTR station. ⊠ *Bowen Rd., between Wan Chai Gap and Stubbs Rds., Wan Chai.*

DID YOU KNOW?

Wan Chai was once one of the five *wan*—areas the British set aside for Chinese residences—but it developed a reputation for vice and attracted sailors on shore leave during the Vietnam War. How times have changed: Wan Chai is still as risqué an area as Hong Kong has to offer, but that says more about the city's overall respectability than it does about the available indulgences. For all its bars and massage parlors, Wan Chai is now so safe that it seems a pale version of the "Wanch" of Richard Mason's novel *The World of Suzie Wong.* Today many venture to the area for arts and culture at the Hong Kong Academy for Performing Arts and the Hong Kong Arts Centre.

CAUSEWAY BAY

Shoppers crowd the streets of Causeway Bay, the area east of Wan Chai, seven days a week. The action happens within a five-block radius of the intersection of Hennessy Road and Percival Street, where you'll find pockets of mazelike malls full of clothing, jewelry, and gadgets. There are also lots of restaurants in the area, as well as upstairs cafés (inside commercial and residential buildings) that are often populated by teens and twentysomethings.

TOP ATTRACTIONS

Fodor's Choice ★

Happy Valley Racecourse. The biggest attraction east of Causeway Bay for locals and visitors alike is this local legend, where millions of Hong Kong dollars make their way each year. The exhilarating blur of galloping hooves under jockeys dressed in bright silk jerseys is a must-see. The races make great Wednesday nights out on the town. Aside from the excitement of the races, there are restaurants, bars, and even a racing museum to keep you amused. The public entrance to the track is a 20-minute walk from Causeway Bay MTR Exit A (Times Square), or simply hop on the Happy Valley tram, which terminates right in front. ⊠ *Sports Rd. at Wong Nai Chung Rd., Happy Valley, Causeway Bay* ⊠ *HK$10* ⊙ *Wed. 6–11:30 pm during racing season* Ⓜ *Causeway Bay, Exit A.*

Victoria Park. Hong Kong Island's largest park is a welcome breathing space on the edge of Causeway Bay. It's beautifully landscaped and has recreational facilities for soccer, basketball, swimming, lawn bowling, and tennis. At dawn every morning hundreds practice tai chi chuan here. During the Mid-Autumn Festival it's home to the Lantern Carnival, when the trees are a mass of colorful lights. Just before Chinese New Year (late January to early February), the park hosts a huge flower market. On the eve of Chinese New Year, after a traditional family dinner at home, much of Hong Kong happily gathers here to shop and wander into the early hours of the first day of the new year. ⊠ *1 Hing Fat St., Causeway Bay* ☎ *2890–5824* ⊕ *www.lcsd.gov.hk* ⊠ *Free* ⊙ *24 hours* Ⓜ *Tin Hau, Exit A2.*

Hope that luck will be a lady and stick with you at Happy Valley Racecourse.

WORTH NOTING

Causeway Bay Typhoon Shelter. Hong Kong's maritime past and present are much in evidence on Causeway Bay's waterfront. Beginning in 1883, those who lived on sampans and old-fashioned junks gathered during bad weather in the Causeway Bay Typhoon Shelter, the first of its kind in the city. Most boat-dwellers have moved to dry land, so these days yachts and speedboats moor here. A few traditional sampans, crewed primarily by elderly women, still ferry owners to their sailboats. ⊠ *Near entrance of Cross Harbour Tunnel, Causeway Bay* Ⓜ *Causeway Bay, Exit D1.*

Noonday Gun. A block east of the Royal Hong Kong Yacht Club stands the Noonday Gun, which Noël Coward made famous in his song *Mad Dogs and Englishmen*. It's still fired by a Jardine Matheson employee at noon every day. It is said that the tradition began when a Jardine employee fired a gun in salute of the company's head arriving at the port, angering an officer of the Royal Navy. ⊠ *Victoria Park Rd., Causeway Bay* Ⓜ *Causeway Bay, Exit D1.*

DID YOU KNOW?

Opium-smuggler-turned-investment-bank Jardine Matheson once had its warehouses in Causeway Bay. The company moved to Central decades ago, but left a legacy of street names: there's Jardine's Bazaar and Jardine's Crescent, two of Causeway Bay's best shopping streets, and Yee Wo Street with the firm's Chinese name.

EASTERN

The densely populated neighborhoods east of Causeway Bay are largely residential and commercial, with a good number of shopping malls and restaurants that cater to residents. You'll also find art galleries and bookshops installed in converted industrial buildings, and some fascinating museums that are well worth seeking out.

TOP ATTRACTIONS

Law Uk Folk Museum. This restored Hakka house was once the home of the Law family, who arrived here from Guangdong in the mid-18th century. It's the perfect example of a triple-*jian*, double-*lang* residence. Jian are enclosed rooms—here, the bedroom, living room, and workroom at the back. The front storeroom and kitchen are the *lang*, where the walls don't reach up to the roof, and thus allow air in. Although the museum is small, informative texts outside and displays of rural furniture and farm implements inside give a powerful idea of what rural Hong Kong was like. It's definitely worth a trip to bustling industrial Chai Wan, at the eastern end of the MTR, to see it. Photos show what the area looked like in the 1930s—these days a leafy square is the only reminder of the woodlands and fields that once surrounded this buttermilk-color dwelling. ⊠ *14 Kut Shing St., Chai Wan, Eastern* ☎ *2896–7006* ⊕ *www.lcsd. gov.hk* ✑ *Free* ☉ *Fri.–Wed. 10–6* Ⓜ *Chai Wan, Exit B.*

WORTH NOTING

FAMILY **Museum of Coastal Defence.** The Lei Yue Mun Fort makes for an appropriate home for the Museum of Coastal Defence. The museum is in the redoubt, a high area of land overlooking the narrowest point of the harbor; you take an elevator and cross an aerial walkway to reach it. As well as the fascinating historical displays indoors, there's a historical trail complete with tunnels, cannons, and observation posts. ⊠ *175 Tung Hei Rd., Shau Ki Wan, Eastern* ☎ *2569–1500* ⊕ *hk. coastaldefence.museum* ✑ *HK$10; free Wed.* ☉ *Fri.–Wed. 10–5* Ⓜ *Shau Ki Wan, Exit B2.*

2

KOWLOON

Sightseeing
★★★★
Dining
☆★★★
Lodging
★★★★
Shopping
☆★★★

Just across the harbor from Central, this piece of Chinese mainland takes its name from the string of mountains that bound it in the north: *gau lung,* "nine dragons" (there are actually eight mountains; the ninth represents the boy emperor who named them). Kowloon is less sophisticated than its island-side counterpart, but its dense, gritty, urban fabric can feel more authentically Chinese. It's also the backdrop for Hong Kong's best museums and most interesting spiritual sights, as well as street upon street of hard-core consumerism in every imaginable guise. There are several neighborhoods here that are easy to get to and well worth exploring.

TSIM SHA TSUI

You'll probably come to this district hugging the waterfront at the southern tip of Kowloon (in Chinese the name means "pointed sandy mouth") to see one or more of Hong Kong's top museums. These collections are within easy reach of one another amid high-rises, hotels, shops, and Kowloon Park, a coveted parcel of green space. One of the best things to see in Tsim Sha Tsui (often referred to simply as TST) is Central: there are fabulous cross-harbor views from the **Star Ferry Pier** as well as from the ferries themselves. The sweeping pink-tile **Hong Kong Cultural Centre** and the Former Kowloon–Canton Railway clock tower are the first landmarks along the breezy pedestrian **TST East Promenade**, which starts at the Avenue of Stars and stretches a couple of miles east. ■ TIP➔ Visit the promenade at 8 pm for the Symphony of Lights,

a quirky show in which more than 40 skyscrapers light up on cue as a commentator introduces them in time to a musical accompaniment.

TOP ATTRACTIONS

Fodor's Choice ★ **Hong Kong Museum of Art.**
⇨ *See highlighted feature in this section.*

2

Hong Kong Museum of History. For a comprehensive hit of history, this museum's popular Hong Kong Story should do the trick. The exhibit starts 400 million years ago in the Devonian period and makes its way all the way through to the 1997 Handover, with spectacular life-size dioramas that include village houses and a shopping street in colonial times. The ground-floor Folk Culture section offers an introduction to the history and customs of Hong Kong's main ethnic groups. Upstairs, gracious stone-walled galleries whirl you through the Opium Wars and the beginnings of colonial Hong Kong. Don't miss the chilling account of life under the Japanese occupation or the colorful look at Hong Kong life in the '60s. ■ TIP➔ Unless you're with kids who dig models of cavemen and bears, skip the prehistory and dynastic galleries.

Budget at least two hours to stroll through—more if you linger in every gallery and make use of the interactive elements. Pick your way through the gift shop's clutter to find local designer Alan Chan's T-shirts, shot glasses, and notebooks. His retro-kitsch aesthetic is based on 1940s cigarette-girl images. To get here from the Tsim Sha Tsui MTR walk along Cameron Road, then left for a block along Chatham Road South. A signposted overpass takes you to the museum. ⊠ *100 Chatham Rd. S, Tsim Sha Tsui* ☎ *2724–9042* ⊕ *hk.history.museum* ☞ *HK$10; free Wed.* ⊙ *Mon. and Wed.–Fri. 10–6, weekends and holidays 10–7* Ⓜ *Tsim Sha Tsui, Exit B2.*

FAMILY **Kowloon Park.** These 33 acres, crisscrossed by paths and meticulously landscaped, are a refreshing retreat after a bout of shopping. In addition to playgrounds, a fitness trail, soccer pitch, aviary, and maze garden, on Sunday and public holidays there are stalls with arts and crafts, as well as a kung fu corner. ⊠ *22 Austin Rd., Tsim Sha Tsui* ☎ *2724–3344* ⊕ *www.lcsd.gov.hk* ☞ *Free* ⊙ *5 am–midnight* Ⓜ *Tsim Sha Tsui MTR, Exit A1; Jordan, Exit C1.*

WORTH NOTING

Avenue of Stars. You have to look down to appreciate the city's walk of fame. Countless local film stars have pawed the wet concrete—you may not recognize many names unless you're a fan of Hong Kong films, but the homage shows how big the local film industry is. ⊠ *TST East Promenade, outside InterContinental Hong Kong, Tsim Sha Tsui* ⊕ *www.avenueofstars.com.hk* Ⓜ *Tsim Sha Tsui, Exit E.*

FAMILY **Hong Kong Science Museum.** The hands-on exhibits are kid-friendly and include an energy machine and a miniature submarine, as well as cognitive and memory tests. That said, this is more of a rainy-day time-killer than a must-see. ⊠ *2 Science Museum Rd., corner of Cheong Wan Rd. and Chatham Rd., Tsim Sha Tsui* ☎ *2732–3232* ⊕ *hk.science.museum* ☞ *HK$25; free Wed.* ⊙ *Mon.–Wed. and Fri. 10–7, weekends and holidays 10–9* Ⓜ *Tsim Sha Tsui, Exit B2.*

GETTING ORIENTED

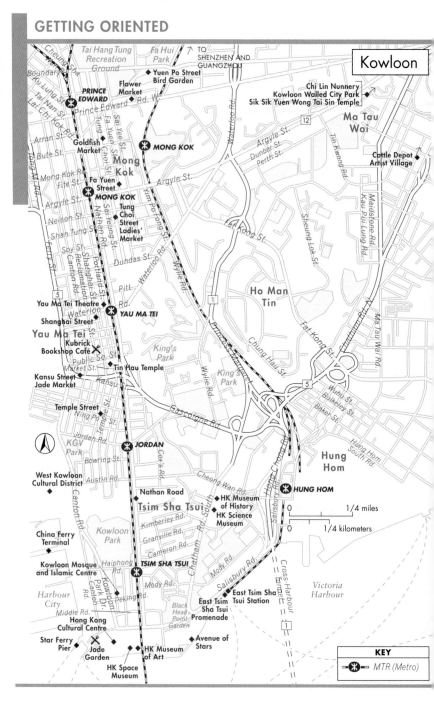

Kowloon

KEY

⊷❋⊶ _MTR (Metro)_

2

GETTING AROUND

The most romantic passage from Hong Kong Island to Tsim Sha Tsui (TST) is by Star Ferry. There are crossings from Central every 6 to 12 minutes and a little less often from Wan Chai.

TST is also accessible by MTR. Underground walkways connect the station with the Tsim Sha Tsui East station on the East Rail Line, where trains depart every 10 to 15 minutes for the eastern New Territories. The Kowloon Airport Express station is amid a construction wasteland west of TST, connecting with Austin station on the West Rail. Hotel shuttles link the area to the rest of Kowloon.

The MTR is your best bet for Jordan, Yau Ma Tei, Mong Kok, and other sights in far-flung Kowloon, including Wong Tai Sin Temple, and Chi Lin Nunnery.

QUICK BITES

Jade Garden. Jade Garden is a popular dim sum eatery. Come early on weekends. ⊠ *4th fl., Star House, opposite Star Ferry Concourse, Tsim Sha Tsui* ☎ *2730–6888* ⊕ *www.maximschinese.com.hk.*

Kubrick Café. Arty tomes surround the tables at the Kubrick Café. It's attached to the city's best art-house cinema, Broadway Cinematheque. Tuck into sandwiches, pastas, and cakes. The coffee's great, too. ⊠ *Broadway Cinemathèque, 3 Public Square St., Yau Ma Tei* ☎ *2384–8929* ⊕ *www.kubrick.com.hk.*

THE TERRITORY

From the Star Ferry Pier the Tsim Sha Tsui (TST) waterfront extends a few miles to TST East. Shops and hotels line Nathan Road, which runs north from the waterfront through the market districts of Jordan, Yau Ma Tei, and Mong Kok. Wong Tai Sin Temple and Chi Lin Nunnery are just to the east of Mong Kok.

TAKING IT IN

Hong Kong Foodie Tours. Traveling gourmands may want to join a tour with Hong Kong Foodie, which promises stops in some of Hong Kong's most celebrated restaurants as well as some hole-in-the-wall gems. There is a Central and Sheung Wan tour that's popular, as well as a half-day tour through historic Sham Shui Po. The latter includes 10 tastings at decades-old family-run diners with bites of quintessential Hong Kong snacks, such as freshly baked buns, milk tea, rice rolls, and egg noodles. Bring an appetite! ⊠ *New Victory House, 93–103 Wing Lok St., Sheung Wan, Western* ☎ *2850–5006* ⊕ *www.hongkongfoodietours.com* ⊠ *HK$690 per person* Ⓜ *Sheung Wan.*

HONG KONG MUSEUM OF ART

✉ *10 Salisbury Rd., Tsim Sha Tsui* ☎ *2721–0116* ⊕ *hk.art. museum* ✍ *HK$10* ⊙ *Mon.– Wed. and Fri. 10–6, weekends 10–7* Ⓜ *Tsim Sha Tsui MTR, Exit F.*

TIPS

■ Traditional Chinese landscape paintings are visual records of real or imagined journeys—a kind of travel-ogue. Pick a starting point and try to travel through the picture, imagining the journey the artist is trying to convey.

■ There is a collection search system on the first floor, as well as a research center.

■ Check the website for the schedule of more detailed visits to specific galleries—they change every month. If you prefer a little more guidance, consider an English-language audio guide: it's informative, if a little dry, and it costs only HK$10.

An extensive collection of Chinese art is packed inside this boxy tiled building on the Tsim Sha Tsui waterfront in Kowloon. The collections contain a heady mix of Qing ceramics, 2,000-year-old calligraphic scrolls, and contemporary canvases. It's all well organized into thematic galleries with clear, if uninspired, explanations. Hong Kong's biggest visiting exhibitions are usually held here as well. The museum is a few minutes from the Star Ferry and the Tsim Sha Tsui MTR stop.

Highlights

The Chinese Antiquities Gallery is the place to head if ceramics are your thing. A series of low-lit rooms on the third floor houses ceramics from the Ming and Qing dynasties. Unusually, they're displayed by motif rather than by period: dragons, phoenixes, lotus flowers, and bats are some of the auspicious designs. Bronzes, jade, lacquerware, textiles, enamel, and glassware complete this collection of decorative art.

In the **Chinese Fine Art Gallery** you get a great intro-duction to Chinese brush painting, often difficult for the western eye to appreciate. Landscape paintings from the 20th-century Guangdong and Lingnan schools form the bulk of the collection, and modern calligraphy also gets a nod.

The **Contemporary Hong Kong Art Gallery** on the sec-ond floor showcases a mix of traditional Chinese and western techniques. Paintings account for most of the pieces from the first half of the 20th century, when local artists used the traditional mediums of brush and ink in innovative ways. Western techniques dominate later work, the result of Hong Kong artists' having spent more time abroad.

FAMILY **Hong Kong Space Museum.** A structure behind the art museum that looks like an oversize golf ball sliced in half houses a planetarium, a solar telescope, and an Omnimax theater. It's all fairly unremarkable, though, and children under 3 aren't allowed to view the Omnimax shows. ✉ *10 Salisbury Rd., Tsim Sha Tsui* ☎ *2721–0226* ⊕ *hk.space. museum* 🎫 *HK$10* ⊙ *Mon. and Wed.–Fri. 1–9, weekends and holidays 10–9* Ⓜ *Tsim Sha Tsui MTR, Exit F.*

Kowloon Mosque and Islamic Centre. Hong Kong's largest Islamic worship center stands in front of Kowloon Park. Visitors can call ahead to arrange for a tour or simply drop by the building, which was designed by noted Indian architect I. M. Kadri. In addition to prayer halls, the complex includes a medical clinic and a library. ✉ *105 Nathan Rd., Tsim Sha Tsui* ☎ *2724–0095* ⊕ *kowloonmosque.com* 🎫 *Free* ⊙ *5 am–10 pm* Ⓜ *Tsim Sha Tsui, Exit A1.*

Nathan Road. Running for several miles, this street is filled with hotels, restaurants, malls, and boutiques—retail space is so costly that the southern end is dubbed the Golden Mile. The mile's most famous tower block is ramshackle Chungking Mansions, packed with cheap hotels and Indian restaurants. The building was a setting for local director Wong Kar-Wai's film *Chungking Express.* To the left and right are mazes of narrow streets with even more shops selling jewelry, electronics, clothes, souvenirs, and cosmetics. ✉ *Nathan Rd. between Salisbury Rd. and Boundary St., Tsim Sha Tsui* Ⓜ *Tsim Sha Tsui, Jordan, Yau Ma Tei, Mong Kok, Prince Edward.*

West Kowloon Cultural District. Though a little bit farther west than Tsim Sha Tsui's main attractions, the West Kowloon Cultural District makes for a nice change of pace. The entire project is slated to be completed in 2017, but already the grassy harbor-front park offers a nice getaway from Kowloon's crowded corners. It hosts music concerts, food festivals, arts exhibits—whatever's on the docket. Rent a bike and pedal around for some fresh air and striking harbor views. ✉ *West Kowloon Waterfront Promenade, Tsim Sha Tsui* ⊕ *www.westkowloon.hk* ⊙ *Daily 6 am–11 pm* Ⓜ *Kowloon Station, Exit D.*

YAU MA TEI

North of Tsim Sha Tsui the vibrant area of Yau Ma Tei teems with people and is home to several street markets. The area of Yau Ma Tei around Jordan Road blends into the neighboring district, and the Jordan MTR stop is a good place to start your exploring.

TOP ATTRACTIONS

Temple Street. In the heart of Yau Ma Tei, Temple Street is home to Hong Kong's biggest night market. Stalls selling kitsch of all kinds set up in the late afternoon in the blocks north of Public Square Street. Fortune-tellers, open-air cafés, and street doctors also offer their services here. ✉ *Temple St. between Jordan Rd. and Kansu St., Yau Ma Tei* Ⓜ *Yau Ma Tei, Exit C; Jordan, Exit A.*

Tin Hau Temple. This incense-filled site is dedicated to Taoist sea goddess Tin Hau, queen of heaven and protector of seafarers. The crowds here

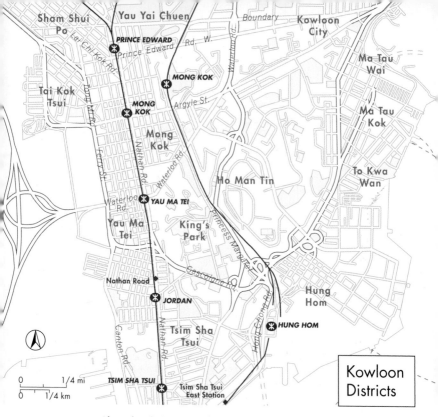

testify to her being one of Hong Kong's favorite deities—indeed, this is one of over 100 temples dedicated to her. Like all Tin Hau temples, this one once stood on the shore. Kowloon reclamation started in the late 19th century, and now the site is more than 3 km (2 miles) from the harbor. The main altar is hung with gold-embroidered cloth and usually piled high with offerings. There are also two smaller shrines inside the temple honoring earth god Tou Tei and city god Shing Wong. Surrounding Temple Street night market is a fortune-telling hot spot: you may well be encouraged to have a try with the chim. Each stick is numbered, and you shake them in a cardboard tube until one falls out. A fortune-teller asks you your date of birth and makes predictions from the stick based on numerology. Alternatively, you could have a mystically minded bird pick out some fortune cards for you. ■TIP→ Agree on a price before your fortune, as bargaining with fortune-tellers is common. ⊠ Market St., between Temple St. and Nathan Rd., Yau Ma Tei ☎ 2385–0759 ⊙ Daily 7–5:30 Ⓜ Yau Ma Tei, Exit C.

WORTH NOTING

Kansu Street Jade Market. From priceless ornaments to plastic pendants, if it's green and shiny, it's here. Quality and prices at the stalls vary hugely, so if you're not with a jade connoisseur, stick with the cheap and cheerful. ⊠ *Kansu St. between Battery St. and Reclamation St., Yau Ma Tei* ☒ *Free* ⊘ *Daily 10–5* Ⓜ *Yau Ma Tei, Exit C.*

Shanghai Street. Traditional trades are plied along this street. There are blocks dominated by tailors or shops selling Chinese cookware or everything you need to set up a household shrine. Nearby Ning Po Street is known for its paper kites and for the colorful paper and bamboo models of worldly possessions (boats, cars, houses) that are burned at Chinese funerals. ⊠ *Shanghai St. between Jordan Rd. and Argyle St., Yau Ma Tei* Ⓜ *Yau Ma Tei, Exit C.*

Yau Ma Tei Theatre. The government transformed this former movie theater (which screened adult films for years before being abandoned) into a 300-seat venue for Chinese opera performances. Some of the shows have English supertitles. A historic redbrick building around the corner on Shanghai Street serves as the theater's administration building. ⊠ *6 Waterloo Rd., Yau Ma Tei* ☎ *2264–8108* ⊕ *www.lcsd.gov.hk/ymtt* ⊘ *Daily 1–8* Ⓜ *Yau Ma Tei, Exit B2.*

MONG KOK

Mong Kok lives up to its Chinese name, which translates roughly as "busy corner." Long city blocks here are known for bustling markets that sell clothing, flowers, pets, and temple goods. The neighborhood is the epicenter of Hong Kong street fashion—the trends that originate from these bustling streets are known as "MK style." Mong Kok is technically the last district of Kowloon: Boundary Street marks the beginning of the New Territories, though these days the urbanized areas are known as New Kowloon.

WORTH NOTING

Fa Yuen Street. Parallel to Tung Choi Street Ladies' Market, this street is sneaker central, lined with shoe shops selling some brands you know and lots more you don't. If you're not sporty, the stretch between Mongkok Road and Nullah Road offers cheap versions of the latest clothing fashion trends. ⊠ *Fa Yuen St. between Mongkok Rd. and Shan Tung St., Mong Kok* ☒ *Free* Ⓜ *Mong Kok, Exit D3.*

Flower Market. Stalls containing local and imported fresh flowers, potted plants, and even artificial blossoms cover Flower Market Road, as well as parts of Yuen Po Street, Yuen Ngai Street, Prince Edward Road West, and Playing Field Road. ⊠ *Flower Market Rd. between Yuen Ngai St. and Yuen Po St., Mong Kok* ☒ *Free* ⊘ *Daily 7–7* Ⓜ *Mong Kok East, Exit C; Prince Edward, Exit B1.*

FAMILY **Goldfish Market.** A few dozen shops at the northern end of Tung Choi Street, starting at the intersection with Nullah Road, sell the ubiquitous fish, which locals believe to be lucky. There are other types of animals as well. ⊠ *Tung Choi St. and Nullah Rd., Mong Kok* ☒ *Free* ⊘ *10:30–10* Ⓜ *Mong Kok East, Exit C; Prince Edward, Exit B2.*

Tung Choi Street Ladies' Market. Despite the name, the stalls here are filled with no-brand clothing and accessories for both sexes. The shopping is best between Dundas and Argyle. ⊠ *Tung Choi St. between Dundas St. and Argyle St., Mong Kok* ☒ *Free* Ⓜ *Mong Kok.*

FAMILY **Yuen Po Street Bird Garden.** Adjacent to the Flower Market, this street has more than 70 stalls selling different types of twittering, fluttering birds. Pretty wooden birdcages, starting from about HK$500, are also on offer. ⊠ *Yuen Po St. between Boundary St. and Prince Edward Rd. W, Mong Kok* ⊙ *Daily 7 am–8 pm* Ⓜ *Mong Kok East, Exit C; Prince Edward, Exit B1.*

NORTHERN KOWLOON

There's much to do in Kowloon beyond Tsim Sha Tsui and Mong Kok. Wong Tai Sin Temple and Chi Lin Nunnery, just a few subway stops to the east of Mong Kok, are two of Hong Kong's must-do spiritual sights. The Kowloon Walled City Park and Cattle Depot Artist Village are surrounded by fairly uninspiring residential and commercial districts but still worth a trip.

TOP ATTRACTIONS

Fodor'sChoice **Chi Lin Nunnery.**
★   ⇨ *See highlighted listing in this section.*

Kowloon Walled City Park. One of Hong Kong's most beautiful parks, Kowloon Walled City Park is designed in Qing-dynasty style. In previous centuries it was a walled military site, then a notorious slum. Today the major attraction is the Yamen—the imperial government administrative building—the only remaining structure from the original Walled City and an example of southern Chinese architecture of the 19th century. There are also a number of traditional gardens on the grounds, and eight zones showcasing different flora that you can see on free 45-minute guided tours on weekends. Hong Kong's Thai community is based in the streets south of the park, and there are countless hole-in-the-wall Thai restaurants. Bus 113 stops nearby, or take the MTR to Kowloon Tong and take a cab. ⊠ *Tung Tau Tsuen Rd. between Junction Rd. and Tung Tsing Rd., Northern Kowloon* ☎ *2716–9962* ⊕ *www.lcsd.gov.hk* 🎫 *Free* ⊙ *6:30 am–11 pm.*

▌ **DID YOU KNOW?** Only the occasional patch of daylight was visible from the labyrinthine alleys of the Kowloon Walled City, Hong Kong's most notorious slum. Originally a 19th-century Chinese fortress, the city wasn't included in the British lease of the New Territories, thus it remained part of China and out-of-bounds to the Hong Kong police. The Triads—organized-crime organizations comparable to the Mafia—ruled its unlicensed doctors and dentists, opium dens, brothels, gambling houses, and worse.

Fodor'sChoice **Sik Sik Yuen Wong Tai Sin Temple.** There's a practical approach to prayer at
★   one of Hong Kong's most exuberant places of worship. Here the territory's three major religions—Taoism, Confucianism, and Buddhism—are all celebrated under the same roof. You'd think that ornamental religious buildings would look strange with highly visible vending machines and LCD displays in front of them, but Wong Tai Sin pulls it off in cacophonous style. The temple was established in the early 20th century, on a different site on Hong Kong Island, when two Taoist masters arrived from Guangzhou with the portrait of Wong Tai Sin—a famous

CHI LIN NUNNERY

⊠ *5 Chi Lin Dr., Northern Kowloon* ☎ *2354–1888*
💺 *Free* ⊗ *Nunnery daily 9–4, lotus pond garden daily 7–7*
Ⓜ *Diamond Hill, Exit C2.*

2

TIPS

■ Left of the Main Hall is a don't-miss hall dedicated to Avalokitesvra, better known in Hong Kong as Kwun Yum, goddess of mercy and childbearing, among other things. She's one of the few exceptions to the rule that bodhisattvas are represented as asexual beings.

■ Be sure to keep looking up—the latticework ceilings and complicated beam systems are among the most beautiful parts of the building. Combine Chi Lin Nunnery with a visit to Sik Sik Yuen Wong Tai Sin Temple, only one MTR stop or a short taxi ride away.

Not a single nail was used to build this nunnery, which dates back to 1934. Instead, traditional Tang Dynasty architectural techniques involving wooden dowels and bracket work hold everything together. Most of the 15 cedar halls house altars to bodhisattvas (those who have reached enlightenment)—bronze plaques explain each one.

Highlights

Feng shui principles governed construction. The buildings face south toward the sea, to bring abundance; their backs are to the mountain, a provider of strength and good energy. The temple's clean lines are a vast departure from most of Hong Kong's colorful religious buildings—here painted wood and gleaming Buddha statues are the only adornments.

The **Main Hall** is the most imposing—and inspiring—part of the monastery. Overlooking the smaller second courtyard, it honors the first Buddha, known as Sakyamuni. The soaring ceilings are held up by cedar columns that support the roof—no mean feat, given that its traditionally made clay tiles make it extremely heavy.

Courtyards and gardens, where frangipani flowers scent the air, run beside the nunnery. The gardens are filled with bonsai trees and artful rockeries. Nature is also present inside: the various halls and galleries all look onto two courtyards filled with geometric lotus ponds and manicured bushes. Neighboring Nan Lian Garden, built in the same style, is adorned with pretty pavilions and more than 60 types of plants. A famous vegetarian restaurant serves up excellent set meals and dim sum. Proceeds from the restaurant fund the Chi Lin Nunnery.

Sik Sik Yuen Wong Tai Sin Temple is one of Hong Kong's most famous Taoist temples.

monk who was born around AD 328—that still graces the main altar. In the '20s the shrine was moved here and expanded over the years.

Start at the incense-wreathed main courtyard, where the noise of many people shaking out *chim* (sticks with fortunes written on them) forms a constant rhythm. After wandering the halls, take time out in the Good Wish Garden—a peaceful riot of rockery—at the back of the complex. At the base of the complex is a small arcade where soothsayers and palm readers are happy to interpret Wong Tai Sin's predictions for a small fee. At the base of the ramp to the Confucian Hall, look up behind the temple for a view of Lion Rock, a mountain in the shape of a sleeping lion. ■TIP→ If you feel like acquiring a household altar of your own, head for Shanghai Street in Yau Ma Tei, the Kowloon district north of Tsim Sha Tsui, where religious shops abound. ⊠ *Wong Tai Sin Rd., Northern Kowloon* ☎ *2327–8141* ⊕ *www.siksikyuen.org.hk* ☜ *Donations expected. Good Wish Garden HK$2* ☉ *Daily 7–5:30* Ⓜ *Wong Tai Sin, Exit B2 or B3.*

WORTH NOTING

Cattle Depot Artist Village. A former slaughterhouse has been transformed into an artistic hub housing a number of artists' studios, galleries, and theater groups, including 1a Space and On & On Theatre Workshop Company. Individual artists and galleries keep erratic hours, and what you see will depend on who's open to the public at any given time. Take the MTR to Jordan and catch a cab, or take a bus that goes through To Kwa Wan, such as the 101. ⊠ *63 Ma Tau Kok Rd., To Kwa Wan, Northern Kowloon* ☎ *2848–6230* ⊕ *www.heritage.gov.hk* ☜ *Free* ☉ *Daily 10–10.*

DAY TRIPS

Updated by
Kate Springer

Beyond all the towering skyscrapers and bustling markets, 70% of Hong Kong's land is rural, rugged, and relatively unspoiled. Easy day trips from one of the most startlingly busy and modern metropolises in the world take you to pristine beaches, hillside forests, and still-quiet fishing villages. No matter what sort of experience you crave, Hong Kong's vast and efficient transport network makes it easy to get around.

Beach lovers usually head to the south side of Hong Kong Island, where the seaside towns of Shek O and Stanley are surrounded by popular stretches of sand. But you never get too far from civilization in Hong Kong—the ever-popular Ocean Park, an aquarium and water park, is also set amid the beautiful Southside scenery.

Lantau is the largest of Hong Kong's more than 260 islands, and has long been a favorite getaway for city dwellers who want to escape to the forested landscapes and mountain vistas. The island is home to the world's favorite mouse, at Hong Kong Disneyland, as well as one of the world's largest Buddhas, the Tian Tan Buddha at Ngong Ping. Near these sights are towering peaks offering mountain hikes, and nice beaches backed by quiet fishing villages. You can take in the scenery from the Ngong Ping 360 cable car, a 5¾-km (3½-mile) ride filled with fantastic views of Lantau's steep northern coast.

Many of Hong Kong's lush, trail-laced parks are tucked away in the New Territories, on the eastern side of Kowloon. Here you can also catch glimpses of traditional life in rustic villages, visit incense-filled temples, or lie on pristine beaches.

SOUTHSIDE

Sightseeing
☆☆★★

Dining
☆☆★★

Lodging
☆☆★★

Shopping
☆☆☆★

For all the unrelenting urbanity of Hong Kong Island's north coast, the south coast is a rolling landscape of green hills dropping down to picturesque bays and sandy beaches. With beautiful sea views, Southside is a breath of fresh air—literally and figuratively—and coveted turf for some of Hong Kong's wealthiest residents. The pace is slower than it is in more congested parts of the city, and there are lots of sea breezes and opportunities to take sampan rides, play a round of golf, swim, or simply enjoy the scenery.

TOP ATTRACTIONS

FAMILY **Ocean Park.** Most Hong Kongers have fond childhood memories of this aquatic theme park. It was built by the omnipresent Hong Kong Jockey Club on 170 hilly acres overlooking the sea just east of Aberdeen. Highlights include the resident pandas, an enormous aquarium, and the Ocean Theatre, where dolphins and seals perform. Youngsters love thrill rides like the gravity-defying Hair Raiser. The park is accessible by a number of buses, including the 629 and 629A; get off at the stop after the Aberdeen tunnel. ■ TIP➜ If you have kids, plan to spend the whole day here. ⊠ *Ocean Park Rd., Aberdeen, Southside* ☎ *3923–2323* ⊕ *www.oceanpark.com.hk* ⬚ *HK$320* ⊙ *Daily 10–7:30.*

Stanley. This peninsula town lies south of Deep Water and Repulse bays. There's great shopping in the renowned Stanley Market, full of casual clothes, cheap souvenirs, and cheerful bric-a-brac. Stanley's popular beach is the site of the Dragon Boat Races every June. To get here from Exchange Square Bus Terminus in Central, take Bus 6, 6A, 6X, 66, 64, or 260. ⊠ *Southside.*

WORTH NOTING

Aberdeen. Aberdeen's harbor contains about 3,000 junks and sampans, and each might be home to several generations of one family. During the Tin Hau Festival in April and May, hundreds more boats converge along the shore. On Aberdeen's side streets you'll find outdoor barbers hard at work and any number of dim sum restaurants serving up dishes you won't find at home. You'll also see traditional sights like the Aberdeen Cemetery, with its enormous terraced gravestones, and yet another shrine to the goddess of the sea: the Tin Hau Temple. ⊠ *Southside.*

Ap Lei Chau Island. A bridge connects Aberdeen with Ap Lei Chau Island (Duck's Tongue Island), where you'll find popular shopping malls like designer-packed Horizon Plaza. ⊠ *Southside.*

Deep Water Bay. Just east of Ocean Park is this lovely beach that's often overlooked by tourists, though weekends can get a bit more crowded.

South China Sea

0 ⊢——⊣ 2 miles
0 ⊢——⊣ 2 kilometers

TAKING IT IN	TRANSPORTATION FROM CENTRAL TO ...
It's best to pick one hub out here, and explore in and around it: Aberdeen with its junks and sampans on the southwest coast; Stanley and its market on the south-central coast; or Shek O with its beaches and parkland far to the southeast.	**Aberdeen:** 30 minutes via Bus 70 or 91. (Ap Lei Chau is 15 minutes from Aberdeen on Bus 90, 90B or 91; 10 minutes by sampan).
	Deep Water Bay: 25 minutes via Bus 6, 6A, or 260.
	Ocean Park: 35 minutes via Bus 629.
	Repulse Bay: 30 minutes via Bus 6, 6A, 6X, or 260.
Gray Line Tours. This company offers seven-hour day trips of Hong Kong Island including Man Mo Temple, Victoria Peak, Aberdeen Fishing Village, and Stanley Market. A dim sum lunch is included in the HK$690 price. ☎ 2368–7111 ⊕ www.grayline. com.hk.	**Shek O:** 50 minutes via MTR to Shau Kei Wan and then Bus 9 to the last stop.
	Stanley: 40 minutes via Bus 6, 6A, 6X, 66, 260.
	Note that express buses skip Aberdeen and Deep Water Bay, heading directly to Repulse Bay and Stanley. Buses run less frequently in the evening, so it's more convenient to grab a taxi (they're everywhere, unless it is 4 pm, when taxi drivers change shifts).

Choi Wan

Happy Valley

Hong Kong Island

Tung Lung Chau

Talbong Channel

Deep Water Bay

The Black Sheep Restaurant

The Verandah at Repulse Bay

Shek O

D'AGUILAR PENINSULA

Middle Island

Ng Fan Chau

Repulse Bay

Tai Tam Bay

Stanley

Chung Hom Wan

Stanley Market

Cape D'Aguilar

Kau Pei Chau

Round Island

Stanley Bay

Bluff Head

Sheung Sze Mun

Sung Kong

Beaufort Island

Po Toi Islands

Castle Rock

Po Toi

Mat Chau

Southside

In Stanley Market there are dozens of cheap local and international eateries. For more upscale yet still casual joints, head to Stanley Main Road.

Black Sheep Restaurant. A favorite place for lunch, drinks, or just alfresco lounging is pleasantly small and offers an eclectic menu and a relaxed vibe. ⊠ *330 Shek O Village Rd., Shek O, Southside, Hong Kong, China* ☎ *2809–2021.*

The Verandah at the Repulse Bay. Treat yourself to British-style high tea at the elegantly appointed Verandah restaurant. Tea is served Wednesday to Saturday from 3 to 5:30 and Sunday from 3:30 to 5:30. ⊠ *Repulse Bay Hong Kong, 109 Repulse Bay Rd., Southside* ☎ *2292–2822* ⊕ *www. therepulsebay.com* ⊙ *Closed Mon. and Tues.*

Deep Water Bay Golf Club. Deep Water Bay is flanked to the north by the Deep Water Bay Golf Club, which is owned by the Hong Kong Golf Club. The most convenient course to play if you're staying on Hong Kong Island has 18 challenging holes. It's technically a members-only club (some of Hong Kong's richest businessmen play here), but it's casual, and visitors with handicap certificates can reserve a tee time on weekdays. On top of the HK$1,200 greens fee, club rentals will cost you another HK$450, and a caddy another HK$225. The club also has two restaurants, one serving Chinese fare, the other western dishes. ⊠ *19 Island Rd., Deep Water Bay* ☎ *2812–7070* ⊕ *www.hkgolfclub.org* ⊞ *HK$1,200.*

Repulse Bay is one of Hong Kong's most popular beaches, and it's very easy to reach from Central.

It's a good place to have a barbecue or swim under the watchful eye of a lifeguard. Leafy trees provide ample shade, and there's a great view of the Ocean Park cable car. To get here, take Bus 6, 6A, or 260 from Exchange Square Bus Terminus in Central. **Amenities:** food and drink; lifeguards; parking (fee); showers; toilets; water sports. **Best for:** swimming; sunset; walking. ⊠ *Southside* ☎ *2812–0228.*

Repulse Bay. The beach in this tranquil neighborhood is large and wide, but be warned: it's the first stop for most visitors to Southside. Two huge statues of Tin Hau—goddess of the sea—at the east end of the beach were built in the 1970s. Worshippers had planned to erect just one statue, but worried she'd be lonely. Look for a famous apartment building with a hole through it—following the principles of feng shui, the opening allows the dragon that lives in the mountains behind to readily drink from the bay. To get here, take Bus 6, 6A, 6X, 66, or 260 from Exchange Square Bus Terminus in Central. **Amenities:** food and drink; lifeguards; parking (fee); showers; toilets; water sports. **Best for:** sunset; swimming; walking. ⊠ *Beach Rd. at Seaview Promenade, Repulse Bay, Southside* ☎ *2812–2483.*

FAMILY **Shek O.** The seaside locale is Southside's easternmost village. Every shop sells the same inflatable beach toys—the bigger the better, it seems. Cut through town to a winding road that takes you to the "island" of Tai Tau Chau, really a large rock with a lookout over the South China Sea. You can hike through nearby Shek O Country Park, where the bird-watching is great, in less than two hours. To get here from Central, take the MTR to Shau Kei Wan (Exit A3), then take Bus 9 to the last stop (about 30 minutes). ⊠ *Southside.*

3

LANTAU ISLAND

Sightseeing
★★★★

Dining
☆☆★★

Lodging
☆☆☆★

Shopping
☆☆☆★

Manic development is changing Lantau, but the island is still known as the "lungs of Hong Kong" because of the abundant forests, relative dearth of skyscrapers, and laid-back attractions—beaches, fishing villages, and hiking trails. At Ngong Ping, a mini-theme park sits at the base of the island's most famous sight, the Tian Tan Buddha. Hong Kong Disneyland sits on the northeast coast, near the airport. At 147 square km (57 square miles), Lantau is almost twice the size of Hong Kong Island, so there's room for all this development, and the island remains a welcome green getaway.

TOP ATTRACTIONS

FAMILY **Hong Kong Disneyland.** Though Hong Kong's home to Mickey Mouse is tame compared with other Magic Kingdoms, it's fast bringing Mai Kei Lo Su—as the world's most famous mouse is known locally—to a mainland audience. Younger kids will find plenty of amusement, but their older siblings and parents will have to settle for just one thrill ride, Space Mountain. If you need to visit a theme park in Hong Kong, Ocean Park in Aberdeen is a better bet. ⊠ *Fantasy Rd., Lantau Island* ⊕ *park.hongkongdisneyland.com* ☒ *HK$450* ⊙ *Daily 9–9* Ⓜ *Disneyland Resort.*

Fodor'sChoice **Tian Tan Buddha.**

★ ⇨ *See highlighted listing in this chapter.*

WORTH NOTING

Cheung Sha Beach. Three kilometers (2 miles) of golden sand make Cheung Sha Beach one of Hong Kong's longest stretches of sand. It gets breezy at this spot 8 km (5 miles) southwest of Mui Wo, so it's popular

TIAN TAN BUDDHA

✉ *Ngong Ping, Lantau Island* ☎ *2985-5248* ⊕ *www.plm.org.hk* 🍴 *Monastery and path free. Walking with Buddha: HK$40* ⊙ *Buddha daily 10–5:30, monastery and path daily 8–6* Ⓜ *Tung Chung, Exit B.*

TIPS

■ You can get here on the Ngong Ping 360 gondola from a terminal adjacent to the MTR station in Tung Chung or via Bus 2 from Mui Wo or Bus 23 from Tung Chung.

■ The only way to the upper level, right under the Buddha, is through an underwhelming museum inside the podium. You only get a couple of feet higher up.

■ The booth at the base of the stairs is only for tickets for lunch—wandering around the Buddha is free.

■ The monastery's vegetarian restaurant is a clattering canteen with uninspiring fare. Pick up sandwiches at the Citygate Mall, Tung Chung, or eat at a restaurant in Ngong Ping Village.

Hong Kongers love superlatives, even if making them true requires strings of qualifiers. So the Tian Tan Buddha, also known as the Big Buddha, is the world's largest Buddha—that's seated, located outdoors, and made of bronze. Just know the vast silhouette is impressive. A set of 268 steep stairs leads to the lower podium, essentially forcing you to stare up at all 202 tons of Buddha as you ascend. At the top, cool breezes and fantastic views over Lantau Island await.

Highlights

Po Lin Monastery. It's hard to believe today, but from its foundation in 1927 through the early '90s, this monastery was virtually inaccessible by road. These days, it's at the heart of Lantau's biggest attraction. The monastery proper has a gaudy orange temple complex. Still, it's the Buddha people come for.

Wisdom Path. This peaceful path runs beside 38 halved tree trunks arranged in an infinity shape on a hillside. Each is carved with Chinese characters that make up the Heart Sutra, a 5th-century Buddhist prayer that expresses the doctrine of emptiness. The idea is to walk around the path—which takes five minutes—and reflect. Follow the signposted trail to the left of the Buddha.

Ngong Ping Village. People were fussing about this attraction before its first stone was laid. Ngong Ping Village is a moneymaking add-on to the Tian Tan Buddha. Walking With Buddha is intended to be a 20-minute-long educational stroll through the life of Siddhartha Gautama, the first Buddha, but it's more of a multimedia extravaganza that shuns good taste with such kitsch as a self-illuminating Bodhi tree and piped-in incense. No cost has been spared in the dioramas that fill the seven galleries—ironic, given that each represents a stage of the Buddha's path to enlightenment and the eschewing of material wealth.

with windsurfers. Upper Cheung Sha Beach is equipped for barbecues, and there is also a refreshment stand. Sunset here is a perfect end to a sun-drenched day. ■ **TIP→ There are only 50 taxis on the entire island, which you should keep in mind when things get busy.** To get here, take the ferry from Central's Pier 6 to Mui Wo, and then hop on Bus 1 or 2 for about 25 minutes. **Amenities:** food and drink; lifeguards; parking (fee); showers; toilets; water sports. **Best for:** sunset; swimming; walking. ⊠ *South Lantau Rd., Lantau Island* ☎ *2980–2114.*

Lantau Peak. The most glorious views of Lantau—and beyond—are from atop Lantau Peak, but at 3,064 feet, the mountaintop experience is not for the faint-hearted. The ascent up the mountain that locals call Fung Wong Shan requires a strenuous 7½-mile hike west from Mui Wo, or you can begin at the Po Lin Monastery—still a demanding two hours. You can also take Bus 23 to a trail that is closer to the summit, and climb from Stage 3 of the Lantau Trail. The most striking views are at sunrise, particularly between December and February, when the air is dry and the sky is clear. ⊠ *Lantau Island.*

DID YOU KNOW?

Lantau is connected to the Kowloon Peninsula by the world's longest rail-carrying suspension bridge, the 4,518-foot Tsing Ma Bridge. Airport Express and MTR trains run through the sheltered lower level; a highway runs on top, affording stunning views of the Pearl River Delta to the west.

Tai O. Tucked away on the western end of Lantau, this fishing village inhabited largely by the *tanka* (boat people), some of whom still live in stilt houses, is a great place to spend a few hours. There's a temple dedicated to Kwan Tai, god of war, that was established in the 15th century. Remains of salt pans line part of the shoreline, and a look seaward sometimes rewards you with a sighting of a rare Hong Kong pink dolphin. The 1902 Tai O Police Station, on the village's southwest tip, has been restored and converted into the Tai O Heritage Hotel, a great place for tea or a meal. ⊠ *Lantau Island.*

GETTING ORIENTED

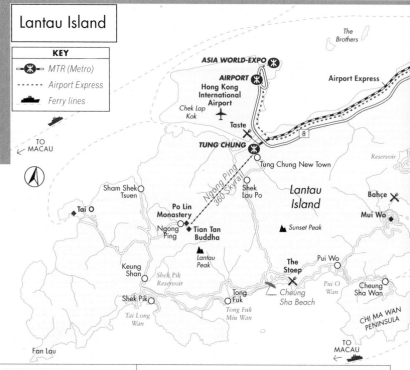

Lantau Island

KEY
- ━━●❋●━━ *MTR (Metro)*
- - - - - - *Airport Express*
- ▰▰▰ *Ferry lines*

The Brothers

ASIA WORLD-EXPO ❋

AIRPORT ❋
Hong Kong
International
Airport

Airport Express

Chek Lap
Kok

Taste ✕

8

TO
MACAU

TUNG CHUNG ❋

Tung Chung New Town

Reservoir

Sham Shek○
Tsuen

Shek
Lau Po○

*Lantau
Island*

Bahçe ✕

Tai O ◆

Po Lin
Monastery

Ngong ◆ Tian Tan
Ping   Buddha

▲ Sunset Peak

Mui Wo ◆

*Ngong Ping
360 Skyrail*

▲
*Lantau
Peak*

Pui Wo○

Keung
Shan○

*Shek Pik
Reservoir*

The
Stoep
✕

*Pui O
Wan*

Cheung○
Sha Wan

Shek Pik○

Tong○
Fuk

Cheung
Sha Beach

*Tong Fuk
Miu Wan*

CHI MA WAN
PENINSULA

*Tai Long
Wan*

Fan Lau

⊙

TO
MACAU
← ▰▰▰

THE TERRITORY	TOURS TO TAKE IT IN
Lantau is connected to Kowloon by the lengthy Tsing Ma Bridge. Most Lantau roads lead to and from Tung Chung, the new high-rise town on the north shore, just west of the bridge and close to Hong Kong International Airport. The Tung Chung Road winds through the mountains and connects northern Lantau with the southern coast. Here the South Lantau Road stretches from the town of Mui Wo (where ferries from Central arrive) in the east to Tai O in the west, passing Cheung Sha Beach and Ngong Ping.	**Hong Kong Dolphinwatch.** Candy-pink dolphins might sound like something Disney cooked up, but Lantau's cutest residents are the endangered species *Sousa chinensis,* native to the Pearl River estuary. Only 60 or so are left in Hong Kong, but experienced ecotourism company Hong Kong Dolphinwatch has a 97% sighting rate on its four-hour cruises. The price is HK$420, which includes return transportation to Tsim Sha Tsui. ☎ *2984–1414* ⊕ *www.hkdolphinwatch.com.* **Splendid Tours.** To see Lantau's big sights whistle-stop style, try Splendid Tours. A daylong trip (HK$800, including lunch) takes in the Tsing Ma Bridge, Tai O Village, and Ngong Ping. ☎ *2316–2151* ⊕ *www.splendid.hk.*

TSING YI

SUNNY BAY · Tsing Ma Bridge · Shek Wan · Tsing Yi

DISNEYLAND · Hong Kong Disneyland · Yam · Pa Tau Kwu

Discovery Bay

Discovery Bay · Siu Kau Yi Chau · Green Island

Tai Shui Hang · Peng Chau · Kennedy Town

Silvermine Bay · Sunshine Island (Chau Kung To) · Hong Kong Island

Hei Ling Chau

Yung Shue Wan

Cheung Chau

Tung Wan

TO → HONG KONG

0   2 miles
0   2 kilometers

GETTING AROUND

The speediest way to get to Lantau from Central is the MTR's Tung Chung line (HK$24), which takes about half an hour. Far more pleasant is the 35-minute ferry from Central to Mui Wo (get a window seat for the views).

New World First Ferry. These ferries to Mui Wo depart every 30 to 40 minutes from Central's Pier 6. The cost is HK$15.20 to HK$42.90 each way. ☎ 2131–8181 ⊕ www.nwff.com.hk.

Ngong Ping 360. The most direct (and daring) way to reach the giant statue and monastery at Ngong Ping is on the Ngong Ping 360, a view-filled 25-minute gondola ride that departs from a terminal adjacent to the MTR station in Tung Chung. If you're not scared of heights, splurge on one of the "crystal" cabins, which have glass floors for the best views. ☎ 3666–0606 ⊕ www.np360.com.hk ✉ HK$105 one way; HK$150 round-trip ⊙ Weekdays 10–6, weekends 9–6:30.

QUICK BITES

Bahçe Turkish Restaurant. You're spoiled for choice on the Mui Wo waterfront, but this cozy Turkish café is a good bet. You can make a meal out of several meze (small snacks)—the flaky phyllo triangles are delicious—or beef up with a kebab. At night the place is more like a bar. ✉ Mui Wo Centre, 3 Ngan Wan Rd., Mui Wo, Lantau ☎ 2984-0222.

The Stoep. For lunch on Cheung Sha Beach—or on Lantau in general—everyone agrees: these outdoor tables facing the beach (the name means "patio") is the place. It's run by South Africans, and the food's a mix of Mediterranean standards and South African–style barbecued meat—try the mixed grill. ✉ 32 Lower Cheung Sha Village Rd., Lantau ☎ 2980-2699 ⊕ www.thestoep.com.

Taste. If you're hiking, stop off in Tung Chung for provisions. Deli counters in the huge branch of the local supermarket Taste have sushi, sandwiches, salads, baked goods, and fruit. ✉ Citygate Mall, 20 Tat Tung Rd., Lantau ☎ 2109-4500.

THE NEW TERRITORIES

Sightseeing
☆★★★

Dining
☆★★★

Lodging
☆☆★★

Shopping
☆☆★★

With rustic villages, incense-filled temples, green hiking trails, and pristine beaches, the New Territories are a favorite Hong Kong getaway. Sha Tin, Tuen Mun, and other "new towns" house more than half a million residents apiece, making them feel like their own cities. Even so, it's still easy to get away from the urban congestion, visit lush parks, and glimpse traditional rural life in restored walled villages and ancestral clan halls.

TOP ATTRACTIONS

Fodor's Choice   **Hong Kong Heritage Museum.**

⇨ *See highlighted feature in this section.*

Ten Thousand Buddhas Monastery. You climb some 400 steps to reach this temple, but look on the bright side: for each step you get about 32 Buddhas. The uphill path through dense vegetation is lined with 500 life-size golden Buddhas in all kinds of positions. Be sure to bring along water and insect repellent. Prepare to be dazzled inside the main temple, where walls are stacked with gilded ceramic statuettes. There are actually nearly 13,000 here, made by Shanghai artisans and donated by worshippers over the decades. Kwun Yam, goddess of mercy, is one of several deities honored in the crimson-walled courtyard.

Look southwest on a clear day and you can see nearby **Amah Rock,** which resembles a woman with a child on her back. Legend has it that this formation was once a faithful fisherman's wife who climbed the mountain every day to wait for her husband's return, not knowing he'd drowned. Tin Hau, goddess of the sea, took pity on her and turned her to stone.

The temple is in the foothills of Sha Tin, in the central New Territories. Take Exit B out of Sha Tin station, walk down the pedestrian ramp, and take the first left onto Pai Tau Street. Keep to the right-hand side

HONG KONG HERITAGE MUSEUM

✉ *1 Man Lam Rd., Sha Tin, New Territories* ☎ *2180–8188* 🌐 *www.heritagemuseum.gov. hk* 🎫 *HK$10; free on Wed.* 🕐 *Mon. and Wed.–Fri. 10–6; weekends and holidays 10–7* Ⓜ *Che Kung, Exit A; Sha Tin, Exit A.*

TIPS

■ Look for the audio tours in English, which are available for special exhibitions.

■ There's lots of ground to cover: prioritize the New Territories Heritage, the T.T. Tsui Gallery, and the Cantonese Opera Halls, all permanent displays, then move on to the temporary history and art exhibitions if time permits.

■ The museum is a five-minute signposted walk from Che Kung Temple station. If the weather's good, walk back along the leafy riverside path that links the museum with Sha Tin station, in New Town Plaza mall, 15 minutes away.

This fabulous museum is Hong Kong's largest, yet it still seems a well-kept secret: chances are you'll have most of its 12 massive galleries to yourself. They ring an inner courtyard, which pours light into the lofty entrance hall.

Highlights

The **New Territories Heritage Hall** is packed with local history—6,000 years of it. See life as it was in beautiful dioramas of traditional villages—one on land, the other on water (with houses on stilts). The last gallery documents the rise of massive urban New Towns.

In the **T.T. Tsui Gallery of Chinese Art**, exquisite antique Chinese glass, ceramics, and bronzes fill hushed second-floor rooms. The curators have gone for quality over quantity. Look for the 3½-foot-tall terra-cotta *Horse and Rider*, a beautiful example of the figures enclosed in tombs in the Han Dynasty (206 BC–AD 220). The Tibetan religious statues and *thankga* paintings are unique in Hong Kong.

The **Cantonese Opera Heritage Hall** is all singing, all dancing, and utterly hands-on. The symbolic costumes, tradition-bound stories, and stylized acting of Cantonese opera can be impenetrable: the museum provides simple explanations and stacks of artifacts, including century-old sequined costumes that put Vegas to shame. Don't miss the virtual makeup display, where you get your on-screen face painted like an opera character's.

Kids love the **Children's Discovery Gallery,** where hands-on activities for 4- to 10-year-olds include putting a broken "archaeological find" together. The Hong Kong Toy Story charts more than a century of local toys.

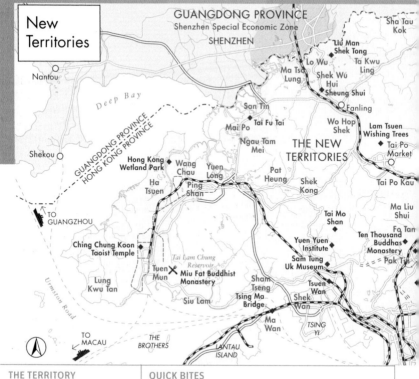

New
Territories

GUANGDONG PROVINCE
Shenzhen Special Economic Zone

SHENZHEN

Sha Tau
Kok

Nantou

Liu Man
Shek Tong

Lo Wu   Ta Kwu
Ma Tso   Ling
Lung   Shek Wu
Hui
Sheung Shui

Deep Bay

San Tin

Tai Fu Tai
Mai Po

Fanling

Wo Hop   Lam Tsuen
Shek   Wishing Trees

Ngau Tam
Mei

THE NEW
TERRITORIES

Tai Po ◆
Market

Shekou

Hong Kong
Wetland Park

Wang
Chau   Yuen
Long

GUANGDONG PROVINCE
HONG KONG PROVINCE

Ha
Tsuen   Ping
Shan

Pat
Heung   Shek
Kong

Tai Po Kau

TO
GUANGZHOU

Ching Chung Koon
Taoist Temple

Tai Lam Chung
Reservoir

Lung
Kwu Tan

Tuen
Mun   Miu Fat Buddhist
Monastery

Tai Mo
Shan

Yuen Yuen
Institute

Sam Tung
Uk Museum

Ma Liu
Shui

Fo Tan
Ten Thousand
Buddhas ◆
Monastery

Pak Tin

Urmston Road

Siu Lam

Sham
Tseng

Tsing Ma
Bridge

Tsuen
Wan

Shek
Wan

TO
MACAU

THE
BROTHERS

Ma
Wan

TSING
YI

LANTAU
ISLAND

THE TERRITORY	QUICK BITES

THE TERRITORY

The New Territories borders mainland China to the north. Sai Kung Peninsula lies to the east. Places worth visiting are a fair distance from each other, so day trips here take some planning. It's best to choose two or three sights to visit in a day, allowing 15–30 minutes of travel time between each, depending on whether you're going by bus or taxi. Note that fewer people speak English away from the city center.

QUICK BITES

Sai Kung Town's waterfront has a plethora of outdoor seafood restaurants.

Chuen Kee Seafood. If you love fish, head straight for the Sai Kung waterfront to get a taste of the village's seafood offerings along what's known as "Seafood Street." The low-key string of eateries here serve up all manner of fresh feasts—choose your lunch from the tanks and have it grilled or panfried to order. For one of the best bets, snag a seat at Chuen Kee Seafood. ⊠ 51–55 Hoi Pong St., Sai Kung, Lantau ☎ 2791–1195.

Honeymoon Dessert Shop. If you have a sweet tooth, drop by the famous Honeymoon Dessert Shop for such sugary delights as mango pudding, chilled sago coconut soup, and banana crepes. Go on, you deserve it. ⊠ 9-10ABC Po Tung Rd., Sai Kung, New Territories ☎ 2792–4991 ⊕ www. honeymoon-dessert.com.

KEY

✈ MTR (Metro)	
------- Light rail	
🚢 Ferry lines	

TAKING IT IN

The best way to see some of the smaller villages is on an organized tour. Gray Line's five-hour Heritage Tour (US$60) takes you to the Man Mo Temple, Lam Tsuen Wishing Trees, and other cultural sights. Gray Line also has half-day tours that stop at the Lam Tsuen Wishing Trees and Tai Po Market, among other places in the New Territories.

Walk Hong Kong. Run by Gabi Baumgartner and Marco Foehn—two expats who have decades of insight into Hong Kong's history and culture—Walk Hong Kong offers walking and hiking tours all over the territory. For maritime and military history buffs, the team counts World War II specialist Martin Heyes among its guides, who walks travelers through the city's past conflict zones. There are also several birdwatching tours, as well as an informative half-day New Territories Heritage Walk that explores walled villages, ancient pagodas and ancestral clan halls. ☎ 9187-8641 ⊕ www.walkhongkong. com 💲 Rates from HK$450 per person.

GETTING AROUND

Between the bus and MTR, you can get close to many sights. Set off on the MTR from Central to Tsuen Wan; from there, taxis, buses, and minibuses will take you to places such as the Yuen Yuen Institute and Tai Mo Shan. For Sha Tin and other spots in the east, take the MTR to Kowloon Tong; transfer to the East Rail line and head to Sha Tin station. To reach the Sai Kung Peninsula, take the MTR from Central to Choi Hung, then the green Minibus 1A to Sai Kung Town.

To tour at your own pace, consider hiring a car and driver.

Ace Hire Car. This rental agency charges HK$250 per hour for a four-seater Benz. ☎ 2893-0541 ⊕ www.acehirecar. com.hk.

The road is paved with golden Buddhas on the path to the Ten Thousand Buddhas Monastery.

of the road and follow it around to the gate where the signposted path starts. ■TIP→ Don't be confused by the big white buildings on the left of Pai Tau Road. They are ancestral halls, not the temple. ⊠ *221 Pai Tau Village, Sha Tin, New Territories* 🖂 *Free* ⊙ *Daily 9–5:30* Ⓜ *Sha Tin, Exit B.*

WORTH NOTING

The Chinese University of Hong Kong Art Museum. Located in the Institute of Chinese Studies building, the museum has paintings and calligraphy from the Qing period to modern times. There are also collections of bronze seals, carved jade flowers, and ceramics from South China. Take the East Rail line to University station, then a campus bus or taxi. ⊠ *Institute of Chinese Studies Bldg., Tai Po Rd., Sha Tin, New Territories* ☎ *3943–7416* ⊕ *www.cuhk.edu.hk/ics/amm* 🖂 *Free* ⊙ *Mon.– Sat. 10–5, Sun. 1–5* Ⓜ *University, Exit D.*

Ching Chung Koon Taoist Temple. This temple has room after room of altars filled with the heady scent of incense. On one side of the main entrance is a cast-iron bell with a circumference of about 5 feet—all large monasteries in ancient China rang such bells at daybreak to wake the monks and nuns for a day of work in the rice fields. On the other side of the entrance is a huge drum that was used to call the workers back in the evening. Inside, some rooms are papered with small pictures; the faithful pay to have these photos displayed so they can see their dearly departed as they pray. Hundreds of dwarf shrubs, ornamental fishponds, and pagodas bedeck the grounds. The temple sits adjacent to the Ching Chung MTR Light Rail station near the town of Tuen Mun.

The entrance isn't obvious, so ask for directions. ⊠ *Tsing Chung Koon Rd., Tuen Mun, New Territories* ☎ *2462–1507* Ⓜ *Siu Hong, Exit B.*

Hong Kong Wetland Park. This vast wetland reserve is home to numerous species of native wildlife, including Hong Kong's own star crocodile, Pui Pui. The reserve has several walks, many suitable for families with children, including a boardwalk through a mangrove habitat and a butterfly garden. The park has a visitor center, which includes an auditorium and several indoor galleries, as well as a café, play area, and souvenir shop. ⊠ *Wetland Park Rd., Tin Shui Wai, New Territories* ☎ *2708–8885, 3152–2666* ⊕ *www.wetlandpark.com* ☝ *HK$30* ✆ *Wed.–Mon. 10–5* Ⓜ *Tin Shui Wai.*

Lam Tsuen Wishing Trees. People from throughout Hong Kong come to these two banyan trees to make wishes and offerings. Some burn joss sticks and incense; others used to throw an orange—tied to a wish written on a piece of paper—up into a tree (if it caught on a branch the wish would come true). Unfortunately, the weight of the oranges caused several branches to fall off and the practice has ended. Now, when people visit the trees—often during exam time or when the health of a loved one is in jeopardy—they tie the joss paper onto nearby wooden racks. Take the East Rail line to Tai Po Market train station, then take Bus 64K or 64P, or Minibus 25K. ⊠ *Lam Tsuen Village, New Territories* ☎ *2638–3678.*

Liu Man Shek Tong Ancestral Hall. In the far northern New Territories—just south of Shenzhen—a small unmarked path in the village of Sheung Shui leads to this ancestral hall. It was built in 1751 for the rich and prosperous Liu clan, and was one of few such halls that survived the Cultural Revolution. A restoration preserved the spectacular original roof and ornamentation, but substituted concrete walls to take the weight off rickety pillars—at some cost to the site's aesthetic unity. Take the East Rail Line to Sheung Shui, then Bus 70X, and alight at the Sheung Shui Bus Terminus on Jockey Club Road. ⊠ *Mun Hau Tsuen, Sheung Shui, New Territories* ☎ *2208–4400* ☝ *Free* ✆ *Wed., Thurs., and weekends 9–1 and 2–5* Ⓜ *Sheung Shui.*

Pak Tai Temple. In the 19th century Cheung Chau Island was a haven for pirates like the notorious Cheung Po Tsai, whose treasure cave is reportedly on the island's southwest tip. The temple here is dedicated to Pak Tai, the god of the sea, who is supposed to have rid the island of pirates. The renovated temple originally dates to 1783, when an image of Pak Tai was brought to appease the spirits of people killed by pirates, thought to be the source of bubonic plague outbreaks. Apparently he did the trick: he remains the island's favorite deity. Beside the main altar are four whalebones from the nearby sea. ■ TIP➜ Make a full day of your trip to Cheung Chau, a gorgeous island with several temples. A walk around the island takes in several temples and the pirate cave. New World First Ferry sails to Cheung Chau twice hourly from Central Ferry Pier 5. Normal ferries take 55 minutes, fast ones 35. Turn left from the Cheung Chau ferry pier and walk ½ km (¼ mile) along waterfront Praya Street, until you see the temple to your right, over a playground. ⊠ *End of Pak She St., Cheung Chau Island, New Territories* ☎ *2981–0663* ⊕ *www.ctc.org.hk* ✉ *Free* ⊙ *Daily 7–5.*

Sai Kung Peninsula. To the east of Sha Tin, the Sai Kung Peninsula is home to one of Hong Kong's most beloved nature preserves, Sai Kung Country Park. It has several hiking trails that wind through majestic hills overlooking the water. The hikes through the hills surrounding High Island Reservoir are also spectacular. Seafood restaurants dot the waterfront in Sai Kung Town as well as the tiny fishing village of Po Toi O in Clear Water Bay. At Sai Kung Town you can rent a sampan that will take you to one of the many islands in the area for a day at the beach. Take the MTR to Diamond Hill (Exit C2) and take Bus 92 to Sai Kung Town. Instead of taking the bus, you can also catch a taxi along Clearwater Bay Road, which will take you into forested areas and land that's only partially developed, with Spanish-style villas overlooking the sea. This excursion will take a full day, and you should only go if it's sunny. ⊠ *Sai Kung Peninsula, Kowloon.*

Sam Tung Uk Museum. A walled Hakka village from 1786 was saved from demolition to create this museum. It's in the middle of industrial Tsuen Wan, in the western New Territories, and its quiet courtyards and small interlocking chambers contrast with the nearby residential towers. It looks more like a large home than a village—not surprisingly, the name translates as "Three Beam House." Rigid symmetry dictated the construction: the ancestral hall and two common chambers form a central axis flanked by private areas. Traditional furniture and farm tools are on display. ∎TIP➜ **Head through the courtyards and start your visit in the exhibition hall at the back, where a display gives helpful background on Hakka culture and pre-industrial Tsuen Wan—explanations are sparse elsewhere. You can also try on a Hakka hat.** ⊠ *2 Kwu Uk La., Tsuen Wan, New Territories* ☎ *2411–2001* ⊕ *www.heritagemuseum. gov.hk* ✉ *Free* ⊙ *Wed.–Mon. 10–6* Ⓜ *Tsuen Wan, Exit B3.*

Sha Tin Racecourse. This popular race track is newer (it opened in 1978) and larger (the capacity is over 83,000) than the one in Happy Valley, and it's a spectacular place to watch a race. It's one of the world's most modern courses and, as such, is the venue for all championship events. Racing season is from September through June. The racecourse has its own stop on the MTR East Rail line that is open only on race days. ⊠ *Near Tai Po Rd., Sha Tin, New Territories* ☎ *2966–6520* ⊕ *www. entertainment.hkjc.com* ✉ *HK$10* Ⓜ *Racecourse.*

Tai Fu Tai Mansion. It's worth the trek almost to the mainland China border to visit this 19th-century home of merchant and philanthropist Man Chung-luen. The surefire path to becoming a big shot in Imperial China was passing civil service examinations, but few people from Hong Kong—which was hicksville at the time—made the grade. Man Chung-luen proved the exception in 1875. Congratulatory tablets from the emperor hang in the house's entrance hall. The room layout, beautifully decorated doors, and roof ridges are all characteristic of Qing-dynasty architecture. Stained glass and rococo moldings reflect European influences, a result of the British victory over China in the Opium War of 1841. Women could watch guests unobserved from an

upper gallery, which also has an enclosed courtyard for stargazing, charmingly called a "moon playing chamber." To reach the house, cross over the road outside Sheung Shui station (Exit A1) and take Bus 76K toward Yuen Long; alight at San Tin, 5½ km (3½ miles) away. The five-minute walk to the mansion is signposted from there. Alternatively, get a taxi from the station—one way costs HK$40. ⊠ *Wing Ping Tsuen, San Tin, New Territories* ⊕ *www.amo.gov.hk* 🎫 *Free* ☉ *Wed.–Mon. 9–1 and 2–5.*

Tai Mo Shan. The name means Big Hat Mountain, and at 3,140 feet this volcanic outcropping in Tai Mo Shan Country Park is Hong Kong's highest point. The "Foggy Mountain" is covered in clouds almost daily, but when the mist—and pollution—clears, the view stretches all the way to Hong Kong Island. To reach the visitor center, take Bus 51 from Tsuen Wan and get off at the Country Park bus stop. Walk 10 minutes up Tai Mo Shan Road. ⊠ *Tai Mo Shan Rd., Tsuen Wan, New Territories* ⊕ *www.afcd.gov.hk.*

Tai Po Market. The name means "shopping place," which it more than lives up to. In the heart of the region's breadbasket, this utilitarian town's main open-air market is a feast for the eyes, with baskets of lush green vegetables, freshly cut meat hanging from great racks overhead, fish swimming in tanks awaiting selection, and all types of baked and steamed treats. To reach the village, take the MTR East Rail Line to the Tai Po Market stop. ⊠ *Fu Shin St., Tai Po, New Territories* Ⓜ *Tai Po Market.*

Tap Mun Island. A couple of temples and shrines dot what's also known as Grass Island, and beautiful beaches line the shore. Most people have a seafood lunch at the New Hon Kee Seafood Restaurant, run by Loi Lam, a stocky, vivacious fellow who speaks fluent English with a fantastic accent he picked up in Manchester, England. A sampan from Wong Shek Pier in Sai Kung Country Park will speed you to the island. ⊠ *New Territories.*

Yuen Yuen Institute. These pavilions and prayer halls, founded in 1950, bring together the three streams of Chinese thought: Buddhism (which emphasizes nirvana and physical purity), Taoism (nature and inner peace), and Confucianism (following the practical and philosophical beliefs of Confucius). The main three-tier red pagoda is a copy of the Temple of Heaven in Beijing, and houses 60 statues representing the full cycle of the Chinese calendar—you can look for the one that corresponds to your birth year and make an incense offering. To reach the institute, take the MTR to Tsuen Wan (Exit B1) and walk five minutes to Shiu Wo Street, then catch green Minibus 81 to the institute. ⊠ *Lo Wai Rd., Sam Dip Tam, New Territories, Tsuen Wan, China* ☎ *2492–2220* ⊕ *www.yuenyuen.org.hk* 🎫 *Free* ☉ *Daily 9–5* Ⓜ *Tsuen Wan, Exit B1.*

SHOPPING

Updated by
Kate Springer

They say the only way to get to know a place is to do what the locals do. When in Rome, scoot around on a Vespa and drink espresso. When in Hong Kong, shop. For most people in this city, shopping is a leisure activity, whether that means picking out a four-figure party dress, rifling through bins at an outlet, upgrading a cell phone, or choosing the freshest fish for dinner.

Shopping is so sacred that sales periods are calendar events, and most stores close on just three days a year—Christmas Day and the first two days of Chinese New Year. Imagine that: 362 days of unbridled purchasing. Opening hours are equally conducive to whiling your life away browsing the racks: all shops are open until 7 or 8 pm; many don't close their doors until midnight.

It's true that the days when everything in Hong Kong was mind-bogglingly cheap are over. It *is* still a tax-free port, so you can get some good deals. But it isn't just about the savings. Sharp contrasts and the sheer variety of experiences available make shopping here very different from back home.

You might find a bargain or two elbowing your way through a chaotic open-air market filled with haggling vendors selling designer knockoffs, the air reeking of the *chou tofu* ("stinky" tofu) bubbling at a nearby food stand. But then you could find a designer number going for half the usual price in a hushed marble-floor mall, the air scented by the designer fragrances of your fellow shoppers. What's more, in Hong Kong the two extremes are often within spitting distance of each other.

Needless to say, thanks to travelers like you running out of space in their suitcases, Hong Kong does a roaring trade in luggage. No need to feel guilty, though—shopping here is practically cultural research. All you're doing is seeing what local life is really like.

TIPS

BARGAINING 101

Prices are always negotiable at markets, and you can expect discounts in small shops, too, especially for electronics or if you buy several things at once. We usually suggest starting to bargain at half the advertised price: you might end up with anything from 10% to 50% off. Be firm and decisive: walking away from a stall can often produce a radical price drop. Don't let anyone guilt-trip you; no Hong Kong salesperson will sell you anything that doesn't cut them a profit.

HAUTE HONG KONG

Local and regional talent is showcased at Hong Kong Fashion Week, held at the Hong Kong Convention & Exhibition Centre every January and July. For more information on fashion week or featured designers such as Guo Pei, Dorian Ho, and Frankie Xie, visit ⊕ *www.hktdc.com*. To read profiles of Hong Kong designers, visit ⊕ *www.hkfda.org*, the website of the Hong Kong Fashion Designers Association.

COMPARISON SHOP

Prices vary hugely. For big items, do research before the trip and then comparison shop in different districts. Ask clerks to record prices on store business cards: it helps you to keep track and ensures that you get the quoted rate if you return to buy. Keep expectations realistic. A US$5 (about HK$40) pure silk shirt probably isn't pure silk. That said, it may still be a good shirt at a great price.

FINDING THE PERFECT FIT

There are no two ways about it: most Americans stand a few inches taller (and wider) than the average Hong Konger. Finding bigger sizes, particularly at cheap shops, can be frustrating. Tailoring—thank goodness it's affordable here—may be the only way to go.

REAL DEAL

Authentic jade can be tricky for the casual shopper to spot, but a couple of simple tricks can help discern genuine from ersatz. When lifted, jade should be heavier than a similarly sized stone. Hold it to the light, and it should look fibrous, not homogenous. A more full-proof technique relies on the shopkeeper's cooperation. Scratch the surface of the stone in question with a knife, scissors, or whatever is on hand, and it shouldn't leave a mark.

SALES SEASON

Hong Kongers look forward to sales like other people look forward to summer vacation. From late December through February and July through September, prices plummet. It may be retail heaven, but it isn't therapy—shoppers all but wrestle bargains from each other at hot sales like Lane Crawford's or Joyce's. Many shops frown on trying things on during sales. Stand your ground, though, and you'll probably swing a fitting room.

SHOPPING TOURS

Asian Cajun. Tours to choice stores—including little-known shops and private dealers—are available from Asian Cajun. ☎ 9278–4174 ⊕ *www. asiancajun.com*.

Hong Kong Art Walk. The art world's version of a pub crawl, Hong Kong Art Walk is an excellent chance to experience the gallery scene. Held over the course of one evening every year, usually in the spring, it gives ticket holders unlimited access to more than 70 galleries where food and drinks donated by neighboring restaurants help create a festive environment. Partial proceeds go to charity, fine arts graduation shows, and participating artists. ⊕ *www.hongkongartwalk.com.*

Shopping 4 U. Malls, markets, and outlets are a part of tailor-made tours led by Shopping 4 U. Book through **Concorde Travel** (*2524–5121* ⊕ *www.concorde-travel.com*). Daylong tours cost HK$710 per person (10-person minimum). ⊠ *Galuxe Bldg., 8–10 On Lan St., 7th fl., Central.*

TRICKS OF THE TRADE

Be wary of absurd discounts, designed purely to get you in the door. Product switches are also common—after you've paid, they pack a cheaper model. Avoid electronics shops in Tsim Sha Tsui, which have earned fearsome reputations thanks to their relentless bait-and-switch tactics. These neon-lit shops are fun to wander through, but do yourself a favor and stick to accountable chain brands for pricey buys. Check purchases carefully, ensuring that clothes are the size you wanted, jewelry is what you picked, and electronics come with the accessories you paid for. *Always* get an itemized receipt. Without one, forget about getting refunds.

Hong Kong Tourism Board. Shops displaying the Hong Kong Tourism Board's "quality tourism service" sticker (an easily recognizable red junk) are good bets. You can complain about prices or service at one of several HKTB offices strewn throughout the city or submit an inquiry online. Find centers at the Peak, at the Star Ferry concourse in Kowloon, and even at the airport. ⊠ *Peak Piazza, Central* ☎ *2508–1234* ⊕ *www. discoverhongkong.com.*

Hong Kong Consumer Council. For complaints about all shops not approved by the Hong Kong Tourism Board, call the Hong Kong Consumer Council. ⊠ *Room 1410, 14th fl., Kodak House II, 39 Healthy St. East, North Point* ☎ *2929–2222* ⊕ *www.consumer.org.hk* ☉ *Closed weekends.*

WATCH OUT FOR FAKES

The Hong Kong government has seriously cracked down on designer fakes. Depending on how strict the police are being, you may not find the choice of knockoffs you were hoping for. Bear in mind that designer fakes are illegal, and you could get into trouble if you get caught with them going through customs.

FINDING YOUR WAY

With space at a premium, shops and small businesses are tucked into all sorts of places—up the back staircase of a scruffy building, down an alleyway, or on an office tower's 13th floor.

CLOSE UP

What to Shop For in Hong Kong

Calligraphy Supplies. Granted, becoming a master brush painter takes years. But calligraphy equipment makes a wonderful display, even if your brushwork doesn't. Boxed sets of bamboo-handled brushes, porcelain inkwells, and smooth ink stones start at about HK$200 at Yue Hwa.

Kitchen Souvenirs. Remind yourself of all those dim sum meals with souvenirs to dress up your dining room. You'll find black-lacquer chopsticks and brocade place mats in street stalls all over town. Stanley Market has beautiful appliqué table linen. Department stores like Wing On sell cheap bamboo dim sum baskets—good for cooking or storage.

Kung-Fu Equipment. If you're addicted to Jackie Chan action flicks, you'll likely love Kung Fu Supplies Co. Stock up on everything from daggers to kempo gloves while you work on that drop kick.

Personalized Seals. Have your name engraved in Chinese, English, or both

on traditional chops (seals). Made of wood, stone, or even jade, they're usually ornately carved, often with animals of the Chinese zodiac. Sets come with a tub of sticky red ink. Man Wa Lane in Sheung Wan is a great place to find them.

Silkware. Silk dressing gowns and basic cheongsams (silk dresses with Mandarin collars) are a bargain in markets and at Yue Hwa or Chinese Arts & Crafts. For more luxurious versions, try Shanghai Tang or Blanc de Chine, which also do men's Mao jackets. Get some brocade cushion covers for a matching bedroom.

Tea Accoutrement. Yixing teapots like those from homegrown brand Fook Ming Tong will melt even coffee-guzzlers' hearts. For the best brews head to the LockCha Tea Shop in Sheung Wan (it also hosts weekly tea classes). Standard leaves come in pretty tins at local supermarkets, and Yue Hwa has cheap porcelain tea sets.

HONG KONG ISLAND

WESTERN

The past is very much alive in the Western district, one of Hong Kong Island's most traditional neighborhoods, and nowhere more than in its shops. Different streets are known as centers for particular trades. Along Hollywood Road, between Sheung Wan and Central, antique Chinese furniture and collectibles fetch high prices in upscale showrooms. You can get similar-looking items half their price (and less than half their age) at the Cat Street Market on Upper Lascar Row, which also does a brisk trade in communist retro paraphernalia, mah-jongg tiles, and fans. Head up the road behind the Man Mo Temple to find couture boutiques, vintage shops, and hipster hangouts sprouting along burgeoning Square Street and Tai Ping Shan Street. Man Wa Lane is the place for chops (seals carved in stone with engraved initials). Traditional Chinese medicine is the commercial lifeblood of Sheung Wan proper: ginseng, snake musk, birds' nests, and sharks' fins are some of the delicacies available. Locals stock up on less exotic household goods at Sincere and Wing On, two of Hong Kong's oldest and largest department stores.

ANTIQUES AND COLLECTIBLES

Yue Po Chai Antique Co. One of Hollywood Road's oldest shops is at the Cat Street end, next to Man Mo Temple. Its vast and varied stock includes porcelain, stone carvings, and ceramics. ⊠ *Ground fl., 132–136 Hollywood Rd., Sheung Wan, Western* ☎ *2540–4374* ⊘ *Closed Sun.* Ⓜ *Sheung Wan, Exit A2.*

ART

Asia Art Archive. The AAA saw it before the rest of us: contemporary Asian art is big. In 2000 the Asian Art Archive set out to address the lack of information on the emerging field and to record its growth. It provides comprehensive research resources through its website, library, and reading facilities, which are open to the public. ⊠ *11th fl., Hollywood Centre, 233 Hollywood Rd., Sheung Wan, Western* ☎ *2815–1112* ⊕ *www.aaa.org.hk* ⊘ *Closed Sun.* Ⓜ *Sheung Wan.*

Gaffer Ltd. The city's first gallery specializing in studio glass—which is gaining respect in the collecting world—has moved to the Western district and broadened its focus. The two-level gallery still hosts a backdrop of modern glass sculptures by artists from Southeast Asia, Australia, and the United States, but also showcases a variety of paintings from primarily Chinese-Australian artists. Expect everything from watercolor to abstract, pop art to traditional oil. ⊠ *Ground fl., 13 Western St., Sai Ying Pun, Western* ☎ *2521–1770* ⊕ *gaffer.com.hk* Ⓜ *Sheung Wan.*

Hanlin Gallery. For Japanese works of art, antiques, modern ceramics, and woodblocks, visit this refined gallery run by specialist Carlos Prata since 1986. His collection and expertise extend to decorative Chinese art, including fans, textiles, and silver. ⊠ *Ground fl., 185 Hollywood Rd., Sheung Wan, Western* ☎ *2522–4479* ⊕ *www.hanlingallery.com* ⊘ *Closed Sun.* Ⓜ *Sheung Wan, Exit A2.*

Sin Sin Fine Art. Works by diverse emerging and established artists from Indonesia, Thailand, mainland China, Hong Kong, and other Asian and European countries reveal the aesthetic tastes of lively Hong Kong designer and entrepreneur Sin Sin Man. There are also regular exhibitions and artist talks. ⊠ *Ground fl., 53–54 Sai St., Sheung Wan, Western* ☎ *2858–5072* ⊕ *www.sinsin.com.hk* ⊘ *Closed Sun.* Ⓜ *Sheung Wan, Exit A2.*

BEAUTY

Eu Yan Sang. The Sheung Wan area is a quaint and pungent place to shop for traditional Chinese herbs and medicines, but this reliable Asia-wide chain—in operation since 1879—is a more straightforward and sanitized option. There are branches all over Hong Kong, including one past immigration in the airport's Terminal One. ⊠ *Shop 281, 2nd fl., Shun Tak Centre, 200 Connaught Rd. Central, Sheung Wan, Western* ☎ *2914–4882* ⊕ *www.euyansang.com* Ⓜ *Sheung Wan, Exit D.*

CLOTHING

Lee Kung Man Knitting Factory. This hole-in-the-wall shop has a surprisingly long history: it dates back to the early 1920s in Guangzhou, where the brand got its start before moving to Hong Kong. Lee Kung Man uses 1950's-era machines to make simple cotton tees and tanks, but the underwear is what brings shoppers flocking in. Despite a loyal hipster following, the store has kept prices relatively affordable, running between about HK$80 and HK$300 per top. Look for the signature cicada logo or the prancing deer at one of the four shops around town. ✉ *111 Wing Lok St., Sheung Wan, Western* ☎ *2543–8579* ⊕ *leekung-man.com* Ⓜ *Sheung Wan, Exit A2.*

Sin Sin Atelier. Everything Sin Sin does is dynamic, exciting, and unique. Her conceptual, minimalist clothing, jewelry, and accessories retain a Hong Kong character, while drawing from other influences—especially Indonesian. Garments are inspired by international fashion, and her silver jewelry features beautiful geometric designs that she calls "artsy yet wearable." The multitalented Sin Sin has a fine-art gallery across the street and also performs Cantonese opera in venues such as City Hall. ✉ *52 Sai St., off Hollywood Rd. at Cat St. end, Western* ☎ *2521–0308* ⊕ *www.sinsin.com.hk* ⊘ *Closed Sun.* Ⓜ *Sheung Wan, Exit A2.*

Vivienne Tam. You know it when you walk into a Vivienne Tam boutique—the strong Chinese-motif prints and modern updates of traditional women's clothing are truly distinct. But don't let the bold, ready-to-wear collections distract you from the very pretty accessories, which include leather bags and other items with Asian embellishments. Tam, who has seven shops here, is one of the best-known designers in Hong Kong—and, even though she's now based in New York, the city still claims her as its own. ✉ *Shop SG03, PMQ, 35 Aberdeen St., Sheung Wan, Western* ☎ *2721–1818* ⊕ *www.viviennetam.com* Ⓜ *Central, Exit D2.*

CRAFTS

Sang Woo Loong. Born in 1915, Mr. Leung Yau Kam is Hong Kong's oldest lantern maker, and he has refused to move his workshop across the border like all the others. These intricate, handmade works in paper take fantastical forms such as bright-orange goldfish. Their role has changed over his long career from functional to purely decorative, but lanterns are still important in Chinese society. This is especially true during the Mid-Autumn Festival, when children carry their special lanterns outdoors to view the full moon. If you can speak Cantonese—or have mastered charades—ask for one that can pack flat. ✉ *Ground fl., 28 Western St., Sai Ying Pun, Western* ☎ *2540–1369* Ⓜ *Sheung Wan, Exit A2.*

DEPARTMENT STORES

Sincere. Run by the same family for more than a century, this eclectic department store has several local claims to fame: it was the first store in Hong Kong to give paid days off to employees, the first to hire women in sales positions (beginning with the founder's wife and sister-in-law), and the first to establish a fixed-price policy backed up by the regionally novel idea of issuing receipts. Although you probably won't have heard of its clothing or electronics brands, you might come across a bargain in one of its five locations throughout Hong Kong. ✉ *189 Des Voeux Rd. Central, Sheung Wan, Western* ☎ *2544–2688, 2830–1016 Customer Service Hotline* ⊕ *www.sincere.com.hk* Ⓜ *Sheung Wan, Exit E3.*

Wing On. Great values on household appliances, kitchenware, and crockery have made Wing On a favorite with locals on a budget since it opened in 1907. It also stocks clothes, cosmetics, and sportswear—just don't expect to find big brands (or even brands you know). Though prices have risen over time, you *can* count on rock-bottom clearance deals and an off-the-tourist-trail experience. The main store is in Sheung Wan, but you can also hunt for bargains at Wing On's four other Hong Kong locations. ✉ *211 Des Voeux Rd., Sheung Wan, Western* ☎ *2852–1888* ⊕ *www.wingonet.com* Ⓜ *Sheung Wan, Exit E3.*

HOME DÉCOR

Lee Fung China Ware Co., Ltd. Friendly service and a decent selection of Chinese and western-style dinnerware make this a good one-stop shop. It also carries vases and antique reproductions. ✉ *Ground fl., 279 Des Voeux Rd. Central, Sheung Wan, Western* ☎ *2524–0630* ⊕ *Sheung Wan, Exit B.*

Wah Tung China Arts. This reliable manufacturer and retailer of predominantly handcrafted ceramics has been in operation since the early days of trade with the West (1863). There are more than 15,000 items on display in the main showroom, and the overwhelmingly large product line includes antique replicas, vases, dinnerware, figurines, and more—all in classic Chinese motifs. You can also visit the shop in the Lee Roy Commercial Building on Hollywood Road. ✉ *16th fl., Cheung Fat Bldg., 7–9 Hill Rd., Western* ☎ *2873–2272* ⊕ *www.wahtungchina.com* ☽ *Closed Sun.* Ⓜ *Kennedy Town.*

MARKETS

PMQ. Formerly the Hollywood Road Police Married Quarters, this renovated heritage building now plays host to more than 100 of Hong Kong's most celebrated indie designers and artists. Weekend night markets—complete with food, drinks, and live music—are one reason to come. You'll also want to head here for one-of-a-kind items like feminine frocks from Aly & Rachelle, eco-friendly bamboo home ware from Bamboa, edgy clutches and jewelry from Cecilia Ma, quirky Hong Kong–themed accessories from Mail852, and smart menswear from Harrison Wong. Don't worry if you work up an appetite: there are also excellent restaurants on the premises, including Michelin-starred-chef Jason Atherton's newest venture, Aberdeen Street Social, which has earned rave reviews for its welcoming two-story space and British-fusion food. ✉ *35 Aberdeen St., Sheung Wan, Western* ☎ *2870–2335* ⊕ *www.pmq.org.hk* Ⓜ *Sheung Wan, Exit E2.*

Western Market. This redbrick Edwardian-style building in the Sheung Wan district is a declared monument and the oldest existing market building in Hong Kong; when built in 1906 it was used as a produce market. These days its classical facades are filled with kitschy commerce, with a few unmemorable shops selling crafts, toys, jewelry, and collectibles on the ground floor. Skip these and head up the escalator, where you'll find a remarkable selection of fabric: satins, silks, sequins

The dried-seafood shops on Des Voeux Road West promise traditional Chinese cures for all your ailments.

are all here and worth a look. A more authentic experience is lunch, dinner, or high tea in the Grand Stage Ballroom Restaurant on the top floor. After a great Chinese meal you can while away the afternoon with the old-timers trotting around the room to a live band belting out the cha-cha and tango. The restaurant is also a popular spot for weddings and receptions. Visit in the evening and you're likely to snap up cashmere and chiffon while a violin sings overhead. ✉ *323 Des Voeux Rd., Sheung Wan, Western* ☎ *6029–2675* ⊕ *www.westernmarket.com.hk* Ⓜ *Sheung Wan.*

SHOES, BAGS, AND ACCESSORIES

Chocolate Rain. The collections—dreamed up by a Hong Kong fine arts graduate—consist of pieces handcrafted from recycled materials, such as fabrics, bottle lids, paint buckets, and other funky finds. Head here for one-of-a-kind bags, unique iPhone cases, and jewelry, as well as an ever-changing array of works by the designer's friends. ✉ *1st fl., Block A, PMQ, 35 Aberdeen St., Sheung Wan, Western* ☎ *2599–0017* ⊕ *www.chocolaterain.com* Ⓜ *Central, Exit D2.*

Fodor's Choice ★ **Squarestreet.** You might stumble upon this local gem while wandering around Sheung Wan's evolving Po Hing Fong neighborhood. The low-key workshop and boutique features slick Scandinavian watches, shoes, luggage, and lots of handmade leather bags from Swedish designers David Ericsson and Alexis Holm. ✉ *15 Square St., Sheung Wan, Western* ☎ *2362–1086* ⊕ *www.squarestreet.se* Ⓜ *Sheung Wan, Exit A2.*

Sambag. Aussie boutique Sambag touched down in Hong Kong in 2013, bringing its quality leather kicks and colorful summer accessories with it. Find strappy sandals and quality ballet flats in every hue (they're

That's a Wrap

Wander into the pretty Edwardian-style Western Market in Sheung Wan and you'll find the entire second floor bursting with pure silk shantung, cotton-piqué shirting, French lace, silk brocade, velvet, damask, and printed crepe de chine—just some of the exquisite, reasonably priced fabrics available in Hong Kong. Although professional sourcing agents spend most of their time in Sham Shui Po on the Kowloon side, Western Market's vast selection is more than adequate. Thai silk costs a bit more here than in Bangkok but is still much cheaper than in the United States or Europe.

Chinese Arts & Crafts and Yue Hwa Chinese Products Emporium have great selections of Chinese brocades and other fabrics. Look also for Chinese hand-embroidered and -appliquéd linen and cotton in Stanley Market. ■ TIP➔ When buying a hand-embroidered item, check that the edges are properly overcast; if not, it's probably machine made. You'll be looking for reasons to buy lots of the blue-and-white, patterned Chinese country fabrics at Mountain Folkcraft. Just check to see that you can bring your bolts on the plane; shipping costs may cancel out any discount.

priced at around HK$1,000 per pair), along with beachy cover-ups, floppy hats, and totes of all sizes. ⊠ *Ground fl., 6 Po Yan St., Sheung Wan, Western* ☎ *2968–1285* ⊕ *www.sambag.com.au* Ⓜ *Sheung Wan, Exit A2.*

Fodor'sChoice ★ **Select 18 and Mido Eyeglasses.** Across from the sprawling Oolaa restaurant, two of Hong Kong's best vintage hangouts are in one convenient store. Select 18 has everything from typewriters to 1970s Hermès blouses. If you can tear yourself from the heaps of jewelry and handbags, a treasure trove awaits. Tucked in back, you'll find literally thousands of retro-styled specs from Mido Eyeglasses, priced from a couple of hundred to several thousand Hong Kong dollars. The big question: tortoise-shell cat eyes or classic wayfarers? ⊠ *18 Bridges St., Sheung Wan, Western* ☎ *2858–8803* ⊕ *Sheung Wan, Exit A2.*

W.O.A.W. Quirky travel gear, handsome leather goods, hipster accessories: W.O.A.W. (World of Amazing Wonders) stocks an array of smart and stylish items. Started by serial entrepreneur, clothing designer, and all-around cool guy Kevin Poon, this lifestyle concept store promises to surprise you with up-and-coming brands like Native Union (a techy design brand pumping out funky and functional gadgets), plus some staple international picks like Hershel bags and Karen Walker shades. ⊠ *11 Gough St., Sheung Wan, Western* ☎ *2253–1313* ⊕ *www.woawstore. com* Ⓜ *Sheung Wan, Exit E2.*

SPECIALTY STORES

Fodor'sChoice ★ **LockCha Tea Shop.** Beloved by connoisseurs, LockCha Tea House is a peaceful little enclave in the Flagstaff House Museum of Tea Ware. LockCha has a reputation for brewing high-quality fair-trade teas sourced directly from farmers; happily, it also has a charming retail shop in Sheung Wan, where you can purchase these plus beautiful teapots. ⊠ *Upper ground fl., 290B Queen's Rd. Central, Sheung Wan, Western* ☎ *2805–1360* ⊕ *www.lockcha.com* ☉ *Daily 11–7* Ⓜ *Sheung Wan, Exit A2.*

CENTRAL

New York, London, Paris, Milan... Central. When it comes to big malls, big labels, and big spenders, Central is true to its name. Where else can you find a mall with a whole floor dedicated to Armani or calculate the Pradas per square mile? Spacious, golden-hue centers like the IFC Mall, Landmark, and Prince's Building are the fashion hunting grounds of Hong Kong's well-to-do and all places to visit if your shopping list reads like the directory pages in *Vogue*.

WHY PAY RETAIL?

As Central becomes Sheung Wan, a little lane called Wing Kut Street (between Queen's Road Central and Des Voeux Road) is home to costume-jewelry showrooms and wholesalers, many of whom accept retail customers and offer bargain-basement prices.

When you're ready to experience a different side of Central, head out of the malls and down to the stalls on Li Yuen streets East and West for cheap souvenirs like silk dressing gowns. Ribbons, buttons, wigs, fluffy boas, and sequins come in colors you didn't know existed on steep Pottinger Street, a costumer's dream. Alternatively, ride three minutes uphill on the Mid-Levels Escalator, and step off onto Hollywood Road. This century-old antiques hub bisects the districts known as SoHo (South of Hollywood Road) and NoHo (North of Hollywood Road). On the former's winding, low-rise streets and the latter's charismatic lanes, artsy boutiques, interior-design stores, and trendy restaurants await.

If you can't resist the call of malls (or merely want to return to air-conditioned comfort), check out the Admiralty neighborhood, just east of Central. It's synonymous with Pacific Place. Locals come here for the designer labels, while tourists come to stock up on souvenirs at Chinese Arts & Crafts. Elevated walkways connect it to Lab Concept, a hip network of shops that shares a building with the Queensway Plaza shopping arcade, as well as two lesser retail havens: the Admiralty and United centers.

ANTIQUES AND COLLECTIBLES

Altfield Gallery. If only your entire home could be outfitted by Altfield. Established in 1980, the elegant gallery carries exquisite antique Chinese furniture, Asia-related maps and topographical prints, Southeast Asian sculpture, and decorative arts from around Asia, including silver and rugs. Altfied Interiors, on nearby Queen's Road, features a selection of larger furniture pieces, framed art, and contemporary home accessories. ⊠ *2nd fl., Shop 248–249, Prince's Bldg., 10 Chater Rd., Central* ☎ *2537–6370* ⊕ *www.altfield.com.hk* Ⓜ *Central.*

Arch Angel Antiques. Ask for Bonnie Groot, who will enthusiastically and knowledgeably guide you through the three floors of fine ceramics, furniture, ancestor portraits, and more. Across the road, the Groots have opened the Arch Angel Art Gallery, which specializes in contemporary

Vietnamese and Southeast Asian art. ⊠ *Ground fl., 53–55 Hollywood Rd., Central* ☎ *2851–6848* Ⓜ *Central.*

Chine Gallery. Dealing in antique furniture, artifacts, and rugs from China, this dark, stylish gallery has been around since the 1980s. It has a solid reputation among international dealers and collectors, thanks in part to its expert in-house art consultants who can help navigate the extensive collections. The company also offers a "Treasure Hunting" sourcing service to help find unique items, plus repair and maintenance services. ⊠ *42A Hollywood Rd., Central* ☎ *2543–0023* ⊕ *www.chinegallery.com* Ⓜ *Central.*

> **LAW ON YOUR SIDE**
>
> Although mainland law forbids that any item more than 120 years old leave China, the SAR (Special Administrative Region, which Hong Kong is) isn't held to this rule. It's perfectly legal to ship your antique treasures home.

Honeychurch Antiques. Highly respected dealers Lucille and Glenn Vessa (one of the few accredited appraisers here) were the first to set up shop on Hollywood Road nearly half a century ago. The gallery has managed to keep its original location, with a front-row seat to the neighborhood's transformation into the art hub it is today. Currently helmed by John and Laurie Fairman, who started their own Honeychurch 40 years ago in Seattle, the shop still provides fine Chinese, Japanese, and Southeast Asian antique silver, porcelain, and unaltered furniture with four additional floors of show space next door. ⊠ *Ground fl., 29 Hollywood Rd., Central* ☎ *2543–2433* Ⓜ *Central, Exit C.*

Oi Ling Fine Chinese Antiques. This beautiful showroom displays Chinese antique furniture, scholars' items, terracotta, bronze, and archaeological stone works. Owner Oi Ling Chiang gives frequent talks. ⊠ *Ground fl., 58 Hollywood Rd., Central* ☎ *2815–9422* ⊕ *www.oilingantiques. com* Ⓜ *Central, Exit D2.*

Teresa Coleman Fine Arts Ltd. Specialist Teresa Coleman sells embroidered costumes from the Imperial Court, antique textiles, painted and carved fans, lacquered boxes, and engravings and prints in her centrally-located gallery. She has a streetside shop at the same address for walk-ins, but this space is appointment only. ⊠ *Ground fl., 55 Wyndham St., Central* ☎ *2526–2450* ⊕ *www.teresacoleman.com* Ⓜ *Central, Exit D2.*

The Tibetan Gallery. At this extension of Teresa Coleman Fine Arts you'll find antique Tibetan *thangkas* (Buddhist paintings), as well as bronzes, textiles, and exquisite rugs on display. Manager Josephine Chan is also a restoration expert. ⊠ *55 Wyndham St., Central* ☎ *2530–4863* ⊕ *www. thetibetangallery.com* Ⓜ *Central, Exit G.*

Wattis Fine Art. Run by affable expert Jonathan Wattis and his wife Vicky since 1988, Wattis Fine Art specializes in antique maps and prints and photographs of Hong Kong, China, and Southeast Asia. ⊠ *2nd fl., 20 Hollywood Rd., Central* ☎ *2524–5302* ⊕ *www.wattis.com.hk* Ⓜ *Central, Exit D2.*

Cat Street antiques shops in Sheung Wan offer cheaper wares than those on Hollywood Road.

ART

10 Chancery Lane Gallery. A visit here takes you behind the historic Central Police Station, where walls facing the gallery's distinctive space are still topped by broken glass (a common security measure). Since it opened in 2001, the white-walled gallery has spotlighted emerging artists from all over the world, with a primary focus on those from the Asia Pacific area. Owner-curator Katie de Tilly has a particularly keen eye for photography, and the gallery often features the works of established names such as Vietnamese-American fine arts photographer Dinh Q. Lê and pioneering Chinese artist Wang Keping. ⊠ *Ground fl., 10 Chancery La., SoHo, Central* ☎ *2810–0065* ⊕ *www.10chancerylanegallery.com* ☾ *Closed Sun.–Mon.* Ⓜ *Central, Exit D2.*

Connoisseur Art Gallery. This well-known gallery represents a small batch of modern, mostly figurative Chinese artists, though it also showcases the dreamlike work of Swedish painter Dorina Mocan and dabbles in photography. Recent exhibitions have foregrounded farflung talents, such as French artist Christian Gaillard and his unique portraits of Spanish matadors. The gallery started to push out of its—and Hong Kong's—comfort zone with the opening of Connoisseur Contemporary next door in 2008; it features the often controversial creative output of the sociopolitical group referred to as the "eighties generation"—mainland Chinese emerging artists born in the 1980s under the one-child policy and known for subversive works. ⊠ *G3 Chinachem Hollywood Ctr., 1 Hollywood Rd., Central* ☎ *2868–5358* 🖷 *2868–9793* ⊕ *www. connoisseur-art.com* Ⓜ *Central, Exit D1.*

Grotto Fine Art. Director and chief curator Henry Au-yeung writes about, curates, and gives lectures on 20th-century Chinese art. His tucked-away gallery focuses exclusively on local Chinese artists, with an interest in the newest and most avant-garde works. Look for paintings, sculptures, prints, photography, mixed-media pieces, and conceptual installations. ✉ *2nd fl., 31C–D Wyndham St., Central* ☎ *2121–2270* ⊕ *www.grottofineart.com* Ⓜ *Central, Exit G.*

Hanart TZ Gallery. This is a rare opportunity to compare and contrast cutting-edge and experimental art from mainland China, Taiwan, and Hong Kong selected by one of the field's most respected authorities. Unassuming curatorial director Johnson Chang Tsong-zung also co-founded the Asia Art Archive and has curated exhibitions at the São Paolo and Venice biennials. ✉ *4th fl., Room 401, Pedder Building, 12 Pedder St., Central* ☎ *2526–9019* ⊕ *www.hanart.com* Ⓜ *Central, Exit D1.*

Picture This Gallery. It's a one-of-a-kind source for vintage posters (mainly with travel and movie themes), early photography of Hong Kong and elsewhere in China, antique maps, prints and engravings, antiquarian books, and limited-edition reproductions or works by artists such as Dong Kingman. You might imagine a dusty library, but Christopher Bailey's welcoming gallery is spacious, bright, and organized. In recent years Bailey's offerings have shifted toward contemporary photography, featuring exhibitions from the likes of William Furniss, Anton Lyalin, and *National Geographic*'s Matthieu Paley. He has a second shop in the Prince's Building on Chater Road. ✉ *13th fl., Shop 1308, 9 Queen's Rd. Central, Central* ☎ *2525–2820* ⊕ *www.picturethiscollection.com* ⊘ *Closed Sun.* Ⓜ *Central.*

Sandra Walters Consultancy Ltd. A longtime figure on the art scene, Sandra Walters represents a stable of Asian and international artists encompassing a variety of periods and styles. Make an appointment with her or one of her team to advise you on small to significant investments. ✉ *501 Hoseinee House, 69 Wyndham St., Central* ☎ *2522–1137* ⊘ *Closed Sun.* Ⓜ *Central, Exit D2.*

Sotheby's. The respected auction house opened here in 1973 and has operated its own 15,000-square-foot gallery since 2012. Come for lectures, exhibitions, cultural events, and for the rare chance to gaze upon Sotheby's diamonds. If you're feeling flush, consider attending an auction (dates for upcoming ones are posted on the website); paintings, ceramics, watches, and wine are only some of the items that go up on the block. ✉ *5th fl., One Pacific Place, 88 Queensway, Admiralty, Central* ☎ *2524–8121* ⊕ *www.sothebys.com* Ⓜ *Admiralty, Exit C1.*

Yan Gallery. This is the place for Hong Kong–based artist Hu Yongkai's charming, slightly cartoonish depictions of Chinese women in traditional settings (you've almost certainly seen fakes in a Stanley Market stall). Among emerging and established local artists the gallery, which isn't as stuffy as some and more commercial than others, also represents Bob Yan, whose extremely popular and colorful dog portraits are commissioned by private clients. ✉ *1st fl., Chinachem Hollywood*

DID YOU KNOW?

Hong Kong's mix of western and eastern treatments puts the "ah" in spa. You can get a quick manicure, rejuvenate weary feet with traditional Chinese reflexology, or have an extravagant spa experience. Hotel spas stay open a few hours later than the standalone establishments, so you don't have to curtail shopping. With treatments for men and treatment rooms for couples, the boys don't need to feel left out, either. Warning: you'll be spoiled for life.

Centre, 1 Hollywood Rd., Central ☎ *2139–2345* ⊕ *www.yangallery.com* Ⓜ *Central, Exit D2.*

Zee Stone Gallery. The gallery's massive street-level windows still hold court on this sleek bar and restaurant strip. Inside you'll find contemporary, often abstract, paintings from China, with a smattering of work from Burma and Vietnam. ✉ *Ground fl., Chinachem Hollywood Centre, 1 Hollywood Rd., Central* ☎ *2810–5895* ⊕ *www.zeestone.com* Ⓜ *Central, Exit D2.*

BEAUTY

Joyce Beauty. Love finding unique beauty products from around the world? Then this is the place for you, with cult perfumes, luxurious skin solutions, and new discoveries to be made. Bring your credit card—"bargain" isn't in the vocabulary here. There are several locations throughout Hong Kong, but the Central branch is one of the largest. ✉ *Ground fl., New World Tower, 16–18 Queen's Rd. Central, Central* ☎ *2869–5816* ⊕ *www.joyce.com* Ⓜ *Central.*

Mandarin Beauty Salon and Barber Shop. Savor views of Victoria Harbour from the 24th floor while you tame your tresses at the Mandarin Beauty Salon. No-nonsense Betty employs hair-removal techniques that are whispered about in the best of circles, and Samuel So has perfected his famous Shanghainese pedicure over the past 20 years. On the second floor in the Mandarin's 1930s Shanghai–inspired barber shop, your man can enjoy his own grooming, complete with in-mirror TVs and VIP rooms. ✉ *Mandarin Oriental, 5 Connaught Rd., Central* ☎ *2825–4800* ⊕ *www.mandarinoriental.com* Ⓜ *Central.*

Mannings. Found throughout the city, this chain sells everything from shampoo and lotions to emery boards and cough medicine (western and Chinese brands). Some stores have pharmacies. ✉ *Shop 204, IFC Mall, 8 Finance St., Central* ☎ *2523–9672, 2299–3381 customer service and branch information* ⊕ *www.mannings.com.hk* Ⓜ *Hong Kong.*

BOOKS AND STATIONERY

Indosiam Rare Books. Yves Azemar indulges his passion for rare books and prints about former French colonies in Asia in this tiny apartment, which he converted into a library–shop in 2003. The former French schoolteacher is happy to sit and chat about this fascinating genre—the lectures are never boring. ✉ *1st fl., 89 Hollywood Rd., Central* ☎ *2854–2853* Ⓜ *Central, Exit D2.*

Lok Man Rare Books. With thick carpets, club chairs, and wooden shelves bearing an impressive array of tomes, Lok Man Rare Books calls to mind an old private study. Whether you're looking for volumes from the 16th century, pre-1900 classics (like a complete set of Dickens), or recent first and second editions, you just might find it here. The collection runs the gamut from children's favorites to books on wine, food, history, and sport. ✉ *6 Chancery La., SoHo, Central* ☎ *2868–1056* ⊕ *www.lokmanbooks.com* ☼ *Closed Mon.* Ⓜ *Central, Exit D2.*

CAMERAS AND ELECTRONICS

Flow. Track down this tiny gem for secondhand CDs, DVDs, magazines, and wall-to-wall used books in English. The range is extraordinary, and the organizational system baffling, but the owner is knowledgeable, friendly, and willing to poke among the shelves for you. Books here average around HK$40, compared to a few hundred new. ⊠ *1st fl., Shop 1A, 38 Hollywood Rd., SoHo, Central* ☏ *2964–9483* ⊕ *www. flowbooks.net* Ⓜ *Central, Exit D2.*

CLOTHING

Bumps to Babes. Homegrown Bumps to Babes has everything you could possibly need for babies and children, all in one place. In addition to familiar brands of clothing, diapers, toiletries, food, and toys, look for strollers, books, maternity wear, furniture, and more. There's also a Southside branch in Horizon Plaza. ⊠ *5th fl., Pedder Bldg., 12 Pedder St., Central* ☏ *2522–7112* ⊕ *www.bumpstobabes.com* Ⓜ *Central.*

Barney Cheng. One of Hong Kong's best-known local designers, Barney Cheng creates haute-couture designs and prêt-à-porter collections with wit and elegance. When the Kennedy Center in Washington, D.C., hosted an exhibition titled "The New China Chic," Cheng was invited to display his works alongside those by the likes of Vera Wang and Anna Sui. His more recent pieces have drifted toward simplicity, with sophisticated cuts and exotic prints, such as alligator jackets and skirts. Cheng has made many a bride's dream dress, and his masterfully tailored evening gowns range from HK$40,000–HK$100,000, depending on style, detailing, and fabric. Consultations are available by appointment only. ⊠ *12th fl., World Wide Commercial Bldg., 34 Wyndham St., Central* ☏ *2530–2829* ⊕ *www.barneycheng.com* ☾ *Closed Sun.* Ⓜ *Central, Exit D2.*

Classics Anew. Hong Kong is home to myriad specialty tailors, but for something a little different, head to Classics Anew. Designer Janko Lam has won many an eco-fashion award for her lines of reimagined cheongsams. For a more casual take on the traditionally formal dress, she adds her own unique flair: discarded denim. Skeptical? You may have to see these beautiful pieces in person to appreciate the originality, but they're definitely one-of-a-kind finds. Expect to pay between HK$1,000 and HK$1,700 for one of Janko's handmade dresses. ⊠ *Shop H407, Block B, 35 Aberdeen St., SoHo, Central* ☏ *9275–7059* Ⓜ *Central, Exit D2.*

Episode. Locally owned and designed Episode collections focus on accessories and elegant clothing for working women and Hong Kong "taitais" (aka ladies who lunch). Look also for the younger, trendier Jessica collection. Though distinct, both collections pay close attention to current trends in the fashion world. Episode has a second store in Harbour City. ⊠ *22nd fl., Entertainment Bldg., 30 Queen's Rd. Central, Central* ☏ *2921–2010* ⊕ *www.episode-intl.com* Ⓜ *Central, Exit D2.*

Fang Fong Projects. Fang Fong fell in love with the vintage feel of the SoHo district as a design graduate and vowed to move in. She chose a light-filled studio space to display her floaty, 1970s-inspired clothing line, with its bold prints and sexy wisps of lace and silk. She also brought her friends with her, or at least those who suited her vibe. Head here for Japanese kimono-inspired belts and for bags by U.K. brand Dialog, which works with scrap fabric from fair trade sources. ⊠ *Shop 1, 69A Peel St., SoHo, Central* ☏ *3105–5557* Ⓜ *Sheung Wan, Exit E2.*

Hulu 10. Tucked away on historic Glenealy—center of British Hong Kong—Hulu 10 takes traditional Chinese textiles for a contemporary spin. Encased by a beautiful white brick building, the store is warm and welcoming, with dark wood floors and open space. Designed and produced locally, the garments have a throwback vibe, inspired by '60s fashion and iconic artifacts like Xian's Terra-cotta Warriors. Find classic Chinese tunics and silk scarves alongside more modern-looking dresses for the ladies, as well as a leaner selection of children's and menswear. ■ TIP→ This quaint little street snakes above Lower Albert Road and can be tricky to find at first. Start from the Fringe Club at Wyndham's five-way intersection and head uphill. ⊠ *Ground fl., 10 Glenealy, Central* ☎ *2179–5500* ⊕ *www.hulu10.com* ☉ *Closed Sun.* Ⓜ *Central, Exit D1.*

Joyce. Local socialites and couture addicts still thank Joyce Ma, the fairy godmother of luxury retail in Hong Kong, for bringing must-have labels to the city. Others may be catching up, but her Joyce boutiques are still ultrachic havens outfitted with a *Vogue*-worthy wish list of designers and beauty brands. Not so much a shop as a fashion institution, hushed Joyce houses the worship-worthy creations of fashion's greatest gods and goddesses. McCartney, McQueen, Oscar de la Renta: the stock list is practically a mantra. Joyce sells unique household items, too, so your home can live up to your wardrobe. The flagship store is in New World Tower. ⊠ *New World Tower, 16 Queen's Rd. Central, Central* ☎ *2810–1120* ⊕ *www.joyce.com* Ⓜ *Central, Exit G.*

Lace Department Store. You might head straight for the embroidered linens, but back up and review the small spread of children's clothing. You've seen these beautiful, traditional, hand-smocked cotton dresses in elegant European stores, sold at prices to make you faint. Here expect to pay as little as HK$200. As you tour the city, keep an eye out for embroidered-linens specialists who carry similar dresses. ⊠ *17th fl., Crawford House, 70 Queen's Rd. Central, Central* ☎ *2523–8162* Ⓜ *Central.*

Marleen Molenaar Sleepwear. When Hong Kong–based Dutch designer and mother Marleen Molenaar discovered how limited her choices were for children's pajamas and sleepwear, she founded her own label. The gorgeous 100% cotton, high-quality classic European collections are sold around the world, in Lane Crawford's home department, and through her showroom, by appointment. ⊠ *Shop 502, Tak Woo House, 17–19 D'Aguilar St., Central* ☎ *2525–9872* ⊕ *www.marleenmolenaar. com* Ⓜ *Central.*

Fodor'sChoice ★ **Moustache.** Brainchild of Alex Daye and Ellis Kreuger, Moustache is perched atop steep Aberdeen Street on the edge of SoHo. Find reasonably priced lightweight men's cotton shirts, Bermuda shorts, and unique finds from the owners' jaunts around Asia. The ready-to-wear garments are housed in a cozy and charismatic shop that's outfitted with an eclectic mix of maritime accents and vintage curiosities from '70s Hong Kong. You can also order locally made tailored suits and bespoke denim, but expect several weeks of production time. ⊠ *31 Aberdeen St., SoHo, Central* ☎ *2541–1955* ⊕ *www.moustachehongkong.com* Ⓜ *Sheung Wan, Exit E2.*

Sabina Swims. Hong Kong girl Sabina Wong Sutch first opened up shop in the burgeoning NoHo neighborhood in 2003. Since then, she's moved her pretty bikinis, accessories, and resort-wear brands to a more central location. The Sabina Swims collection is cleverly sold as separates, because the designer knows that women aren't always the same size on top and on the bottom. There are also matching swimsuits for mother-and-daughter outings and reversible sun hats in the same materials. ⊠ *7th fl., Union Commercial Building, 12 Lyndhurst Terr., Central* ☎ *2115–9975* ⊕ *www.sabinaswims.com* Ⓜ *Central, Exit D2.*

Fodor'sChoice **Shanghai Tang.** Make your way past the perfumes, scarves, and silk-
★ embroidered Chinese souvenirs to the second floor, where you'll find a rainbow of fabrics at your fingertips. In addition to the brilliantly hued—and expensive—silk and cashmere clothing, you'll see custom-made suits starting at around HK$30,000, including fabric. You can also have a cheongsam (a sexy slit-skirt silk dress with a Mandarin collar) made for around HK$10,000, including fabric. Ready-to-wear Mandarin suits are in the HK$15,000–HK$20,000 range. There are stores scattered across Hong Kong, including the airport's Terminal One. ⊠ *Ground–3rd fl., 1 Duddell St., Central* ☎ *2525–7333* ⊕ *www.shanghaitang.com* Ⓜ *Central, Exit D2.*

Siberian Fur Store Ltd. In general, furs sold by reputable Hong Kong dealers are the ideal combination of high quality and low price. This shop, owned and operated by a prominent local family, is famous for its superior furs and special attention to design. ⊠ *Ground fl., 29 Des Voeux Rd. Central, Central* ☎ *2522–1380* Ⓜ *Central, Exit C.*

Topshop. British fashion favorite Topshop opened a gargantuan space in the middle of the Central Business District in 2013. The 14,000-square-foot flagship store fills two stories, with a constant rotation of 300 new pieces a week. The place gets packed on weekends, so consider booking a free personal-shopping appointment with one of Topshop's stylists. ⊠ *Asia Standard Tower, 59 Queen's Rd. Central, Central* ☎ *2118–5353* ⊕ *www.topshop.com* Ⓜ *Central, Exit D2.*

Vintage HK. As you walk along Hollywood Road past the art galleries and wine bars, take time to wander down the steep side streets. On Peel Street you'll stumble upon this one-of-a-kind treasure, which is marked by a black-and-white sign visible from Hollywood. Inside, crinkly posters, love-worn leather, and a stash of antique knickknacks will transport you to the 1970s and beyond. From retro cameras to clocks, belts to blouses, Dior to Marc Jacobs, this is a trove of near-mint-condition consignment pieces. ⊠ *57–59 Hollywood Rd., SoHo, Central* ☎ *2545–9932* Ⓜ *Central, Exit D2.*

CLOTHING: MEN'S TAILORS

A-Man Hing Cheong Co., Ltd. People often gasp at the very mention of A-Man Hing Cheong, in the Mandarin Oriental Hotel. For some it symbolizes the ultimate in fine tailoring, with a reputation that extends back to its founding in 1898. For others it's the lofty prices that elicit a reaction. Regardless, this is a trustworthy source of European-cut suits, custom shirts, and excellent service. ⊠ *Mezzanine, Mandarin Oriental, 5 Connaught Rd., Central* ☎ *2522–3336* Ⓜ *Central, Exit H.*

Tailor-Made

No trip to Hong Kong would be complete without a visit to one of its world-famous tailors, as many celebrities and dignitaries can attest. In often humble, fabric-cluttered settings, customer records contain the measurements of notables such as Jude Law, Kate Moss, David Bowie, and even Queen Elizabeth II.

TAILORING TIPS

If you've ever owned a custom-made garment, you understand the joy of clothes crafted to fit your every measurement. Hong Kong is best known for men's tailoring, but whether you're looking for a classic men's business suit or an evening gown, these steps will help you size things up.

■ Set Your Style. Be clear about what you want. Bring samples—a favorite piece of clothing or magazine photos. Also, Hong Kong tailors are trained in classic, structured garments. Straying from these could lead to disappointment. There are three basic suit styles. The American cut has a jacket with notched lapels, a center vent, and two or three buttons. The trousers are lean, with flat fronts. The British cut also has notched lapels and two- or three-button jackets, but it features side vents and pleated trousers. The double-breasted Italian cut has wide lapels and pleated trousers.

■ Choose Your Fabric. You're getting a deal on workmanship, so consider splurging on, say, a luxurious blend of cashmere, mink, and wool. When having something copied, though, choose a fabric similar to the original. Take your time selecting: fabric is the main cost factor. Examine fabric on a large scale; small swatches are deceiving.

■ Measure Up. Meticulous measuring is the mark of a superior craftsman, so be patient. And for accuracy, stand as you normally would (you can't suck in that gut forever).

■ Place Your Order. Most tailors require a deposit of 30%–50% of the total cost. Request a receipt detailing price, fabric, style, measurements, fittings, and production schedule. Ask for a swatch to compare with the final product.

■ Get Fit. There should be at least two fittings. The first is for major alterations. Subsequent fittings are supposed to be for minor adjustments, but don't settle for less than perfect: Keep sending it back until they get it right. Bring the correct clothes, such as a dress shirt and appropriate shoes, to try on a suit. Try jackets buttoned and unbuttoned. Examine every detail. Are shoulder seams puckered or smooth? Do patterns meet? Is the collar too loose or tight? (About two fingers' space is right.)

FINDING A TAILOR

■ As soon as you arrive, visit established tailors to compare workmanship and cost.

■ Ask if the work is bespoke (made from scratch) or made-to-measure (based on existing patterns but handmade according to your measurements).

■ You get what you pay for. Assume the workmanship and fabric will match the price.

■ A fine suit requires six or more days to create. That said, be wary but not dismissive of "24-hour tailors." Hong Kong's most famous craftsmen have turned out suits in a day.

Ascot Chang. This self-titled "gentleman's shirtmaker" makes it easy to find the perfect shirt, even if you could get a better deal in a less prominent shop. Ascot Chang has upheld exacting Shanghainese tailoring traditions in Hong Kong since 1953, and now has stores in New York, Beverly Hills, Manila, and Shanghai. The focus here is on the fit and details, from 22 stitches per inch to collar linings crafted to maintain their shape. Among the countless fabrics, Italian 330s three-ply Egyptian cotton by David & John Anderson is one of the most coveted and expensive. Like many shirtmakers, Ascot Chang does pajamas, robes, boxer shorts, and women's blouses, too. It also has ready-made lines of shirts, T-shirts, neckties, and other accessories available for online ordering. Other branches are located in the IFC Mall, Elements Mall, and the Peninsula Hotel. ⊠ *Shop 131, Prince's Bldg., 10 Chater Rd., Central* ☎ *2523–3663* ⊕ *www.ascotchang.com* Ⓜ *Central, Exit H.*

Blanc de Chine. Relying on word of mouth, Blanc de Chine has catered to high society and celebrities, such as actor Jackie Chan, for years. The small, refined tailoring shop neatly displays exquisite fabrics from Switzerland and Japan, lovely ready-made women's wear, menswear, and home accessories. Items here are extravagances, but they're worth every penny. ⊠ *Shop 123, Prince's Bldg., 10 Chater Rd., Central* ☎ *2104–7934* ⊕ *www.blancdechine.com* Ⓜ *Central, Exit K.*

Jantzen Tailor. Catering to expatriate bankers since 1972, this reputable yet reasonable tailor specializes in classic shirts; it also makes suits and women's garments. The comprehensive website displays its commitment to quality, such as hand-sewn button shanks, customizable interlinings, and Coats brand thread. ⊠ *Room 504–505, 5th fl., On Lok Yuen Bldg., 25–27 Des Voeux Rd. Central, Central* ☎ *2570–5901* ⊕ *www.jantzentailor.com* Ⓜ *Central, Exit B.*

Linva Tailors. It's one of the best of the old-fashioned cheongsam tailors, in operation since the 1960s. Master tailor Mr. Leung takes clients through the entire process and reveals a surprising number of variations in style. Prices are affordable, but vary according to fabric, which ranges from basics to special brocades and beautifully embroidered silks. ⊠ *38 Cochrane St., Central* ☎ *2544–2456* ⊗ *Closed Sun.* Ⓜ *Central, Exit D2.*

Practical Tailor. As its name suggests, Practical Tailor is a refreshing change of pace from some of the stuffy and overpriced heavyweights just down the street. Popular among westerners and young professionals, the Shanghainese outfit is run by friendly and attentive co-owners Andy Shum and Jason Chan, who ensure every suit comes fully canvassed and hand stitched, inside and out. Depending on the quality of fabric—Inner Mongolia cashmere and silk from Ermenegildo Zegna will obviously run up the price—men's suits range from roughly HK\$5,000 to HK\$12,000. ⊠ *8th fl., AIE Bldg., 33 Connaught Rd. Central, Central* ☎ *2522–3866* ⊕ *www.penhk.com* Ⓜ *Central, Exit A.*

Yuen's Tailor. Need a kilt? This is where the Hong Kong Highlanders Reel Club comes for custom-made ones. The Yuen repertoire, however, extends to well-made suits and shirts. The tiny shop on an unimpressive gray walkway is filled from floor to ceiling with sumptuous European fabrics. It's a good place to have clothes copied, and prices are competitive. ⊠ *2nd fl., Escalator Link Alley, 80 Des Voeux Rd., Central* ☎ *2815–5388* Ⓜ *Central.*

W. W. Chan & Sons Tailors Ltd. Chan is known for excellent-quality suits and shirts in classic cuts and has an array of fine European fabrics. It's comforting to know that you'll be measured and fitted by the same master tailor from start to finish. The store features a mirrored, hexagonal changing room so you can check every angle. Tailors from here travel to the United States several times a year to fill orders for their customers; if you have a suit made and leave your address, they'll let you know when they plan to visit. ⊠ *Unit B, 8th fl., Entertainment Bldg., 30 Queen's Rd. Central, Central* ☎ *2366–9738* ⊕ *www.wwchan.com* Ⓜ *Central, Exit D2.*

CLOTHING: WOMEN'S TAILORS

Irene Fashions. This popular tailoress may have the same name as the W.W. Chan women's division, but don't confuse the two. Slightly better known, this Irene Fashions' guidance and workmanship attract many expatriate women in search of everything from suits to evening wear. Service in the cluttered atmosphere may be brusque, but it's only because the tailors here know what they're talking about. ⊠ *2nd fl., Welley Bldg., 97 Wellington St., Central* ☎ *2850–5635* ⊘ *Closed Sun.* Ⓜ *Central, Exit D2.*

Irene Fashions. In 1987 the women's division of noted men's tailor W.W. Chan branched off and was renamed Irene Fashions. You can expect the same level of expertise and a large selection of fine fabrics. Experienced at translating ideas and pictures into clothing, in-house designers will sketch and help you develop concepts. Like its parent company, Irene promises that the same tailor will take you through the entire process, and most of the work is done onsite. ⊠ *Unit B, 8th fl., Entertainment Building, 30 Queen's Rd. Central, Central* ☎ *2366–9738* ⊕ *www.wwchan.com* Ⓜ *Central, Exit D2.*

Margaret Court Tailoress. A name frequently passed on by expert Hong Kong shoppers, Margaret Wong's tailoring services run from women's daywear to gowns to Chinese cheongsam. Prices tend to be midrange. ⊠ *8th fl., Winner Bldg., 37 D'Aguilar St., Central* ☎ *2525–5596* Ⓜ *Central, Exit G.*

Perfect Dress Alteration (aka Ann & Bon). Hong Kong's tai-tais bring their couture here for adjustments, as evidenced by the Chanel, Escada, and Versace bags hanging overhead in the little workshop buzzing with the sound of sewing machines. Although primarily known for alterations, it also offers tailoring services for women. ⊠ *2nd fl., Melbourne Plaza, 33 Queen's Rd. Central, Central* ☎ *2522–8838* ⊘ *Closed Sun.* Ⓜ *Central, Exit D2.*

CRAFTS

Mountain Folkcraft. A little old-fashioned bell chimes as you open the door to this fantastic shop filled with handicrafts and antiques from around China. Amid the old treasures, carved woodwork, rugs, and curios, are stunning folk-print fabrics. ■**TIP**➔ **To reach the store from Queen's Road Central, walk up D'Aguilar Street toward Lan Kwai Fong,**

then turn right onto Wo On Lane. ⌧ *Ground fl., 12 Wo On La., Central* ☎ *2523–2817* ⊕ *www.mountainfolkcraft.com* Ⓜ *Central, Exit D1.*

Tittot. This Taiwanese brand has taken modern Chinese glass art global. Glass works here are made using the laborious lost-wax casting technique, employed by artists for centuries to create a bronze replica of an original wax or clay sculpture. The collection—which includes tableware, paperweights, glass Buddhas, and jewelry—can be purchased in Lane Crawford department stores. ⌧ *Lane Crawford, IFC Mall, 8 Finance St., Central* ☎ *2118-3638* ⊕ *www.tittot.com* Ⓜ *Hong Kong, Exit A1.*

DEPARTMENT STORES

Fodor'sChoice
★
Chinese Arts & Crafts. Visit this long-established mainland company to blitz through that tiresome list of presents in one fell swoop. It stocks a huge variety of well-priced clothing, porcelain, and giftware. In direct contrast to the thrill of digging through dusty piles at the open-air Jade Market, Chinese Arts & Crafts provides a clean, air-conditioned environment in which to shop for classic jade jewelry—and the prices aren't too outrageous. Other affordable, easily packable items include appliqué tablecloths and cushion covers or silk dressing gowns. There are four branches in Hong Kong, including this spacious shop in Pacific Place. ⌧ *Shop 220, Pacific Place, 88 Queensway, Admiralty, Central* ☎ *2523–3933* ⊕ *www.cacgift.com* Ⓜ *Admiralty, Exit F.*

Harvey Nichols. When this legendary British retailer announced its Hong Kong opening, locals were skeptical, saying nothing would ever live up to the original London store. But Harvey Nicks quickly had them eating their (Philip Treacy) hats with the sheer volume of hypercool labels the store stocks. The menswear section has been a particularly big hit with local celebs, while local tai-tais (ladies who lunch) have declared the fourth-floor restaurant *the* place for mid-shopping-spree coffee breaks. The flagship store covers 83,000 glorious square feet; and there is a second sprawling location in Admiralty's Pacific Place. ⌧ *The Landmark, 15 Queen's Rd. Central, Central* ☎ *3695–3388* ⊕ *www.harveynichols. com* Ⓜ *Central, Exit G.*

Fodor'sChoice
★
Lane Crawford. This prestigious western-style department store has been the favorite of local label lovers for years—not bad for a brand that started out as a makeshift provisions shop back in 1850. The massive flagship store in the IFC Mall (one of Hong Kong's four Lane Crawford locations) feels like a monument to fashion's biggest names, with exquisitely designed acres divided up into small gallery-like spaces for each designer. In addition to contemporary clothing, the phenomenal brand list covers everything from beauty to home ware. ⌧ *Podium 3, IFC Mall, 8 Finance St., Central* ☎ *2118–3388, 2118–7777 Lane Crawford concierge* ⊕ *www.lanecrawford.com* Ⓜ *Hong Kong, Exit A1.*

HOME DÉCOR

G.O.D. The name of this pioneering lifestyle brand stands for "Goods of Desire," and the items it sells live up to that. G.O.D. plays with ideas, designs, and words drawn from Hong Kong's unique heritage, with imaginative yet functional results. Its huge product range consists mostly of home furnishings and tableware, though there is a renewed

Traditional herbalists mix healing concoctions in Wan Chai shops.

focus on fashion—the collection of original-design Hong Kong tees is particularly cute. Affordable creations, such as red rubber trays for making "double happiness" character ice cubes, Buddha statues irreverently turned into wine stoppers, and old-fashioned Chinese textiles reimagined in modern settings, manage to be both nostalgic and contemporary. ■ TIP➔ Buy a trendy gift or unique vintage-style postcards for the folks back home. ⊠ 48 Hollywood Rd., Central ☎ 2805–1876 ⊕ www.god.com.hk Ⓜ Central, Exit D2.

Homeless. Pleasantly quirky but with a finger firmly on the pulse of the city, this small design brand emporium has its flagship in NoHo (North of Hollywood Road), one of Central's up and coming nooks. The store showcases some of its own in-house creations, but it mostly stocks pieces from modern-day design icons. Come here to pick up a Tom Dixon bowler-hat lampshade or a Pac Man–shape oven glove by Fred. ■ TIP➔ Try its basement café for brunch on Saturday. ⊠ Ground fl., 29 Gough St., NoHo, Central ☎ 2581–1880 ⊕ www.homeless.hk Ⓜ Sheung Wan, Exit E2.

Olive Forrest. Irish expat Olive Forrest has cleverly retained original elements of the former print shop that houses her bright-red store. With a unique sense of style, she brings together Chinese and Tibetan antiques, modern lighting designed in-house, home accessories, high-quality bed linens for children and adults, and a line of colorful contemporary furniture. ⊠ 72 Peel St., SoHo, Central ☎ 2526–0277 ⊘ Closed Mon. Ⓜ Central, Exit D1.

Tai Ping Carpets. Headquartered in Hong Kong, Tai Ping is highly regarded for its custom-made rugs and wall-to-wall carpets. It takes

2½ to 3 months to make specially ordered carpets; you can specify color, thickness, and even the direction of the weave. Tai Ping's occasional sales—where you can find a sampling of ready-made rugs marked down at least 20%—are well worth attending. ✉ *Shop 213, Prince's Bldg., 10 Chater Rd., Central* ☎ *2522–7138* ⊕ *www.taipingcarpets.com* ⊗ *Closed Sun.* Ⓜ *Central, Exit K.*

JEWELRY AND ACCESSORIES

Callixto. If you're searching for local handicrafts and worldly finds, then make a beeline for Callixto. Originally launched by Sasha Dennig as an online boutique in 2011, the store recently opened up a bright pink brick-and-mortar shop with a serious case of wanderlust. Look for jewelry from Greece, bags from India, carpets from Uzbekistan, and knickknacks from around the world. ✉ *11 Mee Lun St., Central* ☎ *6316–9551* ⊕ *www.callixto.com* Ⓜ *Sheung Wan, Exit E2.*

Chow Sang Sang. In addition to its contemporary gold, diamond, jade, and wedding collections for the local market, this manufacturer and retailer also sources international brands. It has more than 370 shops in China. ✉ *37 Queen's Rd. Central, Central* ☎ *3583–4150, 2192–3123 customer service and branch information* ⊕ *www.chowsangsang.com* Ⓜ *Central, Exit D2.*

Chow Tai Fook. Jade is not the only thing you'll see from this local chain founded in 1929. It also has fine jewelry in diamond, jadeite, ruby, sapphire, emerald, 18K gold, and more-traditional pure gold. And don't worry about tracking one down; Chow Tai Fook has more than 85 Hong Kong locations. ✉ *Ground fl., Aon China Bldg., 29 Queen's Rd. Central, Central* ☎ *2523–7128* ⊕ *www.chowtaifook.com* Ⓜ *Central, Exit D2.*

Edward Chiu. Everything about Edward Chiu is *fabulous,* from the flamboyant way he dresses to his high-end jade jewelry. The minimalist, geometric pieces use the entire jade spectrum, from deep greens to surprising lavenders. Inspired in part by Art Deco, Chiu is also famous for contrasting black-and-white jade, setting it in precious metals, and adding diamond or pearl touches. ✉ *Shop 2023, IFC Mall, 8 Finance St., Central* ☎ *2525–2618* ⊕ *www.edwardchiu.com* Ⓜ *Hong Kong, Exit F.*

Eldorado Watch Co Ltd. At this deep emporium of watch brands, seek the advice of one of the older staffers who look like they've been there since the British landed. Brands include Rolex, Patek Philippe, Omega, and Tudor. ✉ *Ground fl., Peter Bldg., 60 Queen's Rd. Central, Central* ☎ *2522–7155* Ⓜ *Central, Exit D2.*

Gallery One. This is the next-best option for midrange pearls if you can't make it to the Jade Market. Gallery One blends into Hollywood Road's backdrop of trinket-filled storefronts, but its selection of Japanese and freshwater pearls stands out. Prices are reasonable, and they will string together whichever combination of pearls and semiprecious stones you choose. Gallery One also carries Tibetan and Buddhist beads in wood and amber, as well as bronze sculptures. ✉ *Ground fl., 31–33 Hollywood Rd., Central* ☎ *2545–6436* Ⓜ *Central, Exit D2.*

Jan Logan. This Australian designer has celebrities wearing her youthful yet elegant designs. Pieces contrast cultured, South Seas, and Tahitian pearls with onyx, diamonds, quartz, and other stones. ✉ *Shop 3007, 3rd fl., IFC Mall, 8 Finance St., Central* ☎ *2918–4212* ⊕ *www.janlogan. com* Ⓜ *Hong Kong, Exit F.*

K.S. Sze & Sons. Powdered elderly ladies who lunch and casually dressed tourists all come to this place, more salon than store, for the same thing: quality pearls, fine jewelry, and excellent service. In addition to classic styles, K.S. Sze works closely with clients on custom orders. ✉ *Shop 108, Prince's Building, 10 Chater Rd., Central* ☎ *2524–2803* Ⓜ *Central, Exit H.*

Kai-Yin Lo. Famous for her Asian-inspired jewelry, Kai-Yin Lo combines contemporary style with ancient Chinese designs and materials such as semiprecious stones and jade. The *International Herald Tribune* has credited her with bridging the gap between fine and fashion jewelry. Sales are by appointment only. ✉ *Block 2, Unit 3, 55 Garden Rd., Central* ☎ *2773–6009* ⊕ *www.kaiyinlo-design.com* Ⓜ *Admiralty, Exit B.*

King Fook Jewellery. When considering jewelry stores, longevity is a good thing. King Fook has been around since 1949, promising stringent quality control, quality craftsmanship, and professional service. Masterpiece by King Fook, the higher-end King Fook line, sells first-grade diamonds and precious jewelry. There are also shops at Pacific Place in Admiralty and The One on Nathan Road. ✉ *Shop G21, Central Bldg., 1–3 Pedder St., Central* ☎ *2526–6733* ⊕ *www.kingfook.com* Ⓜ *Central, Exit G.*

Larry Jewelry. Established in 1967, Larry Jewelry is known for handcrafted pieces made from high-grade precious stones. There is a second store in Causeway Bay. ✉ *Ground fl., 72 Queen's Rd. Central, Central* ☎ *2521–1268* ⊕ *www.larryjewelry.com* Ⓜ *Central, Exit D2.*

Po Kwong Jewelry Ltd. Specializing in strung pearls from Australia and the South Seas, Po Kwong will add clasps to your specifications. They also carry pearl earrings, rings, and pendants. ✉ *18th fl., HK Diamond Exchange Bldg., 8–10 Duddell St., Central* ☎ *2521–4686* ⊕ *www. po-kwong-pearl.com* Ⓜ *Central, Exit K.*

Qeelin. With ancient Chinese culture for inspiration and *In the Mood for Love* actress Maggie Cheung as the muse, something extraordinary was bound to come from Qeelin. Its name was cleverly derived from the Chinese characters for male ("qi") and female ("lin"), and symbolizes harmony, balance, and peace. The restrained beauty and meaningful creations of designer Dennis Chan are exemplified in two main collections: Wulu, a minimalist form representing the mythical gourd as well as the lucky number eight; and Tien Di, literally "Heaven and Earth," symbolizing everlasting love. Classic gold, platinum, and diamonds mix with colored jades, black diamonds, and unusual materials for a truly unique effect. A sweeter addendum to the collection was added in the form of Bo Bo, the panda bear. The IFC Mall store is one of seven in Hong Kong. ✉ *Shop 2059, IFC Mall, 8 Finance St., Central* ☎ *2389– 8863* ⊕ *hk.qeelin.com* Ⓜ *Hong Kong, Exit F.*

Ronald Abram. Looking at the rocks in these windows can feel like a visit to a natural history museum. Large white- and rare-color diamonds sourced from all over the world are a specialty here, but the shop also deals in emeralds, sapphires, and rubies. With years of expertise, Abrams dispenses advice on both the aesthetic merits and the investment potential of each stone or piece of jewelry. ✉ *Mezzanine, Mandarin Oriental, 5 Connaught Rd., Central* ☎ *2525–1234* ⊕ *www. ronaldabram.com* Ⓜ *Central, Exit K.*

Saturn Essentials. If you're looking for a local artisan, a reasonably priced piece of silver, semiprecious stones, and sometimes even gold jewelry— or you just want a chat with a nice lady—visit Maureen "Mo" Gerrard. Her place is just down the street from the hair salon of her son, Paul Gerrard. The shop repairs, cleans, plates, restrings, and polishes, too. ✉ *1st fl., 36 Pottinger St., Central* ☎ *2537–9335* Ⓜ *Central, Exit D2.*

Super Star Jewelry. Discreetly tucked in a corner of Central, Super Star looks like any other small Hong Kong jewelry shop—with walls lined with display cases filled with the usual classic designs (old-fashioned to some) in predominantly gold and precious stones. What makes them stand out are the good prices and personalized service. The cultured pearls and mixed strands of colored freshwater pearls are not all shown, so ask Lily or one of her colleagues to bring them out. ✉ *The Galleria, 9 Queen's Rd. Central, Central* ☎ *2521–0507* Ⓜ *Central, Exit H.*

Tayma Fine Jewellery. Unusual colored "connoisseur" gemstones are set by hand in custom designs by Hong Kong–based jeweler Tayma Page Allies. The collection is designed to bring out the personality of the individual wearer, and includes oversize cocktail rings, distinctive brace- lets, pretty earrings, and more. ✉ *Shop 225, 2nd fl., Prince's Bldg., 10 Chater Rd., Central* ☎ *2525–5280* ⊕ *www.taymajewellery.com* Ⓜ *Cen- tral, Exit K.*

The9thMuse. Boho bags, bold jewelry, stylish sunglasses: The9thMuse is a treasure trove of accessories, sourced by twentysomethings Jing Zhang and Charlotte Hwang. Find jewelry from far-flung destinations that the pair stumbled upon while traveling, plus plenty of guilt-free, socially conscious brands that kick back funds to the creators. ■ **TIP➜** **The sale rack in the back usually has some great deals on purses, scarves, and such—and it's not unlikely you'll find a pop-up shop featuring a local designer.** ✉ *12th fl., One Lyndhurst Tower, 1 Lyndhurst Terr., SoHo, Central* ☎ *2537–7598* ⊕ *www.the9thmuse.com* Ⓜ *Central, Exit D2.*

MALLS AND SHOPPING CENTERS

Fodor's Choice ★ **IFC Mall.** A quick glance at the directory—Tiffany & Co., Kate Spade, Prada, Gieves & Hawkes—lets you know that the International Finance Centre isn't for the faint of pocket. Designer department store Lane Crawford chose to open its flagship store here, and J.Crew followed suit in 2014. Even the mall's cinema multiplex is special: the deluxe theaters have super-comfy seats with extra legroom and blankets for those chilled by the air conditioning. If you finish your spending spree at sunset, go for a cocktail at RED or Isola, two posh rooftop bars with fabulous harbor views. The Hong Kong Airport Express station (with in-town check-in service) is under the mall, and the Four Seasons Hotel connects to it. ■ **TIP➜** **Avoid the mall between 12:30 and 2, when it's flooded with lunching office workers from the two IFC towers.** ✉ *8 Finance St., Central* ☎ *2295–3308, 2295–3308 Hotline* ⊕ *www.ifc. com.hk* Ⓜ *Hong Kong, Exit F.*

Lab Concept. Pacific Place may have put Admiralty on the map, but Lab Concept has breathed new life into the otherwise uneventful neighborhood. This 64,000-square-foot "fashion playground"—from the same masterminds behind Joyce and Lane Crawford—comprises a network of shops in the formerly forgettable Queensway Plaza and is fast becoming a major shopping destination. The white, contemporary space introduces some playful touches you won't find elsewhere, such as blow-dry bars, nail stations, and vending machines selling Jurlique skin-care products. Expect young and edgy brands, including American Apparel, Cheap Monday, Free People, and MO&Co. Beloved beauty brands populate the Facesss department, but the highlight is the mix of must-have boots, heels (even for bigfoot Americans), and accessories at Shoespace. ⊠ *93 Queensway, Admiralty, Central* ☎ *2118–6008* ⊕ *www. labconcepthk.com* Ⓜ *Admiralty, Exit C2.*

Landmark. If you haven't got a boutique in Landmark, you clearly haven't made it in the fashion world, darling. Central's most prestigious shopping site houses Celine, Loewe, Gucci, Joyce Grooming, and Harvey Nichols, among others. Even if your credit-card limit isn't up to a spree here, the hushed Café Landmark is the best place in town to watch well-coiffed tai-tais on the prowl. A pedestrian bridge links the mall with shopping arcades in Landmark Prince's, Landmark Alexandra, Landmark Chater, and the Mandarin Oriental Hotel. ⊠ *15 Queen's Rd. Central, Pedder St. and Des Voeux Rd., Central* ☎ *2500–0555 Customer Service* ⊕ *www.landmark.hk* Ⓜ *Central, Exit G.*

Pacific Place. Once Hong Kong Island's classiest mall, Pacific Place remains popular with well-to-do residents—perhaps because it's quieter and more exclusive than most competitors. High-end international prêt-à-porter fills most of its four floors. When your bags are weighing you down, sandwiches, sushi, and Starbucks are on hand, as is a multiplex cinema. The JW Marriott, the Island Shangri-La, the Conrad, and the Upper House hotels are connected to this plaza, all with enticing afternoon tea options. Elevated walkways join Pacific Place with four arcades: the Admiralty Centre, United Centre, Queensway Plaza, and fashion-forward Lab Concept. ⊠ *88 Queensway, Admiralty, Central* ☎ *2844–8900* ⊕ *www.pacificplace.com.hk* Ⓜ *Admiralty, Exit F.*

Pedder Building. Dwarfed by flashy skyscrapers, the Pedder Building is one of Hong Kong's few remaining true neoclassical-style buildings. Once known for its discounted designer outlets and eclectic tenants, the elegant stone construction reinvented itself with a host of new faces after renovations in 2012. Though several shops kept their coveted spots—Bumps to Babes and swanky haberdasher Armoury, to name a few—the Pedder Building seems to have a voracious appetite for art galleries and exhibition spaces. Ben Brown Fine Arts and Gagosian Gallery survived the transition, joined quickly by Simon Lee, Pearl Lam, and Hanart TZ, with more to come. If you need a break from all the abstract images, new-media installations, and inevitable head scratching, sneak away to Burgundy Etc (a top-end wine retailer) or the Pacific Cigar Company smoking lounge on the fourth floor. ⊠ *12 Pedder St., Central* Ⓜ *Central, Exit D1.*

SHOES, HANDBAGS, AND LEATHER GOODS

Kow Hoo Shoe Company. If you like shoes made the old-fashioned way, then Kow Hoo—one of Hong Kong's oldest, circa 1946—is for you. It also does great cowboy boots (there's nothing like knee-high calf-skin!). Just be sure to make an appointment before you go. ⊠ *2nd fl., Prince's Bldg., 10 Chater Rd., Central* ☎ *2523–0489* ⊕ *kowhoo.com. hk* ⊙ *Closed Sun.* Ⓜ *Central, Exit H.*

Kwanpen. Renowned for its crocodile bags and shoes, Kwanpen has acted as a manufacturer for famous brands since 1938, as well as being a stand-alone retailer. In addition to Pacific Place, it has stores in the 1881 Heritage arcade, IFC Mall, and World Trade Centre. ⊠ *Shop 310, Pacific Place, 88 Queensway, Admirality, Central* ☎ *2918–9199* ⊕ *www.kwanpen.com* Ⓜ *Admiralty, Exit F.*

Lianca. This is one of those unique places that make you want to buy something even if there's nothing you need. Lianca, first and foremost a manufacturer, sells well-made leather bags, wallets, frames, key chains, and home accessories in timeless, simple designs. It's an unbranded way to be stylish. ⊠ *Basement fl., 27 Staunton St., entrance on Graham St., SoHo, Central* ☎ *2139–2989* ⊕ *www.liancacentral.com* Ⓜ *Central, Exit D2.*

Llll Llll Shoes. The Chan Brothers have an illustrious history in Hong Kong and have certainly left a trail of satisfied customers in their wake; however, reviews these days speak of hit and miss experiences there. Prices have also shot up over the last few years (from around HK$1,500 for sandals and HK$2,300 for high heels). Still, when they are good, they are very, very good. ⊠ *1st fl., Tower 2, Shop 75, Admiralty Centre, 18 Harcourt Rd., Central* ☎ *2865–3989* Ⓜ *Admiralty, Exit A.*

Mayer Shoes. Since the 1960s, Mayer has been making excellent custom-order shoes and accessories in leather, lizard, crocodile, and ostrich. Go to them for the classic pieces for which they became famous rather than this season's "it" bag. Prices for ladies shoes start at several hundred U.S. dollars and peak at roughly US$2,000. ⊠ *Mandarin Oriental, 5 Connaught Rd., Central* ☎ *2524–3317* Ⓜ *Central, Exit K.*

On Pedder. This store's brand directory reads like a fashion editor's wish list of world-famous shoe, bag, accessory, and jewelry designers. The main branch can be found in Central's Joyce boutique, but you might see the same brands at Lane Crawford—that's because they're sister companies. For the same aesthetics at lower prices, check out trendy younger sibling Pedder Red at the Gateway Arcade in Harbour City. ⊠ *On Pedder at Joyce, 1st fl., New World Tower, 18 Queen's Rd. Central, Central* ☎ *2118–2323 for branch information* ⊕ *www.onpedder. com* Ⓜ *Central, Exit G.*

Sam Wo. A veteran of this area, Sam Wo sells fashion-inspired leather bags at low prices and without the branding. You'll need a keen eye to spot the must-haves amid all the must-nots. See neighboring stalls for closer interpretations of branded bags. ⊠ *6th fl., 41–47 Queen's Rd. Central, Central* ☎ *2524–0970* ⊙ *Closed Sun.* Ⓜ *Central, Exit D2.*

SPAS

Acupressure and Massage Centre of the Blind. Looking for a good massage without all the glitz? Visit these skilled and affordable blind masseurs trained in acupressure and Chinese massage, conveniently located in the middle of the Central Business District. Expect to pay around HK$240 per hour. ⊠ *2nd fl., Tung Ming Bldg., 40–42 Des Voeux Rd. Central, Central* ☎ *2810–6666* Ⓜ *Central.*

Four Seasons Spa. Enter via a light-wood and stark white hallway into treatment rooms that ooze modern cool. The 2½-hour signature Complete Organic Cleanse treatment, using an energizing eucalyptus salt scrub and a warm clay heating mask, is head-to-toe cleansing for your body and your soul. The serene steam and sauna complex and divine harbor views will also help to alter your mood. ⊠ *6th fl., Four Seasons Hotel, 8 Finance St., Central* ☎ *3196–8900* ⊕ *www.fourseasons.com* Ⓜ *Central.*

Fodor'sChoice ★ **Happy Foot Reflexology Center.** Who knew that pressure on your big toe could help clear your sinuses? Reflexology is Hong Kong's cheap way to relax, and Happy Foot is the legendary place to have it done. The armchairs are comfortable, and the therapists are experts, but don't expect a luxe experience. Interiors are basic, and you'll share a room with other customers. This is reflected in the prices, though: you'll pay about HK$250 for a 50-minute full-body massage or HK$198 for just your feet. There's a second center in Central (on Lyndhurst Terrace), plus more locations in Happy Valley and Wan Chai where you can also get your Happy Foot fix. ⊠ *19th and 20th fl., Century Square, 1 D'Aguilar St., Central* ☎ *2522–1151* ⊕ *www.happyfoot.hk* Ⓜ *Central, Exit D2.*

Fodor'sChoice ★ **The Mandarin Spa & The Oriental Spa.** If you indulge in a single Hong Kong treatment, have it at one of these sister spas in the Mandarin Oriental and Landmark Mandarin Oriental hotels. Designed as a journey from the outer into the inner world, the experience begins at the Landmark on the check-in and fitness floor. You're taken up to the next level and offered a welcome tea, then guided deeper into this haven, where treatments are administered by excellent therapists in serene rooms. Try the signature Time Ritual, a holistic combination of therapies adapted to your specific needs on the day. Treatments here get you access to the vitality pool, the amethyst-crystal steam room, the authentic Turkish hammam, and more. Down the street is the legendary Mandarin Spa, as well as the Mandarin Salon and Barber, which offers traditional favorites. Ask for a famous Shanghainese pedicure with Samuel and his knives (yes, knives!), or see Betty for the traditional eyebrow threading. ⊠ *The Landmark Mandarin Oriental, 15 Queen's Rd. Central, Central* ☎ *2132–0011* ⊕ *www.mandarinoriental.com* Ⓜ *Central.*

Quality Chinese Medical Centre. Acupuncture looks alarming but is painless. Where better to try it than in China? This reputable center is also a good place to learn more about traditional Chinese medicine and herbal remedies. ⊠ *5th fl., Jade Centre, 98 Wellington St., Central* ☎ *2881–8267* ⊕ *www.qualitytcm.com* Ⓜ *Central, Exit D2.*

SPECIALTY STORES

Fook Ming Tong Tea Shop. A local favorite for more than 25 years, Fook Ming Tong is known for excellent service and high-quality longjing, oolong, and jasmine teas that have been painstakingly sourced by tea masters. There are six Hong Kong branches, including the main one in the IFC Mall. ⊠ *Shop 3006, 3rd fl., IFC Mall, 8 Finance St., Central* ☎ *2295-0368* ⊕ *www.fookmingtong.com* ⊙ *Mon.–Sat. 10:30–8, Sun. and holidays 11–8* Ⓜ *Hong Kong.*

WAN CHAI, CAUSEWAY BAY, AND EASTERN

WAN CHAI

No malls, no international chains—Wan Chai provides a change of pace when shopping in Central starts to feel a bit repetitive. Tourists don't come here much, so you can try out your Cantonese at the rock-bottom no-name clothing outlets on the lanes between Johnston Road and Queen's Road East, where everything from underwear to evening wear is available. On Johnston Road itself, shops selling bamboo bird-cages and kung fu gear pay homage to Wan Chai's traditional side, in contrast to the chic modern furniture stores and fashion boutiques that have mushroomed here. Find them spreading into the small meandering Star Street neighborhood behind Three Pacific Place (⊕ *www.starstreet. com.hk*). Rosewood furniture and camphor-wood chests are two of the specialties of the midrange furniture shops on Queen's Road East and Wan Chai Road, near Admiralty. The Suzy Wong stereotype lives on in the marine-filled tattoo parlors lining Lockhart Road. Techno-happy modern Hong Kong is alive and well at the Wan Chai Computer Centre, a collection of dozens of computing outlets on Hennessy Road.

ART

Odd One Out. Part art gallery, part Aussie coffee shop, Odd One Out is an unpretentious addition to the gentrified Star Street precinct. Aiming to bring affordable and approachable art to everyday folks, the down-to-earth gallery café specializes in print and home products that have been handmade by local artists. Expect to spend around HK$55–HK$6,000 on any given piece, which could include stationery, wood cuttings, screen-printed totes, or original art prints made using masterful intaglio and lithography techniques, sans digital shortcuts. ⊠ *34 Sau Wa Fong, Wan Chai* ☎ *2529-3955* ⊕ *www.oddoneout.hk* ⊙ *Closed Mon.* Ⓜ *Admiralty, Exit F.*

CAMERAS AND ELECTRONICS

Wanchai Computer Centre. You can find bargains on computer goods and accessories in the labyrinth of shops spanning several floors. It's not as easy to negotiate prices here as it once was, but there are technicians who can help you put together a computer in less than a day if you're rushed; otherwise, two days is normal. The starting price is around HK$3,000 depending on the hardware, processor, and peripherals you choose. This is a great resource, whether you're a techno-buff who's interested in assembling your own computer (a popular pastime with locals), or a technophobe looking for quality earphones. ⊠ *130 Hennessy Rd., Wan Chai* Ⓜ *Wan Chai, Exit A5.*

CLOTHING

45R. Around since 1978, Japanese brand 45R has garnered a reputation for ultracomfortable, exquisitely crafted jeans. Following the successes of outposts in Paris and New York, a flagship store opened on Star Street in 2008. Amid the minimalist surroundings, find heaps of its famous hand-dyed denim as well as breezy button-downs, wooly sweaters, and understated frocks. ⊠ *Ground fl., Vincent Mansion, 7 Star St., Wan Chai* ☎ *2861–1145* ⊕ *www.45rpm.jp* Ⓜ *Wan Chai, Exit B2.*

Kapok. Hip messenger bags, soft fabrics, funky watches, comfy kicks, music, stationery—Kapok has it all. This bright local favorite is a one-stop shop for classic cotton and knits. Meanwhile, its café and gallery space (just two minutes down the road on Sun Street) serves up steamy French coffee, chocolate croissants, and freshly baked cupcakes. ⊠ *5 St. Francis Yard, Wan Chai* ☎ *2549–9254* ⊕ *www.ka-pok.com* Ⓜ *Wan Chai, Exit B2.*

Russell Street. Gatekeeper of the up-and-coming, Russell Street aims to introduce fresh labels to Hong Kong's style savants. Taking cues from New York and London's top fashion students, as well as established international labels—think Victoria Beckham denim—the boutique showcases eclectic designs ranging from fancy furs to colorful graphic-print dresses. Among the mix of envy-inducing pieces, look for Sophie Hulme's gorgeous leather bags and lively animal-print cardigans from Sibling and Sister. ⊠ *6 St. Francis Yard, Wan Chai* ☎ *2866–0800* ⊕ *www.russell-street.com* Ⓜ *Wan Chai, Exit B2.*

Sonjia by Sonjia Norman. Walk past a local garage and snoozing dogs in this old-style Hong Kong area to find the low-key atelier of Korean-English ex-lawyer Sonjia Norman. The designer crafts quietly luxurious, one-of-a-kind pieces and modified vintage clothing under the Sonjia label. Her clothes are the epitome of understated stealth wealth. An adjacent store houses Norman's home and living collection, including tableware, linens, and all kinds of cushions. ⊠ *Ground fl., 2 Sun St., Wan Chai* ☎ *2529–6223* ⊕ *www.sonjiaonline.com* Ⓜ *Wan Chai, Exit B.*

Vie. Modern and minimalist, Vie's decor is in perfect harmony with its Nordic apparel. The combination boutique and gallery on St. Francis Yard is a spinoff of Vein, and offers up a mix of Scandinavian luxury labels and home accessories. The lineup changes every four to six weeks, but you can usually find at least a dozen stalwart, simple-yet-elegant brands, including Filippa K and Won Hundred. Expect straight lines, a gray-scale palette, and unexpected splashes of color. ⊠ *Shop 2, St. Francis Yard, Wan Chai* ☎ *2804–1038* ⊕ *www.bvein.com* Ⓜ *Wan Chai, Exit B2.*

HOME DÉCOR

Lala Curio. Laura Cheung's grandfather spent a lifetime hand-carving rosewood tables, and her father helmed a wildly successful ceramic manufacturing company, so it's only natural that she carry on the tradition with Lala Curio, an eclectic homeware store in a cool corner of Wan Chai. Cheung's collections tip a hat to ancient Chinese craftsmanship, albeit with a whimsical modern spin; offerings range from pretty lacquer boxes to mosaic-tiled trays and bespoke upholstery. ⊠ *23–33*

Sau Wa Fong, Wan Chai ☎ *2528–5007* ⊕ *www.lalacurio.com* Ⓜ *Wan Chai, Exit A3.*

Nlostnfound Living & Co. Some of the items at Nlostnfound could use a bath, but the clutter has a lot of character. Take the time to browse through the jumble of old-world trinkets—1940s clocks, Shanghai lamps, 20s-era luggage trunks, antique furniture, colorful wind-up walking toys, typewriters, and postcards—and you'll likely unearth something worth salvaging. ⊠ *3 St. Francis Yard, Wan Chai* ☎ *2574– 1328* ⊕ *www.nlostnfound.com* Ⓜ *Wan Chai, Exit A3.*

OVO. Push past a giant weathered steel door to enter this atmospheric, high-ceiling showroom, which feels like a cross between a museum and a temple. Designed by an in-house team, the home furnishings and accessories here are smart and rarely fussy. Beautiful, unvarnished blocks of wood, for example, are proposed as side tables. A few minutes' walk away you'll find the newer **OVO Studio** (*Ground fl., 1 Wan Chai Rd., 2527–6088*), with its more European mix of in-house and international contemporary designs from brands like Tom Dixon, Fritz Hansen, and Andreu World. ⊠ *Ground fl., 16 Queen's Rd. E, Wan Chai* ☎ *2526–7226* ⊕ *www.ovo.com.hk* Ⓜ *Wan Chai, Exit B1.*

Tang Tang Tang Tang. A regular in Hong Kong high society, Sir David Tang recently opened lifestyle boutique Tang Tang Tang Tang (meant to be sung like Beethoven's Fifth). The entrepreneur is also behind classy China Club and iconic Shanghai Tang, so you know this spot is going to be good. Settled right under The Pawn's heritage facade, TTTT is all about throwback colonial decor, with a creative western twist and a touch of whimsy. There are even daily tours of the ground floor (built in 1888 and originally home to the Lo family pawnshop) to show off the preserved staircase and architectural elements. As for the collection, it's all very retro chic—even the rice maker has been classed up beyond recognition. TTTT is great for cheeky gifts, comfy pajamas, funky gadgets, and housewares that marry past and present with eye-catching results. ⊠ *66 Johnston Rd., Wan Chai* ☎ *2525–2112* ⊕ *www. tangtangtangtang.com* Ⓜ *Wan Chai, Exit A3.*

JEWELRY AND ACCESSORIES

Wing On Jewelry Ltd. There's a nostalgic charm to the butterflies, birds, and natural forms fashioned from jade, pearls, precious stones, and gold here. Everything looks like an heirloom inherited from your grandmother. With onsite gemologists and artisans, and a commitment to post-sale service, this store has a long list of repeat customers. If, however, you lean toward Scandinavian aesthetics and clean lines, this probably isn't the place for you. Wing On also has a Causeway Bay branch at 459 Hennessy Road. ⊠ *146 Johnston Rd., Wan Chai* ☎ *2572–2332* ⊕ *www.wingonjewelry.com.hk* Ⓜ *Wan Chai, Exit A3.*

SPECIALTY STORES

Kung Fu Supplies Co. You've seen *Enter the Dragon* a hundred times, and you practice your karate chops daily. Time to get the leather boots, sword, whip, double dagger, studded bracelet, and kempo gloves. Kung Fu Supplies Co. can kit you out. ⊠ *192 Johnston Rd., Wan Chai* ☎ *2891–1912* ⊕ *www.kungfu.com.hk* Ⓜ *Wan Chai, Exit A5.*

Monocle. As if running a magazine, website, and radio station weren't enough, Monocle also has a handful of retail outlets, and Hong Kong devotees of the London-based media brand rejoiced when its store-cum-office opened on Star Street's St. Francis Yard in 2010. Whether shopping for excellent reading material or stylish accessories (picture trendy totes, linen-bound notebooks, greeting cards, and embossed card cases), you'll be in good company. ⊠ *Shop 1, Bo Fung Mansion, 1–4 St. Francis Yard, Wan Chai* ☎ *2804–2323* ⊕ *www.monocle.com* Ⓜ *Wan Chai, Exit A3.*

CAUSEWAY BAY

Hong Kong fashionistas hungry for new labels choose Causeway Bay over Central any day. Quirky-but-cool Asian brands that won't arrive stateside for years are the pull at Japanese department store Sogo and micromalls like the Island Beverley Centre. The low-profile store-fronts on Yiu Wa Street belie its *hot* reputation for homegrown clothing and housewares. Similar up-and-coming boutiques are scattered along Vogue Alley, at the intersection of Paterson and Kingston streets. Megamall Times Square soars behind all this—its mix of designer and midrange gear makes it a good one-stop shopping destination. Other good bets for clothing are the big branches of local chains. Garment prices in the stalls and poky shops along Jardine's Crescent and Jardine's Bazaar are unbeatable; and you can see how real Hong Kongers do their food shopping at the "wet market" (so called because the vendors are perpetually hosing down their produce) at the end of these streets.

BEAUTY

Aroma Natural Skin Care. This store has been the secret weapon of skin regime enthusiasts for years, with stock from some of the industry's most venerated brands, many of them hard to track down. Find your Bioderma, Obagi, and Skin Ceuticals here, as well as the mandatory spectrum of whitening products. ⊠ *Shop 863, Island Beverley, 1 Great George St., Causeway Bay* ☎ *2506–0699* ⊕ *www.aroma-natural.com. hk* Ⓜ *Causeway Bay.*

Kwong Sang Hong. This shop carries Hong Kong's first local cosmetics line, also known as Two Girls Brand. The colorful, old-fashioned packaging, which is reminiscent of traditional Chinese medicines, is more remarkable than the products. That said, the line's classics—including hair oil, talcum powder, and face cream—do make lovely gifts. ⊠ *Shop 207–208, Causeway Place, Hong Kong Mansion, 2–10 Great George St., Causeway Bay* ☎ *2504–1811* ⊕ *www.twogirls.hk* Ⓜ *Causeway Bay, Exit E.*

Sa Sa Cosmetics. The fuchsia-pink signs that announce Hong Kong's best and largest cosmetic discounter will become familiar sights on any shopping expedition. Look for deals on everything from cheap glittery makeup to sleek designer lines. Fragrances are a particularly good buy; prices are usually even lower than those at airport duty-free shops. ⊠ *Shop G01, Hang Lung Centre, 2–20 Paterson St., Causeway Bay* ☎ *2577–2286, 2505–5023 customer service and branch info* ⊕ *www. sasa.com* Ⓜ *Causeway Bay, Exit E.*

10/10 Space. A hidden gem in Causeway Bay, 10/10 Space is a day spa and beauty boutique that offers excellent manis, pedis, head massages, hair styling, and facials. It also sells a slew of hard-to-find products. Look for Malin + Goetz lotions, Apothia aromatic candles, Minx nail varnishes, Eve Lom's line of "stem cell" makeup, and hair-repair goodies from the likes of Christophe Robin. ⊠ *Unit B, 1st fl., Fairview Mansion, 51 Paterson St., Causeway Bay* ☎ *3595–1152* ⊕ *1010space.com. hk* Ⓜ *Causeway Bay, Exit D3.*

CAMERAS AND ELECTRONICS

Broadway. Like its more famous competitor, Fortress, Broadway is a large electronic-goods chain. It caters primarily to the local market, so some staff members speak better English than others. Look for familiar name-brand cameras, computers, sound systems, home appliances, and mobile phones. ⊠ *7th–9th fl., Times Square, 1 Matheson St., Causeway Bay* ☎ *2506–0228* ⊕ *www.ibroadway.com.hk* Ⓜ *Causeway Bay, Exit A.*

Fodor's Choice ★ **Fortress.** Part of billionaire Li Ka-shing's empire, this extensive chain of shops sells electronics with warranties—a safety precaution that draws the crowds. It also has good deals on printers and accessories, although selection varies by shop. You can spot a Fortress by looking for the big orange sign. For the full list of outlets, visit the website. ⊠ *Times Square, Shop 719–721, 7th and 8th fl., 1 Matheson St., Causeway Bay* ☎ *2506–0031* ⊕ *www.fortress.com.hk* Ⓜ *Causeway Bay, Exit A.*

COMPUTERS **DG Lifestyle Store.** An appointed Apple Center, the DG chain carries Mac and iPod products. High-design gadgets, accessories, and software by other brands are add-ons that meld with the sleek Apple design philosophy. ⊠ *Shop 903, 9th fl., Times Square, 1 Matheson St., Causeway Bay* ☎ *2506–1338* ⊕ *www.dg-lifestyle.com* Ⓜ *Causeway Bay, Exit A.*

CLOTHING

G2000. This inexpensive chain carries men's and women's business wear in Asian sizes. It's a great place to look for suits with matching shirts (and ties) for a good price. Expect a mix of city-chic and casual, and especially good fits for anyone petit. ⊠ *Shop 25–30, Excelsior Plaza, 24–26 East Point Rd., Causeway Bay* ☎ *2972–2576* ⊕ *www.g2000. com.hk* Ⓜ *Causeway Bay, Exit E.*

Lu Lu Cheung. A fixture on the Hong Kong fashion scene for decades, Lu Lu Cheung creates designs that ooze comfort and warmth. In both daytime and evening wear, natural fabrics and forms are represented in practical yet imaginative ways. ⊠ *Shop C, 42–48 Paterson St., Causeway Bay* ☎ *2537–7515* ⊕ *www.lulucheung.com.hk* Ⓜ *Causeway Bay, Exit E.*

Olivia Couture. The surroundings are functional, but the gowns, wedding dresses, and cheongsams by local designer Olivia Yip are lavish. With a growing clientele—including socialites looking to stand out—Yip is quietly making a name for herself and her Parisian-influenced pieces. ⊠ *Ground fl., Bartlock Centre, 3 Yiu Wah St., Causeway Bay* ☎ *2838–6636* ⊕ *www.oliviacouture.com* Ⓜ *Causeway Bay, Exit A.*

Pink Martini. Step into this blush-colored boudoir for fresh young fashions with spunk, courtesy of brands like Daily Dolly and Kikka. It also has a small range of costume jewelry, clutches, and jackets, all nicely aimed at bringing out your inner girl. ⊠ *Shop 2, ground fl., Bartlock Centre, 3 Yiu Wa St., Causeway Bay* ☎ *2574–1498* ⊕ *www.pinkmartini. com.hk* Ⓜ *Causeway Bay, Exit A.*

Spy Henry Lau. Local bad boy Henry Lau brings an edgy attitude to his fashion for men and women. Bold and often dark, with a touch of bling, his clothing and accessories lines are not for the fainthearted. In Central, you can visit the SoHo store at 21 Staunton Street. ⊠ *1st fl., Cleveland Mansion, 5 Cleveland St., Causeway Bay* ☎ *2317–6928* ⊕ *www.spyhenrylau.com* Ⓜ *Causeway Bay, Exit E.*

Uniqlo. If you are a Giordano or Bossini fan, don't miss this Japanese chain. Uniqlo carries a wide variety of inexpensive, fashionable casual wear for women, men, and children. New locations have been opening rapidly throughout the city since 2007. Popular items include T-shirts, jeans, and pajamas. ⊠ *Basement and Ground fl., Lee Theatre Plaza, 99 Percival St., Causeway Bay* ☎ *2577–5811* ⊕ *www.uniqlo.com.hk* Ⓜ *Causeway Bay, Exit A.*

DEPARTMENT STORES

Fodor'sChoice
★

City'super. Wherever you're from and whatever you're looking for—whether it's fresh oysters from France or quirky products like bottled water for pets—this gourmet supermarket and variety-store chain is the place to begin your search. In addition to edibles, it carries gadgets, inexpensive jewelry, accessories, and cosmetics. The Times Square location often has international-theme food festivals. ■ TIP➡ Be sure to check out the Japanese imported sweets like Royce's unusual chocolate-covered potato chips. ⊠ *Basement One, Times Square, 1 Matheson St., Causeway Bay* ☎ *2506–2888* ⊕ *www.citysuper.com.hk* Ⓜ *Causeway Bay, Exit A.*

Sogo. A lynchpin of the Causeway Bay shopping scene, Japanese brand Sogo's main branch has 16 floors of clothing, housewares, and personal-care items. The selection of street wear, makeup, and accessories is particularly strong, with a dazzling variety of Asian and international labels represented. A vast basement-level grocery store keeps the Japanese expat community happily fed. ⊠ *555 Hennessy Rd., Causeway Bay* ☎ *2833–8338* ⊕ *www.sogo.com.hk* Ⓜ *Causeway Bay, Exit D.*

HOME DÉCOR

Franc Franc. This Japanese home and living store has everything you'd need to equip your downtown apartment, from bookshelves to bubble bath. The funky, colorfully modern designs and intriguing gadgets will keep all types of shoppers entertained, and it's quite a feat to leave the store with empty hands. ⊠ *2nd fl., Hang Lung Centre, 2–20 Paterson St., Causeway Bay* ☎ *3427–3366* ⊕ *www.francfranc.com* Ⓜ *Causeway Bay, Exit E.*

JEWELRY AND ACCESSORIES

City Chain Co. Ltd. With more than 400 shops in Asia and locations all over Hong Kong, City Chain Co. Ltd. has a wide selection of watches for various budgets, including examples by Ellesse, Cyma, and Armani. ⊠ *Shop 911, 9th fl., Times Square, 1 Matheson St., Causeway Bay* ☎ *2506–3553* ⊕ *www.citychain.com* Ⓜ *Causeway Bay, Exit A.*

MALLS AND SHOPPING CENTERS

Hysan Place. Across the street from Causeway Bay's popular Sogo looms neighborhood newcomer Hysan Place. This gleaming 17-story mall devotes the fourth and fifth floors to Japanese and Korean designers. Try on urban-chic garb from Daily Dolly, Snidel, and Deicy, then head up to the sixth floor for pampering. Dubbed the Garden of Eden, this level is overflowing with name-brand beauty products, lingerie shops, dessert counters, and nail salons. For a fix of fresh air, step out onto the Sky Garden on the fourth level, or slip into the three-level Eslite bookstore to relax with a book and a cuppa. ⊠ *500 Hennessy Rd., Causeway Bay* ☎ *2886–7222* ⊕ *hp.leegardens.com.hk* Ⓜ *Causeway Bay, Exit F2.*

Island Beverley Centre. This hip micromall played a big part in putting Causeway Bay on the fashion map. Shoe-box-size boutiques fill its four cramped floors—some showcase small, local designers; others stock Japanese and Korean brands hard to find overseas. Edgy club wear competes for the space with cutesy numbers for girls who just don't want to grow up. Indeed, many of the clothes look like they'll only fit local schoolgirls, but not to worry: Island Beverley has a great selection of bags, accessories, and jewelry. ⊠ *1 Great George St., Causeway Bay* Ⓜ *Causeway Bay, Exit E.*

Lee Gardens One and Two. These two adjacent malls are a firm favorite with local celebrities. They come as much for the mall's low-key atmosphere—a world away from the bustle of Central—as for the clothes. And with so many big names under one small roof—Gucci, Vivienne Tam, Emporio Armani, and Hermès, to name but a few—who can blame them? The second floor of Lee Gardens Two is taken up with designer kiddie wear. The two buildings, one on either side of Hysan Avenue, are linked by a second-floor footbridge. ⊠ *33 Hysan Ave., Causeway Bay* ☎ *2907–5227* ⊕ *www.leegardens.com.hk* Ⓜ *Causeway Bay, Exit F.*

Fodor'sChoice
★ **Times Square.** This gleaming mall packs most of Hong Kong's best-known stores into 12 frenzied floors, organized thematically. Lane Crawford and Marks & Spencer both have big branches here, as does favored local gourmet grocer City'super. Many restaurants are located in the basement, giving way to names like Fendi and De Beers on the second floor, and midrange options like Zara higher up. The electronics, sports, and outdoors selection is particularly good. An indoor atrium hosts everything from heavy-metal bands to fashion shows to local movie stars. ■TIP➔ Among the dozen or so eateries, innovative SML (or Small Medium Large) is a good pick, thanks to its large terrace and good selection of wines. ⊠ *1 Matheson St., Causeway Bay* ☎ *2118–8900 Customer Service Hotline* ⊕ *www.timessquare.com.hk* Ⓜ *Causeway Bay, Exit A.*

Windsor House Computer Plaza. Clean, wide corridors distinguish this less frantic computer arcade from the others. It has two floors of products with a wide selection of Mac and PC computer games, video games, laptops, desktops, and accessories. This is a reputable center with competitive prices. ⊠ *Basement and 10th fl., Windsor House, 311 Gloucester Rd., Causeway Bay* ☎ *2895–0668* ⊕ *www.windsorhouse.hk* Ⓜ *Causeway Bay, Exit E.*

4

MARKETS

Jardine's Bazaar and Jardine's Crescent. These two small parallel streets are so crammed with clothing stalls it's difficult to make your way through. Most offer bargains on the usual clothes, children's gear, bags, and cheap souvenirs like chopstick sets. The surrounding boutiques are also worth a look for local and Japanese fashions, though the sizes are small. ⊠ *Causeway Bay* Ⓜ *Causeway Bay, Exit F.*

SHOES, HANDBAGS, AND LEATHER GOODS

Milan Station. Even if you're willing to shell out for an Hermès Kelly bag, how can anyone expect you to survive the waitlist? Milan Station resells the "it" bags of yesterday that have been retrieved from Hong Kong's fickle fashionistas. Inexplicably, the shop entrances (there are more than half a dozen here) were designed to look like MTR stations. The concept has been so successful, unimaginatively named copycats have sprung up, such as Paris Station. Discounts vary according to brand and trends, but the merchandise is in good condition. ⊠ *Ground fl., Percival House, 77–83 Percival St., Causeway Bay* ☎ *2504–0128, 2730–8037 customer service* ⊕ *www.milanstation.com.hk* Ⓜ *Causeway Bay, Exit A.*

Prestige Shoe Co. Ltd. Like the Happy Valley shoemakers, Prestige does fashion-forward, acceptable-quality, reasonably priced shoes. Unlike its valley brethren it's more convenient, with several locations around town. ⊠ *1st fl., Island Beverley Centre, 1 Great George St., Causeway Bay* ☎ *2915–6813* Ⓜ *Causeway Bay, Exit E.*

Rabeanco. Locally–based Rabeanco has a reasonably priced line of beautiful, quality bags in Italian leather. Expect designs that are contemporary and colorful, but never flashy or absurd. Buy yours now at one of the seven Hong Kong locations before the world catches on. ⊠ *Shop 4A, ground fl., 33 Sharp St. East, Causeway Bay* ☎ *3586–0281, 2245–5085 customer service and branch information* ⊕ *www.rabeanco.com* Ⓜ *Causeway Bay, Exit A.*

SPAS

SPA by MTM. At this soothing Japanese spa the aesthetic is as important as the physical treatments; each room has a specific identity, and products are custom blended on-site. ⊠ *16th fl., 38 Russell St., Causeway Bay* ☎ *2923–7888* ⊕ *www.spabymtm.com* Ⓜ *Causeway Bay, Exit A.*

EASTERN

DEPARTMENT STORES

Marks & Spencer. Classic, good-quality clothing is what this British retailer has built an empire on—its underwear, in particular, is viewed as a national treasure. Although basics are on the staid side, the newer Per Una, Autograph, and Limited collections are decidedly trendier. Marks & Spencer is also one of the few stores in town to stock a full range of sizes, which includes women's shoes up to a US size 10 and men's up to US size 12. There are branches in many of Hong Kong's malls, the biggest of which is in Cityplaza; most have a British specialty food section, too, with a good range of wines. ⊠ *1st fl., Cityplaza, 1111 Kings Rd., Tai Koo, Eastern* ☎ *2922–7234* ⊕ *www.marks-and-spencer. hk* Ⓜ *Tai Koo, Exit D.*

MALLS AND SHOPPING CENTERS

Cityplaza. An ice-skating rink and a multiplex theater are two of the reasons why Cityplaza is the city's most popular family mall. So popular, in fact, that it's best to steer clear on weekends, when you have to fight through the crowds. Toys and children's clothing labels are well represented, as are midrange local and international adult brands. Cityplaza also has branches of Marks & Spencer (the largest in Hong Kong), local department store Wing On, and Japanese supermarket APiTa. ◾ TIP➔ **Popular Food Republic, with 21 Asian food stalls and mini restaurants, is perfect for a quick bite.** ✉ *18 Tai Koo Shing Rd., Tai Koo, Eastern* ☎ *2568–8665* ⊕ *www.cityplaza.com.hk* Ⓜ *Tai Koo, Exit D1.*

MARKETS

Island East Markets. Every Sunday for most of the year, the Hong Kong Markets Association puts on the Island East Markets in Quarry Bay. The bazaar tends to draw expat crowds, and the prices on gourmet snacks and handmade goods —think jewelry, clothes, shoes, and more—reflect that. Although you probably won't bag a bargain, you will come face-to-face with talented local designers and vendors. Time your visit right and you could catch a live band performing. ◾ TIP➔ **There's also a handy play area for little ones with a fun calendar of activities.** ✉ *Taikoo Place, Tong Chong St., Quarry Bay, Eastern* ☎ *2851–3220* ⊕ *www.islandeastmarkets.org* Ⓜ *Quarry Bay, Exit A.*

SHOES, HANDBAGS, AND LEATHER GOODS

Brand Off Tokyo. This Japanese chain hit town in 2008; like Milan Station, it carries secondhand goods from luxury brands like Louis Vuitton, Hermès, Chanel, and Prada. The shop is also a member of the Association Against Counterfeit Product Distribution, a Japanese organization that uses scientific evidence to determine whether items are genuine or knockoffs. ✉ *1st fl., Shop 120, Cityplaza, 18 Tai Koo Shing Rd., Tai Koo, Eastern* ☎ *2967–6137* ⊕ *www.brandoff.com.hk* Ⓜ *Tai Koo, Exit D1.*

SOUTHSIDE

Southside has a booming art scene these days, with 30 galleries and counting in the area around Wong Chuk Hang. The eponymous market in Stanley Village, however, is the reason many visitors come south. Trawling its crowded tourist-laden lanes for clothes, sportswear, and table linen can take half a day—more if you stop to eat at one of the laid-back waterfront restaurants. Other travelers head straight to Ap Lei Chau, a small residential island on reclaimed land that's home to a vast furniture and fashion warehouse called Horizon Plaza. Reaching the island can be a bit of a headache, depending on tunnel traffic. Board an M590 or 90 bus from the Exchange Square terminus for a 25- to 40-minute drive, or grab a cab and make the trip in about 20 minutes.

ANTIQUES AND COLLECTIBLES

Manks Ltd. Open to walk-ins seven days a week, this warehouse in the Wong Chuk Hang industrial district features 20th-century decorative arts, European antiques, and Scandinavian furniture, all proffered by the delightful Susan Man. For those who'd prefer to stick closer to

CLOSE UP

Shopping Hong Kong's Markets

Chinese markets are hectic and crowded, but great fun for the savvy shopper. The intensity of the bargaining and the variety of goods available are well worth the detour.

Nowadays Hong Kongers may prefer to flash their cash in department stores and designer boutiques, but generally,markets are still the best places to shop. Parents and grandparents, often toting children, go to their local neighborhood wet market almost daily to pick up fresh items such as tofu, fish, meat, fruit, and vegetables.

Some markets have a mishmash of items; others are more specialized, dealing in one particular ware. Prices paid are always a great topic of conversation. A compliment on a choice article will often elicit the price paid in reply, and a discussion may ensue on where to get the same thing at an even lower cost.

GREAT FINDS
The prices we list *below* are meant to give you an idea of what you can expect to pay for certain items. Actual post-bargaining prices will of course depend on how well you haggle, while pre-bargaining prices are often based on how much the vendor thinks he or she can get out of you.

Jade. A symbol of purity and beauty for the Chinese, jade comes in a range of colors. Subtle and simple bangles vie for attention with large sculptures in markets. A lavender jade Guanyin (Goddess of Mercy) pendant runs about HK$260 and a green jade bangle about HK$300 before bargaining.

Silk. You'll find silk items, from purses to slippers to traditional dresses,

at certain markets. A meter of silk brocade (that's slightly more than a yard) costs around HK$35, and the price is generally negotiable only if you buy large quantities.

Mah-Jongg Sets. The clack-clack of mah-jongg tiles can be heard late into the night in many public-housing estates during the summer. Cheap plastic sets go for about HK$40. Far more aesthetically pleasing are ceramic sets in slender drawers of painted cases. These run about HK$250 after bargaining, from a starting price of HK$450.

"Maomorabilia." The Chairman's image is available on badges, bags, lighters, watches, ad infinitum. Pop art–like figurines of Mao and his Red Guards clutching red books are kitschy but iconic. For sound bites and quotes from the Great Helmsman, buy the Little Red Book itself. Pre-bargaining, a badge costs HK$30, a bag HK$50, and a ceramic figurine HK$400. Just keep in mind that many posters are fakes.

Pearls. Many freshwater pearls are grown in Taihu; seawater pearls come from Japan or the South Seas. Some have been dyed and others mixed with semiprecious stones. Designs can be pretty wild, and the clasps are not of high quality, but necklaces and bracelets are cheap. Post-bargaining, a plain, short strand of pearls should cost around HK$50.

Propaganda and Comic Books. Follow the adventures of Master Q, or look for scenes from Chinese history and lots of *gongfu* (Chinese martial arts) stories, like *Longfumun* (Dragon Tiger Gate). Most titles are in Chinese and often in black and white, but can be bargained down to around HK$15.

Retro Finds. Odd items from the prewar '30s to the booming '70s include treasures like antique furniture, wooden toys, and tin advertising signs. Small items such as teapots can be bought for around HK$250. Retro items are harder to haggle for than mass-produced items.

SHOPPING KNOW-HOW

At the Markets: Make sure to put money and valuables in a safe place. Pickpockets and bag slashers are becoming more common. When purchasing, watch out for fake materials (for example, synthetic silk).

Bringin' Home the Goods: Although that faux-Gucci handbag is tempting, remember that some countries have heavy penalties for the import of counterfeit goods. Likewise, that animal fur may be cheap, but you may get fined a lot more at your home airport than what you paid for it. Counterfeits are generally prohibited in the United States, but there's some gray area regarding goods with a "confusingly similar" trademark. Each person is allowed to bring in one such item, as long as it's for personal use and not for resale.

When to Go: Avoid weekends if you can and try to go early in the morning, from 8 am to 10 am, or early evening for the night markets. Rainy days are also good bets for avoiding the crowds and getting better prices.

HOW TO BARGAIN

Successful bargaining requires knowing your prices and never losing your cool. Here's a step-by-step guide to getting the price you want and having fun at the same time.

Do's

■ Start by deciding how much you're willing to pay for an item.

■ Let the vendor know you're interested.

■ The vendor will quote you a price, sometimes using a calculator.

■ At this point it's up to you to express either incredulity or loss of interest. But be forewarned, the vendor plays this game, too.

■ Name a price that's around 50%–60% of the original price—lower if you feel daring.

■ Pass the calculator back and forth until you reach an agreement.

Don'ts

■ Don't enter into negotiations if you aren't seriously considering the purchase.

■ Don't haggle over small sums of money.

■ If the vendor isn't budging, walk away; he'll likely call you back.

■ It's better to bargain if the vendor is alone. He's unlikely to come down on the price if there's an audience.

■ Saving face is everything in China. Remain pleasant and smile often.

■ Buying more than one of something can get you a better deal.

■ Dress down and leave your jewelry and watches in the hotel safe on the day you go marketing. You'll get a lower starting price if you don't flash your wealth.

4

Locals and visitors alike flock to Southside's Stanley Market.

the center of town, there's also a showroom in Wan Chai. ⊠ *3rd fl., The Factory, 1 Yip Fat St., Wong Chuk Hang, Southside* ☎ *2522–2115* ⊕ *www.manks.com.*

ART

Alisan Fine Arts. Founded in 1981 by Alice King, Alisan Fine Arts was one of the first galleries in Hong Kong to promote contemporary Chinese art and is now an established authority. Styles range from traditional to modern abstract, and mediums include oil, acrylic, and Chinese ink. ⊠ *Room 2305, Hing Wai Centre, 7 Tin Wan Praya Rd., Aberdeen, Southside* ☎ *2526–1091* ⊕ *www.alisan.com.hk* ☉ *Closed Sun.*

Art Statements Gallery. On the southern side of Hong Kong island, this gallery often features boundary-pushing conceptual artists from Asia, as well as leading ones from Europe and North America. Since opening it in 2004, founder Dominique Perregaux has brought a fresh perspective to the local art scene. ⊠ *8th fl., Factory D, Gee Chang Hong Centre, 65 Wong Chuk Hang Rd., Aberdeen, Southside* ☎ *2696–2300* ⊕ *www. artstatements.com* ☉ *Closed Sun.*

Plum Blossoms Gallery. In the heart of an up-and-coming cultural district down in Aberdeen, this spacious industrial-chic loft-style gallery displays groundbreaking contemporary Chinese art alongside ancient Asian textiles and rugs. To get the most out of it, ask the refreshingly knowledgeable staff to escort you around. ⊠ *14th fl., Cheung Tak Industrial Bldg., 30 Wong Chuk Hang Rd., Aberdeen, Southside* ☎ *2521–2189* ⊕ *www.plumblossoms.com* ☉ *Closed Sun.*

CLOTHING

Hoi Yuen Emporium Co. Of all the cheaper alternatives to Shanghai Tang, this is the best. It has a fantastic selection of Mao collared jackets for boys and girls. Chinese-style onesies come in muted, non-cartoonish colors, and cost around HK$85. ⊠ *Stanley Market, 64 Stanley Main St., Stanley, Southside* ☎ *2813–0470.*

Joyce Warehouse. Fashionistas who've fallen on hard times can breathe a sigh of relief. Joyce's outlet on Ap Lei Chau, the island offshore from Aberdeen in Southside, stocks last season's duds from the likes of Jil Sander, Max Mara, Phillip Lim, Hugo Boss, and Anna Sui. Prices for each garment are reduced by about 10% each month, so the longer the piece stays on the rack, the less it costs. ⊠ *21st fl., Horizon Plaza, 2 Lee Wing St., Ap Lei Chau, Southside* ☎ *2814–8313* ⊕ *www.joyce.com.*

CRAFTS

Good Laque. Elegant lacquerware makes a wonderful gift. The pieces sold here—tabletop items and picture frames among them—are reasonably priced and come in classic red and black as well as silver and gold. In addition to the Stanley Market store, there's a second one in Ap Lei Chau's Horizon Plaza. ⊠ *Ground fl., Stanley Market, 40–42D Stanley Main St., Stanley, Southside, Hong Kong, China* ☎ *3106–0163.*

HOME DÉCOR

CarpetBuyer Limited. With a modern approach to an age-old business, a son of the Oriental Carpet Trading House family sells high-quality carpets from China, India, Iran, Turkey, Afghanistan, and Pakistan at warehouse prices. ⊠ *17th fl., Unit 1718, Horizon Plaza, 2 Lee Wing St., Ap Lei Chau, Southside* ☎ *2850–5508* ⊕ *www.carpetbuyer.com.*

Mrs. Chan. One of the top children's clothing stalls in Stanley Market sells everything from play-date clothes to Christmas Day bests. Push your way through the piles and hanging examples of tasteful, brand-name pieces for babies, boys, and girls. Come here first, then do some comparison shopping before pulling out your wallet. ⊠ *Market stall opposite Stanley Municipal Services Bldg., 6 Stanley Main St., Stanley, Southside, Hong Kong, China* ☎ *6082–7503.*

MALLS AND SHOPPING CENTERS

Horizon Plaza. With 28 floors of high-end fashion and housewares, the huge Horizon Plaza is a good choice for shoppers who have more taste than money. Joyce, Armani, Ralph Lauren, Diesel, and others all have outlet stores on the upper floors. If you're interested in dressing up your home, Tequila Kola has funky furniture, TREE sells eco-chic items, and Shambala's showroom brims with antique treasures. ⊠ *2 Lee Wing St., Ap Lei Chau, Southside* ☎ *2554–9089.*

MARKETS

Fodor's Choice
★ **Stanley Market.** This was once Hong Kong's most famed bargain trove for visitors, but its ever-growing popularity means that the market in Stanley Village no longer has the best prices around. Still, you can pick up some good buys in sportswear, casual clothing, textiles, and paintings if you comb through the stalls. Good-value linens—especially appliqué tablecloths—also abound. Dozens and dozens of shops line a main street so narrow that awnings from each side meet in the middle,

and on busy days your elbows will come in handy. Weekdays are a little more relaxed. One of the best things about Stanley Market is getting here: the winding bus ride from Central (routes 6, 6X, 6A, or 260) or Tsim Sha Tsui (route 973) takes you over the top of Hong Kong Island, with fabulous views along on the way. ✉ *Stanley, Southside* ⊕ *www. hk-stanley-market.com.*

KOWLOON PENINSULA

Kowloon is home to famous Nathan Road, the postcard image of a busy Hong Kong street, where bright neon lights adorn every building. But Kowloon is also the place for old-school outdoor markets, drawing locals and adventurous visitors who are willing to bargain for their bargains. In addition to good sales at outdoor vending areas like the evocative Temple Street Night Market and the Ladies' Market, cultural shopping experiences abound in places such as the Bird Garden or the Jade Market. ■ **TIP➔ Visiting all the outdoor markets in Kowloon in one day may be exhausting. You're better off picking three sites you want to spend some time in rather than rushing through them all.**

TSIM SHA TSUI

Lighted up in neon and jam-packed with shops, garish Nathan Road is Tsim Sha Tsui's main drag—and "what a drag" is the phrase that often comes to mind when shopping here. Sky-high prices, overcrowded streets, and aggressive street hawkers bent on ripping you off may leave you wishing you'd gone elsewhere. But slip down the side streets and things get better. Granville and Cameron roads are home to cheap clothing outlets, while Japanese imports and young designers fill the boutiques at the funky Rise Shopping Arcade. On the other end of the spectrum, the vast Harbour City complex and colonial-style 1881 Heritage arcade both have a big-name count to rival Central's, though the shoppers tend to be a bit more casual. Bespoke tailoring is another Tsim Sha Tsui specialty; however, it pays to choose a well-established place because quality varies enormously.

BEAUTY

FACES. This sprawling one-stop shop, just a stone's throw from the Kowloon Star Ferry terminal, carries a long list of high-profile and niche beauty brands. ✉ *Shop 202, Ocean Terminal, Harbour City, 5 Canton Rd., Tsim Sha Tsui* ☎ *2118–5622* Ⓜ *Tsim Sha Tsui, Exit L6.*

BOOKS AND MUSIC

Hong Kong Records. You'll find a good selection of current local and international CDs and DVDs at this age-old company. A lower profile also means prices are sometimes lower than in flashier retailers. ✉ *Shop 3320, Gateway Arcade, Harbour City, 3–27 Canton Rd., Tsim Sha Tsui* ☎ *2175–5700* ⊕ *www.hongkongrecords.hk* Ⓜ *Tsim Sha Tsui, Exit A.*

CLOTHING

Collect Point. Hidden away in the basement of Mira Mall, this 22,000-square-foot department store makes you feel like you're shopping in Tokyo. The brand list doesn't cover recognizable names, focusing

DID YOU KNOW?

Hong Kong is a leading producer of pure-gold items, and Nathan Road between Mong Kok and TST is one of the places to buy golden baubles. Local law requires all jewelers to indicate the number of carats and the manufacturer on gold pieces. In addition to checking for these markings, ask for an invoice listing the weight and price of each item.

instead on refreshing alternatives such as Lowrys Farm, Jeanasis, and Global Work. When the hip housewares and cool clothes have worn you out, tuck into Japanese-fusion food at Tokyo-import Wired Café. ✉ *Basement, Mira Mall, 118 Nathan Rd., Tsim Sha Tsui* ☎ *2367–2700* Ⓜ *Tsim Sha Tsui, Exit B1.*

Dorfit. A longtime cashmere manufacturer and retailer, Dorfit caters to a variety of men's, women's, and children's tastes. Knitwear here comes in pure cashmere as well as blends, so be sure to ask which is which. There's a branch at 10 Wellington Street in Central, too. ✉ *6th fl., Mary Bldg., 71–77 Peking Rd., Tsim Sha Tsui* ☎ *2312–1013* ⊕ *www.dorfit. com.hk* Ⓜ *Tsim Sha Tsui.*

Giordano. Hong Kong's version of the Gap is the most established and ubiquitous local source of basic T-shirts, jeans, and casual wear. Like its U.S. counterpart, the brand now has a bit more fashion sense and slick ad campaigns, but prices are still reasonable. Although the flagship store is in Manson House on Nathan Road, you'll have no problem finding one on almost every major street. ■TIP➔ Its line—Giordano Concepts—offers more stylish (and pricier) urban wear in neutral colors like black, gray, and white. ✉ *Ground fl., Manson House, 74–78 Nathan Rd., Tsim Sha Tsui* ☎ *2926–1028* ⊕ *www.giordano.com.hk* Ⓜ *Tsim Sha Tsui, Exit B1.*

Giordano Ladies. If Giordano is the Gap, Giordano Ladies is the Banana Republic, albeit with a more Zen approach. Find clean-line modern classics in neutral black, gray, white, and beige; each collection is brightened by a single highlight color, red one season, blue the next, and so on. Everything is elegant enough for the office and comfortable enough for the plane. ✉ *1st fl., Manson House, 74–78 Nathan Rd., Tsim Sha Tsui* ☎ *2926–1331* ⊕ *www.giordanoladies.com* Ⓜ *Tsim Sha Tsui, Exit B1.*

Initial. This team of local designers creates simple but whimsical men's and women's clothing with a trendy urban edge. The bags and accessories strike a soft vintage tone, fitting the store's fashionably worn interiors, casually strewn secondhand furniture, and sultry jazz soundtrack. ✉ *The Park Lane Hong Kong, 31 Gloucester Rd., Causeway Bay* ☎ *2882–9044* ⊕ *www.initialfashion.com* Ⓜ *Causeway Bay.*

Fodor's Choice ★ **Pearls & Cashmere.** Warehouse prices in chic shopping arcades? It's true. This old Hong Kong favorite is elegantly housed on both sides of the harbor. In addition to quality men's and women's cashmere sweaters in classic designs and in every color under the sun, they also sell reasonably priced pashminas, gloves, and socks, which make great gifts for men and women. In recent years the brand has developed the more fashion-focused line, BYPAC. ✉ *Mezzanine, Peninsula Hotel Shopping Arcade, Salisbury Rd., Tsim Sha Tsui* ☎ *2723–8698* ⊕ *bypac.com* Ⓜ *Tsim Sha Tsui, Exit L4.*

CLOTHING: TAILORS

David's Shirts Ltd. Customers have been enjoying the personalized service of David Chu since 1961. All the work is done in-house by Shanghainese tailors with at least 20 years' experience each. There are more than 6,000 imported European fabrics to choose from, each prewashed. Examples of shirts, suits, and accessories—including 30 collar styles,

12 cuff styles, and 10 pocket styles—help you choose. Single-needle tailoring; French seams; 22 stitches per inch; handpicked, double-stitched shell buttons; German interlining—it's all here. Your details, down to on which side you wear your wristwatch, are kept on file should you wish to use its mail-order service in the future. If you're in Central, The Galleria contains a second branch. ⊠ *Ground fl., Wing Lee Bldg., 33 Kimberley Rd., Tsim Sha Tsui* ☎ *2367–9556* Ⓜ *Tsim Sha Tsui, Exit B2.*

Maxwell's Clothiers Ltd. After you've found a handful of reputable, high-quality tailors, one way to choose between them is price. Maxwell's is known for its competitive rates. It's also a wonderful place to have favorite shirts and suits copied and for straightforward, structured women's shirts and suits. It was founded by third-generation tailor Ken Maxwell in 1961 and follows Shanghai tailoring traditions, while also providing the fabled 24-hour suit upon request. The showroom and workshop are in Kowloon, but son Andy and his team take appointments in the United States, Canada, Australia, and Europe twice annually. The motto of this family business is, "Simply let the garment do the talking." ⊠ *13th fl., Maxwell Centre, 39–41 Hankow Rd., Tsim Sha Tsui* ☎ *2366–6705* ⊕ *www.maxwellsclothiers.com* Ⓜ *Tsim Sha Tsui, Exit A1.*

Mode Elegante. Don't be deterred by the somewhat dated mannequins in the windows. Mode Elegante is a favorite source for custom-made suits among women and men in the know. Tailors here specialize in European cuts. You'll have your choice of fabrics from the United Kingdom, Italy, and elsewhere. Your records are put on file so you can place orders from abroad. It'll even ship the completed garment to you almost anywhere on the planet. Alternatively, you can make an appointment with director Gary Zee, one of Hong Kong's traveling tailors, who makes regular visits to North America, Australia, Europe, and Japan. ⊠ *11th fl., Star House, 3 Salisbury Rd., Tsim Sha Tsui* ☎ *2366–8153* ⊕ *www. modeelegante.com* Ⓜ *Tsim Sha Tsui, Exit L6.*

Fodor's Choice ★ **Sam's Tailor.** Unlike many famous Hong Kong tailors, you won't find the legendary Sam's in a chic hotel or sleek mall. But don't be fooled. These digs in humble Burlington House, a tailoring hub, have hosted everyone from U.S. presidents (back as far as Richard Nixon) to performers such as the Black Eyed Peas, Kylie Minogue, and Blondie. This former uniform tailor to the British troops once even made a suit for Prince Charles in a record hour and 52 minutes. The men's and women's tailor does accept 24-hour suit or shirt orders, but will take about two days if you're not in a hurry. Founded by Naraindas Melwani in 1957, "Sam" is now his son, Manu Melwani, who runs the show with the help of his own son, Roshan, and about 57 tailors behind the scenes. In 2004 Sam's introduced a computerized bodysuit that takes measurements without a tape measure (it uses both methods, however). These tailors also make biannual trips to Europe and North America: schedule updates are listed on the website. ⊠ *Burlington House, 94 Nathan Rd., Tsim Sha Tsui* ☎ *2367–9423* ⊕ *www.samstailor.com* Ⓜ *Tsim Sha Tsui, Exit B2.*

LCX. This spacious store combines local and international fashion, beauty products, and dining under one roof. Clothing brands like

Don't skimp on custom clothing. Rely on the expert tailors listed *in this chapter* for classic, tailor-made Chinese clothing.

American Eagle, French Connection, Jack Wills, and Initial all have their own areas here, as do TonyMoly, Dr.Ci:Labo, Lush, and other cosmetics lines. LCX also has a handful of restaurants, including Gyu-Kaku Japanese and Mou Mou Club. ⊠ *3rd fl., Ocean Terminal, Harbour City, 2–27 Canton Rd., Tsim Sha Tsui* ☎ *2890–5200, 3102–3668 Customer service hotline* ⊕ *www.lcx.com.hk* Ⓜ *Tsim Sha Tsui, Exit A.*

JEWELRY AND ACCESSORIES

Artland Watch Co Ltd. Elegant but uncomplicated, the interior of this established watch retailer is like its service. The informed staff will guide you through the countless luxury brands on show and in the catalogs from which you can also order. Prices here aren't the best in Hong Kong, but they're still lower than at home. ⊠ *Ground fl., Mirador Mansion, 62A Nathan Rd., Tsim Sha Tsui* ☎ *2366–1074* Ⓜ *Tsim Sha Tsui.*

Carat. Forget the cheesy cubic zirconium of the past. One look at its stark showrooms, and you'll see that Carat has mastered the creation and presentation of synthetic gemstones. Hand-assembled in precious-metal settings, the large collection spans various eras of jewelry styles. Harbour City houses its flagship store, but you'll also find Carat in the IFC Mall and eight other Hong Kong locations. ⊠ *Shop 3323A, 3rd fl., Gateway Arcade, Harbour City, 7–27 Canton Rd., Tsim Sha Tsui* ☎ *3101–1510* ⊕ *www.caratlondon.com* Ⓜ *Hong Kong.*

Prince Jewellery and Watch Company. This shop carries timepieces made by more than 50 international brands, including Omega, Chopard, Breguet, and IWC. There's other jewelry on sale as well, which may entertain those accompanying the avid watch shopper. ⊠ *Ground fl.,*

Bo Yip Bldg., 10 Peking Rd., Tsim Sha Tsui ☎ *2369–2123* ⊕ *www. princejewellerywatch.com* Ⓜ *Tsim Sha Tsui, Exit L5.*

TSL Jewellery. One of the big Hong Kong chains, TSL (Tse Sui Luen) specializes in diamond jewelry, and manufactures, retails, and exports its designs. Its range of 100-facet stones includes the Estrella cut, which reflects nine symmetrical hearts and comes with international certification. Although its contemporary designs use platinum settings, TSL also sells pure, bright, yellow-gold items targeted at Chinese customers. ⊠ *G5–G7, Park Lane Shopper' Blvd., Nathan Rd., Tsim Sha Tsui* ☎ *2375–2661* ⊕ *www.tsljewellery.com* Ⓜ *Tsim Sha Tsui, Exit A1.*

MALLS AND SHOPPING CENTERS

Elements. This upscale shopping mall is in the Kowloon West residential and commercial district, just above Kowloon's Airport Express train and check-in station. Beautifully designed, it's divided into five different zones based on the titular elements: metal, wood, water, earth, and fire. This is one-stop shopping as far as international luxury brands are concerned, with Valentino, Prada, and Gucci, just to name a few. ⊠ *1 Austin Rd. West, Tsim Sha Tsui* ☎ *2735–5234* ⊕ *www.elementshk.com* Ⓜ *Kowloon, Exit C2.*

Fodor's Choice   **Harbour City.** The four interconnected complexes that make up Harbour
★   City contain almost 500 shops between them—if you can't find it here, it probably doesn't exist. Pick up a map on your way in, as it's easy to get lost. **Ocean Terminal,** the largest section, runs along the harbor and is divided thematically, with kids' wear and toys on the ground floor, and sports and cosmetics on the first. The top floor is home to white-hot department store LCX. Near the Star Ferry pier, the **Marco Polo Hong Kong Hotel Arcade** has branches of the department store Lane Crawford. Louis Vuitton, Prada, and Burberry are some of the posher boutiques that fill the **Ocean Centre** and **Gateway Arcade,** parallel to Canton Road. Most of the complex's restaurants are here, too. A cinema and three hotels round out Harbour City's offerings. ■ TIP→ Free Wi-Fi is available. ⊠ *Tsim Sha Tsui* ⊕ *www.harbourcity.com.hk* Ⓜ *Tsim Sha Tsui, Exit A1.*

Mira Mall. Not to be confused with the neighboring Miramar Shopping Centre, this mall opened in 2012 as the latest addition to The Mira (a design-driven luxury hotel). With offerings like Twist, Tommy Hilfiger, and Coach, it targets Hong Kong's young elite. Asian talent is a focal point at the four-story galleria, where you'll find Hong Kong–based Ika Butoni and her colorful Indonesian creations. Other noteworthy brands include Noriem, Cocomojo, and Sebago. ■ TIP→ Don't miss the huge Collect Point flagship store in the basement. ⊠ *118 Nathan Rd., Tsim Sha Tsui* ☎ *2315–5868* ⊕ *www.mira-mall.com* Ⓜ *Tsim Sha Tsui.*

Rise Shopping Arcade. Many a quirky Hong Kong street-wear trend is born in this fabulous micromall. Don't let its grubby exterior put you off: the arcade is a haven of Asian cool. Japanese designers are particularly well represented—look for überhip brand A Bathing Ape, which does some of the funkiest T-shirts around. Handmade shoes and oversized retro jewelry are other fixtures, all at bargain prices. ⊠ *5–11 Granville Circuit, off Granville Rd., Tsim Sha Tsui* Ⓜ *Tsim Sha Tsui, Exit B2.*

YAU MA TEI, MONG KOK, AND NORTHERN KOWLOON

The bright-lights–big-city look of Tsim Sha Tsui gives way to housing blocks and tenements hung with aging signs north of Jordan Road. Streets are crowded and traffic is manic, but this down-to-earth chaos is what makes shopping in these north Kowloon neighborhoods rewarding. Well, that and all the bargains at the area's markets. Yau Ma Tei has jade and pearls on Kansu Street; clothing, bric-a-brac, and domestic appliances fill atmospheric Temple Street nightly. If you prefer fixed prices, Yue Hwa's seven-story flagship store is one of the best places in Hong Kong for cheap gifts. Farther north in Mong Kok you'll discover blocks and blocks of brandless garments and accessories at the Fa Yuen Street Ladies' Market. Parallel Tung Choi Street has cut-price sporting goods. Goldfish, flowers, and birds each have their own dedicated market in Prince Edward. By comparison, the cavernous Langham Place megamall feels like an alternate universe.

YAU MA TEI
BOOKS AND MUSIC

Kubrick. Stocking alternative-spirited books, graphic novels, magazines, music, and DVDs in a variety of foreign languages, Kubrick is the closest thing to a bilingual community bookshop you're likely to find in Hong Kong. Coming here will give you a good, if slightly unpolished, sense of the city's contemporary culture. As an added bonus, the store is attached to a cinema that regularly shows art-house flicks and a casual café that occasionally hosts poetry readings or music gigs. ■ TIP➔ When seeking directions, ask for the Broadway Cinemateque. ⊠ *Shop H2, Prosperous Garden, 3 Public Square St., Yau Ma Tei* ☎ *2384–8929* ⊕ *www.kubrick.com.hk* Ⓜ *Yau Ma Tei, Exit C.*

DEPARTMENT STORES

Fodor's Choice
★
Yue Hwa Chinese Products Emporium. This popular purveyor of Chinese goods has 17 stores across Hong Kong, and the flagship one features seven floors laden with everything from clothing and housewares to traditional medicine. The logic behind its layout is hard to fathom, so go with time to rifle around. As well as the predictable tablecloths, silk pajamas, and chopsticks, there are cheap and colorful porcelain sets and offbeat local favorites like mini-massage chairs. The top floor is entirely given over to tea—you can pick up a HK$50 packet of leaves or an antique Yixing teapot stretching into the thousands. ⊠ *301–309 Nathan Rd., Jordan, Yau Ma Tei* ☎ *3511–2222* ⊕ *www.yuehwa.com* Ⓜ *Jordan, Exit A.*

JEWELRY AND ACCESSORIES

Kansu Street Jade Market. Jade in every imaginable shade of green, from the milkiest apple tone to the richest emerald, fills the stalls of this Kowloon market. If you know your stuff and haggle insistently, you can get fabulous bargains. Otherwise, stick to cheap trinkets. Some of the so-called "jade" sold here is actually aventurine, bowenite, soapstone, serpentine, or Australian jade—all inferior to the real thing. ⊠ *Kansu St., off Nathan Rd., Yau Ma Tei* Ⓜ *Yau Ma Tei, Exit A.*

Sandra Pearls. You might be wary of the lustrous pearls hanging at this little Jade Market stall. But the charming owner does, in fact, sell genuine cultured and freshwater pearl necklaces and earrings at reasonable prices. Some pieces are made from shell, which Sandra is always quick to point out, and could pass muster among the snobbiest collectors. ⊠ *Stall 437 and 447, Jade Market, Kansu St., Yau Ma Tei* ☎ *9485–2895* Ⓜ *Jordan, Exit A.*

MARKETS

Fodor's Choice ★ **Temple Street Night Market.** Each evening as darkness falls the lamps strung between the stalls of this Yau Ma Tei street market slowly light up, and the air fills with aromas wafting from myriad food carts. Hawkers try to catch your eye by flinging up clothes; Cantonese opera competes with swelling pop music and the sounds of spirited haggling; fortune-tellers and street performers add another element to the sensory overload. Granted, neither the garments nor the cheap gadgets sold here are much to get excited about, but it's the atmosphere people come for—any purchases are a bonus. The market stretches for almost a mile and is one of Hong Kong's liveliest nighttime shopping experiences. ⊠ *Temple St., Yau Ma Tei* Ⓜ *Jordan, Exit A.*

MONG KOK

CLOTHING

Bossini. As indicated by its brand philosophy—"Be Happy"—this Giordano competitor takes a very similar, light approach to casual clothing for women, men, and children. Expect colorful collections at the flagship store and dozens of other Bossini locations. ⊠ *Ground–3rd fl., 6–12A Sai Yeung Choi St., Mong Kok* ☎ *2710–8466* ⊕ *www.bossini. com* Ⓜ *Mong Kok, Exit E2.*

Me & George. Anyone who loves a good thrift-store rummage will delight in the messy abandon of Me & George (also known as Mee & Gee), not to mention the rock-bottom prices. Clothing here start at HK$10. Yes, you heard right! Expect a mix of poorly made factory rejects and vintage dresses, shoes, and handbags. Fitting is not usually allowed (as is the case with most small fashion import outlets), but staff are often tolerant of quick try-ons in front of a mirror. ⊠ *64 Tung Choi St., Mong Kok* Ⓜ *Mong Kok, Exit E2.*

CAMERAS AND ELECTRONICS

Mong Kok Computer Centre. This labyrinth of small shops and narrow corridors is somewhat claustrophobic, but it has many good deals on computers and software. Ask for a warranty, and read it carefully. ⊠ *8–8A Nelson St., Mong Kok* ☎ *2781–0706* ⊕ *www.mongkokcc.com* Ⓜ *Mong Kok, Exit E2.*

SHAM SHUI PO

Two stops from Mong Kok on the MTR is Sham Shui Po, a labyrinth of small streets teeming with flea markets and wholesale shops where you can buy anything from electronics to computers to clothing. The Golden Computer Arcade, stuffed with small computer hardware shops, is favored by local mouse potatoes. Prices are competitive, but parts usually come without a warranty.

4

MALLS AND SHOPPING CENTERS

Langham Place. The light beige sandstone of Langham Place stands in stark contrast to the pulsating neon signs and crumbling residential blocks around it. Yet the mall—with nearly 200 shops packed into 15 floors—has fast become a fixture on Mong Kok's chaotic shopping scene. It is especially popular with hipsters, who are drawn by the Asian labels in offbeat boutiques ranged around a spiral walkway from the 9th to 12th floors. Extra-long escalators—dubbed "Xpresscalators"—whisk you quickly up four levels at a time. The elegant glass-and-steel skyscraper across the road is the Langham Place Hotel; its stylish dining patio, The Backyard, offers the serenest of outdoor sanctuaries in one of the region's most congested neighborhoods. ⌧ *8 Argyle St., Mong Kok* ☎ *3520–2800* ⊕ *www.langhamplace.com.hk* Ⓜ *Mong Kok, Exit C3.*

WORD OF MOUTH

"Go to the bird market and flower market early in the morning, with a stop at the Jade Market and then a visit to the Wong Tai Sin Temple to get your fortune told, and that is a morning in Kowloon."
—Cicerone

MARKETS

Flower Market. Huge bucketfuls of roses and gerbera spill out onto the sidewalk along Flower Market Road, a collection of street stalls selling cut flowers and potted plants. Delicate orchids and vivid birds of paradise are some of the more exotic blooms. During Chinese New Year there's a roaring trade in narcissi, poinsettias, and bright yellow chrysanthemums—all auspicious flowers. ⌧ *Flower Market Rd., off Prince Edward Rd. W, Mong Kok* Ⓜ *Prince Edward.*

FAMILY **Goldfish Market.** Goldfish are thought to bring good luck in Hong Kong (though aquariums have to be properly positioned for maximum benefit), and this small collection of sellers is a favorite local source. Shop fronts are decorated with bags of glistening, pop-eyed creatures, waiting for someone to take them home. Some of the fish for sale inside are serious rarities and fetch unbelievable prices. ⌧ *Tung Choi St., Mong Kok* Ⓜ *Mong Kok.*

Ladies' Market. Block upon block of tightly packed stalls overflow with clothes, bags, and knickknacks along Tung Choi Street in Mong Kok. Despite the name, items for women, men, and children are for sale. Most offerings are imitations or no-name brands; rifle around enough and you can often pick up some cheap, cheerful basics. Haggling is the rule here: a poker face and a little insistence can get you dramatic discounts. At the corner of each block and behind the market are stands and shops selling the street snacks Hong Kongers can't live without. Pick a place where locals are munching and point at whatever takes your fancy. Parallel **Fa Yuen Street** is Mong Kok's unofficial sportswear market. ⌧ *Tung Choi St., Mong Kok* Ⓜ *Mong Kok, Exit A2.*

Yuen Po Street Bird Garden. Though mostly built as a neighborhood park in which bird-owning residents can meet and "walk" their caged pets, the Urban Renewal Authority also included some 70 stalls to be used by those who lost trade when the famous Hong Lok Street songbird stalls were demolished in a revitalization project in the late nineties. Though

Go fish at the Goldfish Market in Mong Kok.

it sells various kinds of feathered creatures, you can also pick up the picturesque, empty carved cages and put them to better (empty) use in your home decor. Access the main entrance from Boundary Street, a short walk from the Prince Edward MTR station. ⊠ *Yuen Po St., Mong Kok* ☎ *2302–1762* Ⓜ *Prince Edward, Exit B2.*

SHOES, HANDBAGS, AND LEATHER GOODS

Sportshouse. Check out the Sportshouse chain for trendy sneakers and other casual footwear by brands like Nike, Puma, Adidas, Converse, and Birkenstock. ⊠ *Ground fl., 61 Fa Yuen St., Mong ok* ☎ *2332–3099* ⊕ *www.sportshouse.com* Ⓜ *Mong Kok, Exit E2.*

SPAS

Chuan Spa. If it's a quiet moment you're after, your best bet is Chuan Spa, which overlooks the city from the top floor of the Langham Place Hotel. In five-star spa surroundings, you can try cupping (an ancient Chinese acupressure technique), acupuncture, or myofascial therapy (a gentle massage and stretching technique)—all of which aim to promote health and balance by distributing chi (energy) throughout the body. ⊠ *Langham Place Hotel, 555 Shanghai St., Mong Kok* ☎ *3552–3510* ⊕ *www.chuanspa.com.hk* Ⓜ *Mong Kok, Exit C3.*

NORTHERN KOWLOON
CAMERAS AND ELECTRONICS

Golden Computer Arcade. It's the most famous—some would say infamous—computer arcade in town. Know what you want before you go to avoid being dazed by the sheer volume of computer equipment and software. ⊠ *146–152 Fuk Wa St., Sham Shui Po, Northern Kowloon* ☎ *2729–2101* ⊕ *www.goldenarcade.org* Ⓜ *Sham Shui Po, Exit D.*

MALLS AND SHOPPING CENTERS

Fodor's Choice

★

Festival Walk. Although it's located in residential Kowloon Tong, 20 minutes from Central on the MTR, reaching Festival Walk is worth the effort. After all, the mall's stores range from Vivienne Tam to Giordano (Hong Kong's take on the Gap). By day the six floors sparkle with sunlight, which filters through the glass roof. Marks & Spencer and DKNY serve as anchors; Armani Jeans and ck Calvin Klein draw the elite crowds; while Camper and agnès b. keep the trend spotters happy. Hong Kong's best bookstore, Page One, has a big branch downstairs. If you want a respite from the sometimes scorching-hot weather, Festival Walk also has one of the city's largest ice rinks, as well as a multiplex cinema. ⊠ *80 Tat Chee Ave., Northern Kowloon* ☎ *2844–2200* ⊕ *www.festivalwalk.com. hk* Ⓜ *Kowloon Tong, Exit C1.*

> ### ITS GOOD TO BE JADED
>
> The Chinese believe that jade brings luck, and it's still worn as a charm in amulets or bracelets. A jade bangle is often presented to newborns, and homes are frequently adorned with jade statues or other carved decorative items.

Mega Box. This 18-story mall is a great option for family shopping expeditions: those with minimal retail stamina can amuse themselves at the video arcade, the IMAX theater, or the skating rink, and there are also numerous onsite eateries. However, unlike other malls that are in walking distance from MTR stations, visitors need to take a free shuttle here from the Kowloon Bay MTR station. To catch it, exit the MTR station at Exit A and go through Telford Plaza; you can always ask the Plaza concierge if you're confused. Shuttles run about every 10 minutes. ⊠ *38 Wang Chiu Rd., Kowloon Bay, Northern Kowloon* ☎ *2989–3000* ⊕ *www.megabox.com.hk* Ⓜ *Kowloon Bay, Exit A.*

WHERE TO EAT

Updated by
Dorothy So

No other city in the world boasts quite as eclectic a dining scene as Hong Kong. Opulent restaurants opened by celebrity chefs such as Gray Kunz and Joël Robuchon are just a stone's throw from humble local eateries doling out thin noodles and some of the best wonton shrimp dumplings, or delicious slices of tender barbecued meat piled atop bowls of fragrant jasmine rice.

One of the key lessons here is never judge a book by its cover—the most unassuming eateries are often the ones that provide the most memorable meals. At noodle-centric restaurants, fish-ball soup with rice noodles is an excellent choice, and the goose, suckling pig, honeyed pork, and soy-sauce chicken are good bets at the roast-meat shops. A combination plate, with a sampling of meats and some greens on a bed of white rice, is generally a foolproof way to go if you're not sure what to order. Street foods are another must-try; for just a couple of bucks you can sample curry fish balls, skewered meats, stinky tofu, and all sorts of other delicious tidbits. If you have the chance, visit a *dai pai dong* (outdoor food stall) and try the local specialties.

For fine dining with a unique Hong Kong twist, you can always hit up places like the extravagant Mott 32 or try Alvin Leung's one-of-a-kind "X-treme Chinese" fare at Bo Innovation.

Finally, remember that Hong Kong is the world's epicenter of dim sum. While you're here you must have at least one dim sum breakfast or lunch in a teahouse. Those steaming bamboo baskets you see conceal mouthwatering dumplings, buns, and pastries—all as comforting and delicious as they are exotic.

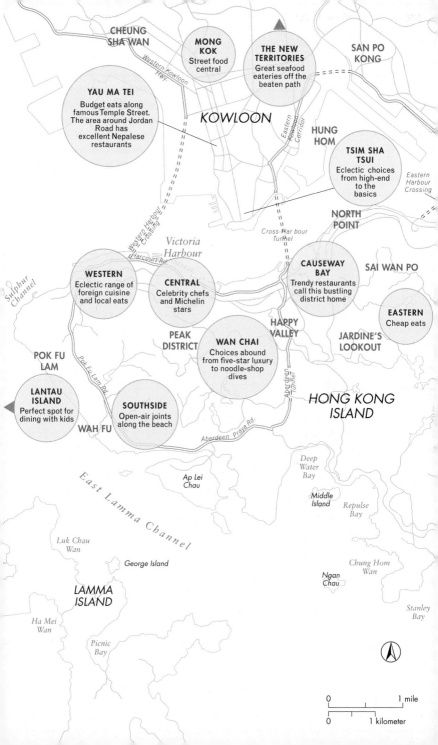

CHEUNG SHA WAN

MONG KOK
Street food central

THE NEW TERRITORIES
Great seafood eateries off the beaten path

SAN PO KONG

Western Kowloon Hwy.

YAU MA TEI
Budget eats along famous Temple Street. The area around Jordan Road has excellent Nepalese restaurants

KOWLOON

HUNG HOM

Eastern Kowloon Corridor

TSIM SHA TSUI
Eclectic choices from high-end to the basics

Eastern Harbour Crossing

Western Harbour Crossing

NORTH POINT

Harcourt Rd.

Cross-Harbour Tunnel

Victoria Harbour

Sulphur Channel

WESTERN
Eclectic range of foreign cuisine and local eats

CENTRAL
Celebrity chefs and Michelin stars

CAUSEWAY BAY
Trendy restaurants call this bustling district home

SAI WAN PO

EASTERN
Cheap eats

PEAK DISTRICT

HAPPY VALLEY

WAN CHAI
Choices abound from five-star luxury to noodle-shop dives

JARDINE'S LOOKOUT

Pok Fu Lam Rd.

POK FU LAM

LANTAU ISLAND
Perfect spot for dining with kids

SOUTHSIDE
Open-air joints along the beach

Aberdeen Tunnel

HONG KONG ISLAND

WAH FU

Aberdeen Praya Rd.

Deep Water Bay

East Lamma Channel

Ap Lei Chau

Middle Island

Repulse Bay

Luk Chau Wan

George Island

Chung Hom Wan

Ngan Chau

LAMMA ISLAND

Stanley Bay

Ha Mei Wan

Picnic Bay

| 0 | | 1 mile |
| 0 | | 1 kilometer |

PLANNING

HOURS

A typical Hong Kong breakfast is often congee (a rice porridge), noodles, or plain or filled buns. Most hotels serve western-style breakfasts, however, and coffee, pastries, and sandwiches are readily available at local coffee shops and western cafés. Lunchtime is between noon and 2 pm; normal dinner hours are from 7 until 11 pm, but Hong Kong is a 24-hour city, and you'll be able to find a meal here at any hour. Dim sum can begin as early as 7:30 am, and though it's traditionally a daytime food, you'll find plenty of specialist restaurants that serve dim sum late into the evening.

PRICES, TIPPING, AND TAX

Many restaurants in Hong Kong serve main dishes that are meant to be shared, so take this into account with respect to prices. It's also worth noting that some specialty dishes are outrageously expensive—abalone, bird's-nest soup, and dried seafood. And when you get your check, don't be shocked that you've been charged for everything, including tea, rice, and those side dishes placed automatically on your table. At upmarket and western-style restaurants tips are appreciated (10% is generous); the service charge on your bill doesn't go to the waitstaff.

RESERVATIONS

Book ahead during Chinese holidays and the eves of public holidays, or at high-end hotel restaurants like Amber or Caprice. Certain classic Chinese dishes (especially beggar's chicken, whose preparation in a clay pot takes hours) require reserving not just a table but the dish itself. Do so at least 24 hours in advance. You'll also need reservations for a meal at one of the so-called private kitchens—unlicensed culinary speakeasies, which are often the city's hottest tickets. Book several days ahead, and be prepared to pay a deposit. Reservations are virtually unheard of at small, local restaurants.

SHARE AND SHARE ALIKE

In China food is meant to be shared. Instead of ordering individual main dishes, it's usual for those around a table—whether a couple or a dozen people—to share several. Four people eating together, for example, might order a whole or half chicken, another type of meat, a fish dish, a vegetable, and fried noodles—all of which would be placed on the table's revolving tray. Restaurants may adjust portions and prices according to the number of diners.

Western-style cutlery is common in many—but not all—upmarket Chinese restaurants in Hong Kong, but what better place to practice your chopstick skills? Serving chopsticks are usually provided for each dish. You should use these to serve yourself and others. If no serving chopsticks are provided, serve yourself using your own chopsticks; just be sure to use the ends that you haven't put into your mouth.

WHAT TO WEAR

Casual dress—sports shirts, T-shirts, clean jeans, and the like—is acceptable almost everywhere in Hong Kong, although shorts and sneakers or flip-flops will feel out of place at trendy venues and five-star restaurants where people dress to impress. Generally, the dress code in Hong Kong is stylish but quite conservative.

WINE OR BEER?

Traditionally, markups on wine have been high here, and wine lists uninspired. French reds have long had a cachet in Hong Kong, but since the repeal of the city's wine tax, the city's wine selection has become increasingly democratic and now includes many New World selections that are often better suited to the local cuisine and the climate. More people are also getting interested in pairing wine with Asian cuisine, and it's not uncommon to see Chinese restaurants—especially the higher-end ones—create tasting menus designed specifically to go with various wines. Many midrange restaurants and private kitchens allow you to bring your own wine for a corkage fee.

For Cantonese food, tea is traditional, but Hong Kong likes its beer—before, during, or after dinner. It's generally light stuff, like Heineken, the locally brewed San Miguel, or a Chinese lager such as the immensely popular Tsing Tao. Craft beers have also taken off. Many pubs import interesting microbrews, and you may also want to try one of the few locally brewed artisanal ales. When it's time to hit the karaoke bars or clubs, though, people switch to stronger spirits. If you like cocktails, check out some of the newer, upscale bars, which take their mixed drinks very seriously.

WHAT IT COSTS IN HK$			
	$	$$	$$$	$$$$
At Dinner	Under HK$100	HK$100–HK$200	HK$201–HK$300	over HK$300

Prices are per person for a main course at dinner and exclude the customary 10% service charge.

HONG KONG ISLAND

Reviews listed alphabetically within neighborhoods.

WESTERN

$$
EUROPEAN
✕ **ABC Kitchen.** Hong Kong is no stranger to continental cuisine, but ABC is in a league of its own. The eatery is made up of a few stand-alone plastic chairs and tables scattered around the Queen Street Cooked Food Market. Despite being sandwiched between a curry stall and a dumpling joint, ABC's owners remain loyal to their classic, European training (the manager and chef both hail from Hong Kong's top restaurants), serving dishes such as roasted suckling pig and foie gras with gooseberry chutney. If you want drinks with your meal, ABC offers a simple wine list and also allows BYOB with no corkage fee. Reservations are highly recommended. $ *Average main: HK$190* ⊠ *Shop CF7, Queen St. Cooked Food Market, 38 Des Voeux Rd. W, Sheung Wan* ☎ *9278–8227* ▭ *No credit cards* ☻ *No lunch Sun.* ✛ *1:B2.*

BEST BETS FOR HONG KONG DINING

Fodor's writers and editors have listed their favorite restaurants by price, cuisine, and experience *below*. You can also search by neighborhood in the following pages.

Fodor's Choice ★

8½ Otto e Mezzo Bombana, $$$$, p. 143

Café Gray Deluxe, $$$$, p. 145

The Chairman, $$, p. 145

Fa Zu Jie, $$$$, p. 147

Little Bao, $, p. 150

Liu Yuan Pavilion, $$, p. 157

Ronin, $$$, p. 152

Serge et Le Phoque, $$$, p. 157

Souvla, $$$, p. 153

Tim Ho Wan, $, p. 178

Tim's Kitchen, $$$, p. 142

Tung Po, $, p. 163

Vasco, $$$$, p. 154

Yau Yuan Xiao Jui, $, p. 176

By Price

$

Capital Café, p. 155

Little Bao, p. 150

Mak's Noodles, p. 151

Tim Ho Wan, p. 178

Tung Po, p. 163

Yau Yuan Xiao Jui, p. 176

$$

ABC Kitchen, p. 139

The Chairman, p. 145

Din Tai Fung, p. 167

Go Koong, p. 170

Liu Yuan Pavilion, p. 157

Wu Kong, p. 161

$$$

Ronin, p. 152

Serge et le Phoque, p. 157

Souvla, p. 153

Tim's Kitchen, p. 142

$$$$

8½ Otto e Mezzo Bombana, p. 143

Amber, p. 144

Bo Innovation, p. 155

Café Gray Deluxe, p. 145

Fa Zu Jie, p. 147

Mandarin Grill + Bar, p. 151

Vasco, p. 154

By Cuisine

ASIAN

Café Malacca, p. 142

Go Koong, p. 170

Islam Food, p. 177

Little Bao, p. 150

CANTONESE

The Chairman, p. 145

Lung King Heen, p. 151

Mott 32, p. 152

Tim's Kitchen, p. 142

Tung Po, p. 163

Yung Kee, p. 154

DIM SUM

Dimdimsum Dimsum Specialty Store, p. 175

Tim Ho Wan, p. 178

Yan Toh Heen, p. 173

FRENCH

Amber, p. 144

Caprice, p. 145

L'Atelier de Joël Robuchon, p. 149

Restaurant Petrus, p. 152

Serge et le Phoque, p. 157

JAPANESE

Ronin, p. 152

Sushi Hiro, p. 161

Yardbird, p. 154

SICHUAN

Chuan Shao, p. 167

San Xi Lou, p. 153

Yun Yan, p. 162

By Experience

BUSINESS DINING

8½ Otto e Mezzo Bombana, p. 143

Amber, p. 144

Gaia, p. 142

Mandarin Grill + Bar, p. 151

CHILD-FRIENDLY

Café Deco, p. 144

Crystal Lotus, p. 165

Mavericks, p. 165

Tai O Lookout, p. 165

GREAT VIEW

Aqua, p. 166

Cuisine Cuisine, p. 146

Inakaya, p. 171

Restaurant Petrus, p. 152

Tai O Lookout, p. 165

MOST ROMANTIC

Caprice, p. 145

Hutong, p. 170

Lucy's, p. 164

The Verandah, p. 164

$
MALAYSIAN

✕ **Café Malacca.** Tucked away in a quiet corner of the Traders Hotel, this unassuming culinary gem serves what is possibly the best Malaysian and Singaporean food in town. You'll find all the classics here, from the piping-hot fried turnip cakes with bean sprouts to spicy beef simmered in coconut milk and aromatic spices. While all dishes satisfy, the main draw is the flavorful fish soup spiked with umami shrimp paste. $ *Average main: HK$90* ✉ *2nd fl., Traders Hotel, 508 Queen's Rd. W, Western* ☎ *2213–6613* ⊕ *www.shangri-la.com/hongkong/traders* ✛ *1:A2.*

$$$$
ITALIAN

✕ **Gaia.** The concept at this trendy restaurant is a re-creation of Rome's Spanish Steps, complete with alfresco seating. The restaurant is particularly popular with the business crowd, many of whom come especially for the excellent antipasti buffet. The authentic pan-Italian fare includes wide pappardelle noodles in rabbit ragout, beef carpaccio with mustard and peppercorns, and the signature thin-crust pizzas topped with everything from hot salami and mozzarella cheese to fresh arugula with prosciutto. $ *Average main: HK$340* ✉ *Ground fl., Grand Millennium Plaza, 181 Queen's Rd. Central, Sheung Wan, Western* ☎ *2167–8200* ⊕ *www.gaiagroup.com.hk* Ⓜ *Sheung Wan* ✛ *1:C4.*

$$
VEGETARIAN

✕ **Grassroots Pantry.** You don't have to be vegetarian to enjoy the food at Grassroots Pantry. The health-conscious, plant-based menu here is full of vibrant flavors and always reflects the season's freshest produce. Try the appetizer platters or the market-inspired stir-fries and pastas. Grassroots also offers a delicious selection of gluten-free desserts. Being healthy never tasted so good. $ *Average main: HK$150* ✉ *12 Fuk Sau La., Sai Ying Pun, Western* ☎ *2873–3353* ⊕ *www.grassrootspantry.com* ◷ *Closed Mon. No dinner Sun.* ✛ *1:A2.*

$$$
CANTONESE
Fodor'sChoice
★

✕ **Tim's Kitchen.** Some of the homespun dishes at this restaurant require at least a day's advance notice, but the extra fuss is worth it. One signature dish pairs a meaty crab claw with winter melon—a clean and simple combo that allows the freshness of the ingredients to shine. The fist-sized crystal king prawn looks unassuming, paired with nothing but a slice of Yunnan ham on a plain, ungarnished plate. Take a bite though, and you'll be amazed at how succulent and delectably creamy it is. Word of warning—some of the more intricate dishes can get pretty pricy. But simpler (and cheaper) options are also available, such as pomelo skin sprinkled with shrimp roe, and panfried flat rice noodles. $ *Average main: HK$300* ✉ *84–90 Bonham Strand, Sheung Wan, Western* ☎ *2543–5919* ⊕ *www.timskitchen.com.hk* ⬥ *Reservations essential* Ⓜ *Sheung Wan* ✛ *1:C2.*

$$$$
FRENCH

✕ **Upper Modern Bistro.** This cool and sophisticated restaurant is a labor of love for Philippe Orrico, a protégé of revolutionary chef Pierre Gagniare. Though classically trained in French cuisine, Orrico takes inspiration from all around the globe. Look out for Asian influences in dishes such as Brittany oysters with ponzu and squab or eggplant rolls seasoned with soy sauce. Another signature is the perfected cooked 63-degree eggs—a dish that Orrico created and serves with amazing ingredients like crabmeat and Bellota ham. $ *Average main: HK$400* ✉ *6–14 Upper Station St., Sheung Wan, Western* ☎ *2517–0977* ⊕ *www.upper-bistro.com* Ⓜ *Sheung Wan* ✛ *1:C2.*

CENTRAL

One of Hong Kong's busiest areas, Central is particularly crazy at lunchtime, when office workers crowd the streets and eateries. Most restaurants have set lunches—generally good values—with speedy service, so everyone gets in and out within an hour. At night the norm is either a formal dinner or a quick bite followed by many drinks, especially in Central's nightlife center, a warren of cobbled backstreets called Lan Kwai Fong. Mostly known as a drinking hole with mediocre dining options, LKF has stepped up its game in the last few years with some serious restaurants, most of which are tucked away in commercial buildings, away from the hustle and bustle of the street-level bars.

For a wider array of choices, head up to SoHo, but be wary of where you go: a lot of these places are average in terms of food and service quality. NoHo is a bit more bohemian, with some excellent hidden, independent culinary gems, especially along Gough Street.

Admiralty, wedged between Central and Wan Chai, is home to large shopping malls, and much of the food is aimed at meeting the lunch needs of workers and shoppers. It's also home to several large hotels and their respective high-end restaurants.

Once a mainstay of the Hong Kong streets, there are now only a little more than 20 licensed dai pai dongs—that is, open-air food stalls specializing in various types of local dishes. These outdoor eateries are popular for their dirt-cheap prices, minimal service, and—of course—their awesome food. There's usually no English menu, so be prepared to point to the dishes at neighboring tables.

$$$$
ITALIAN
Fodor'sChoice
★

✕ **8½ Otto e Mezzo Bombana.** Spearheaded by Umberto Bombana (the former executive chef of the Ritz-Carlton Hong Kong and often lauded as the best Italian chef in Asia), this glitzy space delivers everything it promises. The service is crisp, the wine list is extensive, and the interior is nothing less than glamorous. Most importantly, the authentic Italian food is magnificent. Bombana's famed handmade pastas live up to the hype; the cavatelli with shellfish ragout and sea urchin is particularly delicious. The mains are also solid—the Tajima short rib and beef tenderloin is excellently executed, but the seafood options fare even better. If you can't make up your mind, the degustation menu offers a neat sampling of Bombana's best. $ *Average main: HK$340* ✉ *2nd fl., Landmark Alexandra, 18 Chater Rd., Central* ☎ *2537–8859* ⊕ *www.ottoemezzobombana.com* ⚐ *Reservations essential* ⊗ *Closed Sun.* Ⓜ *Central* ✛ *1:E3.*

$$$$
BRITISH

✕ **Aberdeen Street Social.** Chef Jason Atherton worked at some of the best kitchens in the world before opening the highly successful London restaurant Pollen Street Social in 2011. His culinary empire has since expanded to more than a dozen outlets around the world, with Aberdeen Street Social being one of the more recent additions. This bi-level space is located at the former Police Married Quarters and encompasses a restaurant, café, and bar. Head upstairs to enjoy meticulously plated modern British fare, such as the signature CLT (crab, lettuce, and tomato) and braised ox cheek with roasted bone marrow. You can also grab a table downstairs and try the casual, all-day menu and house special drinks. Ⓢ *Average main: HK$400 ✉ JPC Building, 35 Aberdeen St., Central ☎2866-0300 ⊕ www.aberdeenstreetsocial. hk ⊘ Closed Mon.* Ⓜ *Sheung Wan* ✛ *1:B4.*

$$$$
FRENCH

✕ **Amber.** You'd expect the Landmark Mandarin Oriental to have a stellar restaurant, and Amber will linger in your memories for its modern style, impeccable service, and creative cuisine. Chef Richard Ekkebus's menu of creative European dishes still doesn't fail to impress. The fun begins with the amuse-bouche, which usually

ABOVE-IT-ALL DINING

Central is the place to catch the tram up to the legendary Victoria Peak. A meal in a restaurant at the city's highest point has to be on everyone's itinerary. The trip is justified many times over on clear days, when the views from the top (and en route) are unparalleled. When the clouds are thick and low, though, you won't be able to see a thing—you'll just hear the sounds of the city beneath you.

includes the restaurant's famous foie gras lollipops. You can then look forward to signature creations such as frogs' legs in pastry, or sea urchin set in lobster gelatin with cauliflower, caviar, and crispy seaweed waffles. If you can't make it for dinner, check out the fantastic wine-paired lunch available every weekend. Ⓢ *Average main: HK$850 ✉ 7th fl., Landmark Mandarin Oriental, 15 Queen's Rd., Central ☎2132-0066 ⊕ www.amberhongkong.com ⌔ Reservations essential* Ⓜ *Central* ✛ *1:E4.*

$$$
ITALIAN

✕ **Ammo.** Few places in Hong Kong have the kind of stunning garden views that you'll find at Ammo. Housed in a former ammunition compound (hence the name) that was converted into the Asia Society Hong Kong Center, Ammo's interiors and menus blend the old with the new and East with West, resulting in an impressive and dynamic dining experience. Dishes tout Italian roots, but you'll find plenty of Asian flourishes. Standouts include the quail salad with braised grapes and pancetta, and angel-hair pasta with uni, tomatoes, and garlic chips. Save room for dessert, because the panfried brioche is insanely satisfying. Ⓢ *Average main: HK$300 ✉ 9 Justice Dr., Admiralty, Central ☎2537-9888 ⊕ www.ammo.com.hk ⌔ Reservations essential* ✛ *1:F5.*

$
CHINESE

✕ **Ball Kee.** Despite its unassuming location in an alley, this dai pai dong (outdoor food stall) remains immensely popular due to its delicious stir-fried dishes. The wok-cooked noodle dishes are especially good—thin noodles are cooked until crispy and topped with strips of pork and bean sprouts. Ⓢ *Average main: HK$58 ✉ Staveley St. and Wellington St., Central ☎2544-5923 ▭ No credit cards ⊘ No dinner* ✛ *1:C4.*

$$$
INTERNATIONAL
FAMILY

✕ **Café Deco.** As is often the case where there's a captive audience, dining up at the Peak Galleria mall can be unpredictable—and this huge eatery is no exception. You'll come mostly for the views, though the menu is eclectic enough to keep everyone happy. Menu options traverse four or five continents, and there's also a patisserie offering house-made desserts. Oysters and seafood are the best choices. When you book (and you must), be sure to request a table with a view, as many tables in the place have none, which defeats the purpose of coming here. Ⓢ *Average main: HK$260 ✉ The Peak Galleria, 118 Peak Rd.,*

Central ☎ 2849–5111 🌐 www.cafedecogroup.com ✍ Reservations essential ⊕ 1:C6.

$$$$ CONTEMPORARY Fodor's Choice ★ 🍴 **Café Gray Deluxe.** Celebrated chef Gray Kunz's restaurant offers expertly prepared modern European fare in a casual and relaxed 49th-floor locale that has stunning views of the city. A fan of fresh, seasonal ingredients, Kunz incorporates local produce into the ever-evolving menu whenever possible, and often adds Asian flavorings to excellent effect. Steak tartare shines among the lineup of stellar "first plates," which also include the signature pasta *fiore* served with tangy tomatoes and herbs. The bar boasts a fine selection of creative cocktails, so even if you can't stop by for a sit-down meal, it's worth stopping by for a cocktail and small bite. [$] *Average main: HK$450 ✉ 49th fl., The Upper House, Pacific Place, 88 Queensway, Central ☎ 3968–1106 🌐 www.cafegrayhk.com ✍ Reservations essential* [M] *Admiralty ⊕ 1:F5.*

$$$$ FRENCH 🍴 **Caprice.** The Four Seasons spared no expense in creating this space, bringing in well-known designers and feng shui masters, and the result is a private dining room that might be one of the most spectacular in the world. Guests can see into the entire open kitchen, while floor-to-ceiling windows offer stunning views of Victoria Harbour and beyond. Executive chef Fabrice Vulin hails from France but worked in Geneva and Morocco, and dishes such as the caramelized pigeon breast with North African spices reflect his multicultural influences. The restaurant also boasts an excellent cheese cellar. Even if you're not having a full sit-down meal, you can still enjoy some *fromage* and wine at the adjoining bar and lounge. [$] *Average main: HK$730 ✉ 6th fl., Four Seasons Hotel, 8 Finance St., Central ☎ 3196–8860 🌐 www.fourseasons.com ✍ Reservations essential* [M] *Hong Kong ⊕ 1:E2.*

$ CAFÉ 🍴 **C'est La B.** Indulge your sweet tooth with C'est La B's wide array of gorgeously whimsical cakes and desserts. The sugary creations at this bakery-café are decidedly extravagant and come with playful, tongue-in-cheek names like Better Than Sex (chocolate fudge cake with caramel crunch and red sugar lips) and Blessing in Disguise (carrot and cheesecake with berry glaze). Most cakes are available in miniature portions, so feel free to sample a few. C'est La B operates a second branch in Tsim Sha Tsui. [$] *Average main: HK$80 ✉ 2nd fl., Pacific Place, 88 Queensway, Central ☎ 2536–0173 🌐 www.msbscakery.hk* [M] *Admiralty ⊕ 1:F4.*

$$ CHINESE Fodor's Choice ★ 🍴 **The Chairman.** The restaurant celebrates a return to authentic Cantonese fare. Using only the freshest possible ingredients—from locally reared free-range chicken to wild-caught seafood—this unique eatery focuses on the intrinsic flavors of each ingredient. Appetizers are creative: shredded pig's ear and tripe salad is given an extra crunchy edge with the addition of freshly sliced guava, and razor clams are steamed with pickled lemon and garlic. And it gets even better with the mains. A particular favorite is the signature soy-sauce chicken, perfumed with 18 different fragrant Chinese herbs. Also recommended is the steamed fresh crab, which is steeped in aged ShaoXing wine. [$] *Average main: HK$200 ✉ 18 Kau U Fong, NoHo, Central ☎ 2555–2202 🌐 www.thechairmangroup.com ✍ Reservations essential* [M] *Central ⊕ 1:D3.*

5

Outdoor dining at a dai pai dong

$$$ PERUVIAN 🍴 **Chicha.** Expect complex, chili-fueled flavors from Hong Kong's first Peruvian restaurant. The menu has multicultural influences, from Chinese-style *lomo saltado* (a beef, scallion, and rice stir-fry) to the Spanish paella-like *marisco jugoso* flavored with an umami sea urchin and citrus reduction. Be sure to order the ceviche (cured raw seafood) and a platter of *anticuchos* (grilled skewers) to share; the cod with ponzu miso and chili aioli is close to addictive. If you want to cap your meal off in true Peruvian fashion, finish with a pisco sour at the bar. [$] *Average main: HK$250* ✉ *26 Peel St., Central* ☎ *2561–3336* 🌐 *www.conceptcreations.hk* ✍ *Reservations essential* ✣ *1:B4.*

$$$ INTERNATIONAL 🍴 **Clipper Lounge.** The Mandarin Oriental's Clipper Lounge has long been lauded for serving one of the best afternoon teas in town. Sandwiches and miniature cakes cascade down a multitier stand, and classic scones are served with clotted cream and the restaurant's famed rose-petal jam. The restaurant also offers sumptuous buffet and à la carte options throughout the day. [$] *Average main: HK$258* ✉ *Mezzanine, Mandarin Oriental, 5 Connaught Rd., Central* ☎ *2825–4007* 🌐 *www.mandarinoriental.com* ✣ *1:E3.*

$$$ CHINESE 🍴 **Cuisine Cuisine.** One of the best in the city, this Cantonese restaurant is known for its traditional menu embellished with nouvelle liberties. The restaurant is also loved for its elegant harborside location, which has recently been refurbished into an even sleeker space. In this gorgeous setting, enjoy signature dishes such as sautéed crystal king prawns and fried rice with minced beef and greens. [$] *Average main: HK$250* ✉ *3rd fl., International Finance Center Mall, 8 Finance St., Central* ☎ *2393–3933* 🌐 *www.cuisinecuisine.hk* [M] *Hong Kong* ✣ *1:E2.*

$$$$ CHINESE 🍴 **Duddell's.** Art and food come together in this beautiful two-story establishment, which encompasses a bar, garden terrace, and dining room. The interiors are sophisticated yet inviting, making the perfect backdrop for the year-round art exhibitions hosted at the restaurant. But Duddell's isn't just a feast for the eyes—the Cantonese cuisine here is solid and satisfying and has garnered plenty of praise from locals and visitors alike. Signature items include crispy salted chicken and fried lobster with scallions and shallots. The dim sum lunch here is also quite popular and includes creative dishes like egg-white dumplings with shrimp and caviar. [$] *Average main: HK$330* ✉ *3rd fl., Shanghai Tang Mansion, 1 Duddell St., Central* ☎ *2525–9191* 🌐 *www.duddells.co* [M] *Central* ⊕ *1:D6.*

$$$$ SHANGHAINESE Fodor's Choice ★ 🍴 **Fa Zu Jie.** This place is good—really, *really* good. Tucked away in a nondescript building in a hidden alley off Lan Kwai Fong, this reservations-only private kitchen plates up inventive, French-inspired Shanghainese dishes that are prepped in a polished open kitchen. The prix-fixe menu is tweaked on a regular basis, but you'll probably be treated to trademark items such as drunken quail (cooked in Chinese Hua Diao wine) served with al dente Sanuki udon noodles and plump scallops slicked in shrimp roe oil. The dining room has only a handful of tables, so try to book a few weeks in advance. [$] *Average main: HK$628* ✉ *1st fl., 20A D'Aguilar St., Central* ☎ *3487–1715* ✍ *Reservations essential* 💳 *No credit cards* ⏲ *No lunch. Closed Sun.* [M] *Central* ⊕ *1:C5.*

$$$$ ECLECTIC 🍴 **Fish & Meat.** As its name suggests, this restaurant goes back to the basics by focusing on a few key ingredients. Everything that passes through the kitchen is top grade, whether it's the fresh homemade tagliatelle with chicken and truffle emulsion or the whole roasted Italian sea bass with fennel. Dishes are categorized into small or large plates, but everything is designed to share. Fish & Meat offers decent cocktails, but if you're serious about your drinks, check out its sister bar, Stockton, which is located below the restaurant. [$] *Average main: HK$380* ✉ *1st and 2nd fl., 32 Wyndham St., Central* ☎ *2565–6788* 🌐 *www.fishandmeat.hk* [M] *Central* ⊕ *1:C6.*

$$$$ EUROPEAN 🍴 **Gold by Harlan Goldstein.** The menu here is inspired by the multicultural flavors chef Harlan Goldstein grew up with while living in New York. Italian preparations take precedence, but you'll also find things like salmon crudo with a citrus dressing and crispy falafel served with tahini. The handcrafted pastas are easy favorites, but if you're in the mood to feast, go for the 38-ounce *fiorentina* (steak Florentine style, designed for two) with a side of black-truffle mash. Gold also has a great wine selection, and you can always enjoy a glass on the restaurant's open-air terrace. [$] *Average main: HK$450* ✉ *2nd fl., LKF Tower, 33 Wyndham St., Central* ☎ *2869–9986* 🌐 *www.gold-dining.com* ⏲ *Closed Sun.* [M] *Central* ⊕ *1:C5.*

$$ CHINESE 🍴 **Ho Lee Fook.** Opened by award-winning Sydney-based chef Jowett Yu, this funky eatery is nothing like your average Chinese restaurant. As the tongue-in-cheek name suggests, the food here is bold and playful, inspired by old-school Chinatown classics but with a decidedly modern twist. Standout creations include the Yunnan-style steak tartare with hot-and-sour sauce, as well as the roast Wagyu short ribs with

CHINA'S CUISINES

To help you navigate China's many cuisines, we have used the following terms in our restaurant reviews.

Cantonese: A diverse cuisine that roasts and stir-fries, braises and steams. Spices are used in moderation. Notable dishes include fried rice, sweet-and-sour pork, and roasted goose.

Chinese: Catch-all term used for restaurants that serve cuisine from multiple regions of China; pan-Chinese.

Chinese fusion: Any type of Chinese cuisine with international influences.

Chiu chow: Known for its vegetarian and seafood dishes, which are mostly poached, steamed, or braised. Signature dishes include *popiah* (nonfried spring rolls), baby oyster congee, and fish ball noodle soup.

Hunan: Stewing, frying, braising, and smoking are featured cooking methods. Flavors are spicy, incorporating chili peppers, shallots, and garlic, along with dried and preserved condiments. Signature dishes are Mao's braised pork, steamed fish head with shredded chilies, and spicy eggplant in garlic sauce.

Macanese: An eclectic blend of southern Chinese and Portuguese cooking, featuring the use of salted dried fish, coconut milk, turmeric, and other spices. Common dishes are African-style barbecued chicken with spicy piri piri sauce, pork buns, and curried baked chicken.

Mandarin: China's capital city, Beijing, features cuisine from all over the country. Dishes from the city typically are snack size, featuring ingredients like dark soy paste, sesame paste, and sesame oil. Regional specialties include Peking duck, moo shu pork, and quick-fried tripe.

Northern Chinese: Staples are lamb and mutton, preserved vegetables, and noodles, steamed breads, pancakes, stuffed buns, and dumplings. Common dishes are cumin-scented lamb, congee porridge with pickles, and Mongolian hot pot.

Sichuan: Famed for bold flavors and spiciness resulting from liberal use of chilies and Sichuan peppercorns. Regional dishes include *dan dan* spicy noodles, twice-cooked pork, and tea-smoked duck.

Shanghainese: Cuisine characterized by rich flavors produced by braising and stewing, and the use of alcohol in cooking. Dumplings, noodles, and bread are served more than rice. Signature dishes are baby hairy crabs stir-fried with rice-cake slices, steamed buns and dumplings, and "drunken chicken."

Taiwanese: Diverse cuisine owing to its history and subtropical location. Seafood, pork, rice, soy, and fruit form the backbone of the cuisine. Specialties include "three cups chicken" with a sauce made of soy, rice wine, and sugar; oyster omelets; cuttlefish soup; and dried tofu.

Yunnan: Its cuisine is noted for its use of vegetables, fruit, bamboo shoots, and flowers in its spicy preparations. Signature dishes include rice noodle soup with chicken, pork, and fish.

a jalapeño puree. The cocktail list is just as inspired—try the Cooler, which is made with vodka infused with oolong tea. $ *Average main: HK$170* ✉ *1 Elgin St., Soho, Central* ☎ *2810–0860* ⊕ *www.holeefook. com.hk* ☾ *No lunch. Closed Sun.* Ⓜ *Central* ✛ *1:B4.*

$$$
ITALIAN

✕ **Isola.** Located within the International Finance Center, Isola's floor-to-ceiling windows and harborside terrace afford spectacular views of Hong Kong's famous skyline. The restaurant serves regional Italian fare, with selections like hand-twisted pasta with Parma ham, black truffle, fava beans, and Norcia cheese, or sea bass baked in sea-salt crust. Don't pass up the simple and well-executed stone-baked pizzas. Isola is also as much of a nighttime destination as anything else, and it's worth coming just to sample cocktails in the equally trendy Isobar upstairs. $ *Average main: HK$270* ✉ *3rd and 4th fl., International Finance Centre Mall, 8 Finance St., Central* ☎ *2383–8765* ⊕ *www.gaiagroup.com.hk* Ⓜ *Hong Kong* ✛ *1:E2.*

$$
INDIAN

✕ **Jashan.** This well-established Indian restaurant has kept up with the times, and although you'll still find the spice-scented classics on the menu, the newer dishes with a contemporary twist are the ones that steal the spotlight. Try the *mirchi kebab*—delicious grilled chicken flavored with coriander and chilies and served with a cooling cilantro dip. We also recommend the grilled halibut and the mackerel curry. The restaurant has a wide range of vegetarian specialties that can impress even devout carnivores. For a true Indian feast, drop by for the buffet lunch, which is available from Monday to Saturday. $ *Average main: HK$162* ✉ *1st fl., Amber Lodge, 23 Hollywood Rd., Central* ☎ *3105–5300, 3105–5311* ⊕ *www.jashan.com.hk* ☾ *No lunch Sun.* Ⓜ *Central* ✛ *1:C5.*

$$$
INTERNATIONAL

✕ **Jimmy's Kitchen.** One of the oldest restaurants in Hong Kong, Jimmy's Kitchen opened in 1928 and continues to serve comfort food from around the world in a private-club atmosphere. The handy location just off Queen's Road in Central and a menu that offers a wide selection of dishes—including steak, borscht, goulash, bangers and mash, curry, and burgers—have made Jimmy's a favorite with both Chinese locals and tourists looking for a taste of home. It's not cheap, but it's a good choice for a night out with friends, especially if your group's cravings are pulling you in different directions. $ *Average main: HK$300* ✉ *South China Bldg., 1–3 Wyndham St., Central* ☎ *2526–5293* ⊕ *www. jimmys.com* Ⓜ *Central* ✛ *1:C5.*

$$$
STEAKHOUSE

✕ **La Vache.** In homage to the iconic Relais de Venise restaurant in Paris, this intimate neighborhood brasserie offers only one entrée: steak frites. A typical dinner here includes a green salad, a perfectly grilled entrecôte steak, and unlimited refills of crispy, stick-thin fries. It's probably one of the best deals in town. But if that's not enough food for you, you can always pick up something from the dessert trolley, which features traditional confections such as éclairs and mille-feuilles. $ *Average main: HK$258* ✉ *48 Peel St., SoHo, Central* ☎ *2880–0248* ⊕ *www.lavache. com.hk* ☾ *No lunch Sun.* Ⓜ *Central* ✛ *1:B5.*

$$$$
FRENCH

✕ **L'Atelier de Joël Robuchon.** Joël Robuchon, one of the world's most iconic chefs, claims that his atelier (or "artist's workshop") is for contemporary casual dining. Diners sit on barstools around a counter designed like a modern Japanese sushi bar, so that everyone can watch the chefs at work in the open kitchen. Everything from the freshly baked bread to desserts is immaculately presented. Some dishes are available in small tasting portions so you can try a bit of everything. The quail with foie gras, served with the deservedly famous mashed potatoes, and the sea urchin, in a lobster jelly topped with cauliflower cream, are standouts. Those who don't want to splurge on a full meal should try the superb croissants and cakes at the salon one floor below. [$] *Average main: HK$680* ✉ *Shop 401, The Landmark, 15 Queen's Rd. Central, Central* ☎ *2166–9000* 🌐 *www.robuchon.hk* [M] *Central* ✥ *1:E4.*

$ CHINESE 🍴 **Leaf Dessert.** Visit this outdoor stall for authentic Chinese desserts. Sweet soups made with red bean or ground black sesame are served in both hot and chilled versions. Warmed, chewy, glutinous rice balls heaped with sugar, crushed peanuts, and desiccated coconut are messy but delicious. [$] *Average main: HK$12* ✉ *2 Elgin St., SoHo, Central* ☎ *2544–3795* ✍ *Reservations not accepted* 💳 *No credit cards* ✥ *1:B4.*

$$$ AMERICAN 🍴 **Liberty Exchange Kitchen & Bar.** This two-level restaurant and bar serves modern American food with fine-dining execution and finesse. The menu offers small sharing plates and includes refined yet hearty creations such as crabmeat and chorizo mac and cheese, or buttermilk-fried Cornish hen served with organic honey. The team behind Liberty Exchange also runs a reservations-only kitchen near Lan Kwai Fong called Liberty Private Works, which offers a more personal (and more expensive) experience. [$] *Average main: HK$300* ✉ *2 Exchange Sq., 8 Connaught Pl., Central* ☎ *2810–8400* 🌐 *www.lex.hk* ⏲ *No dinner Sun.* [M] *Hong Kong* ✥ *1:E3.*

$$$ AMERICAN 🍴 **Lily & Bloom.** Enjoy American comfort fare at this Prohibition Era–style restaurant and bar. The upper level—Lily—serves assorted late-night bar bites and classic cocktails made with premium spirits. For a more formal dining experience, head downstairs to Bloom and enjoy catchy Cotton Club tunes and hearty dishes such as Iberico pork chop and hickory-smoked skirt steak. The kitchen at Lily & Bloom stays open until late at night, making this a popular snacking pit stop for Central's party crowd. [$] *Average main: HK$300* ✉ *5th and 6th fl., LKF Tower, 33 Wyndham St., Central* ☎ *2810–6166* 🌐 *www.lily-bloom.com* ⏲ *No dinner Sun.* [M] *Central* ✥ *1:C5.*

$ ECLECTIC Fodor's Choice ★ 🍴 **Little Bao.** Slide into one of the dozen seats at the bar and tuck into the delicious *baos*—fluffy steamed buns sandwiched with all types of delicious ingredients. The braised pork belly is the signature item, but we're partial to the grilled chicken with Japanese pickles. Desserts are in bao form as well, with a thick slab of ice cream as the filling. Carbs aside, the rest of the menu is globally inspired and includes to-share plates such as white-pepper clams, short-rib dumplings, and truffle fries. [$] *Average main: HK$90* ✉ *66 Staunton St., Central* ☎ *2194–0202* 🌐 *www.little-bao.com* ✍ *Reservations not accepted* ⏲ *No lunch. Closed Sun.* [M] *Sheung Wan* ✥ *1:B4.*

$$$$ SEAFOOD 🍴 **Lobster Bar and Grill.** The giant tropical-fish tank at the entrance sets the scene, and, as the name suggests, lobster is the featured ingredient on the menu. It's whipped into soups, served as appetizers, and presented in full glory in numerous entrées. The lobster bisque is creamy yet light, with great chunks of meat at the bottom. The seafood platter—Boston

lobster, seasonal oysters, Alaskan crab, prawns, and fresh clams—doesn't disappoint. If you prefer your shellfish cooked, go for the lobster thermidor or a simple steamed preparation. With a vibe that is at once formal and cozy, the restaurant is also great for before- or after-dinner drinks at the bar and features live jazz performances Monday to Saturday evening. [$] *Average main: HK$400* ✉ *6th fl., Island Shangri-La, Pacific Place, Supreme Court Rd., Admiralty, Central* ☎ *2820–8560* 🌐 *www.shangri-la.com* [M] *Admiralty* ✥ *1:F4.*

$$$ CHINESE 🍴 **Lung King Heen.** This place has made a serious case for being the best Cantonese restaurant in Hong Kong, especially after winning and retaining three Michelin stars every year since 2009. Where other contenders tend to get too caught up in prestige dishes and name-brand chefs, Lung King Heen focuses completely on taste. When you try barbecued suckling pig or crispy shrimp dumplings that are this divine, you'll be forced to reevaluate your entire notion of Chinese cuisine. [$] *Average main: HK$300* ✉ *4th fl., Four Seasons Hotel, 8 Finance St., Central* ☎ *3196–8880* 🌐 *www.fourseasons.com* ✍ *Reservations essential* [M] *Hong Kong* ✥ *1:E2.*

$ CHINESE 🍴 **Mak's Noodles.** Mak's may look like any other Hong Kong noodle shop, but this tiny storefront is one of the best known in town, with a reputation that belies its humble decor. The staff is attentive, and the menu includes a wide range of delicious dishes, such as various sauce-tossed noodles with pork. The real test of a good Cantonese noodle shop, however, is its wontons, and here they're fresh, delicate, and filled with whole shrimp. Don't miss the *sui kau*—a slightly larger and heavier dumpling that has diced mushrooms mixed in to the shrimp filling. [$] *Average main: HK$40* ✉ *77 Wellington St., Central* ☎ *2854–3810* 💳 *No credit cards* [M] *Central* ✥ *1:C4.*

$ VEGETARIAN 🍴 **Mana!.** The guys at Mana! have come up with the concept of "fast slow food"—a convenient and eco-conscious mode of eating that's good for the body and the environment. Utensils and containers are all biodegradable, while the menu brims with plant-based dishes prepared from sustainable organic produce sourced from local farms. Enjoy mixed salads, veggie burgers, and good-for-you shakes and juices. The main attractions are the flatbreads, which are freshly baked in Mana!'s brick oven. They're spread with *za'atar* (a Middle East herb-and-spice mix), then topped with hearty items like roasted veggies, garlic mayo, or hummus. Saving the planet never tasted so delicious. [$] *Average main: HK$90* ✉ *92 Wellington St., Central* ☎ *2851–1611* 🌐 *www.mana.hk* [M] *Central* ✥ *1:C4.*

$$$$ CONTEMPORARY 🍴 **Mandarin Grill + Bar.** This famous dining room at the Mandarin Oriental mixes old-school elegance with chef Uwe Opocensky's progressive gastronomical creations. While the menu sounds straightforward at first, the actual dishes appear like works of art, with plenty of playful flourishes. Perfectly cooked meats are served on plates shaped like giant cookbooks, while the restaurant's famous "flower pot" salad is composed of organic greens arranged in edible soil. It's no wonder that this restaurant has remained a firm fine-dining favorite with the city's discerning foodies. [$] *Average main: HK$695* ✉ *Mandarin*

Oriental, 5 Connaught Rd. Central, Central ☎ *2825–4004* ⊕ *www. mandarinoriental.com* Ⓜ *Central* ✛ *1:E3.*

$$$ ✕ **Mott 32.** Named after a convenience store that was once at the heart
CHINESE   of New York's Chinatown district, Mott 32 embraces the East-meets-
West identity that pervaded early immigrant communities. This is duly
reflected in the interior design, which marries Imperial Chinese fur-
nishings with grungy industrial elements. The menu offers classic Can-
tonese, Beijing, and Sichuan recipes prepared with modern inflections.
Expect only the finest ingredients in dishes from barbecued Iberico
pork cha siu to crab and caviar *xiao long bao* dumplings. Be sure to
try one of the Asian-inspired cocktails, such as the whisky-based Old
Harbor flavored with goji berries and chrysanthemum. Ⓢ *Average main:
HK$270* ⊠ *Basement level, Standard Chartered Bldg., 4–4A Des Voeux
Rd., Central* ☎ *2885–8688* ⊕ *www.mott32.com* Ⓜ *Central* ✛ *1:E3.*

$$$$ ✕ **NUR.** Head chef Nurdin Topham has made it his mission to bring
SCANDINAVIAN   what he calls "nourishing gastronomy" to Hong Kong. His food—
which is heavily influenced by Scandinavian cooking techniques—places
emphasis on taste, nutrition, and sustainable eating. Ingredients are
sourced from local farms whenever possible and are used in the restau-
rant's two tasting menus. Dishes are tweaked regularly to reflect the
season's freshest produce, but dishes like heirloom tomatoes with king
crab or Taiyouran egg with whole grains and shiitake mushrooms have
become house favorites. Ⓢ *Average main: HK$430* ⊠ *3rd fl., Lyndhurst
Tower, 1 Lyndhurst Terr., Central* ☎ *2871–9993* ⊕ *www.nur.hk* ⊗ *No
lunch. Closed Sun.* Ⓜ *Central* ✛ *1:C4.*

$$$$ ✕ **Restaurant Petrus.** Commanding breathtaking views atop the Island
FRENCH   Shangri-La, Restaurant Petrus scales the upper Hong Kong heights of
prestige, formality, and price. This is one of the city's few flagship hotel
restaurants that has not attempted to reinvent itself as fusion—some-
times traditional French haute cuisine is the way to go. Likewise, the
design of the place is in the old-school restaurant-as-ballroom mode.
The kitchen has a particularly good way with foie gras, and the wine
list is memorable, boasting more than 1,500 vintages from some of the
world's best wineries. The dress here is business casual—no jeans, san-
dals, or short-sleeved shirts for men. Ⓢ *Average main: HK$600* ⊠ *56th
fl., Island Shangri-La, Pacific Place, Supreme Court Rd., Admiralty,
Central* ☎ *2820–8590* ⊕ *www.shangri-la.com* Ⓜ *Admiralty* ✛ *1:F4.*

$$$ ✕ **Ronin.** Hidden behind a signless gray door, Ronin is an ultraslick
JAPANESE   *izakaya*-style restaurant that serves some of the most creative seafood
Fodor's Choice   dishes in town. The menu is market driven and always features a selec-
★   tion of fresh sashimi. Most dishes are designed to share. Be sure to
try the deep-fried fish *karaage*, which is perfect for pairing with the
bar's extensive selection of Japanese whiskies, sake, or shochu. Word
of warning: there are only 14 seats at the bar, and reservations are only
accepted via email. You could also head down a few blocks and check
out Ronin's sister restaurant, Yardbird, which serves delicious *yakitori*
(grilled chicken) to an eager, walk-in crowd. Ⓢ *Average main: HK$250*
⊠ *8 Wo On La., at the end of Kau U Fong, Central* ☎ *2547–5263*
⊕ *www.roninhk.com* ⌕ *Reservations essential* ⊗ *No dinner. Closed
Sun.* Ⓜ *Sheung Wan* ✛ *1:C3.*

$$ CHINESE 🍴 **San Xi Lou.** This Mid-Levels eatery is known for the high quality of its spicy Sichuan cuisine. The famous Chongqing spicy chicken is heaped with dried red chili peppers for a sensational tingling, mouth-numbing effect. Another unique creation is the homemade silken tofu, which is bathed in a bright-red spicy broth speckled with chunks of whitefish, chopped scallions, and crunchy roasted peanuts. Those in town during the cold winter months should go for the yinyang hot pot—the fiery-hot side dish is perfect for dunking with thin slices of fat-marbled beef and the local favorite, deep-fried fish skin. [$] *Average main: HK$200* ✉ *7th fl., Coda Plaza, 51 Garden Rd., Central* ☎ *2838–8811* ✍ *Reservations essential* [M] *Central* ✥ *1:D5.*

$ CHINESE 🍴 **Shui Kee.** Fold-up tables and stools are scattered around this small stall, which specializes in cow offal served with noodles in broth. Tender beef brisket and deep-fried wontons are also popular options. [$] *Average main: HK$30* ✉ *2 Gutzlaff St., Central* ☎ *2541–9769* ▭ *No credit cards* ⏲ *No dinner, closed Sun.* [M] *Central* ✥ *1:B4.*

$ CHINESE 🍴 **Sing Heung Yuen.** This outdoor stall has been in operation for well over 30 years, and the canopied tables are pretty much always packed from 8 am to 5:30 pm. The iconic dishes here are the instant ramen noodles or beef and macaroni served in a sweet tomato broth, as well as the toasted, crispy buns drizzled with condensed milk. [$] *Average main: HK$35* ✉ *2 Mee Lun St., Central* ☎ *2544–8368* ✍ *Reservations not accepted* ▭ *No credit cards* ⏲ *No dinner. Closed Sun.* ✥ *1:C3.*

$ CHINESE 🍴 **Sing Kee.** This is one of the rare *dai pai dong* food stalls in the area that stays open late into the evening. The menu is pretty extensive, and the home-style stir-fries are particularly good. Chewy calamari in spicy salt is a classic favorite. The adventurous should try the soy-sauce goose intestines. [$] *Average main: HK$68* ✉ *82 Stanley St., Central* ☎ *2541–5678* ▭ *No credit cards* [M] *Central* ✥ *1:C4.*

$$$ GREEK Fodor's Choice ★ 🍴 **Souvla.** This stylish restaurant and bar serves the delicious flavors of the Mediterranean. Start with a round of warm pita bread and savory dips, such as the addictive *taramasalata* (smoked fish roe blended with lemon and garlic). Other must-try items include the succulent octopus, grilled halloumi cheese, and tender lamb ribs. Of course, you should also try the namesake *souvla*, which is a Greek-style spit-roasted meat. [$] *Average main: HK$300* ✉ *Ho Lee Commercial Bldg., 40 D'Aguilar St., Central* ☎ *2522–1823* 🌐 *www.conceptcreations.hk* [M] *Central* ✥ *1:C5.*

$$$$ EUROPEAN 🍴 **St Betty.** Having found great success in the United Kingdom, restaurateur Alan Yau has returned to his home city with this retro-inspired restaurant concept headed by Australian chef Shane Osborn. The menu combines Osborn's classical culinary training with seasonal Asian ingredients such as soy dressing and fresh wasabi leaves. Meats are done especially well, and diners tend to wax lyrical about the Sagabuta pork loin, as well as the dry-aged rib eye prepared on the Josper grill. Aside from lunch and dinner, St Betty offers a fantastic weekend brunch and Sunday roast menu. [$] *Average main: HK$450* ✉ *2nd fl., IFC Mall, 8 Finance St., Central* ☎ *2979–2100* 🌐 *www.stbetty.com* [M] *Hong Kong* ✥ *1:E2.*

$$$$ ✕**Sushi Sase.** Helmed by veteran chef Satoshi Sase (who hails from the
JAPANESE much-lauded Sushi Zen in Hokkaido, Japan), this high-caliber Japanese
restaurant offers some of the freshest fish in town in a tranquil and
sophisticated setting. Omakase is the way to go here, which means you
leave your meal in the hands of the chefs, allowing them to dictate the
menu according to the best ingredients of the day. The omakase menu
is designed according to the seasons and usually consists of sashimi,
appetizers, and a wide array of nigiri sushi. [$] *Average main: HK$1380*
✉ *Hilltop Plaza, 49 Hollywood Rd., Central* ☎ *2815–0455, 2815–0477*
Ⓜ *Central* ✛ *1:B4.*

$ ✕**Tai Cheong.** This popular bakery was supposed to shut down for
BAKERY good, but there was such an outcry that not only did it remain open, it
expanded to include outlets all across the city. It sells all sorts of pack-
aged and oven-fresh baked goods. The egg tarts, with their buttery crust
and custardy-rich centers, are the main scene stealers, but the thin and
crunchy egg biscuit rolls are also popular. Other local delicacies include
sugar-dusted Chinese doughnuts. [$] *Average main: HK$12* ✉ *35 Lyndhurst Terr., Central* ☎ *8300–8301* ✛ *1:B5.*

$$$$ ✕**Vasco.** This gorgeous restaurant is truly the full package. For start-
SPANISH ers, the space is gorgeous—cool, classy, and intimate at the same time.
Fodor'sChoice More important, though, is that Vasco serves truly inspired Spanish
★ cuisine with global influences. The red Palamos prawns and sea urchin
is a standout, as is the incredibly tender roast pigeon, which is balanced
by tart apple cream. For dessert, a combination of rice and cardamom
rounds off the meal perfectly. Our recommendation is to go for the
chef's tasting menu, which offers the crème de la crème that the restaurant has to offer. If you're looking for something less formal, head
to Vasco's sister restaurant, Isono, one floor below. [$] *Average main:
HK$490* ✉ *6th fl., Block B, PMQ, 35 Aberdeen St., Central* ☎ *2156–
0888, 2156–1818* ⊕ *www.isono-vasco.com.hk* Ⓜ *Central* ✛ *1:B4.*

$$ ✕**Yardbird.** This bustling bi-level eatery is one of the hottest places to
JAPANESE eat. Chef-owner Matt Abergel plates perfectly cooked yakitori (Japa-
nese-style grilled chicken) as well as a repertoire of salads and small
plates designed for sharing. Definitely try the Korean fried cauliflower
(here called KFC) and the liver mousse served with milk bread and
crispy shallots. Drinking is another important part of the experience,
so try the house-brand junmai sake or choose from the well-chosen
Japanese beer and whiskey list. The only downside is that the res-
taurant doesn't take reservations, so arrive early or risk waiting for a
table. [$] *Average main: HK$150* ✉ *33–35 Bridges St., Sheung Wan,
Western* ☎ *2547–9273* ⊕ *www.yardbirdrestaurant.com* ⌁ *Reservations
not accepted* ☉ *No lunch. Closed Sun.* ✛ *1:C3.*

$$$ ✕**Yung Kee.** Close to Hong Kong's famous nightlife and dining district
CHINESE of Lan Kwai Fong, Yung Kee has been a local institution since it first
opened as a food stall in 1942. The food is authentic Cantonese, served
amid riotous decor and writhing gold dragons. Locals come here for
roast goose with beautifully crisp skin and tender meat, as well as dim
sum. Other excellent dishes include the "cloudy tea" smoked pork,
which needs to be reserved a day in advance, and the deep-fried prawns
with mini crab roe. More adventurous palates may wish to check out

the thousand-year-old preserved eggs. [$] *Average main: HK$250* ✉ *32–40 Wellington St, Central* ☎ *2522–1624* 🌐 *www.yungkee.com.hk* [M] *Central* ✣ *1:C5.*

WAN CHAI, CAUSEWAY BAY, AND EASTERN

WAN CHAI

The range of dining options in Wan Chai is extreme—from five-star luxury to noodle-shop dives open into the wee hours.

$$$$ CHINESE 🍴 **Bo Innovation.** The mastermind behind this renowned restaurant is Alvin Leung, who dubs himself the "demon chef" and has the moniker tattooed on his arm. Bo Innovation serves what he calls "X-treme Chinese" cuisine, applying molecular gastronomy, French, and Japanese cooking techniques to traditional Cantonese dishes. The beef and black-truffle *cheung fun* (steamed-rice roll) is a winner, as is the signature xiao long bao (soup dumpling). At dinner you must choose between the multicourse tasting menu, table menu, or chef's menu; à la carte dining is not available. Tables are often full on Friday and Saturday, so book in advance. [$] *Average main: HK$680* ✉ *2nd fl., J Residence, 60 Johnston Rd., Wan Chai* ☎ *2850–8371* 🌐 *www.boinnovation.com* ✍ *Reservations essential* ⏲ *No lunch Sat. Closed Sun.* [M] *Wan Chai* ✣ *2:B4.*

$ CHINESE 🍴 **Capital Café.** It's a blast from the past at this retro Hong Kong café, done up in period '80s and '90s decor, complete with autographed Cantopop idol posters from that era. The food is old-school as well, and you'll find hearty local specialties like elbow macaroni with barbecued pork, milk tea, and toasted sandwiches filled with fluffy scrambled eggs. If you come after 3 pm, try the "principal's toast"—it's black truffle paste and cheese smothered on thick pieces of bread. It's delicious indulgence done the cheap and cheerful way. [$] *Average main: HK$35* ✉ *6 Heard St., Wan Chai* ☎ *2666–7766* 💳 *No credit cards* ✣ *2:D3.*

$$$ SPANISH 🍴 **Catalunya.** This is, without a doubt, one of the finest Spanish restaurants in the city. The experience begins with the space itself, which combines Spain's classical nuances with the contemporary vibe of a cosmopolitan city. There are two main dining rooms where you can enjoy the Catalan-inspired recipes. Highlights from the tapas menu include the *bombas* (deep-fried pork and beef meatballs covered in potato purée and bread crumbs) and the famous ham, cheese, and truffle "bikini" sandwiches. Another must-try is the Segovian-style roasted suckling pig, which is large enough to feed four. Catalunya also offers exceptional weekend brunches with free-flowing sparkling wine. Book early if you want to join the fun. [$] *Average main: HK$285* ✉ *Guardian House, 32 Oi Kwan Rd., Wan Chai* ☎ *2866–7900* 🌐 *www.catalunya.hk* ✍ *Reservations essential* [M] *Wan Chai* ✣ *2:E3.*

$$ CHINESE 🍴 **Che's Cantonese Restaurant.** Smartly dressed locals in the know head for this casually elegant dim sum specialist, which is in the middle of the downtown bustle yet well concealed on the fourth floor of an office building. From the elevator, you'll step into a classy Cantonese world. It's hard to find a single better dim sum dish than Che's crispy pork buns, whose sugary baked pastry conceals the brilliant saltiness of barbecued pork within. Other dim sum to try include pan-fried turnip

cake and a refreshing dessert of cold pomelo and sago with mango juice for a calming end to an exciting meal. $ *Average main: HK$100* ✉ *The Broadway, 54–62 Lockhart Rd., 4th fl., Wan Chai* ☎ *2528–1123* Ⓜ *Wan Chai* ✛ *2:B3.*

$$$ ✕**DiVino Patio.** Located along a stretch of semi-alfresco eateries known
ITALIAN as Brim 28 (named after its waterside location on 28 Harbour Road), DiVino Patio touts rustic, homestyle Italian fare to match its laid-back surroundings. The expansive space is designed like a retro grocery store, and you can purchase gourmet condiments, salumi, and cheeses to enjoy on the go. For eat-in orders, try any of the hand-tossed pizzas, or go for one of the succulent selections from the rotisserie. The spit-roasted Vallespluga game hen is exceptional, with tender meat and crispy skin. The restaurant also has an excellent lunchtime antipasti buffet matched with a rotating choice of mains. $ *Average main: HK$230* ✉ *Causeway Centre, 28 Harbour Rd., Wan Chai* ☎ *2877–3552* ⊕ *www.divinogroup. com* Ⓜ *Wan Chai* ✛ *2:D2.*

$$$$ ✕**Dynasty Restaurant.** Dining on haute Cantonese cuisine at this stunning
CHINESE restaurant with panoramic views over Victoria Harbour is a memorable experience. The chefs here are famed for adapting family-style recipes into elegant dishes, and the service is impeccable yet friendly. The menu changes with the seasons and leans heavily toward fresh seafood, though the barbecued pork is also a must-try. With its high ceilings, old-world charm, and laid-back tempo, Dynasty is one of the rare top-notch restaurants where you can comfortably linger over a meal. $ *Average main: HK$340* ✉ *3rd fl., Renaissance Harbour View Hotel, 1 Harbour Rd., Wan Chai* ☎ *2584–6971* Ⓜ *Wan Chai* ✛ *2:C2.*

$$$ ✕**Han Ga Ram.** Come here for a refined, modern rendition of classic
KOREAN Korean cuisine. Barbecued meats are a must, and we especially recommend the *sam gyup sal* (thick slabs of pork belly). Moving away from the conventional dishes, Han Ga Ram also offers a few newfangled creations such as bulgogi beef and spicy pork sliders, which are available on the lunch menu. Traditionalists may want to wash down their meal with *soju* (a distilled rice liquor), but the staff is also happy to suggest wine pairings to go with each dish. $ *Average main: HK$250* ✉ *27th fl., QRE Plaza, 202 Queen's Rd., Wan Chai* ☎ *2891–5090* ⊕ *www. han-ga-ram.com* Ⓜ *Wan Chai* ✛ *2:C4.*

$ ✕**Kam Fung.** The space is dingy, the tables are cramped, and the staff is
BAKERY brash—but the food makes it all worth it. Kam Fung has been around for more than five decades, serving traditional Hong Kong café fare such as crumbly crusted freshly baked egg tarts, and pineapple buns wedged with a thick slab of butter. Wash everything down with the velvety smooth milk tea after a meal that's cheap, quick, and absolutely satisfying. $ *Average main: HK$25* ✉ *41 Spring Garden Lane, Wan Chai* ☎ *2572–0526* ▭ *No credit cards* ☽ *No dinner.* Ⓜ *Wan Chai* ✛ *2:C4.*

$ ✕**La Crêperie.** This French-owned spot specializes in authentic, thin
FRENCH Breton crêpes filled with all sorts of sweet or savory fillings. Most of the clientele is French, which is a good indication of the authenticity of the food. Fillings for these made-fresh-to-order pancakes range from traditional to experimental; La Complète buckwheat galette is loaded with a classic combination of egg, ham, and deliciously gooey melted

cheese, while L'Italienne has tomato, mozzarella cheese, anchovies, and olives. The dessert crêpe selection is just as wide-ranging. La Crêperie also carries a delicious apple cider—the traditional drink of choice for accompanying galettes in Brittany. $ *Average main: HK$100* ✉ *100 Queen's Rd. E, 1st fl., Wan Chai* ☎ *2529–9280* 🌐 *www.lacreperie.com.cn* 🕒 *Closed Mon.* [M] *Wan Chai* $ *Average main: HK$100* ✉ *69 Jervois St., Sheung Wan, Sheung Wan* ☎ *2679–4666* 🌐 *Sheung Wan* 🕒 *Closed Mon.* ✥ *2:B4.*

$$ CHINESE Fodor's Choice ★

🍴 **Liu Yuan Pavilion.** Often regarded as one of the best Shanghainese restaurants in town, Liu Yuan's cooking style stays loyal to tradition with a no-fuss mentality that has worked in their favor for years. Easy favorites include sweet strips of crunchy eel, pan-fried meat buns, and steamed *xiao long bao* dumplings plumped up with minced pork and broth. Diners also wax lyrical about the house special crispy rice soup and rice crackers smothered in salted egg yolk. Come hungry, since you'll need plenty of room to stomach all of these deliciously carby dishes. $ *Average main: HK$120* ✉ *The Broadway, 54–62 Lockhart Rd., 3rd fl., Wan Chai* ☎ *2804–2000* [M] *Wan Chai* ✥ *2:B3.*

$$$$ CHINESE

🍴 **One Harbour Road.** It's hard to say what's more impressive at the Grand Hyatt's Cantonese showpiece—the interior design (two terraced levels boasting an incredible sense of space and motion), or the view over the harbor from the floor-to-ceiling windows. Unlike many harborside establishments, though, you don't need a window seat to catch the view. And the cuisine is traditional but excellent—order one of the signature barbecued meats and don't be afraid to splurge on seafood. The restaurant offers a wine-pairing menu and there's also a knowledgeable sommelier on hand to provide pairing suggestions for specific dishes. $ *Average main: HK$360* ✉ *7th and 8th fl., Grand Hyatt Hong Kong, 1 Harbour Rd., Wan Chai* ☎ *2584–7722* 🌐 *www.hongkong.grand.hyatt.com* [M] *Wan Chai* ✥ *2:C2.*

$$$ FRENCH Fodor's Choice ★

🍴 **Serge et le Phoque.** With its floor-to-ceiling windows and minimalist decor, this elegant restaurant stands out amid the clamor of Wan Chai's street market. The kitchen serves refined, modern French cuisine, often with minimalist Japanese touches. Dishes on the menu are ever-changing, but may include slow-cooked hen eggs or scallops with *yuzu kosho* (a green chili paste from Japan). Service is friendly and attentive without the stuffiness you'll find in more old-school European restaurants. $ *Average main: HK$300* ✉ *Shop B2, 2 Wan Chai Rd., Wan Chai* ☎ *5465–2000* ✍ *Reservations essential* 🕒 *No lunch* [M] *Wan Chai* ✥ *2:C4.*

$$$ AMERICAN

🍴 **Stone Nullah Tavern.** Tucked away on a quiet street across from the famed Blue House, Stone Nullah Tavern serves new American cuisine that revolves around locally sourced ingredients. The menu changes regularly, but you'll always find unabashedly hearty offerings such as cheddar mac and cheese and the notorious "fat kid cake" (essentially four desserts mixed into one). Adventurous diners will enjoy the wide selection of offal-centric dishes, including crispy pig's head, tripe "fries," and chicken-liver dip served with homemade potato chips. $ *Average main: HK$250* ✉ *69 Stone Nullah La., Wan Chai* ☎ *3182–0128* 🌐 *www.stonenullahtavern.com* 🕒 *No lunch weekdays* [M] *Wan Chai* ✥ *2:C4.*

$$$ SPANISH 🍴 **22 Ships.** Enjoy a fun, communal dining experience at this buzzing tapas bar opened by celebrated chef Jason Atherton. Expect a creative and contemporary menu with to-share dishes from Ibérico pork and foie gras miniburgers to toasted bread filled with ham, truffles, and melty manchego cheese. Be sure to arrive early, since the restaurant only seats 38 people around the open kitchen and by the windows. Fortunately, you can always take advantage of the fantastic sherries and sangrias while you wait for a seat outside. [$] *Average main: HK$230* ✉ *22 Ship St., Wan Chai* ☎ *2555–0722* 🌐 *www.22ships.hk* [M] *Wan Chai* ✣ *2:B4.*

CAUSEWAY BAY

Causeway Bay is one of Hong Kong's busiest shopping districts and has some of the trendiest restaurants in town. It's popular with the younger crowd and is often compared with Tokyo's Shibuya district—and this is also where you'll find some of Hong Kong's best Japanese food, as well as many midprice eateries. The area behind the giant Sogo department store has some great street snacking options. If you fancy a cup of milk tea dotted with black tapioca pearls, this is the place to go, though Causeway also has its fair share of high-end eateries, which are concentrated in the area surrounding Lee Gardens Two, home to many luxury fashion stores.

Some of the most exciting dining options in the area are the upstairs eateries. Hidden away from street view, these venues rely mainly on foodies in the know, but house some of the best eats in the neighborhood.

$$$ JAPANESE 🍴 **Bridges.** You may be familiar with mainstream Japanese sushi and sashimi, but Okinawan cooking is something completely different. Dishes from the Ryukyu Islands carry Chinese and American influences, and you'll find plenty of *chanpuru* (stir-fry) dishes, as well as obscure delicacies like salt and cookie ice cream. The islands are also credited for their bountiful fresh produce; be sure to try the *umi budo* "green caviar" sea kelp and the bitter gourd melon. Carnivores, don't fret—Okinawa's Motobu Wagyu beef and Aguu pork are delicious, well-marbled versions that work well in everything from grills to shabu shabu. [$] *Average main: HK$200* ✉ *Cubus, 1 Hoi Ping Rd., 6th fl., Causeway Bay* ☎ *3428–2131* 🌐 *www.en.com.hk* [M] *Causeway Bay* ✣ *2:G3.*

$ CHINESE 🍴 **Café Matchbox.** The decor, staff uniforms, and—of course—the food all capture the retro vibe of the 1960s Hong Kong *cha chaan teng* (local café). Cantonese pop songs from that era play over the sound system while diners relish bowls of elbow macaroni served in soup and topped with ham and eggs. Other staples include spaghetti served in chicken broth with cha siu pork and green peas. But the sweets here are what really stand out. The egg tarts are rich and custardy, and the French toast is served with a giant slab of butter. Surely the best items, though, are the hotcakes topped with bananas, buttered walnuts, and soft-serve ice cream. [$] *Average main: HK$55* ✉ *8 Cleveland St., Causeway Bay* ☎ *2868–0363* 🌐 *www.cafematchbox.com.hk* [M] *Causeway Bay.* ✣ *2:G2.*

$ CHINESE 🍴 **Dim Sum.** The dim sum menu here goes beyond common Cantonese morsels like *har gau* (steamed shrimp dumplings), embracing dishes more popular in the north, including chili prawn dumplings, Beijing

Hot pot cooking in action

onion cakes, and various steamed buns. Decadent dim sum options, such as abalone pastries, are particularly popular, but also extremely pricey. Lunch reservations are not taken, so there's always a long line, especially on weekends. Arrive early, or admire the antique Chinese decor while you wait. [$] *Average main: HK$70* ✉ *63 Sing Woo Rd., Happy Valley, Causeway Bay* ☎ *2834–8893* [M] *Causeway Bay* ✣ *2:E4.*

$$ STEAKHOUSE 🍴 **Goldfinch Restaurant.** Travel back to the romantic 1960s as you dine at this retro restaurant. Film buffs might recognize this spot as the backdrop to renowned director Wong Kar-wai's most famous films, including *In the Mood for Love*. Like the decor, the food here has remained largely unchanged since the restaurant's heyday, and you'll find local interpretations of western dishes, such as borscht or cream of mushroom soup and gravy-covered steaks served on sizzling iron plates. Don't come here if you're looking for an authentic steak-house experience, though: this place is strictly for those who want to relive the nostalgic charm of Hong Kong's swinging era. [$] *Average main: HK$150* ✉ *13–15 Lan Fong Rd., Causeway Bay* ☎ *2577–7981* ✣ *2:F3.*

$$ CHINESE 🍴 **Hotpot Instinct.** Hot-pot cooking is immensely popular in Hong Kong, and places like Hotpot Instinct are packed even during the steamy summer months. The large menu offers thinly sliced beef, pork, seafood, and a range of house-made fish balls and meatballs, which diners then dip into a boiling vat of broth at their table. [$] *Average main: HK$120* ✉ *The L. Square, 459-461 Lockhart Rd., 6th fl., Causeway Bay* ☎ *2573–2844* 🌐 *www.hotpotinstinct.com* [M] *Causeway Bay* ✣ *2:F3.*

$$ JAPANESE 🍴 **Iroha.** Expert in the art of *yakiniku* (grilled meats), Iroha stocks top-quality ingredients for its tabletop grills. Many go for the premium Wagyu beef selection, but the seafood choices are also worth trying. The

thick-sliced salted beef tongue is legendary. $ *Average main: HK$200* ✉ *Jardine Center, 50 Jardine's Bazaar, 2nd fl., Causeway Bay* ☎ *2882–9877* ⊕ *www.iroha.com.hk* Ⓜ *Causeway Bay* ✛ *2:G3.*

$$
ITALIAN
✕ **Jamie's Italian.** British celebrity-chef Jamie Oliver's first Hong Kong venture may have had a slow start, but its heart is in the right place. The restaurant offers casual, unpretentious Italian cuisine with a heavy emphasis on sustainable, responsibly sourced ingredients. The menu follows the blueprint set out by other Jamie's Italian outlets around the world. House favorites include hearty sharing planks loaded with cured meats, cheeses, pickles, and greens. Other familiar dishes include the famous prawn linguine. $ *Average main: HK$200* ✉ *2nd fl., Soundwill Plaza II–Midtown, 1 Tang Lung St., Causeway Bay* ☎ *3958–2222* ⊕ *www.jamieoliver.com/italian/hongkong* Ⓜ *Causeway Bay* ✛ *2:E3.*

$
INTERNATIONAL
✕ **Lab Made.** You can identify Lab Made by the large crowd that's usually gathered in front of the store. They come for the super-smooth, house-spun ice cream, which is made using liquid nitrogen. The freezing process takes only a minute, which is why everything can be made to order using the freshest ingredients. There are usually only a handful of flavors to choose from, and the menu changes on a weekly basis. If available, go for one of the Hong Kong–inspired flavors, such as beancurd pudding or sweet red-bean soup. $ *Average main: HK$45* ✉ *6 Brown St., Tai Hang, Causeway Bay* ⊕ *www.labmade.com.hk* ▬ *No credit cards* ⊙ *Closed Mon.* Ⓜ *Tin Hau* ✛ *2:H3.*

$
FRENCH
✕ **Ladurée Tea Room.** Foodies were understandably excited when this iconic French patisserie set up shop in Hong Kong. Its pastel-colored macarons come in a rainbow of flavors, such as classic rose and sea-salt caramel. You can enjoy these delectable confections in the sit-down tearoom, or take them to go in one of the gorgeous pastry boxes. $ *Average main: HK$35* ✉ *3rd fl., Times Square, 1 Matheson St., Causeway Bay* ☎ *2509–9377* ⊕ *www.laduree.com* Ⓜ *Causeway Bay* ✛ *2:E3.*

$$
THAI
✕ **Mango Tree.** This eatery has won rave reviews since the first outlet opened in Bangkok. The Hong Kong branch lives up to its predecessor's reputation and boasts a winning formula of designer decor, friendly service, and tasty, refined takes on authentic regional Thai dishes. You can start with char-grilled pork neck before moving on to one of the spicy-and-sweet soups or salads. We also recommend the herb-laden duck and lamb curries, as well as a stir-fried noodle dish to anchor the meal. $ *Average main: HK$180* ✉ *5th fl., Cubus, 1 Hoi Ping Rd., Causeway Bay* ☎ *2577–0828* ⊕ *www.mangotree.com.hk* Ⓜ *Causeway Bay* ✛ *2:F3.*

$
JAPANESE
✕ **Nan Tei.** This *izakaya* offers plate upon plate of *yakitori* and *kushiyaki* (Japanese-style skewered and grilled items) in a decidely relaxed atmosphere. The ox tongue is exceptional—succulent, soft, and flavored with just the right amount of salt. *Kushiyaki* staples, such as chicken wings and shiitake mushrooms, are also excellent. Nightly specials are displayed on a chalkboard. And in true izakaya fashion, Nan Tei offers a well-ranging sake list to accompany the bite-sized noshes. This is a great place for a casual Japanese meal with good food and a couple of drinks. $ *Average main: HK$95* ✉ *Bigfoot Centre, 38 Yiu Wa St.,*

2nd fl., Causeway Bay ☎ *3118–2501* ⊘ *No lunch Sun.* Ⓜ *Causeway Bay* ✛ *2:F3.*

$$$$ ✗ **Seasons by Olivier Elzer.** Chef and cofounder Olivier Elzer cut his teeth
FRENCH   at Pierre Gagnaire and Joël Robuchon's kitchens before opening his solo
venture. The idea is to serve modern French cuisine that pays tribute
to seasonal ingredients. Grab one of the bar seats at the chef's table if
you want an unobstructed view of the action in the open kitchen. The
menu is designed to be flexible, with dishes available in full or half
portions. Standouts include the grilled tuna with five spices and the
langoustine risotto venere with masala butter. The restaurant offers a
set dinner, but you can also create your own four- to eight-course tasting menu. Ⓢ *Average main: HK$470* ⊠ *3rd fl., Lee Gardens Two, 28
Yun Ping Rd., Causeway Bay* ☎ *2505–6228* ⊕ *www.seasonsbyolivier.
com* Ⓜ *Causeway Bay* ✛ *2:G3.*

$$$$ ✗ **Sushi Hiro.** *Uni* (sea urchin), *ikura* (salmon roe), *o-toro* (the fattiest of
JAPANESE   fatty tuna). If these words can make you drool, then you should make
a beeline for Sushi Hiro, hidden in an office building but quite possibly
the best place for raw fish in Hong Kong. The minimalist interior stays
faithful to Japanese style, unlike at some more opulent Hong Kong restaurants. But what really draws in the Japanese crowd here is the freshness of the fish, which you can watch being filleted in front of you at
the sushi bar. Dinner may get pricey, but the restaurant also does some
fantastic lunch deals. Ⓢ *Average main: HK$320* ⊠ *Henry House, 42
Yun Ping Rd., 10th fl., Causeway Bay* ☎ *2882–8752* ⊕ *www.sushihiro.
com.hk* Ⓜ *Causeway Bay* ✛ *2:F3.*

$$$ ✗ **Ta Pantry.** This place started out as a one-table private kitchen in a
ECLECTIC   quiet Wan Chai neighborhood. Due to popular demand, chef-owner
Esther Sham moved to a much larger location. Decked out like a chic
Parisian apartment, the newer space accommodates 48 guests. There
are seven different menus from which to choose, ranging from the Jap-
anese-inspired meal to the Shanghai-style dinner. The latter includes the
famous not-so-Shanghainese foie gras dumplings. Wine connoisseurs
can also take advantage of the extensive selection at Hip Cellar next
door. Ⓢ *Average main: HK$200* ⊠ *5th fl., Block C, Sea View Estate, 8
Watson Rd., Tin Hau, Mong Kok* ☎ *2979–0927* ⊕ *www.ta-pantry.com*
⌕ *Reservations essential* ⊘ *Closed Sun.* ✛ *2:H3.*

$$ ✗ **Tonkichi Tonkatsu Seafood.** This restaurant specializes in *tonkatsu*—
JAPANESE   pork cutlets that are dipped in panko and deep-fried. When it's done
right, as it is here, the pork is crispy on the outside but remains tender
and juicy on the inside. The fillet is sliced up and served with an appe-
tizing, tangy sauce, and goes perfectly with a bowl of steamed rice.
Ⓢ *Average main: HK$200* ⊠ *4th fl., WTC More, 280 Gloucester Rd.,
Causeway Bay* ☎ *2577–6617* ✛ *2:F2.*

$$ ✗ **Wu Kong.** This restaurant serves good Shanghainese fare at reasonable
CHINESE   prices. The signature xiao long bao (soup dumplings) are great, and the
honey ham with crispy bean-curd skin wrapped in soft bread is delicious
and authentic. Be sure to try the tofu dumpling—a unique dish that has
mixed greens enveloped in thin sheets of silken bean curd. (This requires
advance ordering.) We also recommend the Shanghai-style doughnut
on the dessert menu—it's a deep-fried sphere of whipped and fluffy egg

whites stuffed with red bean and bananas. The restaurant also offers several great-value set menus. [$] *Average main: HK$150* ✉ *17th fl., Lee Theatre Plaza, 99 Percival St., Causeway Bay* ☎ *2506–1018* 🌐 *www.wukong.com.hk* [M] *Causeway Bay* ✣ *2:F3.*

$$$$ JAPANESE 🍴 **Xenri D'zen.** A hidden gem in this always-bustling neighborhood, Xenri D'zen follows a strict philosophy of seasonal eating that's inspired by Japan's traditional kaiseki formal dining. The experience is interpreted in a modern manner without detracting from the quality of the food. The multicourse menu usually includes the season's freshest sashimi and sushi, followed by various cooked dishes. The prices aren't necessarily cheap, but a meal here will cost less than at most other Japanese restaurants of a similar caliber. [$] *Average main: HK$500* ✉ *3rd fl., Jardine Ctr., 50 Jardine's Bazaar, Causeway Bay* ☎ *3523–1955* [M] *Causeway Bay* ✣ *2:F3.*

$$ CHINESE 🍴 **Yun Yan.** This is one of Hong Kong's most popular Sichaun restaurants, and the chefs are generous with the spices in dishes like the signature crispy chicken with red chilies and peppercorns. Sliced Mandarin fish with crispy soybean crumbs is another classic. For something with a little less heat but still equally delicious, go for the house-smoked duckling or hand-cut noodles served in a flavorful broth. To end your meal, choose from traditional sweets or newfangled creations like chocolate-and-chili ice cream. [$] *Average main: HK$170* ✉ *10th fl., Times Square, 1 Matheson St., Causeway Bay* ☎ *2375–0800* 🌐 *www.miradining.com/yun-yan* [M] *Causeway Bay* ✣ *2:E3.*

EASTERN

$ CHINESE 🍴 **Mian.** Come to Mian for the Chinese pappardelle—flat egg noodles that are great for holding thick, flavorful sauces. Enjoy these noodles tossed in sweet soy sauce and topped with plum-flavored spareribs and preserved vegetables. The restaurant also serves Taiwanese-style "QQ" noodles, which are made from potato starch and have a springy, al dente bite. If you're up for it, order a side of crunchy pig's ears to go with your bowl of noodles. [$] *Average main: HK$60* ✉ *48 Pan Hoi St., Quarry Bay* ☎ *3482–9981* 💳 *No credit cards* 🕒 *Closed Sun.* [M] *Quarry Bay* ✣ *2:H3.*

$$ FRENCH 🍴 **Plat du Jour.** This cozy bistro stands out as a true gem in a neighborhood dominated by quick-bite eateries and cheap food stalls. Diners can choose between the two- or three-course menu, which features a short but solid selection of classic French dishes. Hearty options range from escargots in garlicky butter to beef bourguignon and the traditional apple tarte tatin. Given the quality of the food, prices are extremely reasonable for both lunch and dinner. [$] *Average main: HK$150* ✉ *21 Hoi Wan St., Quarry Bay, Eastern* ☎ *2789–4200* 🌐 *www.platdujourhk.com* [M] *Quarry Bay* ✣ *2:H3.*

$$ SPANISH 🍴 **Tapeo.** This popular tapas bar is bigger than the original in SoHo, and has a fabulous harborside location, which adds to the laid-back vibe. Authentic Spanish dishes, including ham croquettes and sautéed mushrooms with sherry, are perfect for sharing over glasses of wine. The crispy pork belly is particularly delicious. Tapeo also offers hearty paellas studded with meat and seafood. [$] *Average main: HK$138* ✉ *Lei*

CLOSE UP

Shark's Fin Soup

It makes sense that soup made from a shark's fin—said to be an aphrodisiac—costs so much. Only the promise of increased virility would lead someone to pay HK$1,000 or more for a bowl of the stuff. It actually consists of cartilage from the great beast's pectoral, dorsal, and lower tail fins that has been skinned, dried, and reconstituted in a rich stock form. This cartilage has almost no taste on its own, and is virtually indistinguishable from *tun fun* (cellophane) noodles that are used to create "mock shark's-fin soup."

Selling sharks' fins is a big business, and Hong Kong is said to be responsible for 50% of the global trade. The soup is a fixture at banquets, weddings, and state dinners here. Love potion, elixir, vitality booster, or not, at the very least the dish is high in protein. Recently, however, conservation groups have pointed out that it's also high in mercury. But of even greater concern is the practice of "finning." Since shark meat as a whole isn't valuable, fishermen often clip the fins and dump the rest of the animal back into the sea, and an increasing number of diners—especially the younger crowd—and restaurants are foregoing this dish for environmental reasons.

So, is eating shark's-fin soup a not-to-be-missed Hong Kong experience or a morally reprehensible act? Well, we don't need to take sides in the debate to warn you away from it. Let us repeat: the shark's-fin cartilage *has no taste*. This makes it—and bird's-nest soup, that other tasteless Cantonese delicacy—one of the biggest wastes of money in the culinary universe.

5

King Wan, Site A, 55 Tai Hong St., Sai Wan Ho, Eastern ☎ *2513–0199* 🌐 *www.conceptcreations.hk* [M] *Sai Wan Ho* ✥ *2:H3.*

$ CANTONESE Fodor's Choice ★

🍴 **Tung Po.** Arguably Hong Kong's most famous—if not most perpetually packed—indoor dai pai dong, Tung Po has communal tables large enough to fit 18 guests, and the restaurant's walls are scribbled with its ever-growing list of specials. The food is Hong Kong cuisine with fusion innovations, and you should wash everything down with a cold beer (served here in Chinese soup bowls). Try the spaghetti with cuttlefish, which is flavored with aromatic, jet-black, fresh squid ink. The seafood dishes and stir-fries are all satisfying, but it's really the atmosphere that makes Tung Po a must-visit. Owner Robby Cheung is one of the most delightful characters in the Hong Kong dining biz. Later in the evening, he'll blast the latest pop songs from the sound system. If you're lucky, you might just catch him in one of his moonwalking moods. [$] *Average main: HK$95* ✉ *2nd fl., Java Road Municipal Services Building, 99 Java Rd., Eastern* ☎ *2880–5224, 2880–9399* ✍ *Reservations essential* 💳 *No credit cards* 🕓 *No lunch* [M] *North Point* ✥ *2:H3.*

SOUTHSIDE

The south side of Hong Kong Island is a string of beaches, rocky coves, and luxury developments; the Repulse Bay complex has some good restaurants, most of which boast alfresco seating so diners can take full advantage of the sea breeze. Stanley Village has a much slower pace of life than the one you see in the city. After exploring the market, historic sights, and beaches, have a leisurely meal at one of the top-notch restaurants scattered around, some of which have harbor views. Also on Southside, Shek O is a tiny seaside village with a few decent open-air restaurants.

$$ INTERNATIONAL 🍴 **The Boathouse.** In a gorgeous three-story building, the cozy Boathouse has a lovely view of the waterfront, making it the perfect spot to hang out with friends and family. The menu has a heavy focus on fish, and the bucket of fresh seafood (steamed mussels, prawns, clams, or a combination), served with nicely toasted garlic bread, goes down well with a glass of chilled white wine. Pastas and simple salads are also good bets for casual dining. [$] *Average main: HK$200* ✉ *88 Stanley Main St., Stanley, Southside* ☎ *2813–4467* 🌐 *www.cafedecogroup.com* ✥ *2:E6.*

$$$ MEDITERRANEAN 🍴 **Lucy's.** Hidden inside the famous Stanley Market, this warm, intimate eatery is rarely discovered by tourists. You may feel like you've walked into someone's house when you enter the dining room, but Lucy's is a professionally run restaurant offering excellent home-cooked dishes made from the freshest ingredients. The menu has a Mediterranean slant and often features light salads and grilled meats or fish. Desserts, especially the pecan pudding, are not to be missed. More upscale than most of the beachside restaurants in Stanley, and with lots more character, Lucy's is a perfect end to a relaxed day browsing in the market, and easily your best bet in Stanley. [$] *Average main: HK$250* ✉ *Stanley Market, 64 Stanley Main St., Stanley* ☎ *2813–9055* ✥ *2:E6.*

$ ASIAN 🍴 **Shek O Chinese & Thai Seafood Restaurant.** The seaside village of Shek O, past Stanley, is worth a trip for the large sandy beach and fresh local seafood, and this casual Asian restaurant is an all-time favorite for the quality and variety of food. Come here for simple seaside dining at its best—the menu is extensive, and everything's good and fresh—but prepare for plastic tables and toilets that are best approached with caution. [$] *Average main: HK$90* ✉ *303 Shek O Village, Shek O, Southside* ☎ *2809–4426, 2809–2202* ✥ *2:F5.*

$$$$ EUROPEAN 🍴 **The Verandah.** You won't forget an evening at the Verandah. From the well-spaced tables overlooking the bay to the unobtrusive service to the menu of delicious classics (think French onion soup, Dover sole meunière, and tournedos Rossini), this is an unabashedly regal experience that delivers with finesse at every turn. The beautiful colonial setting is also the perfect place to enjoy a traditional English afternoon tea. Whether you're here for brunch or supper, the food doesn't disappoint, and the wine list is more reasonably priced than you might expect. Note that sleeveless shirts and shorts aren't allowed for men during dinner. [$] *Average main: HK$500* ✉ *The Repulse Bay, 109 Repulse Bay Rd., Repulse Bay, Southside* ☎ *2292–2822* 🌐 *www.therepulsebay.com* ⏲ *Closed Mon. and Tues.* ✥ *2:D5.*

LANTAU ISLAND

You'll wind up on Lantau Island if you're visiting the Big Buddha at Ngong Ping or Disneyland Hong Kong. There are several restaurants within the Disneyland park itself, none of them distinguished, but good if you're traveling with children. The best restaurants are in the hotels. You can reach Lantau by ferry or by one of the many airport-bound buses. But the easiest way to reach the island is by MTR. The Tung Chung line connects from Central and transfers straight to the Disneyland Resort.

$$$
CHINESE
FAMILY
✕ **Crystal Lotus.** The first thing you'll notice here is the most Disney-ish touch: a computer-animated koi pond, where electronic fish dart out of the way as you walk by. Once inside the crystal-studded space, your focus will turn to the food: the pan-Chinese menu includes favorites like Sichuan dan dan noodles, honey-glazed barbecued pork, and double-boiled pear topped with mandarin peel. Kids will get a kick out of the "character dim sum," which includes pork and vegetable buns shaped like *Toy Story*'s little green men, and seafood pancakes bearing the likeness of Mickey Mouse. Make sure to order these in advance. If you wind up in Disneyland, this is by far the best way to dine (unless the kids demand a character meal at the Enchanted Garden in the hotel's lower level). $ *Average main: HK$260* ✉ *Hong Kong Disneyland Hotel, Lantau Island* ☎ *3510–6000* ⊕ *park.hongkongdisneyland.com* Ⓜ *Disneyland Resort* ✛ *3:C1.*

$$
AMERICAN
FAMILY
✕ **Mavericks.** Pui O is famous for its beautiful beach, but not for its dining scene. This seaside restaurant, however, aims to change that by combining a laid-back surfer's attitude with a reverence for top-quality cooking. Locally sourced ingredients feature heavily on the menu, which includes house-ground burgers and nachos made with pork wontons instead of tortilla chips. The restaurant also serves regionally brewed ales and cocktails designed to beat the summer heat. $ *Average main: HK$200* ✉ *Pui O Beach, Lantau* ☎ *5402–4154* ⊘ *Closed Mon.–Thurs. No lunch Fri.* ✛ *3:B2.*

$$
ECLECTIC
FAMILY
✕ **Tai O Lookout.** If you've made your way out to Tai O, this gorgeous glass-roofed restaurant is a great place to enjoy a leisurely afternoon tea or dinner. Formerly the Tai O Police Station, the historic building has been lovingly refurbished, and the restored colonial decor includes authentic wooden furnishings. The menu is short, sweet, and eclectic, offering a mix of Asian and western dishes. Be sure to try the Tai O–inspired items, such as the fried rice and crispy pork-chop bun with shrimp paste. $ *Average main: HK$120* ✉ *Tai O Heritage Hotel, Shek Tsai Po St., Tai O, Lantau Island* ☎ *2985–8383* ⊕ *www. taioheritagehotel.com* ✛ *3:A2.*

KOWLOON PENINSULA

Parts of Kowloon are among the most densely populated areas on the planet and support a corresponding abundance of restaurants. Many hotels, planted here for the view of Hong Kong Island (spectacular at night), also have excellent restaurants, though they're uniformly expensive. Some of the best food in Kowloon is served in backstreet eateries,

A food stall near the Ladies' Market in Kowloon.

where immigrants from Vietnam, Thailand, and elsewhere in Asia keep their native cooking skills sharp.

TSIM SHA TSUI

Tsim Sha Tsui is a foodie's paradise. The high density of hotels here—from the legendary Peninsula Hotel to the chic and modern Mira Hotel—means that there is no shortage of luxury dining options. This district also has several large shopping malls, all filled with restaurants, some better than others. The area is also known for its authentic Korean and Indian cuisine. For the best local eats, though, head to neighboring Yau Ma Tei, especially the Jordan Road area, and to Mong Kok. The eateries here tend to be cramped and noisy, but it's worth exploring for those who want to immerse themselves in the city's local culture.

$$$$ ECLECTIC 🍴 **Aqua.** This trendy restaurant and bar is in the penthouse of the One Peking Road building, and you might hear it referred to by many different names (Aqua Tokyo, Aqua Roma, Aqua Spirit). The menu brings together the East and the West—the Japanese kitchen plates up fresh sashimi, tempura, and innovative sushi rolls, while the restaurant's Italian side offers traditional risottos and pastas with a modern twist. The Japanese offerings usually fare better than the Italian ones, but the thing really worth going to Aqua for is the superb view of the Hong Kong skyline. You might want to just stop in for a drink—the bar stays open until 2 am from Thursday to Saturday. [$] *Average main: HK$380* ✉ *29th and 30th fl., 1 Peking Rd., Tsim Sha Tsui* ☎ *3427–2288* 🌐 *www.aqua.com.hk* [M] *Tsim Sha Tsui* ✣ *3:D5.*

$$ CHINESE 🍴 **Chuan Shao.** This place fires up the grill with skewered items that draw flavor inspiration from Sichuan. The menu is extensive, capping in at more than 100 different choices on any given day (including daily and seasonal specials). Grilled fish is perfect with beer, as are the *tsukune* chicken meatballs. When in season, order grilled oysters, clams, and other seafood items. The folks at Chuan Shao also serve grilled banana and pineapple for dessert. The restaurant is open until late, and there's plenty of beer, so anyone staying at a hotel in the area might just want to keep this place in mind. [$] *Average main: HK$100* ✉ *29–31 Chatham Rd., Tsim Sha Tsui* ☎ *2311–8101* ⏲ *No lunch* [M] *Tsim Sha Tsui* ⊕ *3:F5.*

$$ TAIWANESE 🍴 **Din Tai Fung.** Originally from Taiwan, this global restaurant chain is most famous for its expertly made dumplings. The place is serious about its craft—each dumpling is made from a specified amount of dough and kneaded to a uniform thinness to ensure maximum quality control. The signature steamed *xiao long bao* dumplings arrive piping hot at the table, filled with delectable fatty pork and slurpfuls of flavorful broth. Anyone with a sweet tooth should try the taro-paste dumpling. The excellent food is paired with VIP treatment from the friendly staff, making Din Tai Fung completely worthy of its immense popularity. [$] *Average main: HK$110* ✉ *3rd fl., Silvercord, 30 Canton Rd., Tsim Sha Tsui* ☎ *2730–6928* 🌐 *www.dintaifung.com.hk* [M] *Tsim Sha Tsui* ⊕ *3:E5.*

$$$ CHINESE 🍴 **Dong Lai Shun.** This Chinese restaurant specializes in Beijing and Huaiyang cuisine and is known for its *shuan yang rou* (mutton hot pot). The restaurant offers a host of other great dishes, including traditional Peking duck and the award-winning combination of wok-fried crabmeat, rock lobster, and salted egg yolk served on rice crackers. Appetizers are particularly good—order the smoked eggs and crispy eel. Dong Lai Shun is also famous for its annual hairy crab menu, which is only available in the fall when the shelled delicacy is in season. [$] *Average main: HK$250* ✉ *The Royal Garden, 69 Mody Rd., Tsim Sha Tsui* ☎ *2733–2020* 🌐 *www.rghk.com.hk* ⊕ *3:G5.*

$$$$ MODERN EUROPEAN 🍴 **Felix.** This Philippe Starck–designed, preposterously fashionable scene atop the Peninsula boasts breathtaking floor-to-ceiling views of Hong Kong. The dinner menu is equally stunning, and while rooted in European cooking, includes bright Asian touches as demonstrated by items such as the grilled beef tenderloin with miso powder. The "Felix Experience" menu features some of the chef's most creative dishes and changes on a regular basis. The food here is generally good, but expect it to be quite pricey. Many people come just for cocktails or to try out the most celebrated restroom in Asia—the views across Tsim Sha Tsui are superior to those in the restaurant itself. Note that sleeveless shirts and shorts are not allowed for men. [$] *Average main: HK$480* ✉ *28th fl., The Peninsula Hong Kong, 19–21 Salisbury Rd., Tsim Sha Tsui* ☎ *2696–6778* 🌐 *hongkong.peninsula.com* ✍ *Reservations essential* ⏲ *No lunch* [M] *Tsim Sha Tsui* ⊕ *3:E6.*

$$$ SCANDINAVIAN 🍴 **FINDS.** The name stands for Finland, Iceland, Norway, Denmark, and Sweden, and these Nordic countries are where the restaurant draws its inspiration. Finnish chef Jaakko Sorsa explores the flavors of his home country with dishes such as house-smoked salmon and wild game pâté

The Dim Sum Experience

Dim sum restaurants have always been associated with noise, so don't be dissuaded by the boisterous throngs of locals gathered around large round tables. At one time big metal carts filled with bamboo baskets were pushed around the restaurant by ladies who would shout out the names of the dishes and stamp a mark onto a table's check when it ordered a basket of this or that. This is still the typical dim sum experience outside of China, but in Hong Kong most restaurants require you to order off a form, creating a more sedate and efficient dining experience. Thankfully, many places offer English-translated order forms or menus, although you should ask your waiter about daily specials that might not appear in translation, as those are often some of the most exciting dim sum options. And never forget that most basic principle of Hong Kong ordering: simply point to something you see at a nearby table.

Although dim sum comes in small portions, it's still intended for sharing among several diners. When all is said and done, a group can expect to sample about 10 or 12 dishes, but don't order more than one of any single item. Most dim sum restaurants prepare between 15 and 100 varieties of the more than 2,000 kinds of dim sum in the Cantonese repertoire, daily. These can be dumplings, buns, crepes, cakes, pastries, or rice; they can be filled with beef, shrimp, pork, chicken, bean paste, or vegetables; and they can be bamboo-steamed, panfried, baked, or deep-fried. More esoteric offerings vary vastly from place to place. Abandon any squeamish tendencies and try at least one or two unusual plates, like marinated

chicken's feet or steamed rice rolls filled with pork liver.

You'll be able to find dim sum from before dawn to around 5 or 6 pm, but it's most popular for breakfast (from about 7:30 to 10 am) and lunch (from about 11:30 am to 2:30 pm). Dim sum is served everywhere from local teahouses to high-concept restaurants, but it's often best at casually elegant, blandly decorated midrange spots that cater to Chinese families.

The following is a guide to some of our favorite common dim sum items, but don't let it narrow your mind. It's almost impossible to find a bite of dim sum that's anything less than delicious, and the more unique house specialties can often be the best.

BUNS

■ **Cha siu so:** baked barbecued pork pastry buns; they're less common than the steamed cha siu bao, but arguably even better.

■ **Cha siu bao:** steamed barbecued pork buns are an absolute must. With the combination of soft and chewy textures and sweet and salty tastes, you might forget to remove the paper underneath before eating.

DUMPLINGS

■ **Har gau:** steamed dumplings with a light translucent wrap that conceals shrimp and bamboo shoots.

■ **Siu mai:** steamed pork dumplings are the most common dumplings, and you'll find them everywhere, easily recognizable by their bright yellow wrappers; some are stuffed with shrimp as an additional filling.

MEATS

■ **Ngau yuk yuan:** steamed beef balls, like meatballs, placed on top of thin bean-curd skins and served with vinegar; not the most flavorful option, but a good one for kids or picky eaters.

■ **Pie gwat:** bite-size pieces of succulent pork spare ribs in a black-bean and chili-pepper sauce.

RICE CREATIONS

■ **Har cheong fun:** shrimp-filled rice rolls, whose dough is made in a rice-noodle style; the thick, flat rice rolls are drowned in soy sauce. Other versions include ngau yuk cheong fun (beef filled) and cha siu cheong fun (barbecued pork filled; if available, these are not to be missed).

■ **Ja leung:** similar to cheong fun but filled with a crunchy, deep-fried pastry. The rice-noodle dough is sometimes dotted with chopped scallions. These are served with soy sauce but should also be dunked in sweet sauce and peanut paste. They're delicious but increasingly hard to find.

■ **Ho yip fan:** delicious sticky rice, which is usually cooked with chopped Chinese mushrooms, Chinese preserved sausage, and dried shrimp, and wrapped and steamed in a lotus leaf to keep it moist (don't eat the leaf).

DON'T BE AFRAID OF . . .

■ **Woo tao go:** a glutinous panfried taro cake, sweet enough for dessert but eaten as a savory dish, with delicate undertones that come from preserved Chinese sausage, preserved pork belly, and dried shrimp. Another version of this is *lau bak go*, which is made with turnip instead of taro.

■ **Foong jow:** marinated chicken feet, whose smooth, soft texture is unlike any other. Once you get past the idea that you're sucking the cartilage off a foot, the sensation is wonderful.

■ **Gam cheen to:** cow's stomach served with chunks of daikon and doused in an addictive black-bean sauce with chili.

SWEETS

■ **Dan taht:** tarts with a custard filling, generally served for dessert.

■ **Mong gwor bo deen:** mango pudding that has a consistently glassy texture. The pudding itself is not too sweet and needs to be eaten with condensed milk.

■ **Ma lai go:** This soft and spongy steamed cake is served warm and is popular for its eggy, custardy aroma.

5

served with rowanberry jelly. The menu expands from there to cover other parts of Scandinavia; be sure to try the Danish smørrebrød open-faced sandwiches and the Daim parfait—a crunchy, sticky, layered dessert based on a popular Swedish chocolate bar. Another reason to love FINDS? The restaurant is a firm supporter of eco-conscious eating, and you'll find seafood specials on the menu that have been sustainably sourced. $ *Average main: HK$283* ⊠ *The Luxe Manor, 39 Kimberley Rd., Tsim Sha Tsui* ☎ *2522–9318* ⊕ *www.finds.com.hk* ✛ *3:F4.*

$$ ✕**Gaylord.** This was one of the first Indian restaurants on the Hong
INDIAN   Kong dining scene, and the atmosphere is still intimate and fun, especially on nights when there's live music. The food is packed with authentic spices, and there's an extensive menu for vegetarians. The *chowpatty chaat* is a winning combination of potatoes, chickpeas, and crisp wafers in a spicy dressing, and the chicken tikka masala is almost legendary. Lamb dishes are also done well, especially those in fragrant curry sauce, perfect for scooping up with bits of naan bread, or for spooning over plates of fragrant basmati rice. The restaurant also offers several lunch and dinner menus at excellent value. $ *Average main: HK$130* ⊠ *Ashley Centre, 23–25 Ashley Rd., Tsim Sha Tsui* ☎ *2376–1001* Ⓜ *Tsim Sha Tsui* ✛ *3:E5.*

$$ ✕**Go Koong.** One of the best Korean restaurants in town, Go Koong
KOREAN   covers extensive ground, from raw meats and seafood that are cooked sizzling on the tabletop grills, to kimchi stews and thick pancakes studded with shrimp, squid, and scallions. The complimentary *banchans* (appetizers) are a feast in themselves, with more than 10 different items available every day. Order the smoked duck-breast salad to start, before moving on to more substantial fare such as the tender beef ribs steamed in whole pumpkin. If you still have room at the end of the meal, remember to try the *patbingsoo*—a giant bowl of crunchy shaved ice laced with sweetened red beans and fresh fruit. $ *Average main: HK$200* ⊠ *2nd fl., Toyomall, 94 Granville Rd., Tsim Sha Tsui* ☎ *2311–0901* Ⓜ *East Tsim Sha Tsui* ✛ *3:G4.*

$$ ✕**Hoi King Heen.** If you're looking for stellar Cantonese cuisine, this is
CHINESE   the place for you. The chefs serve a range of modern classics made from the freshest ingredients and influenced by their reverence for natural flavors. There are excellent—and expensive—dishes on the menu like double-boiled bird's nest and braised abalone, but the humbler dishes like smoked vegetarian goose and braised beef brisket with pear really steal the show. Hoi King Heen is a great dinner destination, and the lunchtime dim sum menu is also worth checking out. $ *Average main: HK$200* ⊠ *InterContinental Grand Stanford, 70 Mody Rd., Tsim Sha Tsui* ☎ *2731–2883* ⊕ *www.hongkong.intercontinental.com* Ⓜ *East Tsim Sha Tsui* ✛ *3:H4.*

$$$$ ✕**Hutong.** It's not hard to see why Hutong is one of the hottest tables
CHINESE   in Hong Kong: it has some of the most imaginative food in town. Its beautifully decorated dining room at the top of the dramatic One Peking Road Tower overlooks the entire festival of lights that is the Hong Kong island skyline. Best among the sensational selection of regional Chinese creations are the deboned lamb ribs and the crispy soft-shell crab with dried Sichuan peppers. Subtler dishes include fresh abalone carpaccio

marinated in spring-onion oil, and delicate scallops tossed with pomelo. Hutong also hosts Sunday brunch, which features a limitless supply of northern Chinese specialties and free-flowing bubbly. $ *Average main: HK$368 ⊠ 28th fl., 1 Peking Rd., Tsim Sha Tsui* ☎ *3428–8342* ⊕ *www.aqua.com.hk* ⚲ *Reservations essential* Ⓜ *Tsim Sha Tsui* ⊹ *3:D5.*

$$$$
JAPANESE
✗ **Inakaya.** On the 101st floor of the ICC building, Inakaya flaunts a jaw-dropping, bird's-eye view of the city below, but the interior of the restaurant is equally extravagant—the highlight is the specialized *robatayaki* (the Japanese equivalent to barbecue) room, which has a long counter decorated with baskets of fresh ingredients. Choose your meat or vegetables and the chefs will grill them to order and serve them the traditional way, on long wooden paddles. Because robatayaki is served in bite-sized morsels, prices can add up, but it's a fun and unique experience. If you don't want to splurge on grilled goods, Inakaya also offers other *washoku* (Japanese cuisines) such as sushi and traditional, multicourse *kaiseki* meals. $ *Average main: HK$600 ⊠ 101st fl., International Commerce Centre, 1 Austin Rd. W, Kowloon* ☎ *2972–2666* ⊕ *www.jcgroup.hk* ⊹ *3:D3.*

$$
CHINESE
✗ **Ko Lau Wan Hotpot and Seafood Restaurant.** Anyone seeking an authentic hot-pot experience need look no farther than Ko Lau Wan. Locals flock here for the tender beef and seafood that you cook at your table in a piping-hot pot of broth. The soup selection is quite extensive, but the satay broth and the fish stock with crab are particularly tasty. The owner comes from a fishing village in the New Territories, so there's no wonder the cuttlefish, shrimp balls, sea urchin, amberjack, and abalone are all so tantalizingly fresh. The adventurous should try the geoduck, a giant clam popular among Hong Kongers, which can be eaten raw with soy sauce and wasabi or slightly cooked in soup. $ *Average main: HK$200 ⊠ 1st fl., 21–23 Hillwood Rd., Tsim Sha Tsui* ☎ *3520–3800* ⊗ *No lunch* Ⓜ *Jordan* ⊹ *3:F3.*

$
CHINESE
✗ **Lee Keung Kee.** Bubble-shaped egg waffles are a local specialty in Hong Kong, and Lee Keung Kee offers a delicious version. The waffles here are crisp on the outside but soft and cottony on the inside. $ *Average main: HK$15 ⊠ 178 Nathan Rd., Tsim Sha Tsui* Ⓜ *Tsim Sha Tsui* ⊹ *3:E3.*

$$$$
ITALIAN
✗ **Osteria.** This place flies under the radar, but it does excellent, home-style Italian fare in a sophisticated yet relaxed and inviting environment. The traditional cuisine has won over many homesick Italian expats. The pizzas and pastas are done with respect to classic recipes—the recommended spaghetti mancini is a satisfyingly hearty dish loaded with fresh seafood and a brandy reduction. Starters also hold their own—the beef carpaccio is tender and flavorful, and the other favorite starter, octopus salad, uses dill and olives to bring out its flavors. $ *Average main: HK$350 ⊠ Mezzanine fl., Holiday Inn Golden Mile, 50 Nathan Rd., Tsim Sha Tsui* ☎ *2315–1010* Ⓜ *Tsim Sha Tsui* ⊹ *3:F5.*

$$$$
SEAFOOD
✗ **Oyster & Wine Bar.** Against the romantic backdrop of Hong Kong's twinkling harbor, this is the top spot in town for oyster lovers. More than 20 varieties are flown in daily and displayed around the horseshoe oyster bar, ready for shucking. The staff cheerfully explains the characteristics of the available mollusks and guides you to ones to suit your taste. Also on the menu is an excellent lobster bisque, as well as clams,

mussels, crab, and fish in various preparations. The Dungeness crab cake is another standout, made with sweet and succulently delicious crabmeat. Wine aficionados are also spoiled for choice here, with the extensive wine selection that lines the walls. [$] *Average main: HK$400* ✉ *18th fl., Sheraton Hong Kong Hotel & Towers, 20 Nathan Rd., Tsim Sha Tsui* ☎ *2739–8707* 🕓 *No lunch Mon.–Sat.* [M] *Tsim Sha Tsui* ✥ *3:F6.*

$$$$ ITALIAN 🍴 **Sabatini.** Opened by the acclaimed Sabatini restaurateur brothers, this small corner of Italy with sponge-painted walls and wooden furnishings has a cult following among those who crave authentic Roman cuisine. Linguine Sabatini, the house specialty, is prepared according to an original recipe in a fresh tomato-and-garlic marinara sauce, served with an array of seafood. For dessert, try the famous homemade tiramisu or the refreshing wild-berry pudding. [$] *Average main: HK$450* ✉ *3rd fl., The Royal Garden, 69 Mody Rd., Tsim Sha Tsui* ☎ *2733–2000* 🌐 *www.rghk.com.hk* ✍ *Reservations essential* [M] *East Tsim Sha Tsui* ✥ *3:G5.*

$$ CHINESE 🍴 **Spring Deer.** The pastel blue and green interior make this Peking duck specialist look like something from 1950s Beijing. The crowd, too, is old-school, which only adds to the experience. You'll see locals with noodle dishes, stir-fried wok meat dishes, and so forth, but the Peking duck is the showstopper—it might be the best in town. Even the peanuts for snacking, which are boiled to a delectable softness, go above and beyond the call of duty. This place is extremely popular, so it's best to book your table at least a week in advance. [$] *Average main: HK$170* ✉ *42 Mody Rd., 1st fl., Tsim Sha Tsui* ☎ *2366–4012, 2366–5839* ✍ *Reservations essential* [M] *Tsim Sha Tsui* ✥ *3:F5.*

$$$$ FRENCH 🍴 **St. George.** Hullett House—the former marine police headquarters turned into a boutique hotel—was designed with maxed-out luxury in mind, so it's to be expected that its signature fine-dining French restaurant would be a no-expenses-spared venture. The restaurant is decked out in colonial era–inspired duds, complete with chandeliers and comfy leather sofas. But while the decor pays homage to days gone by, the cuisine is modern, creative, and totally inspired. Guests can look forward to dishes such as tomatoes served eight ways with black garlic, basil, and olive-oil "caviar." Two tasting menus (four or six courses) are available for those who want the full St. George experience. [$] *Average main: HK$600* ✉ *Hullett House, 2A Canton Rd., Tsim Sha Tsui* ☎ *3988–0220* 🌐 *www.hulletthouse.com* ✍ *Reservations essential* 🕓 *Closed Sun.* [M] *Tsim Sha Tsui* ✥ *3:E6.*

$$$$ STEAKHOUSE 🍴 **The Steak House.** This restaurant, with its lively, informal atmosphere and gleaming harbor views, serves the best steak in the city. You can choose from among 10 steak knives and more than a dozen mustards and rock salts—gimmicky, but fun—but the main event is the perfectly cooked, char-grilled meats. The selection is extensive, including Wagyu from Japan, herb-crusted tenderloin from Argentina, the restaurant's own dry-aged beef, and other delicious cuts flown in from the United States—and all of it is lovingly seared on the grill. There isn't a jacket-and-tie policy, but note that shorts, sleeveless shirts, and open shoes are not allowed for gentlemen. [$] *Average main: HK$630* ✉ *InterContinental Hong Kong, 18 Salisbury Rd., Tsim Sha Tsui* ☎ *2313–2323*

hongkong-ic.intercontinental.com ☜ *Reservations essential* ⊘ *No lunch weekends* Ⓜ *Tsim Sha Tsui* ✛ *3:F6.*

$ ✕ **Sun Kee.** This little café might not be the easiest of places to locate,
ASIAN being tucked away in an old complex filled mainly with secondhand camera and wristwatch stores, but it has a cult following, with photos of local celebrity patrons adorning almost every inch of wall space. Most customers come for one thing—the instant noodles blanketed in a rich and creamy melted cheese sauce. These coiled noodles go best with tender slices of grilled pork-neck meat on top of the sauce. It's not exactly healthy eating, but it's definitely satisfying. Ⓢ *Average main: HK$42* ✉ *Champagne Court, 16–20 Kimberley Rd., Tsim Sha Tsui* ☎ *2722–4555* ▭ *No credit cards* Ⓜ *Tsim Sha Tsui* ✛ *3:F4.*

$$ ✕ **Tai Ping Koon.** This is one of the oldest restaurants in Hong Kong,
CHINESE and also one of the first places to serve "soy sauce" Hong Kong–style western cuisine. The decor, staff, and menu seem to have remained unchanged since day one, adding to the nostalgic charm of the place. Steaks are served with dramatic effect on sizzling iron plates and brought to the table by waiters clad in waistcoats. Other menu highlights include the baked Portuguese chicken, the near-perfect stir-fried rice noodles with beef (a classic Hong Kong dish), chicken wings doused in "Swiss sauce" (which has no real Swiss associations), and the enormous baked soufflé that takes 20 minutes to prepare and at least three people to devour. Ⓢ *Average main: HK$100* ✉ *40 Granville Rd., Tsim Sha Tsui* ☎ *2721–3559* *taipingkoon.com* Ⓜ *Tsim Sha Tsui* ✛ *3:F4.*

$$$$ ✕ **Tosca.** Stuck high up the clouds on the 102nd floor of the towering
ITALIAN International Commerce Center, the views at Tosca can be hit-or-miss, depending on how clear the skies are on the day you visit. Fortunately, you'll be preoccupied with the stunning interiors (complete with pretty fountains) and incredible culinary creations. The menu boasts creative Italian fare like sea tiramisu with red-prawn carpaccio, roasted scallops, caviar, and parsley pasta. There's also a degustation menu for those who want a taste of Tosca's finest. Note that sandals, sleeveless shirts, and shorts are not allowed for men. Ⓢ *Average main: HK$450* ✉ *102nd fl., International Commerce Center, 1 Austin Rd. W, Kowloon* ☎ *2263–2270* *www.ritzcarlton.com* Ⓜ *Kowloon* ✛ *3:A4.*

$$$$ ✕ **Whisk.** At the Mira Hotel's flagship restaurant, seasonal ingredients
EUROPEAN are turned into creative European dishes designed to impress. The famous suckling pig arrives with a layer of melt-in-your-mouth meat covered in a sheet of deliciously crispy skin—this is one dish worth trying. Be sure to save room for the flaky apple tart. Aside from à la carte options, the restaurant offers a 6- to 10-course degustation menu inspired by global flavors and ingredients. Another bonus is the extensive wine list, which features some of the world's finest vintages at incredibly reasonable prices. Ⓢ *Average main: HK$600* ✉ *5th fl., The Mira Hotel, 118 Nathan Rd., Tsim Sha Tsui* ☎ *2315–5999* *www. themirahotel.com* ⊘ *Closed Mon. No dinner Sun.* Ⓜ *Tsim Sha Tsui* ✛ *3:E4.*

$$$$ ✕ **Yan Toh Heen.** This Cantonese restaurant in the InterContinental Hong
CHINESE Kong sets formal elegance against expansive harbor views, and the food is at the top of its class. Exquisite is hardly the word for the decor, which

CLOSE UP

A Spot of Tea

Legend has it that the first cup dates from 2737 BC, when *Camellia sinensis* leaves fell into water being boiled for Emperor Shenong. He loved the result, tea was born, and so were many traditions.

Historically, when a girl accepted a marriage proposal she drank tea, a gesture symbolizing fidelity (tea plants die if uprooted). Betrothal gifts were known as "tea gifts," engagements as "accepting tea," and marriages as "eating tea." Traditionally the bride and groom kneel before their parents, offering cups of tea in thanks.

Serving tea is a sign of respect. Young people proffer it to their parents or grandparents; subordinates do the same for their bosses. Pouring tea also signifies submission, so it's a way to say you're sorry. When you're served tea, show your thanks by tapping the table with your index and middle fingers.

Even modern medicine acknowledges that tea's powerful antioxidants reduce the risk of cancer and heart disease. It's also thought to be such a good source of fluoride that Mao Zedong eschewed toothpaste for a green-tea rinse.

TEA TYPES

Pu'er tea, which is known here as *Bo Lei*, is the beverage of choice at dim sum places. In fact, another way to say dim sum is *yum cha*, meaning "drink tea."

Afternoon tea is another local fixation—neighborhood joints with Formica tables, grumpy waiters, and often, menus written only Chinese. Most people go for *nai cha* made with evaporated milk. A really good cup is smooth, sweet, and hung with

drops of fat. An even richer version, *cha chow*, is made with condensed milk. If *yuen yueng* (yin yang, half milk tea and half instant coffee) sounds a bit much, *ling-mun cha* (lemon tea) is also on hand. Don't forget to order peanut-buttered toast or a pineapple bun, often served with a thick slab of butter sandwiched in the middle.

The bubble (or *boba*) tea craze may have died down a bit, but you'll still find plenty street stalls selling the popular Taiwanese drink. These cold brews contain pearly balls of tapioca or coconut jelly. There's also been a return to traditional teas with chains such as Healthworks, which serves healthy blends in MTR stations all over town.

FLAGSTAFF HOUSE MUSEUM OF TEA WARE

All that's good about British colonial architecture is exemplified in the simple white facade, wooden monsoon shutters, and colonnaded verandas of the Flagstaff House Museum of Tea Ware. More than 600 pieces of delicate antique tea ware from the Tang (618–907) through the Qing (1644–1911) dynasties fill rooms that once housed the commander of the British forces.

The best place to put your tea theory into practice is at the **LockCha Tea House** (☎ 2801–7177) in the K.S. Lo Gallery annex of Flagstaff House. It is half shop, half teahouse, so you can sample brews before you buy. ✉ *Hong Kong Park, 10 Cotton Tree Dr., Central* ☎ *2801–7177* ⊕ *www.lockcha.com* ⊙ *Weekdays 10–8, weekends 10–9* Ⓜ *Admiralty MTR, Exit C1.*

Moon cakes are a popular dessert at eateries all over Hong Kong.

mixes contemporary with the traditional and encompasses gorgeous details like jade-colored place settings. Dim sum is done well here during lunch, and if you're looking for more extravagant dishes, there's a vast selection of seafood that includes seasonal crab, poached lobster, and sea whelk. Some dishes, like Peking duck, need to be ordered at least a day ahead. Note that sleeveless shirts, shorts, and sandals are not allowed for men. $ *Average main: HK$400* ⊠ *InterContinental Hong Kong, 18 Salisbury Rd., Tsim Sha Tsui* ☎ *2313–2323* ⊕ *hongkong-ic. intercontinental.com* ⚓ *Reservations essential* Ⓜ *Tsim Sha Tsui* ✛ *3:F6.*

YAU MA TEI, MONG KOK, AND NORTHERN KOWLOON

Yau Ma Tei and Mong Kok have some of the best cheap eats in town, especially the area of Yau Ma Tei around Jordan Road, which is known as Jordan. Jordan has a large Nepalese population in this neighborhood, so look out for excellent authentic Nepalese and Indian food.

These areas may not seem like the most tourist-friendly of places (non-English menus, impatient waiters, etc.) , but you're more likely to score an interesting meal here than anywhere else.

YAU MA TEI

Yau Ma Tei's famed Temple Street is a good place to start. The street hides dai pai dongs and wallet-friendly noodle shops amid the many DVD shops and souvenir stores.

$ ✕ **Dimdimsum Dimsum Specialty Store.** Hidden away near the old Jordan
CHINESE pier, this little sit-down restaurant has excellent dim sum without the insane queues that plague its more famous competitors. That's not to

say that it doesn't get packed during mealtimes; thankfully, the venue stays open until 1 am, so you can sneak in for a late-night dinner when the crowds have dissipated. While it does all the classics, it's the newfangled house creations that are really worth trying. We love the crispy shrimp rice-flour rolls drizzled with soy sauce. The chefs also do black-truffle crab dumplings and golden pastries filled with a combination of apples and cha siu pork. [$] *Average main: HK$20* ✉ *23 Man Ying St., Jordan, Yau Ma Tei* ☎ *2771–7766* 🌐 *www.dimdimsum.hk* 💳 *No credit cards* ✥ *3:D2.*

$ CHINESE 🍴 **Hing Kee Restaurant.** Located on a boisterous stretch of Temple Street, this crowded, open-air eatery is the perfect spot to soak in the local atmosphere. The food isn't amazing, but it's cheap and offers a wide range of choices. Stick to the wok-tossed stir-fries laced with pungent black-bean sauce or spicy chili salt. Hing Kee is also known for its claypot dishes, which are especially comforting during the colder winter months. [$] *Average main: HK$68* ✉ *14–21 Temple St., Yau Ma Tei* ☎ *2384–3647* 💳 *No credit cards* 🕒 *No lunch* [M] *Yau Ma Tei* ✥ *3:E1.*

$ NEPALESE 🍴 **Manakamana Restaurant.** For a dose of Indian and Nepalese food, head to Manakamana. The restaurant serves the essentials, like brightly colored curries and meat-filled steamed *momo* dumplings, as well as plenty of vegetarian options. There's also a decent selection of South Asian beers. Nepalese music completes the atmosphere. [$] *Average main: HK$75* ✉ *165 Temple St., Jordon, Yau Ma Tei* ☎ *2385–2070* 💳 *No credit cards* [M] *Jordan* ✥ *3:E2.*

$ CHINESE 🍴 **Mido Café.** This old-school *cha chaan teng* (local café) has plenty of charm, since the decor hasn't changed much since the '60s. Although prices have gone up somewhat over time, the food still draws plenty of loyal fans. Try the famous baked-pork-chop rice or enjoy a slice of crispy French toast with a cup of milk tea. [$] *Average main: HK$45* ✉ *63 Temple St., Yau Ma Tei* ☎ *2384–6402* 💳 *No credit cards* [M] *Yau Ma Tei* ✥ *3:E1.*

$ CHINESE 🍴 **Tan Ngan Lo.** Chinese herbal teas are served by the bowlful at this Temple Street institution. Some of the bittersweet beverages may not be to everyone's taste, but most of them—such as the five-flower tea—are said to have beneficial medicinal properties and are especially refreshing on a hot day. [$] *Average main: HK$10* ✉ *151 Temple St., Jordan, Yau Ma Tei* ☎ *2384–3744* 💳 *No credit cards* [M] *Jordan* ✥ *3:E2.*

$ CHINESE Fodor's Choice ★ 🍴 **Yau Yuan Xiao Jui.** This tiny storefront may look like any other noodle joint, but its humble appearance belies its culinary prowess. The restaurant serves authentic Shaanxi snacks, which can be best described as some of the heartiest and delicious chow that China has to offer. The handmade dumplings are amazing, especially if they're fattened up with lamb and scallion oil. Then there's the signature *biang biang mien*, which are extremely long and wide al dente noodle sheets designed to be anointed with chili oil, scallions, and marinated spareribs. Definitely check this place out. [$] *Average main: HK$38* ✉ *Keybond Commercial Building, 38 Ferry St., entrance on Saigon St., Jordan* ☎ *5300–2682* 💳 *No credit cards* [M] *Jordan* ✥ *3:D2.*

$ CHINESE 🍴 **Yee Shun Milk Company.** Expect to wait in line if you want to try the famed milk desserts from Yee Shun Milk Company. The velvety-smooth, double-boiled milk pudding is rich and comforting. The ginger-flavored milk pudding has a nice spicy kick, making it the perfect stomach warmer—a must-try if you're visiting Hong Kong in the wintertime. Chocolate and coffee puddings are also available. $ *Average main: HK$35* ⊠ *63 Pilkem St., Jordan* ☎ *2730–2799* ⚏ *No credit cards* ✛ *3:E3.*

MONG KOK

For the best street snacks in town, look no further than Mong Kok, where you'll find curry fish balls, among other snacks. The Tung Choi Street vicinity is especially rich in eateries of this type, selling everything from regional specialties like spicy Chongqing noodles to curry fish balls on bamboo skewers and fragrant egg waffles.

$ ✕ **Delicious Food.** The street stalls of Hong Kong are filled with interest-
CHINESE ing snacks of all shapes and sorts. The intrepid should trek over to Delicious Food for the infamous stinky tofu. $ *Average main: HK$10* ⊠ *30 Nullah Rd., Prince Edward* ☎ *2142–7468* ⚏ *No credit cards* Ⓜ *Prince Edward* ✛ *3:E1.*

$ ✕ **Fei Jie Snacks Stall.** Dundas Street in Mong Kok is filled with street
CHINESE vendors. The Fei Jie Snacks Stall is one of the best, with its dizzying selection of skewered choices ranging from chewy squid to duck gizzard to pig intestine (best eaten with a squirt of mustard). $ *Average main: HK$10* ⊠ *55 Dundas St., Mong Kok* ⚏ *No credit cards* Ⓜ *Mong Kok* ✛ *3:E1.*

$ ✕ **Islam Food.** This halal restaurant may not be the prettiest restaurant
CHINESE you've ever seen, and you should expect to wait a while for a table (lines get extremely crazy during peak meal hours), but we promise that the panfried beef patties (translated as "veal goulash" on the menu) here are well worth the pilgrimage. The browned pastry packets arrive at the table piping hot and bursting with tender minced beef—good luck trying to stop at just one. Other excellent dishes include the delicious lamb brisket curry, panfried mutton dumplings, and the hot-and-sour soup. $ *Average main: HK$55* ⊠ *1 Lung Kong Rd., Kowloon City* ☎ *2382–2822, 2382–8928* ⊕ *www.islamfood.com.hk* ⚏ *No credit cards* ✛ *3:H1.*

$ ✕ **Lung Jie Thai Restaurant.** Dubbed Little Thailand, Kowloon City is
THAI home to some of the best Thai restaurants in town. Lung Jie is one of the more popular choices, and for good reason—the food is excellent and the flavors are authentic. The extensive menu covers all the basics, from stir-fried pad thai noodles to hot-and-sour tom yum soup. For something a little more adventurous, try the raw prawns, which are topped with garlic and chilies and served with a deliciously spicy dipping sauce on the side. $ *Average main: HK$90* ⊠ *18 Nam Kok Rd., Kowloon City* ☎ *2382–1348* ⚏ *No credit cards* ✛ *3:H1.*

$ ✕ **100 Bites.** The miniature cakes here sit like jewels in the pastry case. A
BAKERY lot of the desserts feature Asian ingredients such as green tea and adzuki beans. Japanese-style soufflé pancakes are another house specialty. These fluffy stacks are served with toppings such as fresh strawberries, chocolate shavings, and whipped cream. Sweets aside, 100 Bites also offers pasta-based lunch sets and a tasting menu for dinner. $ *Average*

main: HK$35 ✉ *10th fl., Langham Place Mall, 8 Argyle St., Mong Kok*
☎ *2191–6638* ✛ *3:D1.*

$ × **Pâtisserie Tony Wong.** Opened by one of Hong Kong's best-known
BAKERY pastry chefs, this takeaway bakery offers a gorgeous collection of classic and original French-style gâteaux. The most famous creation here
is the Rose—an elaborate layer cake decorated with edible chocolate
petals. If you don't want to splurge on this signature creation (or if it
sells out by the time you arrive), consider equally tasty treats like the
green-tea opera, raspberry napoleon, or lemon tart. ⓢ *Average main:*
HK$42 ✉ *74 Fuk Lo Tsun Rd., Kowloon City* ☎ *2382–6639* ⊕ *www.*
patisserietonywong.com ✛ *3:H1.*

$ × **Si Sun.** One of the pioneers of American fast-food-style dining in
AMERICAN Hong Kong, Si Sun still looks and feels like an eatery from the swinging '60s. The plastic fixtures have stayed the same over the past few
decades, and the menu doesn't seem to have changed much either. Burgers are geared toward local tastes, and the freshly grilled beef patties
are sandwiched between two soft buns and topped with ketchup and
mayo. Add cheese or a fried egg and your meal will still be a steal. Si
Sun also offers pork and fish fillet burgers, as well as a few rice and
noodles dishes. ⓢ *Average main: HK$23* ✉ *1A Whampoa St., Hung*
Hom, Kowloon City ☎ *2362–1279* ⚐ *Reservations not accepted* ⊟ *No*
credit cards Ⓜ *Hung Hom* ✛ *3:H3.*

$ × **Tim Ho Wan.** This award-winning eatery serves some of the city's best
CHINESE dim sum. Opened by a former Four Seasons Hotel chef, this humble
Fodor's Choice spot makes all of its shrimp dumplings, rice rolls, and baked cha siu
★ buns fresh to order. It's top-quality food at dirt-cheap prices. It's as
popular as ever, so go in midafternoon if you want to beat the crowds.
ⓢ *Average main: HK$30* ✉ *9–11 Fuk Wing St., Sham Shui Po, Mong*
Kok ☎ *2788–1226* ⊟ *No credit cards* Ⓜ *Sham Shui Po* ✛ *3:G1.*

$ × **Tong Pak Fu.** For a perfect warm-weather treat, drop by Tong Pak Fu
CHINESE for the Taiwanese-style shaved snow ice. Blocks of flavored ice (chocolate, milk, fruit, and many others) are put into a special machine that
shaves them into thin, ribbonlike sheets that fold up into a mountainous
heap. The texture is richer and denser than regular shaved ice. This store
also offers other Chinese desserts, including red-bean soup and sesame-
filled dumplings. ⓢ *Average main: HK$25* ✉ *99 Hak Po St., Mong Kok*
☎ *2659–2529* ⊟ *No credit cards* Ⓜ *Mong Kok* ✛ *3:E1.*

$ × **Tso Choi Koon.** If you have a delicate constitution, take a pass on this
CHINESE home-style Cantonese restaurant. Tso Choi (which literally translates
as "rough dishes") is not everyone's cup of tea. Offal lovers, however,
might be interested in trying some of the house favorites: fried pig tripe,
fried pig brain (served as an omelet), double-boiled pig brain—you get
the idea. The older Hong Kong generation still likes this stuff; younger
folks may demur. The wary can opt for creamy congee, fried chicken,
or simple stir-fries. ⓢ *Average main: HK$50* ✉ *17A Nga Tsin Wai Rd.,*
Kowloon City ☎ *2383–7170* ⊟ *No credit cards* Ⓜ *Mong Kok* ✛ *3:H1.*

KOWLOON BAY

$ × **Siu Shun Village Cuisine.** This is one of the few restaurants in town
CHINESE specializing in cuisine from Shunde, an area in the Pearl River Delta. A
collection of tanks at the front of the restaurant display various types of

freshwater fish, which can be ordered steamed, fried, baked, or sautéed. Steamed fish in broth is one of the best ways to enjoy the selection. Sautéed fresh milk is one of Shunde's most renowned dishes—at Siu Shun, it's made with fresh soy milk, egg whites, fresh prawns, and *conpoy* (dried scallops). Don't skip dessert: the double-boiled sweetened milk is reminiscent of a rich, custardy pudding and is a perfectly comforting closure. [$] *Average main: HK$88* ✉ *7th fl., 38 Wang Chiu Rd., Kowloon Bay* ☎ *2798–9738* 🌐 *www.siushun.com* [M] *Kowloon Bay* ✣ *3:H1.*

THE NEW TERRITORIES

Sai Kung in the New Territories is worth a visit, if only for a meal. The many restaurants lining the main street and the giant fish tanks with the dizzying selection of fresh fish, crabs, prawns, clams, and oysters are a sight to behold. Point to your catch of choice and have the kitchen cook it up in any way your stomach desires (stir-fried with spicy salt is the no-fail way to go).

5

$$ SRI LANKAN

🍴 **AJ's Sri Lankan Cuisine.** Sai Kung may be best known for its local seafood joints, but we'll happily shine a light on the city's only Sri Lankan restaurant. Housed in a quaint cottage, AJ's rolls out regional delicacies from the South Asian island country—if you haven't tried it before, Sri Lankan cuisine shares similarities with its neighboring countries, though there are some distinct differences in the use of spices and cooking techniques. Definitely order the *moju*—fried eggplant with onions and chilies. We're also fans of any string hopper (shredded, steamed rice-flour dough) dish that's tossed in a wok with diced meats and spices. [$] *Average main: HK$160* ✉ *14 Sai Kung Hoi Pong St., Sai Kung, New Territories* ☎ *2792–2555* 🌐 *www.aj.srilankan.hk* 🕓 *No lunch weekdays* ✣ *3:F1.*

$ CHINESE

🍴 **Honeymoon Dessert.** Though it's expanded across Asia, Honeymoon Dessert's first-ever store in Sai Kung still draws droves of loyal and new fans alike. The store sells homemade traditional Chinese desserts such as black-sesame sweet soup and the refreshing mango-pomelo sweet soup. It also does newfangled items, including durian pancakes and glutinous rice dumplings dusted with desiccated coconut and filled with fresh mango. In the summer, don't miss out on the wide selection of cooling grass jelly creations. [$] *Average main: HK$35* ✉ *9–10 ABC Po Tung Rd., Sai Kung, New Territories* ☎ *2791–7387* 🌐 *www.honeymoon-dessert.com* 💳 *No credit cards* [M] *Hang Hau* ✣ *3:F1.*

$$ INTERNATIONAL FAMILY

🍴 **Jaspa's.** The food at Jaspa's is delicious and filling, perfect after a day walking in the hills or enjoying the beach. The international menu is wide-ranging enough to satisfy all tastes. The chicken and Peking duck fajitas arrive on your table sizzling hot; grilled snapper with Asian herbs and Parmesan-crusted rack of lamb are also delicious. Enjoy your meal indoors or opt for a table on the alfresco terrace. [$] *Average main: HK$190* ✉ *13 Sha Tsui Path, Sai Kung, New Territories* ☎ *2792–6388* 🌐 *www.casteloconcepts.com* [M] *Hang Hau* ✣ *3:F1.*

$$ SEAFOOD

🍴 **Loaf On.** Off Sai Kung's main drag, this hidden gem stands out as one of the finer seafood joints for those in the know. Unlike its big and boisterous competitors, this tiny store has no flashy fish tanks outside and the number of seats is extremely limited, so it's best to book in advance. The food, however, is a cut above the rest. Try the fish soup—a milky-white broth with a hint of sweetness. There's also the famous deep-fried abalone dusted in chili and salt. Aside from seafood, Loaf On also serves an amazing deep-fried tofu dish that's crisp and golden on the outside and silken, soft, and supple in the center. $ *Average main: HK$200* ⊠ *49 See Cheung St., Sai Kung, New Territories* ☎ *2792–9966* ⌂ *Reservations essential* Ⓜ *Hang Hau* ✛ *3:F1.*

$$$ ✕ **Sha Tin 18.** If you're exploring the Sha Tin neighborhood, consider
CHINESE   visiting Sha Tin 18 for a pan-Chinese feast. The restaurant is equipped with several open kitchens, each with its own culinary specialty. Northern Chinese dishes are best, and you'll find a range of homespun noodles and dumplings, but the traditional Peking duck, which is roasted in-house and served as three separate courses, is also excellent. If you're dropping by for lunch, the extensive dim sum menu should keep you well sated. Save room for dessert, though, because the selection—which includes candied pomelo crème brûlée and pink peppercorn ice cream—is definitely more innovative than your average Chinese eatery. $ *Average main: HK$258* ⊠ *Hyatt Regency Hong Kong, 18 Chak Cheung St., Sha Tin, New Territories* ☎ *3723–1234* ⊕ *www.hongkong.shatin.hyatt.com* Ⓜ *University* ✛ *3:F1.*

$$$ ✕ **Tung Kee Seafood Restaurant.** Lobsters, clams, abalone, crabs, prawns,
SEAFOOD   fish, and everything else from the deep blue sea is here for the tasting on Sai Kung's picturesque harbor. Crustaceans and fish are quickly cooked by steaming and wok frying, but are first presented whole, leaving no doubt as to the freshness of your food. A quick look inside the tank is like a lesson in marine biology. Pick your favorites, and leave the rest to the chef. $ *Average main: HK$300* ⊠ *96–102 Man Nin St., Sai Kung, New Territories* ☎ *2792–7453* ⊕ *www.tungkee.com.hk* Ⓜ *Hang Hau* ✛ *3:F1.*

HONG KONG DINING AND LODGING ATLAS

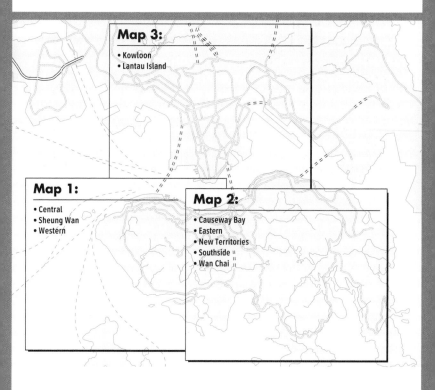

Map 3:
- Kowloon
- Lantau Island

Map 1:
- Central
- Sheung Wan
- Western

Map 2:
- Causeway Bay
- Eastern
- New Territories
- Southside
- Wan Chai

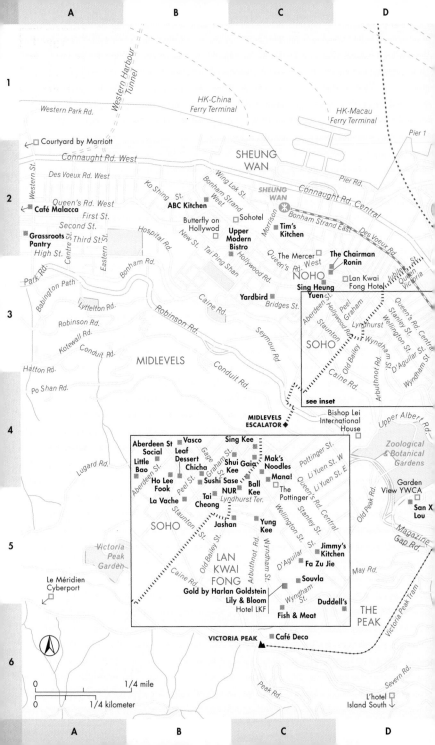

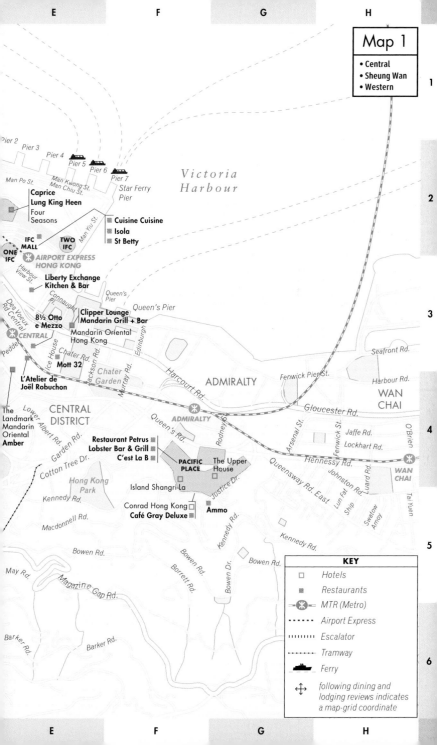

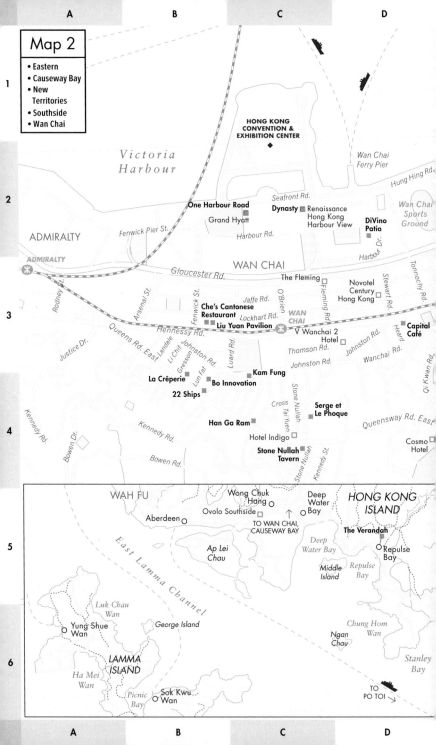

Map 2

- Eastern
- Causeway Bay
- New Territories
- Southside
- Wan Chai

A   B   C   D

1

Victoria Harbour

HONG KONG CONVENTION & EXHIBITION CENTER

Wan Chai Ferry Pier

Hung Hing Rd.

2

ADMIRALTY

ADMIRALTY

Fenwick Pier St.

Seafront Rd.

One Harbour Road
Grand Hyatt

Dynasty ■ Renaissance Hong Kong Harbour View

DiVino Patio

Wan Chai Sports Ground

Harbour Rd.

Harbour Dr.

WAN CHAI

Gloucester Rd.

The Fleming

Novotel Century Hong Kong

Stewart Rd.

Tonnochy Rd.

3

Queens Rd. East

Justice Dr.

Arsenal St.

Fenwick St.

Jaffe Rd.

Che's Cantonese Restaurant

Liu Yuan Pavilion

Lockhart Rd.

Hennessy Rd.

WAN CHAI

V Wanchai 2 Hotel

Thomson Rd.

O'Brien

Fleming Rd.

Johnston Rd.

Johnston Rd.

Wanchai Rd.

Capital Café

Heard St.

IQ Kwan Rd.

4

Kennedy Rd.

Bowen Dr.

Li Chit

Johnston Rd.

Gresson

Lun Fat

Landale

La Crêperie

22 Ships

Bo Innovation

Kam Fung

Han Ga Ram

Hotel Indigo

Stone Nullah Tavern

Cross Tai Yuen

Stone Nullah

Kennedy St.

Stone Nullah St.

Serge et Le Phoque

Queensway Rd. East

Cosmo Hotel

Bowen Rd.

5

WAH FU

Aberdeen ○

Wong Chuk Hang ○

Ovolo Southside □

TO WAN CHAI, CAUSEWAY BAY ↑

Deep Water Bay

○

HONG KONG ISLAND

East Lamma Channel

Ap Lei Chau

Deep Water Bay

Middle Island

Repulse Bay

The Verandah
○ Repulse Bay

Chung Hom Wan

6

Luk Chau Wan

Yung Shue Wan ○

George Island

LAMMA ISLAND

Ha Mei Wan

Picnic Bay

Sok Kwu Wan ○

Ngan Chau

Stanley Bay

TO PO TOI →

A   B   C   D

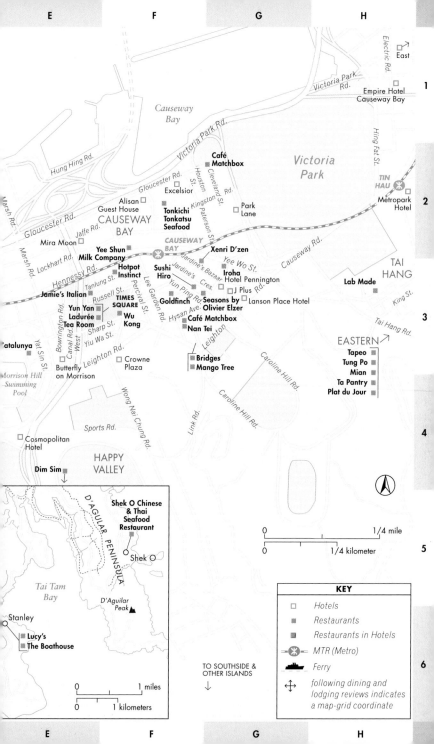

E **F** **G** **H**

→ East
Electric Rd.

1

Victoria Park Rd.

Empire Hotel
Causeway Bay

*Causeway
Bay*

Hung Hing Rd.

*Victoria
Park*

Hing Fat St.

Café
Matchbox

Gloucester Rd.

Houston St.

Cleveland St.

Kingston St.

**TIN
HAU** ⊗

2

Excelsior

Marsh Rd.

Alisan
Guest House

Gloucester Rd.

**CAUSEWAY
BAY**

Jaffe Rd.

Tonkichi
Tonkatsu
Seafood

Paterson St.

Park
Lane

Metropark
Hotel

Mira Moon

Lockhart Rd.

Yee Shun
Milk Company

Xenri D'zen

Yee Wo St.

Causeway Rd.

**TAI
HANG**

Hennessy Rd.

Marsh Rd.

⊗ *CAUSEWAY
BAY*

Jardine's Bazaar

Jardine's Cres.

Iroha

Hotel Pennington

King St.

Lab Made

Hotpot
Instinct

Sushi
Hiro

Yun Ping Rd.

J Plus
Rd.

Tai Hang Rd.

Jamie's Italian

Tanlung St.

Russell St.

Goldfinch

Hysan Ave.

Seasons by
Olivier Elzer

Lanson Place Hotel

3

Yun Yan
Ladurée
Tea Room

**TIMES
SQUARE**

Percival St.

Wu
Kong

Café Matchbox

Leighton Rd.

Nan Tei

EASTERN ↗

Bowrington Rd.

Sharp St.

Canal Rd. West

Yiu Wa St.

Catalunya

Yat Sin St.

Leighton Rd.

Bridges
Mango Tree

Caroline Hill Rd.

Tapeo
Tung Po
Mian
Ta Pantry
Plat du Jour

Morrison Hill
Swimming
Pool

Butterfly
on Morrison

Crowne
Plaza

Link Rd.

Caroline Hill Rd.

4

Wong Nai Chung Rd.

Sports Rd.

Cosmopolitan
Hotel

**HAPPY
VALLEY**

Dim Sim ↓

⬥

D'AGUILAR PENINSULA

Shek O Chinese
& Thai
Seafood
Restaurant

Shek O

*Tai Tam
Bay*

D'Aguilar
Peak ▲

Stanley

Lucy's
The Boathouse

0 _____ 1 miles
0 _____ 1 kilometers

0 _____ 1/4 mile
0 _____ 1/4 kilometer

5

TO SOUTHSIDE &
OTHER ISLANDS
↓

KEY	
☐	*Hotels*
■	*Restaurants*
■	*Restaurants in Hotels*
⊗	*MTR (Metro)*
⛴	*Ferry*
⬌	*following dining and lodging reviews indicates a map-grid coordinate*

6

E **F** **G** **H**

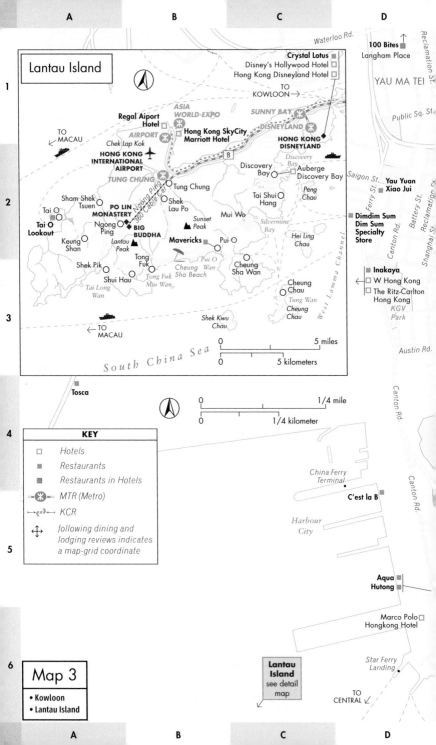

Lantau Island

1
- Crystal Lotus ■
- Disney's Hollywood Hotel □
- Hong Kong Disneyland Hotel □

100 Bites ■
Langham Place

Waterloo Rd.
Reclamation St.

YAU MA TEI

Public Sq. St.

ASIA WORLD-EXPO

TO KOWLOON →

SUNNY BAY ✸

Regal Aiport Hotel □
✸
AIRPORT
✸
Hong Kong SkyCity Marriott Hotel □

DISNEYLAND ✸

HONG KONG DISNEYLAND ◆

TO MACAU ←

Chek Lap Kok

HONG KONG INTERNATIONAL AIRPORT ✈

Discovery Bay
Auberge Discovery Bay □

Discovery Bay

Saigon St.
Yau Yuan ■
Xiao Jui ■

Ferry St.

Battery St.
Reclamation St.
Shanghai St.

TUNG CHUNG ✸

Tung Chung

8

Shek Lau Po

2
Sham Shek
Tsuen

Tai ○
○

Tai O Lookout ■

PO LIN MONASTERY
Ngong Ping
◆ BIG BUDDHA
Lantau Peak ▲

Keung Shan

Tai Shui Hang ○

Peng Chau

Mui Wo

Silvermine Bay

Hei Ling Chau

Canton Rd.

Dimdim Sum Dim Sum Specialty Store ■

Ngong Ping 360 Cable Car

Sunset Peak ▲

Mavericks ■
Pui O ○

Inakaya ■
□ W Hong Kong
□ The Ritz-Carlton Hong Kong

Shek Pik

Tong Fuk

Cheung Sha Wan ○

Cheung Wan
Pui O
Cheung Sha Beach

KGV Park

Shui Hau ○

Tong Fuk
Tong Fuk Miu Wan

Cheung Chau

Austin Rd.

Tai Long Wan

Cheung Chau
Tung Wan

West Lamma Channel

3
TO MACAU ←

Shek Kwu Chau

South China Sea

0 _____ 5 miles
0 _____ 5 kilometers

Tosca ■

0 _____ 1/4 mile
0 _____ 1/4 kilometer

Canton Rd.

KEY

4
□	Hotels
■	Restaurants
■	Restaurants in Hotels
✸	MTR (Metro)
KCR	KCR
↔	following dining and lodging reviews indicates a map-grid coordinate

China Ferry Terminal •

C'est la B ■

Harbour City

Canton Rd.

5

Aqua ■
Hutong ■

Marco Polo □
Hongkong Hotel

Star Ferry Landing •

6
Map 3
- Kowloon
- Lantau Island

Lantau Island
see detail map

TO CENTRAL ↙

A   B   C   D

Dining

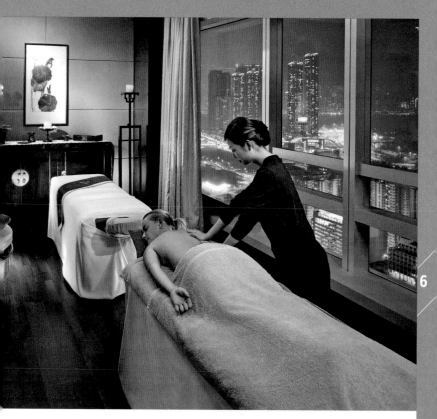

6

WHERE TO STAY

Updated by
Kate Springer

Whether you're a business traveler or a casual tourist, you'll inevitably be caught up with the manic pace of life in Hong Kong. Luckily, hotels are constantly increasing their efforts to provide guests with a restful haven, often bundling spectacular views of the famous skyline and harbor with chic luxury, snazzy amenities, and soothing ambience.

From budget guesthouses to gleaming towers, you're sure to find a style and site to fit your needs. Prices tend to reflect quality of service and amenities as well as location, so it's worth the effort to examine neighborhoods closely when making your choice—you may end up paying the same to stay exactly where you want to be as you would to be off the beaten path.

The rock stars of Hong Kong's hotel industry are perfectly situated around Victoria Harbour, offering unobstructed harbor views, sumptuous spas, and reputable service to compete for the patronage of business-suited jet-setters, and any visitor willing to splurge for uncompromised luxury. Farther up the hills on both Kowloon and Hong Kong Island, cozy hotels seduce travelers who simply want a safe and practical place to crash in a trendy locale.

Travelers familiar with European cities might be surprised by the lack of provenance among Hong Kong hotels—the Peninsula passes as the venerable old-timer in this brashly new city where most hotels are perched in modern towers. And the scene keeps changing: Hong Kong's continued growth as a top tourist destination and business capital means that when it comes to choice of lodging, the next big thing is always around the corner. The Ritz-Carlton, Hong Kong, recently hit the heights when it began hosting guests on the 102nd through 118th floors of the ICC tower in West Kowloon, suggesting that on the Hong Kong hotel scene the sky really is the limit.

PLANNING

CHECKING IN

Typical check-in and checkout times are 2 pm and noon, respectively, although most hotels will be flexible if they are not fully booked and if you make a request in advance. Many major hotel chains have privilege clubs that allow their members to extend their checkout times until the evening, and some hotels now offer completely flexible checkout times, with checkout based on when you check in, rather than a set time. Some hotels also offer you the opportunity to check out online, so you can simply pack up and leave.

CHILDREN

Many hotels allow children under a certain age to stay in their parents' room at no extra charge, and most offer a babysitting service. Remember that many Hong Kong hotels have swimming pools, an attraction that in itself can satisfy young travelers.

EXECUTIVE PRIVILEGE

Most high-end hotels have a VIP executive floor or lounge, and these tend to come with sweeping panoramic views. Complimentary breakfast (not a regular feature in most Hong Kong hotels) and cocktails are usually served in these clubs, while business facilities tend to include Wi-Fi, laser printing, special dedicated concierges, and sometimes a mini-conference room. Entry to these clubs and lounges is based on the type of room you book, although some hotels allow guests staying in less expensive rooms to pay an additional fee for executive privileges.

FACILITIES

Unless stated otherwise in the review, hotels are equipped with elevators and all guest rooms have air-conditioning, TV, telephone, and private bathrooms. Note that bathrooms with showers but no bathtubs are the norm in smaller hotels, so be sure to check if you want a tub. All hotels have designated no-smoking rooms or floors. Many also have designated "special access" rooms for guests in wheelchairs.

Note that the majority of hotels, even the budget ones, now come with in-room Wi-Fi, although some hotels (ironically, often the more expensive ones) charge a fee; almost all hotels now offer free Wi-Fi in public areas. Most moderately priced hotels will offer up-to-date technologies such as plasma screens, entertainment on demand, iPod docks, and sometimes even cell phones. Most hotels are conveniently situated near the MTR subway system, and those that are not will often provide free shuttle services to the nearest station, as well as to popular downtown destinations.

LODGING STRATEGY

The 60-plus selections here represent the best this city has to offer. Scan "Best Bets" on the following pages for top recommendations by price and experience. Reviews are arranged alphabetically within each neighborhood.

PRICES

Prices vary depending on season and occupancy. Most hotels offer their best rates and special offers on their websites—look for long-stay or advanced-purchase discounts, or for that matter, last-minute booking deals. Hong Kong's high seasons are generally May through June and October through November, though rates also go up during certain holiday periods and for events such as the Hong Kong Sevens rugby tournament in March. While many hotels put on lavish breakfast buffets, breakfast is usually extra and not included in basic room rates.

WHAT IT COSTS IN HK$			
	$	$$	$$$	$$$$
For two people	Under HK$1,500	HK$1,500–HK$2,500	HK$2,500–HK$4,000	over HK$4,000

Prices are for two people in a standard double room in high season, excluding 10% service charge and a 3% government tax.

RESERVATIONS

Most hotels have reliable online booking systems, but phone reservations are also accepted, and receptionists speak English.

Specify arrival and departure dates, number of guests, room type (standard, deluxe, suite), and any specific preferences. Make sure to find out what is, and what is not, included in the room rate, such as breakfast, in-room Wi-Fi, and local calls. A credit-card deposit is generally required to secure reservations.

Flights from the United States often arrive in the evening, so it's a good idea to inform the hotel when you plan to arrive. Some hotels will not otherwise hold a booking after 6 pm.

ROOMS WITH A VIEW

It's no secret that the prime waterfront properties have the best views in Hong Kong. On the Kowloon side, hotels in Tsim Sha Tsui and West Kowloon generally have the most compelling skyline views across Victoria Harbour. Because of the curvature of the bay, hotels in Causeway Bay and North Point can also have an equally exhilarating view down the coast of Hong Kong Island as well as of Kowloon. Remember that silence speaks loudly; if the hotel doesn't advertise views, no matter how hip it is, it probably has none. And while more low-profile small hotels are cleverly designing their rooms to optimize limited square footage, nothing opens up a room like a far-reaching view, be it harbor (preferably) or city (high-rise horizons).

USING THE MAPS

Throughout the chapter, you'll see mapping symbols and coordinates (j3:F2) after property names or reviews. To locate the property on a map, turn to the Hong Kong Dining and Lodging Atlas at the end of the Where to Eat chapter. The first number after the ⊕ symbol indicates the map number. Following that is the property's coordinate on the map grid.

WHERE SHOULD I STAY?

	NEIGHBORHOOD VIBE	PROS	CONS
Western	A sprawling neighborhood with hidden alleyways, antiques shops, Chinese medicine markets, temples and hip eateries.	Western is akin to the residential extension of Central, with less traffic and similarly spectacular views. Accessible on foot, and a leisurely tram ride from Central during off-peak hours.	May require steep footwork if your destination is away from the main roads, where the trams and MTR run. Even taxis have difficulty navigating many narrow, one-way streets.
Central	A dense international finance center full of banks, shopping malls, restaurants, and footbridges. High up the escalators, Mid-Levels is an exclusive residential getaway.	Home to major luxury brands' flagship stores, as well as grand hotels, fine dining, and the famous nightlife area, Lan Kwai Fong. Mid-Levels offers quiet views from above the fray.	Congested streets by day, crowded bars by night. Mid-Levels Escalator runs uphill only after morning rush hour.
Wan Chai, Causeway Bay, and Beyond	Wan Chai hosts a strip of street-level bars in addition to the boutique Star Street area. Causeway Bay is the haven of hip young locals who come to eat, shop, and hang out in upstairs cafés.	Wan Chai has stylish restaurants, the convention center, and performing-arts venues. Causeway Bay, home to Victoria Park, is absurdly busy but conveniently situated with hotels in all price ranges.	The Wan Chai bar strip can get seedy, while Causeway Bay is extremely crowded on weekends. Eastern is mostly for business or residents.
Southside	Lower building density means more green space and fewer people, with a relaxing fishing-village atmosphere around Aberdeen.	Proximity to great beaches and treks on Hong Kong Island, as well as to Stanley Market.	Be prepared for a lot of car and bus rides along winding roads, often in slow traffic.
Lantau Island	Hong Kong's largest island hosts disparate attractions: an international airport, an outlet shopping mall, natural scenery, Hong Kong Disneyland, and AsiaWorld-Expo.	Tung Chung, at the end of the MTR line, is the point of access to the Ngong Ping cable car. Those with kids may prefer the resortlike setting inside Disneyland.	Inconvenient for exploring the rest of Hong Kong, as even Tung Chung is a half-hour MTR ride from Central.
Kowloon	The "wild" side of Hong Kong (at least according to Islanders) culminating in the commercial centers of Mong Kok and Tsim Sha Tsui.	Shopping paradise indeed, for both malls and markets. The TST promenade, including the touristy Avenue of Stars, offers endless postcard views of the Hong Kong skyline.	Kowloon is not everyone's idea of a holiday—outside residential areas the streets (even pedestrian) are generally noisy, crowded, and congested.

6

HONG KONG ISLAND

Reviews listed alphabetically within neighborhood.

Hotel reviews have been shortened. For full information, visit Fodors.com.

WESTERN

The steep, narrow streets of Western District, navigated by old-fashioned trams, are a natural setting for new, small hotels catering to those who favor local flavor over opulence. Hotels in Sheung Wan combine transport convenience with an abundance of neighborhood character, while hotels farther out on the main drive focus on sleek efficiency and minimalist style. However, getting to and from usually means passing through high-traffic Central or navigating congested streets, steps, and alleyways.

$ HOTEL 🏨 **Butterfly on Hollywood.** A charming location alone is reason enough to stay in one of these snug but stylishly contemporary rooms in a cozy neighborhood full of antiques shops, galleries, cafés, and up-and-coming restaurants. **Pros:** excellent location for wandering; a 10-minute walk from the hub of Hong Kong nightlife; free Wi-Fi throughout. **Cons:** cramped lobby and few hotel facilities; no views. [$] *Rooms from: HK$1,300* ✉ *263 Hollywood Rd., Sheung Wan, Western* ☎ *2850–8899* 🌐 *www.butterflyhk.com* 🛏 *148 rooms* 🍴 *No meals* [M] *Sheung Wan* ✣ *1:B2.*

$$ HOTEL 🏨 **Courtyard by Marriott Hong Kong.** Tidy and comfortable no-frills rooms are close to Western Tunnel and especially convenient for those with business in Kowloon. **Pros:** business-friendly; free shuttle buses; close to Sheung Wan Ferry Terminal and Western Tunnel; nice views of Kowloon West from upper floors. **Cons:** few dining options in hotel or immediate area; rooms on lower floors look out over a lot of traffic; fitness center but no pool. [$] *Rooms from: HK$1,600* ✉ *167 Connaught Rd. W, Western* ☎ *3717–8888* 🌐 *www.marriott.com/hotels/travel/hkgcy-courtyard-hong-kong* 🛏 *245 rooms* 🍴 *No meals* [M] *Western* ✣ *1:A2.*

$$ HOTEL 🏨 **The Mercer.** Spacious junior suites with kitchenettes (about two-thirds of the accommodations) are the best choice in this needlelike spire, where all rooms come with lots of light, airy views, and contemporary styling. **Pros:** a fun neighborhood to explore; good Japanese restaurant on the ground floor; small open-air pool. **Cons:** cramped lobby; surrounding area can get congested with traffic; glass-walled bathrooms are not popular with some guests. [$] *Rooms from: HK$2,000* ✉ *29 Jervois St., Sheung Wan* ☎ *2922–9988* 🌐 *www.ascottchina.com* 🛏 *55 rooms* 🍴 *No meals* [M] *Sheung Wan* ✣ *1:C2.*

$ HOTEL 🏨 **Sohotel.** It's a toss-up whether the rooms here should be considered basic and no-frills or minimally sleek, but they are extremely functional and nicely tucked away in a colorful neighborhood of galleries and local shops. **Pros:** free Wi-Fi and local calls; subway and Macau Ferry Terminal nearby. **Cons:** few in-hotel facilities; some rooms are tiny. [$] *Rooms from: HK$1,320* ✉ *139 Bonham Strand, Sheung Wan*

BEST BETS FOR HONG KONG LODGING

Fodor's offers a selective listing of quality lodgings at every price point, from the city's best budget guesthouses to its most sophisticated luxury hotels. We've compiled our top recommendations by price and experience.

Fodor's Choice ★

Alisan Guest House, $, p. 199

Bishop Lei International House, $, p. 196

Four Seasons Hotel Hong Kong, $$$$, p. 196

Hop Inn Carnarvon, $, p. 203

Hotel ICON, $$$, p. 203

InterContinental Hong Kong, $$$, p. 204

J Plus Hotel by YOO, $$, p. 201

The Landmark Mandarin Oriental, $$$$, p. 197

Mandarin Oriental Hong Kong, $$$$, p. 197

The Peninsula Hong Kong, $$$$, p. 205

The Ritz-Carlton, Hong Kong, $$$$, p. 206

The Upper House, $$$$, p. 197

W Hong Kong, $$$, p. 206

By Price

$

Alisan Guest House, p. 199

Bishop Lei International House, p. 196

Butterfly on Morrison, p. 199

Hop Inn Carnarvon, p. 203

Hop Inn Hankow, p. 203

Hotel Pennington, p. 201

Lan Kwai Fong Hotel, p. 197

V Wanchai 2, p. 199

$$

Auberge Discovery Bay, p. 207

Hotel Indigo, p. 198

J Plus Hotel by YOO, p. 201

Langham Place, p. 206

Mira Moon, p. 198

Ovolo Southside, p. 207

The Mira, p. 205

$$$

Hotel ICON, p. 203

InterContinental Hong Kong, p. 204

Lanson Place Hotel, p. 201

The Peninsula Hong Kong, p. 205

The Pottinger, p. 197

W Hong Kong, p. 206

$$$$

Four Seasons Hotel Hong Kong, p. 196

The Landmark Mandarin Oriental, p. 197

Mandarin Oriental Hong Kong, p. 197

The Ritz-Carlton, Hong Kong, p. 206

The Upper House, p. 197

By Experience

BEST VIEW

Bishop Lei International House, p. 196

InterContinental Hong Kong, p. 204

The Peninsula Hong Kong, p. 205

The Ritz-Carlton, Hong Kong, p. 206

BEST INTERIOR DESIGN

Hotel ICON, p. 203

Hotel Indigo, p. 198

Hullett House, p. 203

J Plus Hotel by YOO, p. 201

Mira Moon, p. 198

Ovolo Southside, p. 207

The Landmark Mandarin Oriental, p. 197

The Upper House, p. 197

BEST SPA

Auberge Discovery Bay, p. 207

Four Seasons Hotel Hong Kong, p. 196

InterContinental Hong Kong, p. 204

The Landmark Mandarin Oriental, p. 197

Mandarin Oriental Hong Kong, p. 197

The Peninsula Hong Kong, p. 205

BEST POOL

Four Seasons Hotel Hong Kong, p. 196

Grand Hyatt, p. 198

Hotel ICON, p. 203

Hotel Indigo, p. 198

InterContinental Hong Kong, p. 204

W Hong Kong, p. 206

BEST FOR KIDS

Auberge Discovery Bay, p. 207

Cosmopolitan Hotel, p. 200

Disney's Hollywood Hotel, p. 208

Hong Kong Disneyland Hotel, p. 208

Pentahotel Kowloon, p. 206

6

☎ 852/2851–8818 🌐 www.sohotel.com.hk 🛏 37 rooms 🍴 Breakfast [M] Sheung Wan ✥ 1:C2.

CENTRAL

As Hong Kong's financial hub, Central has attracted many fine restaurants, luxury shops, and swank hotels where deals are hatched, closed, and celebrated. Prepare to pay top prices for uncompromising service amid glamorous skyline views. Just up the hill, Lan Kwai Fong nightlife beckons with rowdy release; farther up the escalators, the Mid-Levels offers peaceful respite. Admiralty is a busy traffic-hub extension of Central that climbs into the gentrified heights of Pacific Place, above shopping malls and embassies, to more remote palatial hotel offerings with panoramic views.

$ HOTEL Fodor's Choice ★ **Bishop Lei International House.** If you've ever dreamed of living a life of privilege in the Mid-Levels without having to pay through the nose for it, this is your chance—all the better if you go for a slightly pricier harbor-view room. **Pros:** unique perch near escalators, saving you countless steps up and down to SoHo and Central; good value. **Cons:** escalator runs upward-only after 10 am, so lots of steps down in the morning. *[$] Rooms from: HK$1,200 ✉ 4 Robinson Rd., Mid-Levels, Central ☎ 852/2868–0828 🌐 www.bishopleihtl.com.hk 🛏 228 rooms 🍴 No meals [M] Central ✥ 1:D4.*

$$$$ HOTEL **Conrad Hong Kong.** A gleaming-white, oval-shaped tower rising from the Pacific Place complex offers dramatic views of the harbor and the Peak, along with super convenience for shopping and transport to other parts of Hong Kong. **Pros:** open-air pool area is dramatically backed by towering skyscrapers; elevator whisks guests down to Pacific Place shopping mall. **Cons:** has a bit of a chain hotel feel. *[$] Rooms from: HK$5,300 ✉ Pacific Place, 88 Queensway, Admiralty, Central ☎ 2521–3838 🌐 www.conradhongkong.com 🛏 512 rooms 🍴 No meals [M] Admiralty ✥ 1:F5.*

$$$$ HOTEL Fodor's Choice ★ **Four Seasons Hotel Hong Kong.** Few comforts are neglected, with amenities ranging from sumptuous Chinese-accented furnishings to all sorts of high-tech gadgetry, but the main features are the knockout views of the harbor and Victoria Peak through walls of glass. **Pros:** elite service and attention to detail; outstanding 24-hour business center. **Cons:** breakfast not included in high rates; some views are better than others. *[$] Rooms from: HK$4,500 ✉ International Finance Centre, 8 Finance St., Central ☎ 3196–8888 🌐 www.fourseasons.com/hongkong 🛏 399 rooms 🍴 No meals [M] Central ✥ 1:E2.*

$$ HOTEL **The Garden View – YWCA.** Rooms in this attractive, cylindrical, high-rise guesthouse overlook the peaceful Hong Kong Zoological and Botanical Gardens and are clean, well designed, and affordable. **Pros:** nice park views; value for money; kitchenettes in some suites; walking distance to Central. **Cons:** traffic can get bad during rush hours; limited amenities. *[$] Rooms from: HK$1,800 ✉ 1 MacDonnell Rd., Mid-Levels ☎ 2877–3737 🌐 hotel.ywca.org.hk 🛏 141 rooms 🍴 No meals [M] Central ✥ 1:D5.*

$$ HOTEL **Hotel LKF.** Enthusiastic partygoers can roll out of bed and land in a bar—one is on the 29th and 30th floors of the hotel, others are in the same tower, and dozens of others are on the surrounding Lan Kwai Fong bar strips. **Pros:** at the towering center of Hong Kong's nightlife; pet-friendly; extended-stay discounts. **Cons:** noise through the walls; rowdy neighborhood streets. *$ Rooms from: HK$1,900 ✉ 33 Wyndham St., Lan Kwai Fong, Central ☎ 3518–9688 🌐 www.hotel-lkf.com.hk 🛏 95 rooms 🍴 No meals [M] Central ✥ 1:C5.*

$$$$ HOTEL **Island Shangri-La.** A city icon towering above Pacific Place drips with old-world charm and offers spacious and luxurious accommodations with an Asian twist, along with fine dining and impeccable service. **Pros:** grand lobby; beautiful pool deck with a great close-up view of the skyline; elevator access to Pacific Place Mall. **Cons:** no full-service spa. *$ Rooms from: HK$4,500 ✉ Pacific Place, Supreme Court Rd., Admiralty, Central ☎ 2877–3838 🌐 www.shangri-la.com/island 🛏 565 rooms 🍴 No meals [M] Admiralty ✥ 1:F4.*

$ HOTEL **Lan Kwai Fong Hotel.** The scent of lemongrass and cozy feel of an old Hong Kong apartment building extend to the small but beautiful rooms enlarged by bay windows and plunging views of the surrounding cityscape. **Pros:** hotel and neighborhood have lots of character; free Wi-Fi; complimentary smartphone; some rooms have balconies. **Cons:** narrow roads surrounding the hotel are often congested. *$ Rooms from: HK$1,300 ✉ 3 Kau U Fong, Central ☎ 3650–0000 🌐 www.lankwaifonghotel.com.hk 🛏 162 rooms 🍴 No meals [M] Sheung Wan ✥ 1:D3.*

$$$$ HOTEL Fodor's Choice ★ **The Landmark Mandarin Oriental.** Some of the city's most beautifully designed and spacious rooms are equipped with massive, circular, spa-style bathtubs, the centerpieces of huge, view-filled bathrooms. **Pros:** you can't get more central in Central; elegantly appointed rooms. **Cons:** relatively small lobby; city views only. *$ Rooms from: HK$4,500 ✉ The Landmark, 15 Queen's Rd. Central, Central ☎ 2132–0188 🌐 www.mandarinoriental.com/landmark 🛏 113 rooms 🍴 No meals [M] Central ✥ 1:E4.*

$$$$ HOTEL Fodor's Choice ★ **Mandarin Oriental Hong Kong.** Hong Kong's most famous hotel has lost none of its opulence, colonial charm, and shine over the past 50 years, and is still known for spacious and luxurious accommodations and impeccable service. **Pros:** spacious, open, and beautifully designed rooms; old-world ambience at its finest; exquisite spa. **Cons:** in-room Wi-Fi isn't free. *$ Rooms from: HK$4,500 ✉ 5 Connaught Rd., Central ☎ 2522–0111 🌐 www.mandarinoriental.com/hongkong 🛏 501 rooms 🍴 No meals [M] Central ✥ 1:E3.*

$$$ HOTEL **The Pottinger.** As its name implies, The Pottinger overlooks the historic stony staircase of the same name. **Pros:** centrally located; local touches; big bathrooms; historical elements. **Cons:** no pool; limited amenities; underwhelming views. *$ Rooms from: HK$3,200 ✉ 21 Stanley St., Central ☎ 2308–3188 🌐 www.thepottinger.com 🛏 68 rooms 🍴 No meals ✥ 1:C4.*

$$$$ HOTEL Fodor's Choice ★ **The Upper House.** Even standard rooms in this haven of stylish luxury are suites—tranquil havens of design and indulgence that feature huge window-side bathtubs, walk-in rain showers, a personal iPod touch with everything on it, free minibars, and high-end wine fridges. **Pros:**

high design, and filled with works of contemporary Asian artists; feels worlds away from Central neighborhood below; incredible personalized service. **Cons:** no spa or pool; can be difficult to get a taxi. [$] *Rooms from: HK$4,500* ✉ *Pacific Place, 88 Queensway, Admiralty, Central* ☎ *2918–1838* 🌐 *www.upperhouse.com* 🛏 *117 suites* 🍴 *No meals* [M] *Admiralty* ✣ *1:G4.*

WAN CHAI, CAUSEWAY BAY, AND EASTERN

Wan Chai, the neighborhood made famous in *The World of Suzie Wong,* still has nightlife (and red-light activity), in addition to 24-hour noodle joints and hip new wine bars. Hotels around the Hong Kong Convention and Exhibition Centre may offer great views, but nights can get noisy around Lockhart Road. Causeway Bay is the choice of the young and trendy in search of food and fashion, but is perpetually overcrowded with pedestrians around Times Square. This part of Hong Kong also includes the recreational green spaces of Victoria Park and the Happy Valley Racecourse. Outlying Eastern is strictly about business.

WAN CHAI

$$ HOTEL 🏨 **The Fleming.** Popular among the business crowd, The Fleming offers views of the bustling streets below from clean yet drab rooms. **Pros:** free DVD library; near ferry terminal. **Cons:** standard rooms come with only double beds. [$] *Rooms from: HK$1,600* ✉ *41 Fleming Rd., Wan Chai* ☎ *3607–2288* 🌐 *www.thefleming.com* 🛏 *66 rooms* 🍴 *Breakfast* [M] *Wan Chai* ✣ *2:C3.*

$$$$ HOTEL FAMILY 🏨 **Grand Hyatt Hong Kong.** A direct connection to the Hong Kong Convention and Exhibition Centre makes this a business-first hotel, but leisure travelers also enjoy the elegant rooms,with sweeping harbor views and luxurious touches such as an oversized square bathtub and mirror TV. **Pros:** excellent service; extensive sports facilities; Plateau spa is a beautiful sanctuary; free Wi-Fi. **Cons:** quiet outside the hotel at night; difficult to get reservations in popular restaurant. [$] *Rooms from: HK$5,200* ✉ *1 Harbour Rd., Wan Chai* ☎ *2588–1234* 🌐 *www.hongkong.grand.hyatt.com* 🛏 *539 rooms* 🍴 *No meals* [M] *Wan Chai, Exit A1* ✣ *2:C2.*

$$ HOTEL 🏨 **Hotel Indigo.** A standout boutique addition to the Wan Chai hotel scene, Hotel Indigo boasts serious architectural chops—the exterior resembles a circling dragon—as well as photogenic interiors. **Pros:** free Wi-Fi; eclectic neighborhood; panoramic views; top-notch service; convenient location. **Cons:** pricey drinking and dining options; over-air-conditioned public spaces; tiny fitness center. [$] *Rooms from: HK$2,200* ✉ *242–246 Queen's Rd. E, Wan Chai* ☎ *3926–3888* 🌐 *www.ihg.com/hotelindigo* 🛏 *138 rooms* 🍴 *No meals* [M] *Wan Chai, Exit A3* ✣ *2:C4.*

$$ HOTEL 🏨 **Mira Moon.** If you get a little nostalgic for *Alice in Wonderland* at Mira Moon hotel, you're not totally off the mark: the hypermodern, abstract interiors are meant to depict the legend behind the Mid-Autumn moon festival—a fairy-tale-like Chinese legend revolving around the Moon Goddess of Immortality and a space-traveling jade rabbit. **Pros:** local flavor; excellent restaurant; free Wi-Fi and minibar; complimentary

smartphone. **Cons:** some rooms look into nearby apartments; cab desert; entry-level rooms on small side; check-in at 3 pm. $ *Rooms from: HK$2,100 ⊠ 388 Jaffe Rd., Wan Chai* ☎ *2643–8888* ⊕ *www. miramoonhotel.com* ⌁ *91 rooms* ⊚| *No meals* Ⓜ *Causeway Bay, Exit B* ✛ *2:E2.*

$ ⊡ **Novotel Century Hong Kong.**
HOTEL   Decent harbor views from some rooms compensate for sparse furnishings and the lack of any personality, while a decent business center is handy for those with work to do. **Pros:** near the subway, Wan Chai bars and clubs, and Hong Kong Convention and Exhibition Centre; unaffiliated but delicious Shanghainese restaurant in the basement. **Cons:** dull rooms; can get crowded with tour groups and during business conventions. $ *Rooms from: HK$1,350 ⊠ 238 Jaffe Rd., Wan Chai* ☎ *2598–8888* ⊕ *www. novotelhongkongcentury.com* ⌁ *511 rooms* Ⓜ *Wan Chai* ✛ *2:D3.*

$$$ ⊡ **Renaissance Hong Kong Harbour View Hotel.** These modest guest rooms
HOTEL   in the Hong Kong Convention and Exhibition Centre complex are
FAMILY   simply outfitted with attractive modern decor, and many have harbor views. **Pros:** great harbor views; harborside recreational garden. **Cons:** a walk from the subway but near the Star Ferry. $ *Rooms from: HK$2,800 ⊠ 1 Harbour Rd., Wan Chai* ☎ *2802–8888* ⊕ *www. renaissanceharbourviewhk.com* ⌁ *857 rooms* ⊚| *No meals* Ⓜ *Wan Chai* ✛ *2:C2.*

$ ⊡ **V Wanchai 2 Hotel.** The high ceilings and abacus-inspired lobby decor
HOTEL   bode well for the rest of the contemporary rooms and facilities at V Wanchai 2. **Pros:** close to convention center; good for long stays; sizable rooms. **Cons:** nearby traffic; no views; small bathrooms; limited dining options. $ *Rooms from: HK$1,300 ⊠ 139 Thomson Rd., Wan Chai* ☎ *3948–4800* ⊕ *www.thev.hk* ⌁ *79 rooms* ⊚| *Breakfast* Ⓜ *Wan Chai, Exit A4* ✛ *2:D3.*

CAUSEWAY BAY

$ ⊡ **Alisan Guest House.** Some of these no-frills rooms nestled into an old
B&B/INN   apartment building in Causeway Bay have nice views of the yachts just
Fodor's Choice   across Gloucester Road, and all offer cleanliness, safety, and friendly
★   hospitality at a budget price—plus each room has the convenience of an en suite washroom and shower. **Pros:** friendly, English-speaking staff; good location; free Wi-Fi. **Cons:** small rooms and windows; basic decor; surcharge to pay with credit card. $ *Rooms from: HK$520 ⊠ Flat A, 5th fl., Hoi To Court, 275 Gloucester Rd., Causeway Bay* ☎ *2838–0762* ⊕ *www.alisanguesthouse.com* ⌁ *25 rooms* ⊚| *No meals* Ⓜ *Causeway Bay* ✛ *2:F2.*

$ ⊡ **Butterfly on Morrison.** Standard rooms are small and housed on
HOTEL   lower floors with no views, so consider upgrading to a larger room on the upper floors where the surrounding skyline and Happy Valley

Racecourse form a dramatic backdrop. **Pros:** chic contemporary-style rooms, some with decent neighborhood views. **Cons:** few in-hotel facilities. $ *Rooms from: HK$1,300* ⊠ *39 Morrison Hill Rd., Causeway Bay* ☎ *3962–8333* ⊕ *www.butterflyhk.com* ↴ *98 rooms* ⦿❘ *No meals* Ⓜ *Causeway Bay* ✛ *2:E4.*

$$ ⛻ **Cosmo Hotel.** The Cosmopolitan's little next-door neighbor appeals
HOTEL   to guests who enjoy trendy, contemporary design as well as the allure of the popular ground-floor Nooch Bar, with its lush, red-velvet booths and lavish cocktails. **Pros:** cheerful rooms in one of three mood colors—orange, green, or yellow; 24-hour check-in and checkout; guests can use facilities of the Cosmopolitan next door. **Cons:** surrounded by busy streets. $ *Rooms from: HK$1,600* ⊠ *375–377 Queen's Rd. E, Wan Chai* ☎ *3552–8388* ⊕ *www.cosmohotel.com.hk* ↴ *142 rooms* ⦿❘ *No meals* Ⓜ *Causeway Bay* ✛ *2:D4.*

$$ ⛻ **Cosmopolitan Hotel.** Kid-friendly services extend to family-sized rooms
HOTEL   that sleep up to five and even suites filled with stuffed animals and
FAMILY   electronic games; adults enjoy a choice of 11 pillows and many other personal touches. **Pros:** great shuttle services; packages to Ocean Park and other kid-friendly amenities; good in-house restaurant and bar; free Wi-Fi; extremely reasonable rates. **Cons:** surrounded by insanely busy streets with little pedestrian appeal. $ *Rooms from: HK$1,800* ⊠ *387–397 Queen's Rd. E, Wan Chai* ☎ *3552–1111* ⊕ *www. cosmopolitanhotel.com.hk* ↴ *454 rooms* ⦿❘ *No meals* Ⓜ *Causeway Bay* ✛ *2:E4.*

$$ ⛻ **Crowne Plaza Hong Kong.** Overlooking Happy Valley and the sur-
HOTEL   rounding hillsides through floor-to-ceiling double-glazed windows, the sleek superior rooms are equipped with surround-sound DVD systems and 42-inch flat screens; suites afford especially panoramic views through three walls of windows. **Pros:** great outdoor pool has a nice view; short walk from Times Square and shopping streets. **Cons:** racing fans get better track views at nearby Cosmopolitan. $ *Rooms from: HK$2,100* ⊠ *8 Leighton Rd., Causeway Bay* ☎ *3980–3980* ⊕ *www. cphongkong.com* ↴ *263 rooms* ⦿❘ *No meals* Ⓜ *Causeway Bay* ✛ *2:F4* ✛ *2:F3.*

$ ⛻ **Empire Hotel Hong Kong, Causeway Bay.** A quiet locale just east of Vic-
HOTEL   toria Park is enhanced by soothingly decorated guest rooms, where the amenities include posh glass-walled showers. **Pros:** quiet neighborhood; beautiful west-facing views; free WiFi. **Cons:** small rooms and windows; no pool or gym; situated away from the action. $ *Rooms from: HK$1,400* ⊠ *8 Wing Hing St., Causeway Bay* ☎ *3692–2333* ⊕ *www. empirehotel.com.hk* ↴ *280 rooms* ⦿❘ *No meals* Ⓜ *Tin Hau* ✛ *2:H1.*

$$ ⛻ **Excelsior.** Some rooms are spacious, with splendid views of the bay,
HOTEL   and other rooms are smaller with close-up street views, but all have a light, contemporary design and are moderately priced compared with other high-end hotels (especially in the center of Causeway Bay). **Pros:** excellent location for exploring bustling Causeway Bay. **Cons:** no pool; faces one of the most congested main roads in the city. $ *Rooms from: HK$1,999* ⊠ *281 Gloucester Rd., Causeway Bay* ☎ *2894–8888* ⊕ *www.mandarinoriental.com/excelsior* ↴ *884 rooms* ⦿❘ *Breakfast* Ⓜ *Causeway Bay* ✛ *2:F2.*

$ ⌂ Hotel Pennington. Smack in the midst of Causeway Bay's business
HOTEL venues and frenetic shopping scene, Hotel Pennington offers comfortable accommodations at reasonable prices. **Pros:** decent views from
higher floors; connecting rooms for families; nice terrace bar. **Cons:**
crowded neighborhood; business-centric; compact rooms. $ *Rooms
from: HK$1,400* ⌂ *13–15 Pennington St., Causeway Bay* ☎ *3970–0688*
⊕ *www.hotelpennington.com.hk* ➶ *79 rooms* ⦾ *No meals* Ⓜ *Causeway Bay, Exit F* ✢ *2:G3.*

$$ ⌂ J Plus Hotel by YOO. Designer Philippe Starck's incredible ability to
HOTEL blend seemingly unblendable themes makes every corner an exercise
Fodor'sChoice in eye candy, but it isn't all style over substance: each white-swathed
★ room is like a mini suite, full of cozy corners and splashes of color
that combine Old Hong Kong, *Alice in Wonderland*, and everyday
practicalities. **Pros:** great value for money; a design geek's dream; complimentary breakfast; kitchenettes; self-laundry facilities. **Cons:** no
views. $ *Rooms from: HK$1,500* ⌂ *1–5 Irving St., Causeway Bay*
☎ *3196–9000* ⊕ *www.jplushongkong.com* ➶ *56 rooms* ⦾ *Breakfast*
Ⓜ *Causeway Bay* ✢ *2:G3.*

$$$ ⌂ Lanson Place Hotel. The understated, striking design promotes a sense
HOTEL of calm, from the relaxing lounge-library to guest quarters that feel like
exclusive apartments and come with kitchenettes and cleverly designed
living areas. **Pros:** attractive, distinctive surroundings; business center;
gym. **Cons:** no harbor views; no substantial dining. $ *Rooms from:
HK$2,600* ⌂ *133 Leighton Rd., Causeway Bay* ☎ *3477–6888* ⊕ *hong-kong.lansonplace.com* ➶ *194 rooms* ⦾ *No meals* Ⓜ *Causeway Bay*
✢ *2:G3.*

$$ ⌂ Metropark Hotel Causeway Bay. The views of the skyline and adjacent
HOTEL Victoria Park are beautiful, whether enjoyed from the simple but effectively designed modern rooms with all the basics or the pleasant rooftop
pool. **Pros:** spectacular views for less; across from Victoria Park. **Cons:**
limited facilities; small lobby; few in-room amenities. $ *Rooms from:
HK$1,500* ⌂ *148 Tung Lo Wan Rd., Causeway Bay* ☎ *2600–1000*
⊕ *www.metroparkhotel.com* ➶ *266 rooms* ⦾ *No meals* Ⓜ *Tin Hau*
✢ *2:H2.*

$$ ⌂ Park Lane. Guest rooms are as airy as the views at this elegant land-
HOTEL mark overlooking Victoria Park, with glass-topped furnishings and
glass walls that accent the open outlooks over greenery, the harbor,
and the skyline. **Pros:** sprawling views; close to Causeway Bay shopping; free Wi-Fi. **Cons:** often crowded; no pool; showing its age in
places. $ *Rooms from: HK$2,430* ⌂ *310 Gloucester Rd., Causeway
Bay* ☎ *2293–8888* ⊕ *www.parklane.com.hk* ➶ *826 rooms* ⦾ *Breakfast*
Ⓜ *Causeway Bay* ✢ *2:G2.*

EASTERN

$$ ⌂ East. Regulars, many of whom are business travelers, appreciate being
HOTEL comfortably away from the Island's bustling madness while enjoying
such perks as the minimalist-chic guest rooms and rooftop deck. **Pros:**
free Wi-Fi; beautiful rooftop lounge and deck; good fitness center; excellent harbor views. **Cons:** quiet residential surroundings; little nearby
nightlife. $ *Rooms from: HK$1,650* ⌂ *29 Taikoo Shing Rd., Tai Koo,*

6

Eastern ☎ *3968–3968* 🌐 *www.east-hongkong.com* 🛏 *345 rooms* 🍴 *No meals* [M] *Tai Koo* ⊕ *2:H1.*

KOWLOON

If you enjoy rubbing elbows with the locals in chatty all-day noodle stalls just as much as shuffling through touristy pedestrian night markets and malls, Kowloon is the place to be. Postcard skyline views abound from harbor-front hotels in Tsim Sha Tsui, a 10-minute ferry ride away from Hong Kong Island, with a calmer atmosphere heading eastward toward Hung Hom.

TSIM SHA TSUI

The southern tip of the Kowloon peninsula is the birthplace of the Golden Mile, and upholding its reputation is a cluster of luxury hotels around the southern end of Nathan Road. Postcard skyline views from posh suites overlooking Victoria Harbour provide an oasis of serenity above the bustling and boisterous neighborhood below.

$$ HOTEL 🏨 **BP International.** These small and no-frills rooms in a modern tower on the north side of Kowloon Park come with a bonus: views over an extensive swath of greenery or the harbor. **Pros:** coffee shop, restaurant, and lounge on premises; self-service coin laundry. **Cons:** can get crowded with business and tour groups; few amenities. [$] *Rooms from: HK$1,500* ✉ *8 Austin Rd., Tsim Sha Tsui* ☎ *2376–1111* 🌐 *www.bpih.com.hk* 🛏 *529 rooms* 🍴 *No meals* [M] *Tsim Sha Tsui* ⊕ *3:E4.*

$$ HOTEL 🏨 **Butterfly on Prat.** Pleasant rooms done in soothing earth tones and natural wood are a restful retreat from oft-rowdy Prat Avenue, overflowing with restaurants, bars, and clubs—meaning guests don't have to venture far to explore Hong Kong nightlife. **Pros:** friendly staff; colorful, practical rooms; fridge, microwave, and electric kettles in rooms. **Cons:** limited views; rowdy neighborhood; no restaurant and few amenities. [$] *Rooms from: HK$1,500* ✉ *21 Prat Ave., Tsim Sha Tsui* ☎ *3962–8888* 🌐 *www.butterflyhk.com* 🛏 *122 rooms* 🍴 *No meals* [M] *Tsim Sha Tsui* ⊕ *3:F5.*

$$ HOTEL 🏨 **Harbour Grand Kowloon.** For many guests a long list of amenities makes up for an isolated-from-action locale: most of the large, comfortable, contemporary rooms have harbor views, and the year-round outdoor pool, spa, gym, and array of lounges and restaurants are spectacular. **Pros:** harborfront location on the peaceful side of the promenade; extensive business center. **Cons:** no easy subway access. [$] *Rooms from: HK$2,200* ✉ *Whampoa Garden, 20 Tak Fung St., Hung Hom, Tsim Sha Tsui* ☎ *2621–3188* 🌐 *www.harbourgrand.com/kowloon* 🛏 *554 rooms* 🍴 *No meals* [M] *Hung Hom* ⊕ *3:H4.*

$$ HOTEL 🏨 **Holiday Inn Golden Mile.** Most views from the basic, medium-size rooms involve an up-close look at your neighbors, but being in the heart of Tsim Sha Tsui is the main attraction, along with such perks as a refreshing outdoor pool area with sauna and steam rooms. **Pros:** multiple dining options include a Cantonese restaurant, Italian restaurant, and popular buffet. **Cons:** no views; can get crowded with groups. $ Rooms from: HK$2,000 ⊠ 50 Nathan Rd., Tsim Sha Tsui ☎ 2369–3111 ⊕ holidayinn.com/hongkong-gldn ⇗ 614 rooms ⦿ No meals Ⓜ Tsim Sha Tsui ✛ 3:F5.

$
HOTEL
Fodor's Choice
★

Hop Inn Carnarvon. One of the city's most charming and personable budget locations exudes loads of character in tidy, comfortable rooms that are well organized and individually decorated with lots of color by local artists. **Pros:** fun, beautifully original decor for budget lodgings; friendly staff; ultracool common room and outside deck; private bathrooms. **Cons:** not too many amenities, but the price is right. $ Rooms from: HK$650 ⊠ 9th fl., James S. Lee Mansion, 33–35 Carnarvon Rd., Tsim Sha Tsui ☎ 2881–7331 ⊕ www.hopinn.hk ⇗ 27 rooms ⦿ No meals Ⓜ Tsim Sha Tsui ✛ 3:F5.

$
HOTEL

Hop Inn Hankow. Much like the affiliated Hop Inn Carnarvon, this appealing guesthouse is a budget traveler's dream, with loads of personality in the guest rooms designed by local artists. **Pros:** friendly service and amazing personality for budget lodgings; private bathrooms. **Cons:** no common hangout areas; small elevator. $ Rooms from: HK$400 ⊠ Flat A, 2nd Fl., Hanyee Building, Hankow Rd., Tsim Sha Tsui ☎ 2881–7331 ⊕ www.hopinn.hk ⇗ 9 rooms ⦿ No meals Ⓜ Tsim Sha Tsui ✛ 3:E5.

$$$
HOTEL
Fodor's Choice
★

Hotel ICON. Here's a stunning design statement, from the vertical garden hanging above the lobby café to the stylish, panoramic lounge on the top floor—and in between are gorgeous, view-filled guest rooms outfitted with cozy woods, natural fabrics, and all the high-tech amenities. **Pros:** a designer's dream; dedication to guest experience; tranquil feel with no tour groups allowed; complimentary smartphones with free mobile data. **Cons:** surrounding area is thick with crowds at times. $ Rooms from: HK$2,600 ⊠ 17 Science Museum Rd., Tsim Sha Tsui ☎ 3400–1000 ⊕ www.hotel-icon.com ⇗ 262 rooms ⦿ No meals Ⓜ Tsim Sha Tsui East ✛ 3:G4.

$
HOTEL

Hotel Panorama by Rhombus. True to the name, each of the contemporary-style guest rooms is on a corner, allowing breathtaking harbor and city views through floor-to-ceiling windows. **Pros:** sophisticated experience in an old neighborhood; pet-friendly; executive lounge and other facilities geared to business travelers. **Cons:** no spa or pool; even no-smoking rooms may smell of smoke. $ Rooms from: HK$1,048 ⊠ 8A Hart Ave., Tsim Sha Tsui ☎ 3550–0388 ⊕ www.hotelpanorama.com.hk ⇗ 324 rooms ⦿ No meals Ⓜ East Tsim Sha Tsui ✛ 3:F5.

$$$$
HOTEL

Hullett House. Ten huge suites occupy a former colonial marine police headquarters dating back to the 1880s, and each re-creates a different era of Hong Kong history with bold, artistic flair showcasing Asian and colonial styles—while pampering guests with 21st-century technology and luxury. **Pros:** historic surroundings; complimentary minibar; Bentley transfer included; notable restaurants and bars on the ground floor. **Cons:** public areas can get crowded. $ Rooms from: HK$6,500 ⊠ 2A Canton Rd., 1881 Heritage, Tsim Sha Tsui ☎ 3988–0000 ⊕ www.hulletthouse.com ⇗ 10 suites ⦿ Breakfast Ⓜ Tsim Sha Tsui ✛ 3:E6.

$$
HOTEL

Hyatt Regency Hong Kong, Tsim Sha Tsui. At this location boxed in by high-rises, only the upper-floor rooms have memorable views, but all are cozy retreats done in olive and brown tones with burgundy

6

armchairs and classic photos of Hong Kong on the walls. **Pros:** close to the action and Minden Street bar scene; good dining options; complimentary smartphones with unlimited data and local calls. **Cons:** busy shopping-mall surroundings; partial harbor views. [$] *Rooms from: HK$2,300* ✉ *18 Hanoi Rd., Tsim Sha Tsui* ☎ *2311–1234* 🌐 *www.hongkong.tsimshatsui.hyatt.com* 🛏 *381 rooms* 🍴 *No meals* [M] *Tsim Sha Tsui* ✣ *3:F5.*

$$$ HOTEL Fodor's Choice ★ 🏨 **InterContinental Hong Kong.** Its location at the tip of the Kowloon peninsula ensures panoramic, front-row harbor views from most of the contemporary rooms, designed with Asian accents that include deep, sunken tubs in the marbled bathrooms. **Pros:** exceptional views; modern design; extravagant spa. **Cons:** the Avenue of Stars just outside can get crowded during the nightly Symphony of Lights show. [$] *Rooms from: HK$3,000* ✉ *18 Salisbury Rd., Tsim Sha Tsui* ☎ *2721–1211* 🌐 *www.hongkong-ic.intercontinental.com* 🛏 *503 rooms* 🍴 *No meals* [M] *Tsim Sha Tsui* ✣ *3:F6.*

$$$ HOTEL 🏨 **Kowloon Shangri-La.** You might feel like a '70s tycoon amid murals, fountains, and crystal chandeliers in the lobby, and the feeling extends to the spacious rooms decorated in warm colors with armchairs, rich wooden furniture, bay windows, and nice marbled bathrooms. **Pros:** warm hospitality; attention to detail; quality Chinese restaurant; excellent business facilities. **Cons:** less exciting garden views on lower floors. [$] *Rooms from: HK$3,200* ✉ *64 Mody Rd., Tsim Sha Tsui* ☎ *2721–2111* 🌐 *www.shangri-la.com/kowloon* 🛏 *688 rooms* 🍴 *No meals* [M] *Tsim Sha Tsui East* ✣ *3:G5.*

$$$ HOTEL 🏨 **The Langham.** Attractive luxury is apparent everywhere, from the opulent, European-baroque-style lobby to warmly decorated guest rooms, each finished with hardwood floors and silk drapes, and many with such touches as separate sitting areas and marble bathrooms with deep tubs and walk-in showers. **Pros:** one of the better buffet breakfasts in Hong Kong (included in some room rates); excellent dining options. **Cons:** limited city views; surrounded by heavy traffic. [$] *Rooms from: HK$2,600* ✉ *8 Peking Rd., Tsim Sha Tsui* ☎ *2375–1133* 🌐 *www.hongkong.langhamhotels.com* 🛏 *499 rooms* 🍴 *No meals* [M] *Tsim Sha Tsui* ✣ *3:E5.*

$$ HOTEL 🏨 **The Luxe Manor.** In the absence of views, rooms are a show in themselves, with audacious design themes (gold picture frames flying across the walls) that don't sacrifice comfort and luxury. **Pros:** a trippy experience for the eyes; close proximity to more mellow nightlife and easy shopping. **Cons:** no views; lobby feels deserted at times. [$] *Rooms from: HK$1,800* ✉ *39 Kimberley Rd., Tsim Sha Tsui* ☎ *3763–8888* 🌐 *www.theluxemanor.com* 🛏 *159 rooms* 🍴 *No meals* [M] *Tsim Sha Tsui* ✣ *3:F4.*

$$ HOTEL 🏨 **Marco Polo Hongkong Hotel.** Spacious rooms with sweeping views of Hong Kong Island are near the shopping hub along Canton Road and linked to Harbour City's immense shopping complex. **Pros:** westward views; convenient to Star Ferry and other transport. **Cons:** full in late March during the Hong Kong Rugby Sevens tournament; boisterous crowds during German Bierfest. [$] *Rooms from: HK$2,300* ✉ *Harbour City, Canton Rd., Tsim Sha Tsui* ☎ *2113–0088* 🌐 *www.*

marcopolohotels.com ⮎ *665 rooms* ⦿| *Some meals* M *Tsim Sha Tsui* ✛ *3:D6.*

$$ $ ⊞ **The Mira.** Streamlined-sleek guest rooms have touches of modern
HOTEL buzz everywhere (glass-pod showers, laptop safes, free smartphones),
but the excellent service and guest-friendly facilities make this much
more than a design showplace. **Pros:** hip, seen-and-be-seen vibe; good
in-house dining; great spa with pool; 24-hour gym. **Cons:** lobby can be
a little too active at times. $ *Rooms from: HK$2,400* ⊠ *118 Nathan*
Rd., Tsim Sha Tsui ☎ *2368–1111* ⊕ *www.themirahotel.com* ⮎ *492*
rooms ⦿| *No meals* M *Tsim Sha Tsui* ✛ *3:E4.*

$$$ $ ⊞ **The Peninsula Hong Kong.** Even in a city with so many world-class
HOTEL hotels, the Peninsula manages to stand apart from the rest, an oasis of
Fodor's Choice old-world glamour—opened in 1928 and the flagship for the luxury
★ Peninsula brand—with Kowloon and harbor views that'll make you
feel like you own Hong Kong. **Pros:** legendary dining and service; state-
of-the-art room facilities; tons of character; extensive on-site facilities;
free Wi-Fi and VOIP calls. **Cons:** rooms are pricey. $ *Rooms from:*
HK$4,000 ⊠ *Salisbury Rd., Tsim Sha Tsui* ☎ *2920–2888* ⊕ *www.*
peninsula.com ⮎ *354 rooms* ⦿| *No meals* M *Tsim Sha Tsui, Exit L3*
✛ *3:E6.*

$$ $ ⊞ **Royal Garden.** A comfortable business hotel built around a towering
HOTEL garden atrium happens to be a particularly good place for world-class
dining, with four notable restaurants on-site, though the spacious, sleek,
and soothing guest rooms do not have views. **Pros:** excellent pool; dis-
tinguished restaurants. **Cons:** no views from rooms. $ *Rooms from:*
HK$2,000 ⊠ *69 Mody Rd., Tsim Sha Tsui* ☎ *2721–5215* ⊕ *www.rghk.*
com.hk ⮎ *420 rooms* ⦿| *No meals* M *Tsim Sha Tsui East* ✛ *3:G5.*

$$ $ ⊞ **Sheraton Hong Kong Hotel & Towers.** Such perks as good dining and
HOTEL the chance to sip champagne in a bubbling rooftop Jacuzzi enhance
the warm and modern guest rooms, many with city and harbor views.
Pros: beautiful art-filled lobby and public spaces; pleasant, contemporary room decor; excellent business and fitness facilities; classy shopping arcade. **Cons:** at the dense and congested southern end of Nathan
Road. $ *Rooms from: HK$1,900* ⊠ *20 Nathan Rd., Tsim Sha Tsui*
☎ *2369–1111* ⊕ *www.sheraton.com/hongkong* ⮎ *782 rooms* ⦿| *No*
meals M *Tsim Sha Tsui* ✛ *3:E6.*

$ ⊞ **Stanford Hillview Hotel.** Straightforward and relatively no-frills rooms
HOTEL are set above busy Tsim Sha Tsui on a hillside below the Hong Kong
Observatory, providing a nice retreat and pleasant views. **Pros:** free
Wi-Fi; quiet; stately renovated building; excellent all-day buffet in the
Hillview Cafe. **Cons:** small, simple rooms. $ *Rooms from: HK$1,045*
⊠ *Observatory Rd., Knutsford Terrace, Tsim Sha Tsui* ☎ *2722–7822*
⊕ *www.stanfordhillview.com* ⮎ *177 rooms* ⦿| *No meals* M *Tsim Sha*
Tsui ✛ *3:F4.*

YAU MA TEI, MONG KOK, AND WESTERN KOWLOON

As you venture up and off Kowloon's central artery of Nathan Road
through Yau Ma Tei, accommodations tend to be older and cheaper
until you reach the grand hotels dominating the shopping malls in Mong
Kok. Western Kowloon—centered around classy Elements shopping

mall, Western Waterfront Promenade, and ICC tower—is the high-end up-and-coming exception.

YAU MA TEI

$$ **Eaton.** Rooms above a theater and shopping complex come in a variety of welcoming styles, from an East-meets-West decor in some to airy, **HOTEL** bright, functional contemporary design in others—all are set up for maximum comfort and relaxation. **Pros:** comfortable rooms in a relatively convenient location; free WiFi. **Cons:** Nathan Road can be overwhelming with traffic, crowds, and noise. ⓢ *Rooms from: HK$1,500* ✉ *380 Nathan Rd., Yau Ma Tei* ☎ *2782–1818* ⊕ *hongkong.eatonhotels. com* ⇆ *465 rooms* ⓧ *No meals* Ⓜ *Yau Ma Tei* ✛ *3:E2.*

MONG KOK

$$ **Langham Place.** At this sleek glass-and-steel box that transformed **HOTEL** a once seedy block, whimsical sculptures of Mao's Red Guards greet **FAMILY** you at the entrance, and luxurious guest rooms feature floor-to-ceiling windows, mirrored walls, mood lighting, and glass-walled marble bathrooms. **Pros:** great spa and pool; loads of shopping at adjoining high-end mall; good choice of in-house bars and restaurants. **Cons:** very busy surroundings; loud neighborhood. ⓢ *Rooms from: HK$1,600* ✉ *555 Shanghai St., Mong Kok* ☎ *3552–3388* ⊕ *hongkong.langhamplacehotels.com* ⇆ *665 rooms* ⓧ *No meals* Ⓜ *Mong Kok* ✛ *3:D1.*

WESTERN KOWLOON

$ **Pentahotel Kowloon.** Tucked away off a narrow street, Pentahotel is **HOTEL** deceivingly large, with 32 floors and 695 rooms. **Pros:** great for families; **FAMILY** green and city views; huge pool; free shuttle-bus services. **Cons:** out-of-the-way neighborhood; crowded with groups from China; no minibars. ⓢ *Rooms from: HK$1,200* ✉ *19 Luk Hop St., San Po Kong, Northern Kowloon* ☎ *3112–8222* ⊕ *www.pentahotels.com* ⇆ *695 rooms* ⓧ *No meals* Ⓜ *Diamond Hill, Exit A2* ✛ *3:H1.*

$$$$ **The Ritz-Carlton, Hong Kong.** From the world's highest hotel, perch-**HOTEL** ing on the 102nd through 118th floors of the ICC skyscraper in West **FAMILY** Kowloon, every large and luxurious guest room enjoys a stupendous **Fodor'sChoice** vantage point. **Pros:** earth-shattering views; top-class service and ameni-★ ties. **Cons:** pricey; surrounding Kowloon area lacks nightlife. ⓢ *Rooms from: HK$4,700* ✉ *International Commerce Center, 1 Austin Rd. W, Kowloon City* ☎ *2263–2263* ⊕ *www.ritzcarlton.com/en/Properties/ HongKong* ⇆ *312 rooms* ⓧ *No meals* Ⓜ *West Kowloon, Exit C2* ✛ *3:D3.*

$$$ **W Hong Kong.** A hip, young vibe prevails, but guest rooms are veri-**HOTEL** table urban oases—soundproof and spacious, alternately colorful or **Fodor'sChoice** sleek on even and odd floors, with mood lighting, surround audiovi-★ sual systems, big mirrors, and even bigger views of the harbor. **Pros:** friendly service; spacious and colorful rooms; panoramic views; exciting bars and restaurants. **Cons:** noisy atmosphere outside rooms; removed shopping-mall location. ⓢ *Rooms from: HK$3,100* ✉ *1 Austin Rd. W, Kowloon Station, Kowloon* ☎ *3717–2222* ⊕ *www.whotels.com/ hongkong* ⇆ *393 rooms* ⓧ *No meals* Ⓜ *West Kowloon* ✛ *3:D3.*

SOUTHSIDE

Southside feels relatively removed from the more frequented northern coast of Hong Kong Island, due to less direct transport routes. On the upside, it's only a short drive to popular south-coast destinations such as Aberdeen, Ocean Park, Repulse Bay beach, Shek O, and Stanley Market.

$ HOTEL **L'hotel Island South.** These towering 37 floors offer clean and modern rooms, and though the surroundings are industrial, water and lush greenery views, along with an outdoor pool and casual ambience throughout, provide a nice getaway feel. **Pros:** south coast views; close to Southside attractions; free shuttle service to city center; spacious gym. **Cons:** Aberdeen tunnel traffic; very little nightlife nearby. [$] *Rooms from: HK$1,000* ✉ *55 Wong Chuk Hang Rd., Aberdeen, Southside* ☎ *3968–8888* 🌐 *www.lhotelislandsouth.com* 🛏 *432 rooms* 🍴 *No meals* [M] *Aberdeen* ✥ *1:D6.*

$$ HOTEL **Le Méridien Cyberport.** Though most guests belong to the convention crowd gathering at nearby Cyberport, bright and spacious guest rooms break out of the business mode with a hip vibe and generously sized windows for sea gazing; corner suites enjoy especially sensational sea views. **Pros:** vast sunset views over bay and sea; five restaurants; outdoor pool; bathrooms with walk-in showers. **Cons:** isolated location on south side of island. [$] *Rooms from: HK$1,600* ✉ *100 Cyberport Rd., Pok Fu Lam, Southside* ☎ *2980–7788* 🌐 *www.lemeridien.com/hongkong* 🛏 *170 rooms* 🍴 *No meals* [M] *Pok Fu Lam* ✥ *1:A6.*

$$ HOTEL **Ovolo Southside.** For art and design enthusiasts, Ovolo Southside is a fantastic base for exploring the burgeoning Wong Chuk Hang enclave. **Pros:** green views; close to beaches and art galleries; excellent CiRQLE restaurant; free minibar; great rooftop bar; 24-hour gym **Cons:** out-of-the-way location; common areas can get crowded; small entry-level rooms; design not for everyone. [$] *Rooms from: HK$1,500* ✉ *64 Wong Chuk Hang Rd., Aberdeen, Southside* ☎ *3460–8100* 🌐 *www.ovolohotels.com* 🛏 *162 rooms* 🍴 *Breakfast* ✥ *2:C5.*

LANTAU ISLAND

The main advantage to staying on Lantau Island is its proximity to the airport and SkyPier for late-night arrivals or early-morning departures, or to AsiaWorld-Expo if you're here on business. Most visitors come to Lantau by MTR as a day trip; popular attractions include Disneyland, the Ngong Ping cable-car ride, the Tian Tan Buddha, scenic hikes and beaches, and outlet shopping at Citygate mall. For the more adventurous, the island is also home to remote fishing villages, reached by ferry and roads less traveled. Gentrified Discovery Bay beach, easily accessible by ferry from Central, hosts dragon boat races every spring.

$$ HOTEL FAMILY **Auberge Discovery Bay.** Need an escape from the city? **Pros:** family-friendly; comprehensive facilities; sea and mountain views; near beaches **Cons:** 25-minute ferry ride from Central. [$] *Rooms from: HK$1,600* ✉ *88 Siena Ave., Discovery Bay, Lantau Island* ☎ *2295–8288* 🌐 *www.aubergediscoverybay.com* 🛏 *325 rooms* 🍴 *No meals* ✥ *3:C2.*

$$ ⚇ **Disney's Hollywood Hotel.** This is Disneyland, so the focus is on kids—
RESORT   from Chef Mickey restaurants to the piano-shaped pool to well-stocked
FAMILY   playrooms—but adults might enjoy the theme of silver-screen glamour
that extends to art-deco styling in the cocktail lounge and the small but
comfortable guest rooms. **Pros:** good value; a children's paradise; Dis-
covery Bay restaurants are just minutes away; near airport. **Cons:** cut
off from other Hong Kong attractions; corniness factor; generic theme-
park ambience. Ⓢ *Rooms from: HK$2,100* ⊠ *Hong Kong Disneyland
Resort, Lantau Island* ☎ *3510–5000* ⊕ *www.hongkongdisneyland.com*
⤳ *601 rooms* ⦿ *No meals* Ⓜ *Disneyland Resort* ✛ *3:C1.*

$$$ ⚇ **Hong Kong Disneyland Hotel.** Modeled in Victorian style after the
RESORT   Grand Floridian at Florida's Disney resort, this hugely popular resort
FAMILY   is beautifully done, from the spacious rooms with balconies overlook-
ing the sea to kids' activities hosted by Disney characters. **Pros:** great
for kids; handy to airport; free Wi-Fi. **Cons:** cut off from the rest of
Hong Kong; can seem crowded at times. Ⓢ *Rooms from: HK$3,100*
⊠ *Hong Kong Disneyland Resort, Lantau Island* ☎ *3510–6000* ⊕ *www.
hongkongdisneyland.com* ⤳ *415 rooms* ⦿ *No meals* Ⓜ *Disneyland
Resort* ✛ *3:C1.*

$$ ⚇ **Hong Kong SkyCity Marriott Hotel.** Perks at this standard-issue airport
HOTEL   hotel are views of the picturesque Nine Eagles golf course or the South
China Sea, a footbridge that conveniently connects to AsiaWorld-Expo,
and free shuttle service to and from Disneyland and Citygate Outlets
mall in Tung Chung. **Pros:** comfortable if generic ambience; spacious
rooms good for families. **Cons:** tiny spa; low-ceilinged indoor-pool area.
Ⓢ *Rooms from: HK$1,588* ⊠ *1 Sky City Rd. E, Hong Kong Inter-
national Airport, Lantau* ☎ *3969–1888* ⊕ *www.skycitymarriott.com*
⤳ *658 rooms* ⦿ *No meals* Ⓜ *Asia World Expo* ✛ *3:B1.*

$$ ⚇ **Regal Airport Hotel.** One of the world's largest airport hotels is more
HOTEL   than just a place to sleep before the next flight— rooms have terrific
views of planes landing from afar, or overlook the swimming pool, and
the spa has pleasant alfresco areas for relaxation. **Pros:** direct airport
access via indoor moving walkway; refreshing pool and spa facilities;
24-hour gym. **Cons:** far removed from Hong Kong sights. Ⓢ *Rooms
from: HK$1,950* ⊠ *9 Cheong Tat Rd., Hong Kong International Air-
port, Lantau Island* ☎ *2286–8888* ⊕ *www.regalhotel.com/regal-airport-
hotel* ⤳ *1,171 rooms* ⦿ *Breakfast* Ⓜ *Airport* ✛ *3:B1.*

7

NIGHTLIFE AND PERFORMING ARTS

Updated by Charley Lanyon

A riot of neon announces Hong Kong's nightlife districts. Clubs and bars fill to capacity, evening markets pack in shoppers looking for bargains, restaurants welcome diners, cinemas pop corn as fast as they can, and theaters and concert halls prepare for full houses.

The neighborhoods of Wan Chai, Lan Kwai Fong, Sheung Wan, and SoHo are packed with bars, pubs, and nightclubs that cater to everyone from the hippest trendsetters to bankers ready to spend their bonuses and more laid-back crowds out for a pint. Partying in Hong Kong is a way of life; it starts at the beginning of the week with a drink or two after work, progressing to serious barhopping and clubbing on the weekends. Wednesday is a big night out here, too. Work hard, play harder is the motto in Hong Kong, and people follow it seriously.

Because each district has so much to offer, and since they're all quite close to each other, it's perfectly normal to pop into two or three bars before heading to a nightclub. You simply cannot go home without a Hong Kong nightlife story to tell.

PLANNING

HK magazine is distributed free each Friday. *Time Out Hong Kong* costs HK$18 and is published every other Wednesday. Another good source of nightlife and cultural information is the daily English-language newspaper the *South China Morning Post* with its nightlife magazine *48 Hours*.

WHERE TO GO

From champagne decadence to sports bars lined with peanut shells, each of Hong Kong's districts has its own distinct nighttime personality. Even on a single street, dress codes and drink prices can vacillate wildly. The bar- and pub-lined streets of Lan Kwai Fong, Wan Chai, and Kowloon are fairly casual, though shorts and flip-flops will limit your options. A beer or a mixed drink will cost from HK$50 to HK$80. The Central, SoHo, and Wyndham Street areas are home to classy bars and glamorous nightclubs where a cosmopolitan mix of high rollers and partiers comes out to play. Drinks are expensive, and a martini might set you back more than HK$100.

Nightclubs range from down-to-earth dives with boisterous cover bands to hermetically sealed pleasure palaces packed with models and millionaires. The venues listed here tend to be smaller and more intimate than their high-octane megaplex cousins. Cover charges, if levied, can be steep, from HK$120 to HK$250, but often include a drink or two. If you're prepared to pay a steep minimum for bottle service (HK$1,000 to HK$10,000 depending on the venue), you can reserve a table for your party at some of these swanky establishments. Door trolls abound, so dress up to get in and blend in—shorts, flip-flops, and sneakers are definite no-nos.

WHEN TO GET THERE

Around-the-clock liquor licenses are common, so strict closing times are not. Bars start closing around 2 am, clubs around 4 am, with some still hopping around sunrise. Happy hours are from midafternoon to 8 or 9 pm on weekdays. Closing times listed refer to Friday, Saturday, and the eves of public holidays; you can expect things to wind down an hour or two earlier midweek. Bars are typically open nightly, but nightclubs are closed or quiet on Sunday and Monday.

MEMBERS ONLY

Many bars and clubs have a "members-only" policy, but don't let this deter you. It's mostly a way of prioritizing the guest list on busy nights or get around no-smoking regulations. It can also mean that you're required to pay a cover charge, usually in the region of HK$150 to HK$200, including a drink on the house.

STAYING SAFE

All premises licensed to serve alcohol are supposedly subject to stringent fire, safety, and sanitary controls, although at times this is hard to believe, given the overcrowding at the hippest places. Think twice before succumbing to the city's raunchier hideaways. If you stumble into one, check out cover and table charges *before* you get too comfortable. If you don't have a table, pay for each round of drinks as it's served (in cash rather than by credit card).

Hong Kong is an extremely safe place, but, as in many destinations, the art of the out-of-towner rip-off has been perfected. If you're unsure, visit places signposted as approved by the Hong Kong Tourism Board.

LATE-NIGHT TRANSPORTATION

The clean and reliable subway (MTR) shuts down at around 1 am, depending on your location. Taxis are your only way home after that. They are relatively cheap and can easily be flagged down on the street; when the light on the car roof is on, it's available for hire. If the cab has an "out of service" sign over its round "for hire" neon sign on the dashboard, it means it's a cross-harbor taxi. Fares start at HK$22.

HONG KONG'S TOP FIVE NIGHTLIFE SPOTS

dragon-i: The door's clipboard-wielding glamazons will not make entry easy, but this remains the kingpin of the big Central clubs, and second home to the city's extravagant elite.

Fatty Crab: This New York transplant has one of the hottest bars in town, with excellent cocktails, beautiful people, and old-school hip-hop on the sound system. Try the signature Pickle Backs: a shot of bourbon followed by pickle brine.

Felix: Aqua Spirit may be trendier, but Philippe Starck–designed Felix, at the Peninsula, is an institution. The best view of the skyline is marketing currency in Kowloon, and this penthouse bar really matches its claim.

Le Jardin: This no-rules watering hole is off the beaten track near the heart of LKF. Don't let the greenery and fairy lights fool you: on a good night Le Jardin can be as wild as they come.

Solas: Stronghold of Wyndham Street's after-dark action, Solas is great if you're looking for somewhere loud and lively to meet new people over well-mixed drinks.

NIGHTLIFE

HONG KONG ISLAND

WESTERN

As rents rise and progress is made on the new MTR extension, neighborhoods in the western district of the island—Sheung Wan, Sai Ying Pun, and Kennedy Town—are exploding with restaurants, bars, and art galleries. Today Western, as it's called, is undoubtedly the hippest part of Hong Kong.

BARS

The Black Star. This New York–style pub has a loyal following thanks to its excellent cocktails, a good selection of beers, and friendly service. It's a no-frills place, located across from the Sheung Wan MTR station. ⊠ *81 Wing Lok St., Sheung Wan, Western* ☎ *2399–0207* ⊕ *www.theblackstar.hk* Ⓜ *Sheung Wan.*

Club 71. This bohemian diamond-in-the-rough was named in tribute to July 1, 2003, when half a million Hong Kongers successfully rallied against looming threats to their freedom of speech. Tucked away on a terrace down a side street, the quirky, unpretentious bar is a mainstay of artists, journalists, and left-wing politicians. The outdoor area closes around midnight. ⊠ *67 Hollywood Rd., Sheung Wan, Western* ☎ *2858–7071* Ⓜ *Central.*

Fodor'sChoice
★ **Missy Ho's.** The hippest spot in Kennedy Town, Missy Ho's has made a name for itself as much for the swing hanging from the ceiling and dress-up closet as for its Asian-inspired cocktails. Dark but inviting, it's the kind of place where the bartender will urge you to enjoy tequila shots on a Tuesday night. The crowd tends to be mostly young people

looking to party, but all will feel welcome. A sign that Hong Kong's nightlife epicenter is moving ever westward, the bar comes into its own on weekends when it is often full to the brim with revelers. ⊠ *Sincere Western House, 48 Forbes St., Kennedy Town, Western* ☎ *2817–3808* ⊕ *www.casteloconcepts.com.*

Fodor'sChoice **Ping Pong 129.** Housed in an old table-tennis parlor, Ping Pong 129
★ is one of the hottest bars in up-and-coming Sai Ying Pun. The place serves gin and tonics in oversized wine goblets and features works by local artists on the walls. It offers an array of Spanish-inspired snacks. ⊠ *Nam Cheong House, 129 Second St., Western* ☎ *9158–1584* ⊕ *www. pingpong129.com.*

208. One of Hong Kong's favorite after-work watering holes, 208 sits in the middle of trendy Sheung Wan, The place serves up spot-on classic cocktails alongside authentic antipasti. Sit outside and enjoy a cocktail or three with a mostly local crowd. ⊠ *208 Hollywood Rd., Sheung Wan, Western* ☎ *2549–0208* ⊕ *www.208.com.hk* Ⓜ *Sheung Wan.*

GAY AND LESBIAN SPOTS
Volume Beat. A friendly, mixed crowd of gays, lesbians, and their friends enjoys this club's free admission and open-door policy. New Arrivals Wednesdays are a staple of the scene, welcoming tourists and newbies and attracting locals with free vodka between 7 and 9 pm. Weekends are reliably hyper, with dance anthems filling the floor until the wee hours. Regular events include '70s and '80s retro nights and quiz nights. ⊠ *62 Jervois St., Sheung Wan, Western* ☎ *2799–2883* Ⓜ *Sheung Wan.*

CENTRAL
On weekends the streets of Lan Kwai Fong are liberated from traffic, and the hordes from both sides of the street merge. A five-minute walk uphill is SoHo. Back in the '90s it took local businesses some effort to convince district councilors that the sometimes vice-associated moniker (which in this case stands for South of Hollywood Road) was a good idea, but Hong Kong is now proud of this *très* chic area, a warren of streets stuffed with commensurately priced restaurants, bars, and late-night boutiques. Midway between Lan Kwai Fong's madness and SoHo's bohemian glamour is Wyndham Street, home to an array of sophisticated bars, nightclubs, and restaurants, and strict domain of the over-25s.

BARS
Armani Privé. The Armani brand has made its mark on Chater House, bringing a taste of Milan to Hong Kong. The big draw here is a wide, gorgeous deck with skyscraper views, chic outdoor seating, and an impressive—if pricey—list of cocktails. Go into the bar and turn right up the stairs. ⊠ *2nd fl., Chater House, 8 Connaught Rd., Central* ☎ *3583–2828* ⊕ *www.armaniprive-hk.com* Ⓜ *Sheung Wan.*

Back Bar. On Wan Chai's trendy Ship Street, the dimly lit Back Bar is the place for top-of-the-line cocktails and delicious Spanish-influenced bar snacks. It gets very crowded, so come early. ⊠ *1–7 Ship St., behind Ham and Sherry, Wan Chai* ☎ *2555–0628* ⊕ *www.hamandsherry.hk* ☞ *Wan Chai.*

Lan Kwai Fong

CLOSE UP

A curious, L-shape cobblestone lane in Central is the pulsating center of nightlife and dining in Hong Kong. Lan Kwai Fong, or just LKF, is a spot that really shines after the sun goes down. You can start with a late-afternoon drink at any number of bars, then enjoy some of the territory's finest dining before stopping at a nightclub to dance the night away.

For such a small area, Lan Kwai Fong has an incredibly broad range of nightlife, with dozens of bars, restaurants, and clubs within just a few blocks. Since most of the ground-floor establishments spill out onto the pavement, there's an audible buzz about the place, lending it a festive air that's unmatched elsewhere in Hong Kong. Whether it's corporate financiers celebrating their latest million-dollar deals at La Dolce Vita or humbler office workers having drinks with their buddies at Le Jardin, there's a place here to suit every taste.

The same "something for everyone" motto extends to the plethora of upmarket restaurants in Lan Kwai Fong. From Asia there are Chinese, Thai, Japanese, and Vietnamese restaurants, while European food can be found at French and Italian establishments. If your wallet's feeling a little light from your latest shopping expedition, take heed of the excited waiters waving to potential customers along Wing Wah Lane (affectionately known as Rat Alley). Here you'll find rowdy Indian, Thai, and Malaysian restaurants that serve piping-hot dishes at reasonable prices.

Lan Kwai Fong used to be a hawkers' neighborhood before World War II. Its modern success is largely due to Canadian expatriate Allan Zeman, an eccentric figure who has been dubbed the "King of Lan Kwai Fong" by the local media. Today he not only owns dozens of other restaurants and bars, but also the buildings they're in. He claims to have about 100 restaurants, and although he doesn't actually own them all, he acts as the landlord for most of them. LKF's restaurants are now simply a hobby for Zeman, whose business empire includes everything from property development to fashion.

New Year's Eve is undoubtedly the busiest time for Lan Kwai Fong. Thousands of people line the tiny area to celebrate and party. You'll notice a strong police presence moving the human traffic through the streets and keeping an eye out for any trouble-makers. This is mainly to prevent another tragedy such as the one in the early 1990s when 21 people were crushed to death as a massive throng veered out of control as it ushered in a new year. Now when large crowds are anticipated—usually New Year's Eve, Christmas Eve, and also Halloween—the police carefully monitor the number of people entering the area.

Call it progress, or a type of survival-of-the-strongest evolution, but this trendy neighborhood has seen as many establishments open as close down. New spots are constantly in development, or old places under refurbishment. Regardless of the changes, Lan Kwai Fong is always alive with scores of people and places to be merry.

—Eva Chui Loiterton

Partiers vie for elbow room on Lan Kwai Fong, Central's nightlife hub.

The Blck Brd. This whisky bar (pronounced "blackbird") has become the go-to watering hole for a more creative crowd. The design is bachelor-pad chic, with exposed brick walls, Chesterfield sofas on gray, tiled floors, and an outdoor terrace with long wood tables and potted palm trees. Take the elevator up to the sixth floor of 8 Lyndhurst Terrace, a building worth noting for its variety of bars and restaurants. ⊠ *8 Lyndhurst Terrace, 6th fl., Central* ☎ *2545–8555* ⊕ *www.theblckbrd. com* Ⓜ *Central.*

Club 97. A local institution, Club 97 offers extremely generous pours and some of the best service in the city. Very loud and open late, this is not the place for an early evening. ⊠ *9 Lan Kwai Fong, Central* ☎ *2816–1897* Ⓜ *Central.*

The Cutty Sark. Named after the legendary British tea clipper in homage to Hong Kong's colonial history, this small pub in SoHo is a cozy, reliable spot with a nautical theme. It's a good place for a pint on weekend afternoons too, when locals gather around the streetside tables with their dogs. ⊠ *20 Elgin St., SoHo, Central* ☎ *2868–1250* Ⓜ *Central.*

The Envoy. So popular you'll need a reservation, this see-and-be-seen bar in the Pottinger Hotel packs them in with expertly mixed cocktails, comfy seating areas, and the exclusive feel of a British gentlemen's club. Head to the outdoor terrace, where you can enjoy a selection of East-meets-West snacks. ⊠ *3rd fl., Pottinger Hotel, 74 Queen's Rd. Central, Central* ☎ *2308–3188* ⊕ *www.theenvoy.hk* Ⓜ *Sheung Wan.*

Fatty Crab. This New York transplant has become a Hong Kong hot spot because of its great cocktails and old-school hip-hop on the stereo. Snack on a pork-belly bao as you mingle among the beautiful people.

Fatty Crab is credited with bringing pickle-back bourbon—with a shot of pickle brine—to Hong Kong. Make sure you say hi to the owner's dog, Bear. ✉ *1113 Old Bailey St., Central* ☎ *2521–2033* ⊕ *www.fattycrab.com.hk* Ⓜ *Central.*

Fu Lu Shou. An amazing rooftop terrace has turned this bar and restaurant in a nondescript commercial building on Hollywood Road into one of the hippest spots in town. The boldly colored mural urging patrons to "Eat, Drink, and Be Prosperous" and the bar covered with mah-jongg tiles add just the right amount of retro cool. The menu boasts cocktails based on traditional local flavors, but the bartenders are also adept at turning out the classics. If the front door is locked, just call and ask for the code. ✉ *7th fl., 31 Hollywood Rd., Central* ☎ *2336–8812* Ⓜ *Central.*

Fodor's Choice ★ **Globe.** In a trendy SoHo space, this British-expat hangout evokes the feel of southwest London. The owner is a beer fanatic, and the place boasts one of the best selections in Hong Kong. It's a fun and convivial spot with a mix of ages and a pretty even split between expats and locals. You can book the sectioned-off "chill-out" area to watch live sports coverage with a group of friends. Good luck trying to get the proprietors to turn on the World Series or the Super Bowl, though. Soccer and rugby reign supreme here, and you'll have to share the TV. ✉ *45–53 Graham St., SoHo, Central* ☎ *2543–1941* ⊕ *www.theglobe.com.hk* Ⓜ *Central.*

Honi Honi. Tongue-in-cheek Honi Honi is a sleeker, more sophisticated take on the classic tiki bar, with fruit-filled cocktails and a DJ spinning island rhythms. Aside from the over-the-top South Pacific decor, the main draw is the plam-fringed outdoor terrace. Tables fill up fast, so get here early. ✉ *3rd fl., Somptueux Central, 52 Wellington St., Central* ☎ *2353–0885* ⊕ *honihonibar.com* Ⓜ *Central.*

Ivan The Kozak. This is one of Hong Kong's best-kept secrets, serving authentic Russian food in a charmingly kitschy setting. The real draw is the "ice bar," a collection of vodkas in a walk-in refrigerator that has been painted with scenes from the old country. To get in the *Dr. Zhivago* mood, don one of the complimentary fur coats. The drinks are cheap and very good, and the experience is unlike anything else in Hong Kong. ✉ *46–48 Cochrane St., Central* ☎ *2851–1193* Ⓜ *Central.*

The Keg. As the name implies, beer and more beer is the beverage of choice at this small pub. It's designed to resemble the inside of a keg, with interiors finished in wood, copper, and polished steel. Large wooden barrels serve as tables, and the floors are covered with discarded peanut shells. Sports coverage rules the TV screens. ✉ *52 D'Aguilar St., Lan Kwai Fong, Central* ☎ *2810–0369* Ⓜ *Central.*

La Cabane. The beating heart of Hong Kong's French community, La Cabane specializes in organic and biodynamic wines. On weekends the crowds spill into the street, with patrons enjoying glasses of affordable but hard-to-find wines and dining on French-influenced fare. ✉ *62 Hollywood Rd., Central* ☎ *2776–6070* ⊕ *www.lacabane.hk* Ⓜ *Central.*

Le Jardin. The leafy setting belies the down-and-dirty vibe at this casual bar with a terrace overlooking the colorful dining strip known locally as "Rat Alley." This refreshingly low-key bar is a little tricky to find:

walk through the dining area and up a flight of steps. The place is packed on weekends. ✉ *10 Wing Wah La., Lan Kwai Fong, Central* ☎ *2877–1100* Ⓜ *Central.*

Le Tambour. You'll feel like you've stepped into a Parisian wine bar. Le Tambour offers great vintages and excellent casual French fare—all of it at reasonable prices. The atmosphere is laid-back, and French is the language of choice. This place is a guaranteed good time, especially when there's live music. ✉ *52A Peel St., Central* ☎ *3114–6320* ⊕ *www.tambour.com.hk* ☞ *Central.*

Lux. Decorated in a lush shade of red, this two-story establishment boasts a busy street-level bar with windows overlooking the crowds in Lan Kwai Fong. The daily happy hour is popular with the after-work crowd. Head upstairs and you'll find modern European fare, with signature dishes including roasted lobster spaghetti. ✉ *The Plaza, 21 D'Aguilar St., Lan Kwai Fong, Central* ☎ *2868–9538* ⊕ *www.luxhongkong.com* Ⓜ *Central.*

MO Bar. A destiation for Hong Kong's big spenders, this plush bar in the Landmark Mandarin Oriental appeals to a more civilized crowd. You'll pay top dollar for the signature drinks (up to HK$200), but the striking, sleek, and super modern interior makes it almost worthwhile. The ground-floor location means the best views will be of the other well heeled patrons but that's ok, this is a place to be seen as much as see. ✉ *Landmark Mandarin Oriental, 15 Queen's Rd. Central, Central* ☎ *2132–0077* ⊕ *www.mandarinoriental.com/landmark/fine-dining/mo-bar* Ⓜ *Central.*

Racks MDB. The grungy pool hall turned hipster haven keeps packing them in with great music, reasonable prices, and an unpretentious vibe. It's good for a game of pool, darts, or beer pong. It seems everyone, even celebrity-chef Anthony Bourdain, goes to Racks. ✉ *Winning Centre, 46–48 Wyndham St., Central* ☎ *2868–0400* Ⓜ *Central.*

RED Bar. Although its shopping-mall location, self-service policy, and incongruous affiliation with the next-door gym may not seem appealing, once you arrive you'll throw all your preconceived notions into the harbor. On the roof of IFC Mall, RED's outdoor terrace has breathtaking views of the city, making it a relaxing place for watching the sunset. The entire rooftop seating area is public space—a rarity in Hong Kong—so do what the locals do: buy your drinks from the CitySuper downstairs and enjoy one of the best views in the city on the cheap. ✉ *4th fl., Two IFC, 8 Finance St., Central* ☎ *8129–8882* ⊕ *www.pure-red.com* Ⓜ *Hong Kong.*

Sevva. With a stunning view of Central's glittering valley of skyscrapers, this cool and elegant rooftop bar is, despite often appalling service, always busy on Friday and Saturday nights. If you're feeling indulgent, come for dessert (the cakes are among the city's best) and stay for cocktails. Most of Sevva's well-heeled clientele prefer to drink outside on the spacious terrace, but there are also cozy couches inside. A dress code of smart casual applies. ✉ *25th fl., Prince's Bldg., 10 Chater Rd., Central* ☎ *2537–1388* ⊕ *www.sevva.hk* Ⓜ *Central.*

Fodor's Choice
★

Solas. Positioned a floor below the dance club dragon-i, this always-crowded bar is Wyndham Street's party central. Expect a mostly expat crowd of twenty- and thirtysomethings who come straight from work in their business suits. With good music—everything from electronic dance music to Katy Perry—and a well-lubricated crowd, Solas is a great place to cut loose. The interior is dark and extremely basic, but the party routinely spills into the street out front. ✉ *60 Wyndham St., SoHo, Central* ☎ *3162–3710* ⊕ *www.solas.com.hk* Ⓜ *Central.*

Staunton's Wine Bar & Cafe. Adjacent to Hong Kong's famous outdoor escalator is this popular bistro-style café and bar. As the weekend aproaches the place gets crowded, but it's still the perfect place to people-watch from the balcony. You can come for a drink at night or coffee during the day. It's also a Sunday-morning favorite for nursing hangovers over brunch. ✉ *10–12 Staunton St., SoHo, Central* ☎ *2973–6611* ⊕ *www.stauntonsgroup.com* Ⓜ *Central.*

Stormies. This hectic boozer in the center of heaving Lan Kwai Fong is packed to bursting every weekend. It's saved from being just another soulless Lan Kwai Fong dive thanks to a killer oldies sound track and a ready-for-anything crowd. Come ready to dance. ✉ *46 D'Aguilar St., Lan Kwai Fong, Central* ☎ *2845–5533* ⊕ *www.cafedecogroup.com* Ⓜ *Central.*

DANCE CLUBS

Azure. Head skyward to this cosmopolitan club at the top of the Hotel LKF. The downstairs lounge features pool tables, comfy couches, and a sound track of ambient tunes. Upstairs, you can take in the harbor from the smoking terrace or dance to funky house music inside. Don't miss the excellent espresso martinis. ✉ *29th fl., Hotel LKF, 33 Wyndham St., Central* ☎ *3518–9330* ⊕ *www.azure.hk* Ⓜ *Central.*

Fodor's Choice
★

dragon-i. Around for more than a decade, dragon-i has lost none of its popularity, which is rare for a nightclub in Hong Kong. Have a drink on the deck or step inside the vivid red playroom, which doubles as a Chinese restaurant earlier in the day. It's the domain of the city's young, rich, and beautiful (if not necessarily classy) crowd, and attracts a busy roster of international acts and DJs. ✉ *The Centrium, 60 Wyndham St., Central* ☎ *3110–1222* ⊕ *www.dragon-i.com.hk* Ⓜ *Central.*

Drop. This pint-size gem is *the* after-hours party spot in Central. Hidden down an alley beside a late-night food stand, its obscure location only adds to the speakeasy feel. Drop gets crowded on weekends and it can be hard to get inside, so it's best to arrive early and wait for the party to pop off. ✉ *Basement level, On Lok Mansion, 39–43 Hollywood Rd., Central* ☎ *2543–8856* ⊕ *www.drophk.com* Ⓜ *Central.*

Fly. This club attracts a younger crowd, making it one of Central's rowdier nightlife spots. The music tends to be more varied than the commercial fare at other clubs, encouraging visits from a lively mix of local and international talent. Get here early for a perch on the low-slung black sofas. ✉ *24–30 Ice House St., Central* ☎ *2810–9902* ⊕ *www.clubfly.com.hk* Ⓜ *Central.*

Oma. The owner is good friends with the people behind the now-shuttered Midnight & Co., so expect the same great electronic dance music, international DJs alongside local talent, and parties that go all night. The space is a bit of a dank hole, but thanks to the top-of-the-line sound system and strong drinks, nobody seems to notice or care. ⊠ *Basement level, Harilela House, 79 Wyndham St., Central* ☎ *2521–8815* Ⓜ *Central.*

Tastings. Oenophiles will discover like minds at this vanguard of the city's burgeoning (and very serious) wine scene. Tucked in an alley off Wellington Street, the bar stocks more than 160 wines. About 40 are always available for sampling through an Enomatic wine dispenser, which the sommeliers use to draw from rare wines without uncorking the entire bottle. Head toward the door's blue glow to find the place. Enjoy the spread of fine cheeses and Italian antipasti before the tasting begins. ⊠ *Basement level, 27 and 29 Wellington St., Central* ☎ *2523–6282* ⊕ *tastings.hk* Ⓜ *Central.*

Varga Lounge. Named after the Peruvian painter of pinup girls, this is a colorful, eclectic little spot for a cocktail. Large groups can take over the upstairs lounge, with its bright walls and 1950s-inspired art. Downstairs, the popular bar opens onto the street. ⊠ *36 Staunton St., SoHo, Central* ☎ *2104–9697* ⊕ *www.vargaloungehk.com* Ⓜ *Central.*

Volar. By midnight the line outside this club is more like a scrimmage. The maze of low-ceilinged basement rooms hosts a young, hip crowd and a genuinely eclectic mix of music ranging from electro-house to hip-hop to rock-and-roll mash-ups. Volar boasts one of Hong Kong's best sound systems and the clout to draw some of the best DJs from overseas. ⊠ *38–44 D'Aguilar St., Lan Kwai Fong, Central* ☎ *2810–1510* Ⓜ *Central.*

GAY AND LESBIAN SPOTS

Propaganda. Off a quaint cobblestone street is a popular gay nightclub with an art-deco bar area that hosts quite the flirt fest. The sunken dance floor has poles on either side for go-go boys. The place is pretty empty during the week, and on weekends the crowds arrive well after midnight. The entrance is in an alleyway called Ezra Lane, which runs parallel to Hollywood Road. ⊠ *Basement level, 1 Hollywood Rd., Central* ☎ *2868–1316* Ⓜ *Central.*

MUSIC CLUBS

Grappa's Cellar. This cavernous basement restaurant clears its tables regularly for some of the best live-music gigs in town. Whether the performers are visiting indie bands or homegrown jazz performers, the huge dance floor and rowdy second-level bar make it difficult not to have fun. The swinging Stray Katz Big Band plays on the first Saturday of each month. ⊠ *Basement level, Jardine House, 1 Connaught Pl., Central* ☎ *2521–2322* Ⓜ *Central.*

WAN CHAI

Wan Chai is the pungent night flower of the nocturnal scene, where the way of life served as inspiration for the novel *The World of Suzie Wong*. It now shares the streets with hip wine bars, salsa sessions, and after parties that continue past sunrise. The seedy "hostess bars" in this neighborhood are easy to spot, with curtained entrances guarded by old ladies on stools and suggestive names in neon. But some things

CLOSE UP

Late-Night Bites

The Flying Pan. Nix that looming hangover with a greasy fry-up before you hit the sack. The Flying Pan is a popular 24-hour diner, equally busy at 3 am and 3 pm on weekends. Eggs any style come with two picks from a huge list of sides including grits, blintzes, baked beans, and fruit salad. The truly greedy can order the Kitchen Sink, which is a taste of everything. There's another branch at 81–85 Lockhart Road in Wan Chai. ⊠ *9 Old Bailey St., Central* ☎ *2140–6333* ⊕ *www.the-flying-pan.com* Ⓜ *Central.*

Hay Hay Kitchen. A brightly lit oasis on Lockhart Road, Hay Hay is best known for its Hong Kong–style noodles and rice plates. The *char siu hor fun* (barbecue pork noodles in soup) is a popular late-night dish. Pay the cashier on your way out. ⊠ *Hay Wah Bldg., 72–86 Lockhart Rd., Wan Chai* ☎ *2143–6183* Ⓜ *Wan Chai.*

Tsui Wah. While locals head to the three-story Tsui Wah at any time of the day, the late-night crowds are the happiest. Service is quick and there's a huge menu of typical Chinese fare such as fried rice and noodles as well as western dishes such as steak and pasta. It's noisy and bright, but the crowds just keep on coming. You may even find the odd celebrity chowing down on beef brisket noodles at 2 am. ⊠ *15–19 Wellington St., Central* ☎ *2525–6338* ⊕ *www.tsuiwah.com* Ⓜ *Central.*

—Eva Chui Loiterton

never change: the busiest nights are still when there's a navy ship in the harbor on an R&R stopover.

BARS

The Canny Man. This is Hong Kong's only old-school Scottish pub, decked out in timber and red-tartan furnishings. The bar serves an impressive collection of 180 single malts and 28 artisanal beers, alongside a roster of guest ales that changes regularly. In the basement of the nondescript Wharney Guang Dong Hotel, there's a dartboard, pool table, and live sports on the video screens. There's also a full menu that includes delicacies like haggis balls. ⊠ *Basement level, Wharney Guang Dong Hotel, 57–73 Lockhart Rd., Wan Chai* ☎ *2861–1935* ⊕ *www. thecannyman.com* Ⓜ *Wan Chai.*

Carnegie's. Named after Scottish steel baron Andrew Carnegie, whose family sailed to America in the late 1800s, this rock-and-roll bar lives up to its name. Although Carnegie himself probably didn't imagine bartop dancing at an establishment bearing his name, the Scottish owners feel that his love of music lives on in this pub. Avoid Wednesday nights, when the place is wall-to-wall teenagers in search of cheap drinks. ⊠ *53–55 Lockhart Rd., Wan Chai* ☎ *2866–6289* ⊕ *www.carnegies.net/ hongkong/* Ⓜ *Wan Chai.*

Mes Amis. In the heart of Wan Chai, this high-ceilinged bar has bifold doors that open onto the busy street corner, meaning that you won't miss any of the action outside. The perpetual crowd inside is on display to passersby outside. ⊠ *83–85 Lockhart Rd., Wan Chai* ☎ *2527–6680* ⊕ *www.mesamis.com.hk* Ⓜ *Wan Chai.*

Rio. A nice alternative to the dives of Wan Chai, sophisticated Rio has a plush bar with low-key live music and a dance club complete with a light-up floor. On weekends the party runs until very late. ⊠ *Hang Shun Mansion, 68–82 Jaffe Rd., Wan Chai* ⊕ *www.rioclub.hk* Ⓜ *Wan Chai.*

Wooloomooloo. This sleek rooftop bar, named after the Australian aboriginal word for "young male kangaroo," provides a respite from the Wan Chai crowds. There's a downstairs steak house, but the real draw is the alfresco bar. The breezy terrace and a panoramic view over Happy Valley have made it a favorite. ⊠ *31st fl., 256 Hennessy Rd., Wan Chai* ☎ *2893–6960* ⊕ *www.wooloo-mooloo.com* Ⓜ *Wan Chai.*

DANCE CLUBS

Dusk Till Dawn. Loud, energetic cover bands get the dance floor jumping on Wednesday to Saturday nights. Popular with expats, it can get crowded, but patrons are usually having too much fun to care. ⊠ *76–84 Jaffe Rd., Wan Chai* ☎ *2528–4689* Ⓜ *Wan Chai.*

Joe Bananas. The days of all-night partying are gone: Joe Bananas has reopened as a gentler version of the boisterous place it used to be. There's almost always a live band, and the the doors stay open until the wee hours. The handsome space is considered a Hong Kong landmark, and is still worth a visit. ⊠ *23 Luard Rd., Wan Chai* ☎ *2537–4618* ⊕ *www.joebananas.hk* Ⓜ *Wan Chai.*

CAUSEWAY BAY

BARS

ToTT's and Roof Terrace. Also known as Talk of the Town, this restaurant and bar takes up the 34th floor of one of Hong Kong's legendary hotels. Today, it's best known for its Sunday brunch buffet, where live jazz and free-flowing champagne complement daytime views of Victoria harbor. At night, a classic cocktail on the outdoor terrace is one of the area's classier offerings. ⊠ *34th fl., The Excelsior, 281 Gloucester Rd., Causeway Bay* ☎ *2837–6786* ⊕ *www.mandarinoriental.com/excelsior* Ⓜ *Causeway Bay.*

KOWLOON

Central and Wan Chai are undoubtedly the king and queen of nightlife in Hong Kong. If you're staying in a hotel, however, or having dinner across the water in Kowloon, Ashley Road and Knutsford Terrace, both in Tsim Sha Tsui, still make for a fun night out. If cocktails on the water with a view of the harbor sounds like your kind of thing, check out the *Aqua Luna.*

TSIM SHA TSUI

BARS

All Night Long. This Knutsford Terrace staple hosts a talented Filipino cover band that mainly works hits from the '80s and '90s. Drinks are a little overpriced, but there's an impressive sound system that prompts a loud sing-along from the crowd. Spanish-style artwork adorns the red-and-yellow walls. ⊠ *9 Knutsford Terr., Tsim Sha Tsui* ☎ *2367–9487* Ⓜ *Tsim Sha Tsui.*

Aqua Luna. As one of the city's last traditionally crafted vessels, or junks, the plush *Aqua Luna*'s dramatic appearance and red sails make her easy to spot. Step off dry land from the piers in Kowloon or Central, order a gin and tonic, and take in the shimmering harbor sights for 45 minutes. The HK$195 price tag includes one drink, and a snack menu is available. The ferry runs every hour from 5:30 pm daily. ◼TIP→ The more expensive 7:30 cruise lets you watch the city's nightly Symphony of Lights show from the harbor. ⊠ *Hong Kong Cultural Center, Public Pier No. 1, Tsim Sha Tsui* ☎ *2116–8821* ⊕ *www.aqua.com.hk.*

Fodor's Choice   **Aqua Spirit.** Inside an impressive curvaceous skyscraper, this very cool
★   bar sits on the mezzanine level of the top floor. The high ceilings and glass walls offer up unrivaled views of Hong Kong and the surrounding harbor filled with ferries and ships. Tables are placed in front of the windows, so you never have to crane your neck to see the skyline. ⊠ *30th fl., One Peking, 1 Peking Rd., Tsim Sha Tsui* ☎ *3427–2288* ⊕ *www.aqua.com.hk* Ⓜ *Tsim Sha Tsui.*

Dada. This bar in the eccentric Luxe Manor hotel is a tribute to surrealism: a side gallery boasts two original etchings by Salvador Dalí. References to that artist and other greats like Magritte abound. A dark and spacious bar area is anchored by a central counter, from which bottles of absinthe glimmer. ⊠ *2nd fl., Luxe Manor, 39 Kimberly Rd., Tsim Sha Tsui* ☎ *3763–8778* ⊕ *www.dadalounge.com.hk* Ⓜ *Tsim Sha Tsui.*

Delaney's. This Irish pub has interiors that were shipped here from the Emerald Isle, and the mood is as authentic as the furnishings. Guinness and Delaney's ale (a specialty microbrew) are on tap, and there's a traditional Irish menu. The crowd includes some Irish regulars, so get ready for spontaneous outbursts of fiddling and other Celtic traditions. ⊠ *Basement fl., 71–77 Peking Rd., Tsim Sha Tsui* ☎ *2301–3980* ⊕ *www.delaneys.com.hk* Ⓜ *Tsim Sha Tsui.*

Fodor's Choice   **Felix.** High up in the Peninsula Hong Kong, this bar is immensely pop-
★   ular with visitors. It not only has a brilliant view of the island, but the dramatic interiors are by the visionary designer Philippe Starck. Another memorable feature: the men's room also has windows with great city views. If you feel like dancing, head to the dramatic Crazy Box, which has padded walls and illuminated tables. ⊠ *28th fl., Peninsula Hong Kong, Salisbury Rd., Tsim Sha Tsui* ☎ *2696–6778* ⊕ *hongkong.peninsula.com* Ⓜ *Tsim Sha Tsui.*

Ned Kelly's Last Stand. Come to this boisterous Australian watering hole, named for the continent's notorious bushranger, for an exuberant Dixieland jazz outfit that often leads the crowd in a rowdy singalong. The band plays from 9:30 pm to 1 am nightly. Arrive early for decent seats and a chance to sample the pub meals. ⊠ *11A Ashley Rd., Tsim Sha Tsui* ☎ *2376–0562* Ⓜ *Tsim Sha Tsui.*

NORTHERN KOWLOON
BARS

Woobar. This fashionable space is in keeping with the hotel's chic and fun aesthetic. Wednesday nights you can opt for free-flowing wine and a selection of tasty cheeses. The lychee martinis are excellent. ⊠ W

Hong Kong, 1 Austin Rd. W, Northern Kowloon ☎ *3717–2222* ⊕ *www. woobarhongkong.com* Ⓜ *Kowloon.*

PERFORMING ARTS

The city's arts and culture scene is quite lively, with innovative music, dance, and theater among the regular offerings. Small independent productions as well as large-scale concerts take to the stage across the territory every weekend.

FILM

Hong Kong cinema still projects an image of classic martial arts and prolific Triad flicks, with a few auteurs capturing the nuanced poetry of life in the former British colony. Inside the territory, however, silly romantic comedies with pop stars, gory–sexy ghost films, cheesy slapstick throwaways, and a handful of thoughtful independent films also populate the screens. It goes without saying that you can learn a lot about Hong Kong by watching its local flicks in situ.

Broadway Cinematheque. The train-station design of this art house has won awards. Inside the foyer, a departure board displays the showings: primarily foreign and independent films, with a few Hollywood productions to round out the roster. You can read the latest reel-world magazines from around the globe at Kubrick, the café-bookshop next door. ✉ *Prosperous Garden, 3 Public Square St., Yau Ma Tei* ☎ *2388–3188* ⊕ *www.cinema.com.hk* Ⓜ *Yau Ma Tei.*

Grand Cinema. This cinema in the upscale Elements Mall in West Kowloon boasts massive screens, a kicking sound system, and vibrating seats, making it the ideal place to watch a big-budget blockbuster. Facilities include a café, restaurant, and a gallery space hosting film-related exhibitions. ✉ *2nd fl., Elements Mall, 1 Austin Rd. W, Kowloon* ☎ *3983–0033* ⊕ *www.thegrandcinema.com.hk.*

Fodor's Choice ★ **Hong Kong Film Archive.** Don't underestimate the popularity of old black-and-white films in a modern auditorium—buy your tickets in advance, as these classic regularly sell out. The theater screens rarities from the impressive archive of reels dating back decades. Conscientiously curated film programs are often accompanied by exhibitions in a separate gallery downstairs, as well as lively panel discussions featuring film critics and directors. ✉ *50 Lei King Rd., Sai Wan Ho, Eastern* ☎ *2734–9009* ⊕ *www.filmarchive.gov.hk* Ⓜ *Sai Wan Ho.*

Hong Kong International Film Festival. The annual Hong Kong International Film Festival brings together some of the finest film-industry talent from all over the globe. The festival usually occurs in mid-May, offering two weeks worth of movie screenings, exhibitions, and seminars, some hosted by world-renowned actors and filmmakers. As a supplement to the main festival, the Hong Kong International Film Festival Society also holds a Summer International Film Festival in the middle of August. ☎ *2970–3300* ⊕ *www.hkiff.org.hk.*

For a unique evening out, nab tickets to the Chinese opera.

PERFORMANCE CENTERS

Fringe Club. The pioneer of Hong Kong's alternative-arts scene has been staging excellent independent theater, music, and art productions since opening in 1983. The distinctive brown-and-white-stripe colonial structure was built as a cold-storage warehouse in 1892, and the painstaking renovation has earned awards. Light pours through huge windows into the street-level Anita Chan Lai-ling Gallery, with its small, well-curated exhibitions. It has its own bar, the Fringe Dairy, which claims to be the only jazz and cabaret space in Hong Kong. Productions are sometimes in Cantonese, so check the program carefully. ⊠ *2 Lower Albert Rd., Central* ☎ *2521–7251 general inquiries, 3128–8288 Hong Kong Ticketing box office* Ⓜ *Central.*

Hong Kong Academy for Performing Arts. Many of Hong Kong's most talented performers studied at this academy's schools of drama, music, dance, television, and film. It has five theaters and a gallery, so there's always something going on. Productions are staged in the Lyric Theatre, the smaller Drama Theatre, and the tiny Studio Theatre. The two concert halls host choice classical or traditional Chinese music performances. When the weather's pleasant, take in a show at the garden amphitheater. ⊠ *1 Gloucester Rd., Wan Chai* ☎ *2584–8500* ⊕ *www. hkapa.edu* Ⓜ *Wan Chai.*

Hong Kong Arts Centre. A hodgepodge of activities takes place in this deceptively bleak concrete tower, financed with horse-racing profits donated by the Hong Kong Jockey Club. The split-level Pao galleries house year-round exhibitions of art and crafts. Thematic cycles of art-house flicks run in the basement agnès b. CINEMA. Community theater

CLOSE UP

Chinese Opera

There are 10 **Cantonese opera** troupes headquartered in Hong Kong, as well as many amateur singing groups. Some put on performances of "street opera" in, for example, the Temple Street Night Market almost every night, while others perform at temple fairs, in City Hall, or in playgrounds under the auspices of the Urban Council. Those unfamiliar with Chinese opera might find the sights and sounds of this highly complex and sophisticated art form a little strange. Every gesture has its own meaning; in fact, there are 50 gestures for the hand alone.

Props attached to the costumes are similarly intricate and are used in exceptional ways. For example, the principal female often has 5-foot-long pheasant-feather tails attached to her headdress; she shows anger by dropping the head and shaking it in a circular fashion so that the feathers move in a perfect circle. Surprise is shown by what's called "nodding the feathers." You can also "dance with the feathers" to show a mixture of anger and determination. Orchestral music punctuates the singing. It's best to attend with someone who can translate the gestures for you; or you can learn more at the Cantonese Opera Halls in the Hong Kong Heritage Museum.

The highly stylized **Peking opera** employs higher-pitched voices than Cantonese opera. Peking opera is an older form, more respected for its classical traditions; the meticulous training of the several troupes visiting Hong Kong from the People's Republic of China each year is well regarded. They perform in City Hall or at special temple ceremonies. You can get the latest programs from the Hong Kong Cultural Centre.

—Eva Chui Loiterton

groups are behind much of the fare at the Shouson Theatre and smaller McAulay Studio, though international drama and dance troupes sometimes appear. The new Comix Home Base showcases local comedians. From Wan Chai MTR, cross the footbridge to Immigration Tower, then dogleg left through the open plaza until you hit Harbour Road. The center is on the left. ⌧ 2 Harbour Rd., Wan Chai ☎ 2582–0200 ⊕ www. hkac.org.hk 🎫 Free Ⓜ Wan Chai.

Hong Kong City Hall. The performances at City Hall, ranging from the New York Philharmonic to the Bee Gees, and from the Royal Danish Ballet to the People's Liberation Army Comrade Dance Troupe, are varied but consistently excellent. Two buildings make up the chunky '60s-era complex, divided by a World War II memorial garden and shrine. The 1,500-seat concert hall and a smaller theater are in the low-rise block, as is the massive Maxim's City Palace, a clattering restaurant with good dim sum. The high-rise building has an exhibition space and a smaller recital hall. Performances are usually held Friday and Saturday evenings. ⌧ 5 Edinburgh Pl., Central ☎ 2921–2840 ⊕ www.lcsd.gov. hk ☉ Daily 9 am–11 pm Ⓜ Central.

Hong Kong Cultural Centre. The Hong Kong Cultural Centre's 2,000-seat concert hall, an oval-shaped space fitted with an adjustable acoustic canopy and curtains, houses an 8,000-pipe Austrian organ, one of the world's largest. The Grand Theatre often hosts visiting Broadway musicals, opera, and ballet, while cozier plays take place in the Studio Theatre. Exhibitions are occasionally mounted in the atrium. ✉ *10 Salisbury Rd., Tsim Sha Tsui* ☎ *2734–2009* ⊕ *www.hkculturalcentre. gov.hk* ☉ *Daily 9–11* Ⓜ *Tsim Sha Tsui*

Hong Kong Philharmonic Orchestra. Look out for performances by the world-class Hong Kong Philharmonic Orchestra, which plays everything from classical to avant-garde, as well as contemporary music by Chinese composers. Past soloists have included Vladimir Ashkenazy, Rudolf Firkusny, and Maureen Forrester. ☎ *2721–2030* ⊕ *www.hkpo.com.*

Kwai Tsing Theatre. It might be in the sticks, but the Kwai Tsing Theatre is a major player in the cultural scene. Sunlight pours into the atrium through a curving glass facade that looks onto a plaza where performances are often held. Inside, the 900-seat theater provides a much-needed middle ground between the massive spaces and tiny studio theaters at other venues. And if the likes of Philip Glass and the Royal Shakespeare Company can schlep out here, 25 minutes by MTR from Central, so can you. ✉ *12 Hing Ning Rd., Kwai Chung, New Territories* ☎ *2408–0128* ⊕ *www.lcsd.gov.hk/ktt* ☉ *Daily 9 am–11 pm* Ⓜ *Kwai Fong.*

SIDE TRIP TO
MACAU

WELCOME TO MACAU

TOP REASONS TO GO

★ **Discover the Ruins of São Paulo.** The church facade, all that remains of a former center of learning, is a symbol of Macau.

★ **Take a seat in Senado Square.** A bench here is the perfect perch from which to watch Macau's comings and goings while admiring the colonial surroundings.

★ **Explore the A-Ma Temple.** It's steeped in Macau's culture and history. Search for the Lucky Money Pool, then wash your hands in the blessed water before heading to the casinos.

★ **Place Your Bets.** Even if you don't gamble, take a peek inside the Hotel Lisboa, a classic Macau landmark, or the newer and splashier Venetian Macao, a sprawling complex where gondoliers glide down indoor canals and luxury shopping abounds.

★ **Say "Spaaahhh."** Macau's spas have ultra-indulgent treatments and world-class facilities—with prices to match. But for many the pampering is well worth the expense.

1 The Macau Peninsula. You'll experience authentic Macau in vintage Portuguese squares and in European-style sidewalk cafés, as well as in Buddhist temples, with their red lanterns and fragrant joss sticks. In this exotic place where two worlds collide, don't be surprised to find a pink colonial building housing a Chinese herbal-medicine shop.

2 Taipa. The Portuguese presence on Macau dates from the mid-1500s, but the island of Taipa wasn't occupied until the mid-1800s. It remained a garrison and a pastoral retreat until the 1970s, when it was linked to Macau by bridge. Today some parts retain a village feel, while others are crowded with soulless high-rises.

3 Coloane. Although it's now attached to its smaller sister island, Coloane is still less populated and more intimate than Taipa. Few tourists venture this far south; however, those who do will discover parks, beaches, and golf links, as well as unchanged Portuguese architecture and cobblestone streets.

0 — 1/2 mi
0 — 800 meters

Av. Conselhe Bo

Inner Harbour

R. Visconde

R. do Almirante

R. Sergio

R. Padre A

A Ma Temple

Sai Van

GUANGDONG PROVINCE

CHINA

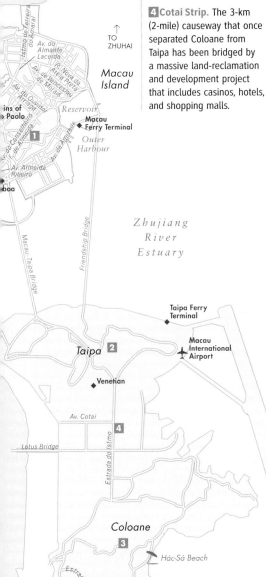

4 **Cotai Strip.** The 3-km (2-mile) causeway that once separated Coloane from Taipa has been bridged by a massive land-reclamation and development project that includes casinos, hotels, and shopping malls.

GETTING ORIENTED

Macau, a Special Administrative Region (SAR) of the People's Republic of China, is on the western bank of the Pearl River Delta, about an hour from Hong Kong by hydrofoil. It consists of the Macau Peninsula, and Taipa and Coloane on a nearby island. The Cotai area, a glitzy, Vegas-like strip of hotels and casinos that began development in 2006, lies between Taipa and Coloane and merges the two. Most people visit Macau to gamble, eat cheap seafood, and shop. But don't over-look its timeless charms and unique culture, born from centuries of both Portuguese and Chinese influence.

8

Updated by
Kate Springer

Enter the desperate, smoky atmosphere of a Chinese casino, where frumpy players bet an average of five times more than the typical Vegas gambler. Sit down next to grandmothers who smoke like chimneys while playing baccarat—the local game of choice—with visiting high rollers. Then step out of the climate-controlled chill and into tropical air that embraces you like a warm, balmy hug. Welcome to Macau.

The many contrasts in this tiny enclave of 555,000 people serve as reminders of how different cultures have embraced one another's traditions for hundreds of years. Though Macau's population is 95% ethnic Chinese, there are still-vibrant pockets of Portuguese and Filipino expats. And some of the thousands of Eurasians—who consider themselves neither Portuguese nor Chinese, but something in between—can trace the intermarriage of their ancestors back a century or two.

Macau's old town, while dominated by the buildings, squares, and cobblestone alleyways of colonial Portugal, is tinged with eastern influences as well. In Macau you can spend an afternoon exploring Buddhist temples before feasting on a dinner of *bacalhau com natas* (dried codfish with a cream sauce), grilled African chicken (spicy chicken in a coconut-peanut broth—a classic Macanese dish), Chinese lobster with scallions, or fiery prawns infused with Indian and Malaysian flavors. Wash everything down with *vinho verde,* the crisp young wine from northern Portugal, and top it all off with a traditional Portuguese *pastel de nata* (egg-custard tart) and dark, thick espresso.

PLANNING

THE BASICS

The Macau Government Tourist Office (MGTO) is well managed.

To enter Macau, Americans and Canadians need only a valid passport for stays of up to 30 days, while EU citizens can stay for 90.

The Macanese *pataca* (MOP) has a fixed exchange rate of MOP$1.032 to HK$1 and roughly MOP$8 to US$1. Patacas come in 10, 20, 50, 100, 500, and 1,000 MOP banknotes plus 1, 2, and 5 MOP coins. A pataca is divided into 100 *avos*, which come in 10-, 20-, and 50-avo coins. Hong Kong dollars are accepted in Macau on a 1:1 basis.

Contacts **Macau Government Tourist Office** (*MGTO*). ✉ *335–341, Alameda Dr. Carlos d'Assumpção* ☎ *853/2833–3000 in Macau, 8238–8680 in Hong Kong* ⊕ *www.macautourism.gov.mo.*

LANGUAGE

Chinese and Portuguese are Macau's official languages. Cantonese and Mandarin are widely spoken. English is unreliable outside tourist areas.

GETTING TO MACAU

AIR TRAVEL

International flights (from Asia) come into Macau, but there are no planes from Hong Kong. Sky Shuttle offers 15-minute helicopter flights between Hong Kong's Shun Tak Centre and the Macau Ferry Terminal; they leave every 30 minutes from 9 am to 11 pm daily and cost HK$4,100, with a surcharge of HK$400 on holidays. Reservations are essential.

Contacts **Macau International Airport** ☎ *853/2886–1111* ⊕ *www.macau-airport.com/en.* **Sky Shuttle** ☎ *853/2872–7288 Macau Terminal* ⊕ *www. skyshuttlehk.com.*

FERRY TRAVEL

Ferries travel between Hong Kong and Macau every 15 minutes with a reduced schedule from midnight to 7 am. Economy/ordinary and super/deluxe seats cost between HK$169 and HK$420; VIP cabins range from HK$1,192 (four seats) to HK$1,788 (six seats). Weekday traffic is usually light, so you can buy tickets right before departure. Weekend tickets often sell out, so make reservations. You can book tickets up to 90 days in advance with China Travel Service agencies (⊕ *www.ctshk. com*) or directly with CotaiJet and TurboJET by phone or online. You must pick up tickets at the terminal at least a half hour before departure.

Most ferries leave from Hong Kong's Shun Tak Centre (which is connected to the Sheung Wan MTR station), though limited service is available at Kowloon's Hong Kong China Ferry Terminal in Tsim Sha Tsui. In Macau most ferries dock at the main Macau Ferry Terminal, but CotaiJet services the terminal on Taipa. The trip takes one hour each way. Buses, taxis, and free shuttles to most casinos and hotels await on the Macau side.

Contacts **CotaiJet** ☎ *853/2885–0595 in Macau, 2359–9990 in Hong Kong* ⊕ *www.cotaijet.com.mo.* **TurboJET** ☎ *2859–3333 information* ⊕ *www.turbojet. com.hk.*

GETTING AROUND MACAU

BUS TRAVEL

Public buses are clean and affordable. Trips to anywhere on the Macau Peninsula cost MOP$3.20; service to Taipa is MOP$4.20, and service to Coloane is MOP$5. Buses run from 6:30 am to midnight, and require exact change upon boarding. But you can get downtown for free, via hotel or casino shuttles, from the official Border Gate crossing just outside mainland China, from the airport, and from the Macau Ferry Terminal.

CAR TRAVEL

As in Hong Kong, driving in Macau is on the left-hand side of the road. Road signs are in Chinese and Portuguese only. Rental cars with Avis are available at the Grand Lapa Macau. Regular cars start around MOP$750 for a full day. Book three to four days in advance for weekend rentals.

TAXI TRAVEL

Taxis are inexpensive but not plentiful in Macau. The best places to catch a cab are the major casinos—the Wynn Macau, the Lisboas, the Sands Macao, and the Venetian Macao. Carry a bilingual map or ask the concierge at your hotel to write the name of your destination in Chinese. All taxis are metered, air-conditioned, and reasonably comfortable. The base charge is MOP$15 for the first 1.6 km (1 mile) and MOP$1.50 per additional 755 feet. Trips between Coloane and either the Macau Peninsula or Taipa incur respective surcharges of MOP$5 and MOP$2. Drivers don't expect a tip.

WHAT IT COSTS IN MOP$

	$	$$	$$$	$$$$
Restaurants	Under MOP$100	MOP$100–MOP$200	MOP$201–MOP$300	over MOP$300
Hotels	Under MOP$1,100	MOP$1,100–MOP$1,850	MOP$1,851–MOP$2,800	over MOP$2,800

Restaurant prices are per person for a main course at dinner and exclude the customary 10% service charge. Hotel prices are for two people in a standard double room in high season, excluding 10% service charge and 3% government tax.

TOURS

Macau is compact, and you can see the highlights on your own with relative ease, so taking an organized tour isn't really necessary. But if you do want to sign on for one, check out your options at the travel counters of the main ferry terminals in either Macau or Hong Kong. Some offer tours in multiple languages.

Cotai Travel. Based at the Venetian Macao-Resort-Hotel, Cotai Travel runs daily tours from 9 am to 1 pm that include the Macau Tower, the A-Ma Temple, the Taipa Houses-Museum, and Senado Square for MOP$400 per person. ⊠ *Shop 1028, 1st fl., Venetian Macao-Resort-Hotel* ☎ *853/8118–2933* ⊕ *www.venetianmacao.com.*

Estoril Tours. Whether you're interested in bungee jumping off the Macau Tower, wandering through Coloane Village, or spending a day visiting museums, Estoril Tours can customize a private group outing for you. ⊠ *Shop 3711A, 3rd fl., Shun Tak Centre, 200 Connaught Rd., Sheung Wan, Western, Hong Kong, Hong Kong–China* ☎ *853/2559–1028* ⊕ *www.estoril.com.mo.*

EXPLORING MACAU

Macau is a small place, where on a good day you can drive from one end to the other in 30 minutes. This makes walking the ideal way to explore winding city streets, nature trails, and long stretches of beach. Most of Macau's population lives on the peninsula attached to mainland China. The region's most famous sights are here—Senado Square, the Ruins of St. Paul's, A-Ma Temple—as are most of the luxury hotels and casinos. As in the older sections of Hong Kong, cramped older buildings stand comfortably next to gleaming new structures.

THE MACAU PENINSULA

Chances are you'll arrive at the Macau Ferry Terminal after sailing from Hong Kong. There's not much to see around the terminal itself, so hop into one of the many waiting casino or hotel shuttles (free) and head straight downtown, less than 10 minutes away. From there it's a short walk to the city's historic center, along the short stretch of road named Avenida Almeida Ribeiro, more commonly known as San Ma Lo, which is Macau's commercial and cultural heart.

TOP ATTRACTIONS

Fodor'sChoice
★
Fortaleza da Guia (*Guia Fortress*). This fort, built between 1622 and 1638 on Macau's highest hill, was key to protecting the Portuguese from invaders. You can walk the steep, winding road up to it or take a five-minute cable-car ride from the entrance of Flora Garden on Avenida Sidónio Pais. From the drop-off point, follow the signs for the **Guia Lighthouse**—you can't go in, but you can get a good look at the gleaming white exterior that's lit every night. Next to it is the **Guia Chapel**, built by Clarist nuns to provide soldiers with religious services. Restoration work in 1996 uncovered elaborate frescoes mixing western and Chinese themes. They're best seen when the morning or afternoon sun floods the chapel, which is no longer used for services. The views from here are among the best, sweeping across all of Macau. ⊠ *Guia Hill, Downtown* ☎ *853/8399–6699* ⊡ *Free* ☉ *Daily 9–5:30.*

Igreja de São Domingos (*St. Dominic's Church*). The cream-and-white interior of one of Macau's most beautiful churches takes on a heavenly golden glow when illuminated for services. St. Dominic's was originally a convent founded by Spanish Dominican friars in 1587. In 1822 China's first Portuguese newspaper, *The China Bee,* was published here, and the church became a repository for sacred art in 1834 when convents were banned in Portugal. ■**TIP→ Admission to all churches and temples is free, though donations are suggested.** ⊠ *Largo de São Domingos, Downtown* ☉ *Daily 10–6.*

Fodor'sChoice
★
Largo do Senado (*Senado Square*). Open only to pedestrians and paved in shiny black-and-white tiles, this has been the charming hub of Macau for centuries. Largo do Senado is lined with neoclassical-style colonial buildings painted in bright pastels. The **Edifício do Leal Senado** (Senate Building), which gives the square its name, was built in 1784 as a municipal chamber and continues to be used by the government today. An elegant meeting room on the first floor opens onto a magnificent

Continued on page 238

CLOSE UP

A Casino Crawl in Macau

These days casinos are as much a part of the character of Macau as its cobblestone streets. Don't expect dusty, dodgy caverns, though. This neon-clad city is all glam and glitz, chandeliers and sommeliers. Win or lose, checking out casinos is all part of the fun of being in Macau, and this itinerary includes some cultural sights, too.

PLANNING

Where to Stay: MGM Macau, Wynn Macau, Altira Macau

Where to Eat and Drink: Margaret's Café e Nata, Portas Do Sol, Il Teatro, Robuchon au Dôme, 38 Lounge

Where to Play: The Hotel Lisboa, The Grand Lisboa, Wynn Macau, Altira Macau

What to See: Senado Square, Ruins of St. Paul's Cathedral, Grand Prix Museum, Wine Museum, The House of Dancing Water

ITINERARY

1. Margaret's Café e Nata. Start the day with a warm, flaky egg tart.

2. Largo do Senado. You almost have to go home with the obligatory Ruins of St. Paul's Cathedral photo. Saunter through Senado Square for a quick hit of history.

3. Wynn Macau. Break from the madding crowds and head to this swish address. With thick, beige drapes and plush furniture, the casino offers VIP treatment.

4. Hotel Lisboa. The infamous basement corridors and sparkling gaming floors of the Lisboa sister hotels are just a few blocks from the Wynn Macau.

5. Portas do Sol. Spend any remaining change you have left on dim sum. The pork buns and soup dumplings won't disappoint.

6. Grand Prix Museum. A bit farther north, you'll find colorful Formula 3 cars and memorabilia, as well as Macau's Wine Museum next door.

7. Cotai Strip. Fast and furious in its own right, Cotai is constantly expanding. Despite a stream of incoming resort-cum-casino complexes, the Venetian Macao remains the highlight, with 2,000-odd slot machines and more than 600 gaming tables.

8. The House of Dancing Water. Snag tickets to the city's most mesmerizing show, staged in City of Dreams.

9. Robuchon au Dôme. If you hit the jackpot, head to this French dining room for an unforgettable meal—and price tag to match.

10. 38 Lounge. Even if you end up with a thinner wallet, you can still cap the day with tapas and cocktails on the top floor of the Altira Macau. The views are fabulous—and free.

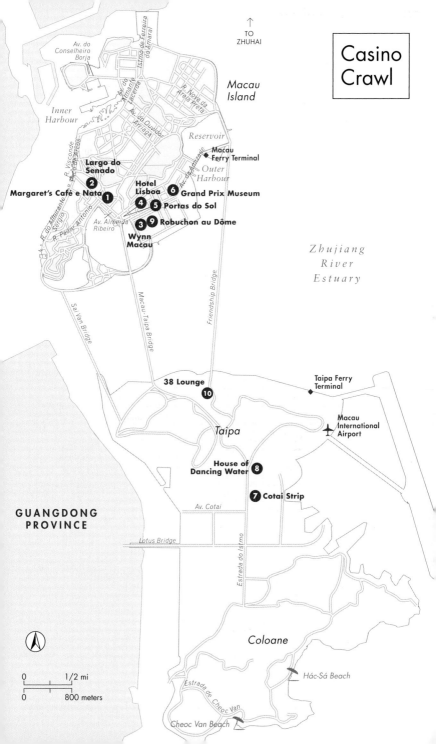

↑
TO
ZHUHAI

Casino Crawl

Av. do Conselheiro Borja

Inner Harbour

Macau Island

Reservoir

◆ **Macau Ferry Terminal**

Outer Harbour

Largo do Senado

2

Margaret's Café e Nata

1

Hotel Lisboa

6 **Grand Prix Museum**

4 **5** **Portas do Sol**

3 **9** **Robuchon au Dôme**

Wynn Macau

Zhujiang River Estuary

Sai Van Bridge

Macau-Taipa Bridge

Friendship Bridge

38 Lounge
10

◆ **Taipa Ferry Terminal**

✈ **Macau International Airport**

Taipa

House of Dancing Water **8**

7 **Cotai Strip**

Av. Cotai

GUANGDONG PROVINCE

Lotus Bridge

Estrada do Istmo

Coloane

Hác-Sá Beach

Estrada de Cheoc Van

Cheoc Van Beach

0   1/2 mi

0   800 meters

CLOSE UP

Exploring Macau's Culture

Macau's historical reputation may have been eclipsed by an ever-expanding matrix of casinos, but this former Portuguese colony has much to offer in the way of heritage and beauty. From the cobblestone streets to colonial facades, museums to Moorish architecture, fortresses to street food, Macau remains a city of color, character, and top-notch cuisine.

PLANNING

Where to Stay: Pousada de São Tiago, Pousada de Mong-Há, the Grand Lapa Macau

Where to Eat and Drink: A Lorcha, Margaret's Café e Nata, Restaurante Fernando, MacauSoul

What to See: Senado Square and the Ruins of St. Paul, Fortaleza do Monte, Guia Hill, A-Ma Temple, Moorish Barracks

ITINERARY

1. Leitaria I Son. Fortify yourself by ordering a Macau-style smoothie made with frothy milk and fresh juice at one of Senado Square's favorite cafés.

2. Largo do Senado. See everything or just the standouts, which include the House of Holy Mercy, St. Dominic's Church, and, of course, the Ruins of St. Paul's Cathedral and neighboring Na Tcha temple.

3. Fortaleza do Monte. Admire the 17th-century hilltop fort; then peruse the exhibits at the adjoining museum to see how Macau has evolved.

4. Margaret's Café e Nata. Heading northeast along Avenida da Amizade, pop in for a quick lunch. Choose from flaky egg tarts, pastries, and made-to-order sandwiches.

5. Guia Hill. Take the short cable-car ride up Guia Hill, or lace up your sneakers and hike past quirky shrubs manicured to resemble dragons. Once at the top, you'll be rewarded by stunning views of all Macau.

6. Largo do Barra. Anchoring Barra Square, the A-Ma Temple was built in 1488 for the goddess of the sea. After seeing it, visit the Maritime Museum (also on the square) and the nearby Mandarin's House.

7. Pousada de São Tiago. If you're feeling peckish, stop by The Terrace at this romantic former fort for a refreshing tipple or old-school high tea.

8. Moorish Barracks. Originally housing a regiment from Goa to bolster local police, this neoclassical and Moghul complex has stood since 1874.

9. A Lorcha. Just off of Barra Square, the ever-popular Macanese eatery serves up hearty favorites in a friendly atmosphere. It's best to make reservations.

10. MacauSoul. End the day by lingering over a glass of Portuguese wine—and perhaps listening to live music—at this jazzy venue back in Senado Square.

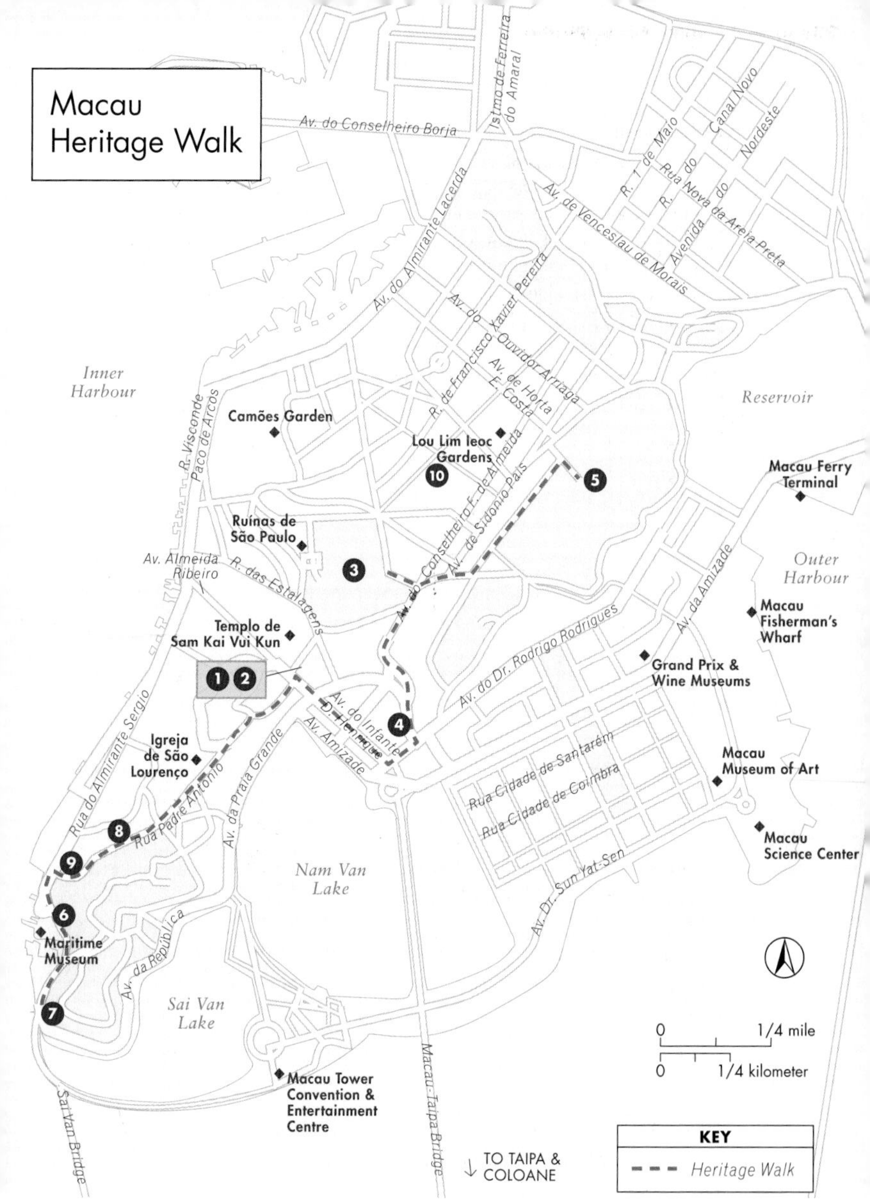
Macau
Heritage Walk
Av. do Conselheiro Borja
Istmo de Ferreira do Amaral
R. 1 de Maio
Canal Novo
Rua do Nordeste
R. Rua Nova da Areia Preta
Avenida do
Av. de Venceslau de Morais
Av. do Almirante Lacerda
Av. do Ouvidor Arriaga
R. de Francisco Xavier Pereira
Av. de Horta E. Costa
Inner Harbour
Reservoir
R. Visconde Paço de Arcos
Camões Garden
Lou Lim Ieoc Gardens
10
5
Macau Ferry Terminal
Ruínas de São Paulo
3
Av. do Conselheiro F. de Almeida
Av. de Sidónio Pais
Outer Harbour
Av. Almeida Ribeiro
R. das Estalagens
Av. da Amizade
Macau Fisherman's Wharf
Templo de Sam Kai Vui Kun
Av. do Dr. Rodrigo Rodrigues
1 2
Grand Prix & Wine Museums
4
Av. do Infante D. Henrique
Av. Amizade
Rua do Almirante Sergio
Igreja de São Lourenço
Av. da Praia Grande
Rua Cidade de Santarém
Rua Cidade de Coimbra
Macau Museum of Art
Rua Padre António
8
Macau Science Center
9
Nam Van Lake
Av. Dr. Sun Yat-Sen
6
Maritime Museum
Av. da Republica
7
Sai Van Lake
0
1/4 mile
0
1/4 kilometer
Macau Tower Convention & Entertainment Centre
Sai Van Bridge
Macau-Taipa Bridge
↓ TO TAIPA & COLOANE
KEY
Heritage Walk

A Lorcha **9**
Fortaleza do Monte **3**
Guia Hill **5**
Largo do Barra **6**
Largo do Senado **2**
Leitaria I Son **1**
MacauSoul **10**
Margaret's Café e Nata **4**
Moorish Barracks **8**
Pousada de São Tiago **7**

library based on one in the Mafra Convent in Portugal, with books neatly stacked on two levels of shelves reaching to the ceiling; art and historical exhibitions are frequently hosted in the beautiful foyer and garden. Alleys adjacent to the square are packed with restaurants and shops. ■TIP→ Visit on a weekday to avoid the crowds, and try to come back at night, when locals of all ages gather to chat and the square is beautifully lit. ⊠ *Downtown.*

> ### WORLD HERITAGE
>
> "The Historic Centre of Macau" is listed as a UNESCO World Heritage Site. The term "center" is misleading, though, as the site is really a collection of churches, buildings, and neighborhoods that colorfully illustrate Macau's 400-year history. Included in it are China's oldest examples of western architecture and the region's most extensive concentration of missionary churches.

NEED A BREAK?

Leitaria i Son. Look for the small cow sign marking the out-of-the-ordinary Leitaria i Son milk bar. The decor is cafeteria-style and spartan, but the bar whips up frothy glasses of fresh milk from its dairy and blends them with all manner of juices: papaya, coconut, apricot, and more. ⊠ *Largo do Senado 7, Downtown* ☎ *853/2857–3638.*

Margaret's Café e Nata. Not far off the main drag but somewhat hidden down an alleyway, Margaret's Café e Nata offers a cool—albeit increasingly crowded—place to sit, outside under fans and awnings, with some of the best custard tarts in town, plus fresh juices, sandwiches, homemade tea blends, and pizza slices. ⊠ *Rua Comandante Mata e Oliveira, Downtown* ☎ *853/2871–0032.*

Fodor'sChoice ★ **Macau Tower Convention & Entertainment Centre.** Rising above peaceful San Van Lake, this 338-meter (1,109-foot) freestanding tower recalls Sky Tower, a similar structure in New Zealand—and it should, as both were designed by New Zealand architect Gordon Moller. The Macau Tower offers a variety of thrills, including the Tower Climb, which challenges the strong of heart and body with a two-hour ascent on steel rungs 100 meters (328 feet) up the tower's mast for incomparable views of Macau and China. Other thrills include Skywalk X, an open-air stroll around the tower's exterior—without handrails; SkyJump, an assisted, decelerated 233-meter (765-foot) descent; and the world's highest bungee jump. More subdued attractions inside the tower include a mainstream movie theater and a revolving restaurant (the 360° Café) serving lunch, high tea, and a dinner buffet. ⊠ *Largo da Torre de Macau, Downtown* ☎ *853/2893–3339* ⊕ *www.macautower.com.mo* 🎫 *MOP$788 for Skywalk X to MOP$1,888 for the Tower Climb; MOP$2,888 for bungee jump; photos extra.* ☉ *Observation deck, weekdays 11–7:30, weekends 11–10.*

Fodor'sChoice ★ **Ruínas de São Paulo** (*Ruins of St. Paul's Cathedral*). Only the magnificent, towering facade, with its intricate carvings and bronze statues, remains from the original Church of Mater Dei, built between 1602 and 1640 and destroyed by fire in 1835. The sanctuary, an adjacent college, and

Mount Fortress—all Jesuit constructions—once formed East Asia's first western-style university. Now a tourist attraction, the ruins are the widely adopted symbol of Macau. Snack bars and shops are clustered at the foot of the site. Tucked behind the facade of São Paulo is the small **Museum of Sacred Art and Crypt**, which contains statues, crucifixes, and the bones of Japanese and Vietnamese martyrs. There are also some intriguing Asian interpretations of Christian images, including samurai angels and a Chinese Virgin and Child. ✉ *Top end of Rua de São Paulo, Downtown* ☏ *853/8399–6699* 🎫 *Free* ⊙ *Daily 8–5.*

Santa Casa da Misericordia (*The Holy House of Mercy*). Founded in 1569 by Dom Belchior Carneiro, Macau's first bishop, the Holy House of Mercy is the China coast's oldest Christian charity, and it continues to take care of the poor with soup kitchens and health clinics, as well as providing housing for the elderly. The exterior, with its imposing white facade, is neoclassical, but the interior is done in a contrasting opulent, modern style. A reception room on the second floor contains paintings of benefactress Marta Merop. ✉ *2 Travessa da Misericordia, Downtown* ☏ *853/2857–3938* 🎫 *MOP$5* ⊙ *Tues.–Sun. 10–1 and 2:30–5:30.*

Fodor's Choice ★ **Templo de A-Ma.** The tiered A-Ma Temple is one of Macau's oldest and most picturesque buildings. Properly Ma Kok Temple but known to locals as simply A-Ma, the structure originated during the Ming Dynasty (1368–1644) and was influenced by Confucianism, Taoism, and Buddhism, as well as local religions. Vivid red calligraphy on large boulders tells the story of the goddess A-Ma (also known as Tin Hau), the patron of fishermen. A small gate opens onto prayer halls, pavilions, and caves carved directly into the hillside. ✉ *Rua de São Tiago da Barra, Largo da Barra, Downtown* ⊙ *Daily 7–6.*

Templo de Na Tcha. This small Chinese temple was built in 1888, during the Macauan plague, in the hope that it would appeal to a mythical Chinese character who granted wishes and could save lives. The **Troço das Antigas Muralhas de Defesa** (Section of the Old City Walls), all that remains of Macau's original defensive barrier, borders the left side of the temple. These crumbling yellow walls were built in 1569 and illustrate the durability of *chunambo,* a local material made from compacted layers of clay, soil, sand, straw, crushed rocks, and oyster shells. ✉ *Top end of Rua de São Paulo, Downtown* ⊙ *Daily 8–5.*

WORTH NOTING

Camões Garden. Macau's most popular park is frequented from dawn to dusk by tai chi enthusiasts, palm readers, lovers, students, and men huddled over Chinese chessboards with their caged songbirds nearby. The gardens, which were developed in the 18th century, are named after Luís de Camões, Portugal's greatest poet, who was banished to Macau for several years during the 16th century. A rocky niche shelters a bronze bust of him in the park's most famous and picturesque spot, Camões Grotto. At the grotto's entrance a bronze sculpture honors the friendship between Portugal and China. A wall of stone slabs is inscribed with poems by various contemporary writers, praising Camões and Macau. In **Casa Garden,** a smaller park alongside Camões Garden, the grounds of a merchant's estate are lovingly landscaped with a variety of flora

8

and bordered with a brick pathway. A central pond is stocked with lily pads and lotus flowers. ✉ *13 Praça Luis de Camões, Downtown* ☉ *Daily 6 am–10 pm.*

Casa do Mandarim (*The Mandarin's House*). The Mandarin's House—Macau's largest representation of Guangdong residential architecture—covers 43,055 square feet and includes more than 60 rooms. Built in 1869 and refurbished in 2010, the compound melds Chinese and western architectural elements. It was once home to Zheng Guanying, a famous literary figure of the late Qing Dynasty, who finished his influential masterpiece *Words of Warning in Times of Prosperity* under this roof. ✉ *10 Travessa de António da Silva, Downtown* ☎ *853/2896–8820* ⊕ *www. wh.mo/mandarinhouse/en* 🎫 *Free* ☉ *Thurs.–Tues. 10–6.*

Fortaleza do Monte (*Mount Fortress*). On the hill overlooking the ruins of São Paulo and affording great peninsular views, this renovated fort was built by the Jesuits in the early 17th century. In 1622 it was the site of Macau's most legendary battle, when a priest's lucky cannon shot hit an invading Dutch ship's powder supply, saving the day. The interior buildings were destroyed by fire in 1835, but the outer walls remain, along with several large cannons and artillery pieces. Exhibits at the adjoining **Macau Museum** (daily 10–6, MOP$15) take you through the territory's history, from its origins to modern development. ✉ *Monte Hill, Downtown* ☎ *853/2835–7911* ⊕ *www.macaumuseum. gov.mo* 🎫 *Free* ☉ *Daily 6 am–7 pm.*

FAMILY **Grand Prix Museum.** Inaugurated in 1993 to celebrate the 40th anniversary of the Macau Grand Prix, this museum tells the stories of the best drivers from every year, but the highlights are the actual race cars on display. More than 20 Formula vehicles are exhibited in the hall, of which the centerpiece is the red-and-white Formula Three car driven by the late champion Aryton Senna. ✉ *431 Rua Luis Gonzaga Gomes, Downtown* ☎ *853/8798–4108* 🎫 *MOP$10 for adults* ☉ *Wed.–Mon. 10–6* ☉ *Closed Tues.*

Heritage Exhibition of a Traditional Pawn Shop. This impressive re-creation documents the important role that pawnshops have played in Macau for hundreds of years. ✉ *396 Av. Almeida Ribeiro, Downtown* ☎ *2892–1811* ⊕ *www.macaumuseum.gov.mo* 🎫 *MOP$5* ☉ *Daily 10:30–7; closed 1st Mon. of month.*

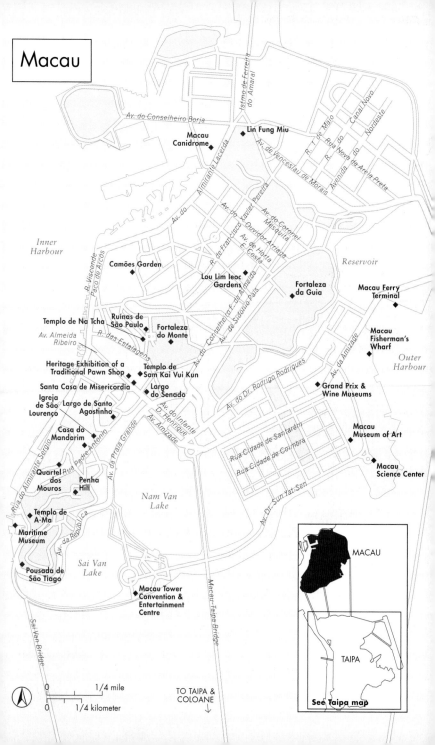

Igreja de São Lourenço (*Church of St. Lawrence*). One of Macau's three oldest churches, the Church of St. Lawrence was founded by Jesuits in 1560 and has been lovingly rebuilt several times. Its present appearance dates to 1846. It overlooks the South China Sea amid pleasant, palm-shaded gardens. Families of Portuguese sailors used to gather on the front steps to pray for the sailors' safe return; hence its Chinese name, Feng Shun Tang (Hall of the Soothing Winds). Focal points of its breathtaking interior are the elegant wood carvings, striking stained-glass windows, a baroque altar, and crystal chandeliers. ⊠ *Rua de São Lourenço, Downtown* ☎ *8399–6699* ◷ *Daily 10–5.*

Largo de Santo Agostinho. Built in the pattern of traditional Portuguese squares, St. Augustine Square is paved with black-and-white tiles laid out in mosaic wave patterns and lined with leafy overhanging trees and lots of wooden benches. It's easy to feel as if you're in a European village, far from South China. One of the square's main structures is the **Teatro Dom Pedro V,** a European-style hall with an inviting green-and-white facade built in 1859. It's an important cultural landmark for Macanese and was regularly used until World War II, when it fell into disrepair. The 300-seat venue once again hosts concerts and recitals—especially during the annual Macau International Music Festival—as well as important public events, the only times you can go inside. It does, however, have a garden that's open daily, and admission is free. **Igreja de Santo Agostinho (Church of St. Augustine)**, to one side of the square, dates from 1591, and has a grand, weathered exterior and a drafty interior with a high turquoise-colored wood-beam ceiling (open daily 10–6). There's a magnificent stone altar with a statue of Christ on his knees, bearing the cross, with small crucifixes in silhouette on the hill behind him. The statue, called Our Lord of Passos, is carried in a procession through the streets of downtown on the first day of Lent. ⊠ *Off R. Central, Downtown.*

Lin Fung Miu. Built in 1592, the Temple of the Lotus honors several Buddhist and Taoist deities, including Tin Hau (goddess of the sea), Kun Iam (goddess of mercy), and Kwan Tai (god of war and wealth). The front of the temple is embellished with magnificent clay bas-reliefs of renowned figures from Chinese history and mythology. Inside are several halls, shrines, and courtyards. The temple is best known as a lodging place for Mandarins traveling from Guangdong Province. Its most famous guest was Commissioner Lin Zexu, whose confiscation and destruction of British opium in 1839 was largely responsible for the First Opium War. ⊠ *Av. do Almirante Lacerda, Downtown* ◷ *Daily 7–5.*

Lou Lim Ieoc Gardens. These beautiful gardens were built in the 19th century by a Chinese merchant named Lou Kau. Rock formations, water, vegetation, pavilions, and sunlight were all carefully considered, and the balanced landscapes are the hallmark of Suzhou garden style. The government took possession and restored the grounds in the mid 1970s, so that today you can enjoy tranquil walks among delicate flowering bushes framed with bamboo groves and artificial hills. A large auditorium frequently hosts concerts and other events, most notably recitals during the annual Macau International Music Festival. Adjacent to the gardens a European-style edifice contains the **Macau Tea Culture House,** a small museum with exhibits on the tea culture of Macau and China (Tues.–Sun. 9–7, free). ⊠ *10 Estrada de Adolfo Loureiro, at Av. do Conselheiro Ferreira de Almeida, Downtown* ☎ *853/2882–7103* 🖃 *Free* ⊘ *Daily 6–9.*

Macao Museum of Art. The large, boxy museum is as well known for its curving, rectangular framed roof as it is for its calligraphy, painting, copperware, and international film collections. It's Macau's only art museum, and has five floors of eastern and western works, plus important examples of ancient indigenous pottery found at Coloane's Hác-Sá Beach. ⊠ *Macao Cultural Centre, Av. Xian Xing Hai, Outer Harbour* ☎ *853/8791–9814* ⊕ *www.artmuseum.gov.mo* 🖃 *MOP$5 (free Sun.)* ⊘ *Tues.–Sun. 10–6:30.*

FAMILY **Macau Fisherman's Wharf.** This sprawling complex of rides, games, and other minor attractions has a Disney-esque vibe. The centerpiece is the Roman Amphitheatre, which hosts outdoor performances, but the main draws are the lively themed restaurants on the west side: Afri-Kana (⇨ *Where to Eat)* for one, serves up Macau's best African brews and barbecues. Come for the food and stay after dark, as Fisherman's Wharf is most active at night. ⊠ *Av. da Amizade, at Av. Dr. Sun Yat-Sen, Outer Harbour* ☎ *853/8299–3300* ⊕ *www.fishermanswharf. com.mo* 🖃 *Admission free, games MOP$1–MOP$32* ⊘ *Open 24 hours.*

Maritime Museum. Looking like a ship, with jutting white slats and port-hole windows, this handsome building across from the A-Ma temple is a great place to spend an interesting hour brushing up on seafaring history. A row of fountains out front soothes you almost as much as the calm, cool interior. Multimedia exhibits cover fishermen, merchants, and explorers from Portugal, South China, and Japan. Look for compasses, telescopes, and sections of ships. There's even a small aquarium gallery with local sealife. Try your hand at astronomic navigation—which sailors have used for thousands of years—by looking up at the top floor's nifty celestial dome ceiling. ⊠ *1 Largo do Pagode da Barra, Inner Harbour* ☎ *853/2859–5481* ⊕ *www.museumaritimo.gov.mo* 🖃 *MOP$10 ($5 Sun.)* ⊘ *Wed.–Mon. 10–5:30.*

Quartel dos Mouros (*Moorish Barracks*). The elegant yellow-and-white building with Moorish architectural influences built onto a slope of Barra Hill is the Moorish Barracks. It now houses the Macau Maritime Administration, but was originally constructed in 1874 for Indian police regiments brought into the region, a reminder of Macau's historic relationship with the state of Goa. Although the barracks are not open to the public, visitors can tour the ornamented veranda. ⊠ *Barra Hill, Inner Harbour* ☎ *853/8399–6699* 🖃 *Free* ⊘ *Daily 9–6.*

Templo de Sam Kai Vui Kun. Built in 1750, this temple is dedicated to Kuan Tai, the bearded, fierce-looking god of war and wealth in Chinese mythology. Statues of him and his two sons sit on an altar. A steady stream of people comes to pray and ask for support before they go wage battle in the casinos. May and June see festivals honoring Kuan Tai throughout Macau. ⊠ *10 Rua Sui do Mercado de São Domingos, Downtown* ⊘ *Daily 8–6.*

A BIT OF HISTORY

In 1557 the Portuguese took over Macau, making it the first European colony in East Asia. Called "A Ma Gao" by the Chinese (in honor of the patron goddess of sailors, A-Ma), its name was adapted to "Macau" by the Portuguese. For more than a century the port thrived as the main intermediary in the trade between Asia and the rest of the world: ships from Italy, Portugal, and Spain came here to buy and sell Chinese silks and tea, Japanese crafts, Indian spices, African ivory, and Brazilian gold.

In addition to international trade, Macau became an outpost for western religions. St. Francis Xavier successfully converted large numbers of Japanese and Chinese to Christianity and used Macau as a base of operations. In the 1500s and 1600s many churches were built, including an ambitious Christian college. Today in Macau this religious legacy can be seen in the array of well-preserved churches.

Macau's age of prosperity ended in the 1800s, when the Dutch and British gained control of most trading routes to East Asia. After the British victory over China in the 1814 Opium War, the huge, deep-water port of Hong Kong was established, and Macau was relegated to a quiet, sleepy port town. Macau did, however, remain important to Chinese refugees during both World Wars and the Cultural Revolution. With the widespread introduction of legalized gambling in the 1960s, Macau became a freewheeling place, where gambling, espionage, and crime reigned in the long shadow of modern, wealthy Hong Kong.

Today textile, furniture, electronics, and other exports join a world-class tourism industry in making Macau prosperous. Just before the 1999 handover to the Chinese government, the Portuguese administration launched a staggering number of public works. A huge international airport was built on a reclaimed island, and new bridges were built to connect Macau's two islands. Recent years also saw the construction of two artificial lakes in the Outer Harbour along the Praia Grande and another in Cotai. These projects and the continuing developments have transformed Macau into a location rife with casinos and luxury resorts.

Wine Museum. In the same building as the Grand Prix Museum, this spot has more than 1,100 wines on display; some are almost 200 years old. You'll learn about production techniques and the importance of *vinho* (wine) in Portuguese culture. Several varieties are on hand for impromptu tastings. ⊠ *431 Rua Luis Gonzaga Gomes, Downtown* ☎ *853/8798–4188* ⬛ *MOP$15, including wine tasting* ☉ *Wed.–Mon. 10–6* ☉ *Closed Tues.*

TAIPA

The island of Taipa is directly south of peninsular Macau and connected to it by three long bridges. Macau's two universities, scenic hiking trails, and international airport are all here. Like downtown Macau, Taipa has been greatly developed in the past few years, yet it

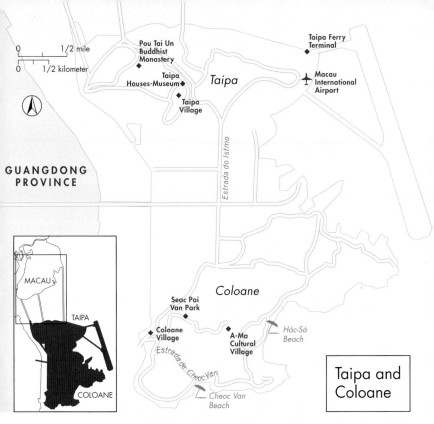

Taipa and
Coloane

retains a visual balance between old Macau charm and modern sleek-
ness. Try to visit on a weekend, so you can shop for clothing and crafts
in the traditional flea market that's held every Sunday from morning
to evening in Taipa Village.

Pou Tai Un Buddhist Monastery. The region's largest temple is part of
a functioning monastery with several dozen monks. The classically
designed structure has an ornate main prayer hall and central pavilions with sculptures, fish ponds, and banyan trees. Monks tend the
vegetable plots that supply the popular onsite vegetarian restaurant.
■TIP➜ It's best to have your concierge write down the address before
you go, as this monastery is a little bit off the beaten track. ⊠ *Estrada
Lou Lim Leok, Taipa* ☎ *853/2881–1007* ✉ *Free* ☉ *Daily 9–5* ☉ *Restaurant closed Sun.*

Taipa Houses-Museum. These five sea-green buildings are interesting
examples of Porto-Chinese architecture and were originally residences
of wealthy local merchants. They now house changing art exhibitions.
Paths lead into the beautiful adjoining **Carmel Garden,** where palm trees
provide welcome shade. Within the garden stands the brilliant white-
and-yellow **Nossa Senhora do Carmo** (Church of Our Lady of Carmel),
built in 1885 and featuring a handsome single-belfry tower. ⊠ *Av. da
Praia, Carmo Zone, Taipa* ☎ *853/2882–7103* ⊕ *housesmuseum.iacm.*

READY, SET, GO!

Grand Prix racing, which began in Macau in 1954, is the region's most glamorous annual sporting event. In mid- to late November the city is pierced with the sound of super-charged engines testing the 6.2-km (3.8-mile) Guia Circuit, which follows city roads along the Outer Harbour to Guia Hill and around the reservoir. The route is as challenging as that of Monaco, with rapid gear changes demanded at the right-angle Statue Corner, the Doña Maria bend, and the Melco hairpin. Cars achieve speeds of 275 kph (171 mph) on the straightaways, with the lap record approaching two minutes, 10 seconds. The premier event is the Formula 3 Macau Grand Prix, but there are also races for motor-cycles and production cars. If you plan to visit Macau during this time, beware of the logistical disruption that results from the race, including rerouting of main roads and lack of hotel vacancies.

gov.mo ✉ *Museum MOP$5, free Sun.; garden free* ☉ *Museum Tues.–Sun. 10–6; garden daily, 24 hours.*

Fodor's Choice ★ **Taipa Village.** The narrow, winding streets are packed with restaurants, bakeries, shops, temples, and other buildings with traditional South Chinese and Portuguese design elements. The aptly named Rua do Cunha (Food Street) has many great Chinese, Macanese, Portuguese, and Thai restaurants. Several shops sell homemade Macanese snacks, including steamed milk pudding, almond cakes, beef jerky, durian ice cream, and coconut candy. ✉ *Taipa.*

OUTDOOR ACTIVITIES

Whether you prefer a leisurely walk through a park or conquering steep hills on foot or by bike, Taipa has the region's best trails. The rewards for heading up Taipa Grande and Taipa Pequena, the island's two largest hills, are majestic views. The Taipa Grande trail starts at Estrada Colonel Nicolau de Mesquita, near the United Chinese Cemetery. The Taipa Pequena trail starts at Estrada Lou Lim Ieoc (Lou Lim Ieoc Gardens) behind the Regency Hotel. Be sure to wear rugged hiking shoes, use bug repellent, and, if possible, bring a mobile phone for emergency calls. The most popular place to rent bicycles is the shop at the bus stop outside the Civic and Municipal Affairs Bureau in Taipa Village on Largo Camões, where you can also find trail maps.

COLOANE

Centuries ago Coloane was a wild spot, where pirates hid in rocky caves and coves, awaiting their chance to strike at cargo ships on the Pearl River. Early in the 20th century the local government sponsored a huge planting program to transform Coloane from a barren place to a green one. The results were spectacular—and enduring. Today this side of the island is idyllic, with lush hills and clean sandy beaches. Once connected to Taipa by a thin isthmus, Coloane is now fused with Taipa via the huge Cotai reclaimed land project, where the "Strip" was completed in

2010. Regardless of the recent development boom, Coloane remains the destination of choice for anyone seeking natural beauty and tranquillity.

FAMILY
Fodor's Choice
★

A-Ma Cultural Village. A huge complex built in a traditional Qing Dynasty style pays homage to Macau's namesake, the goddess of the sea. The vibrancy and color of the details in the bell and drum towers, the tiled roofs, and the carved marble altars are truly awe-inspiring. It's as if you've been transported back to the height of the Qing Empire and can now see temples in their true state of greatness. Other remarkable details include the striking rows of stairs leading to Tian Hou Palace at the entrance. Each row features painstakingly detailed marble and stone carvings of auspicious Chinese symbols: a roaring tiger, double lions, five cranes, the double phoenix, and a splendid imperial dragon. The grounds here also have a recreational fishing zone and an arboretum with more than 100 species of local and exotic flora.

Behind A-Ma Cultural Village, **Coloane Hill** rises 170 meters (560-feet); it is crowned by a gleaming white-marble statue of A-Ma that's 21 meters (68 feet) tall and visible from miles away. You can make the short hike up to the top or take one of the shuttle buses that leave from the base of the hill every 30 minutes. ⌧ *Off Estrada de Seac Pai Van, Coloane Island South* ☼ *Daily 8–6.*

Fodor's Choice
★

Coloane Village. Quiet, relaxed Coloane Village is home to traditional Mediterranean-style houses painted in pastels, as well as the baroque-style Chapel of St. Francis Xavier and the Taoist Tam Kung Temple. The narrow alleys reveal surprises at every turn; you may well encounter fishermen repairing their junks or a baptism at the chapel. At the village's heart is a small square adorned with a fountain with a bronze Cupid. The surrounding Macanese and Chinese open-air restaurants are among the region's best; some are the unheralded favorites of chefs visiting from Hong Kong and elsewhere in Asia. ⌧ *Coloane Island West.*

FAMILY

Seac Pai Van Park (*Coloane Park*). This large park has extensive gardens, ponds, and waterfalls, and a large walk-in aviary with more than 200 bird species chirping and flying about. There are lots of things of interest to children, including playgrounds, a mini zoo, and an interactive museum with exhibits on nature and agriculture. ⌧ *Off Estrada de Seac Pai Van, Coloane Island West* ☼ *Daily 8–6.*

CASINOS

In February 2006 Macau surpassed Las Vegas in gambling revenue. By June 2008 Macau's casinos were turning over 2.6 times the revenue of their Vegas Strip counterparts. Small wonder that international casino groups have swarmed the region, and they continue to drive Macau's explosive double-digit growth.

From the late 1960s until 2001, Macau native Dr. Stanley Ho—Macau's biggest taipan (Chinese for "big boss")—owned all the casinos, becoming one of the world's wealthiest people. One of the first steps the Chinese government took after the 1999 handover was to break up Dr. Ho's monopoly and award casino licenses to several consortiums from Las Vegas. The grand plan to transform Macau from a quiet town that

Rickshaws await gamblers leaving the Casino Lisboa, the gaming den that started it all.

offered gambling into one of the world's top gaming destinations has become a reality.

THE SCENE

Gambling is lightly regulated, so there are only a few things to remember. No one under age 18 is allowed into casinos. Most casinos use Hong Kong dollars in their gaming and not Macau patacas, but you can easily exchange currencies at cashiers. High- and no-limit VIP rooms are available on request, where minimum bets range from HK$50,000 to HK$100,000 per hand. You can get cash from credit cards and ATMs 24 hours a day, and every casino has a program to extend additional credit to frequent visitors. Although most casinos don't have strict dress codes outside of their VIP rooms, men are better off not wearing shorts or sleeveless shirts. Minimum bets for most tables are higher than those in Las Vegas, but there are lower limits for slots and video gambling.

The players here may not look sophisticated: don't be fooled. Many of Macau's gamblers are truly hard-core. Average bets are in the hundreds per hand, and many people gamble until they're completely exhausted or completely broke, usually the latter.

Macau is also famous for gambling's sister industries of pawnshops, loan sharks, seedy saunas, and prostitution. This underbelly is hidden, though. You won't encounter such things unless you seek them out.

THE CASINOS

Gone are the days of Macau's dark and dingy underground gaming parlors. Over the past few years American-style casinos have been mushrooming like mad, primarily in Macau's NAPE (zona Nova de Aterros do Porto Exterior), or New Reclamation Area, in the Outer Harbour district between the main ferry terminal and the historic center. The foreign exports are most likely to please both casual tourists and serious players for their variety of gaming and other entertainment, relatively clean and well-lit atmosphere, free 24/7 accessibility, and overall glamour-resort experience.

DOWNTOWN

Casino Lisboa. Opened in 1970 by Dr. Stanley Ho, this iconic Macau gaming den is replete with ancient jade ships in the halls, gilded staircases, and more baccarat tables than you can shake a craps stick at. It's great for a few rounds of dai-siu—dice bets over cups of iced green tea. Most of the gamblers are from neighboring Guangdong province, and Cantonese is the lingua franca. Other popular pastimes at this storied casino revolve around international fine-dining venues and colorful coffee shops, if you care to wander around a maze of marbled floors and low ceilings. ⊠ *Av. de Lisboa, Downtown* ☎ *853/2888–3888* ⊕ *www.hotelisboa.com.*

Galaxy StarWorld. As you enter the StarWorld empire you're greeted by tall girls in high heels, while a mariachi band serenades you from across the lobby. The gaming floors are small and have a couple of Chinese-style diners if you get peckish, but the cool Whisky Bar on the 16th floor of the adjacent hotel is an atmospheric place to either begin or end your evening. The neon-blue building is just across from the Wynn Macau and down the block from the MGM Macau. Live lobby entertainment and local holiday attractions add a kitschy, friendly feel. ⊠ *Av. da Amizade, Downtown* ☎ *853/2838–3838* ⊕ *www.starworldmacau.com.*

Grand Lisboa. The main gaming floor, notable for its glowing egg statue, features more than 430 tables, about 800 slot machines, and a sexy Paris cabaret show that runs every 15 minutes. The second floor has additional gambling opportunities as well as a great bar. The Grand Lisboa has a variety of dining choices, too. Options range from the baroque Don Alfonso 1890 to the Round-the-Clock Coffee Shop. If the slots have been kind, celebrate by having a divine dinner on-site at Robuchon au Dôme *(⇨ Where to Eat)* or The Eight *(⇨ Where to Eat)*: both have earned three Michelin stars. ⊠ *2–4 Av. de Lisboa, Downtown* ☎ *853/2838–2828* ⊕ *www.grandlisboa.com.*

MGM Macau. A stylish part of Macau's gambling scene offers lavish lounges, Dale Chihuly glass sculptures, Portuguese-inspired architecture, and fine dining. The gambling floor itself is popular with high rollers from Hong Kong, including business tycoons who are just in for a few days. One of the owners, Pansy Ho, is the daughter of Macau's "gambling godfather," Dr. Stanley Ho; she is a high-octane business professional in her own right and a woman's classy touch shows up in this place's glitz-and-glam energy and high-society appeal. ⊠ *Av. Dr. Sun Yat-Sen, Downtown* ☎ *853/8802–8888* ⊕ *www.mgmmacau.com.*

8

The opulent MGM Macau is like a fantasy trip to Portugal.

Fodor's Choice ★ **Wynn Macau.** Listen for theme songs such as "Diamonds are Forever," "Luck Be a Lady," or "Money, Money" as Wynn's outdoor Performance Lake dazzles you with flames and fountain jets of whipping water every 15 minutes from 11 am to midnight. Inside the "open hand" structure of Steve Wynn's Macau resort, the indoor Rotunda Tree of Prosperity also wows guests with feng shui glitz. Wynn's expansive, brightly lit gaming floor, fine dining, buffet meals, luxury shops, deluxe spa, and trendy suites make this one of the swisher resorts in Macau. ✉ *Rua Cidade de Sintra, Downtown* ☎ *853/2888–9966* ⊕ *www.wynn macau.com.*

MACAU OUTER HARBOUR

Fodor's Choice ★ **Sands Macao.** This was the largest casino on earth until its sibling, the Venetian, stole the spotlight. It's also the first casino you'll see on the peninsula even before disembarking from the ferry. Past the sparkling 50-ton chandelier over the entrance, the grand gaming floor is anchored by a live cabaret stage above an open bar and under a giant screen. Several tiers are tastefully linked with escalators leading to the high-stakes tables upstairs. The friendly atmosphere and handy location, just across from Fisherman's Wharf and near the bar street in NAPE, make this a good place to warm-up for your big night out. ✉ *203 Largo de Monte Carlo, Outer Harbour* ☎ *853/2888–3330* ⊕ *www.sands.com.mo.*

MACAU INNER HARBOUR

Ponte 16. In the swinging seaside days of the 1950s, Macau's western port, or Ponte 16, is where all the action was. When the eastern port opened in the mid-1960s, the area fell into decay, but with the 2008 opening of Ponte 16, this legendary Latin Quarter has seen new momentum. The resort-casino has attracted Hong Kong and Taiwanese pop stars, mainland mass-market gamblers, and VIPs from Beijing and Shanghai. Probably because of the relatively isolated location, the atmosphere tends to be casual, and you can expect a winning combination of gorgeous views of the Inner Harbour as well as 109 gaming tables and 300-plus slot machines. ⊠ *4th fl., Rua do Visconde Paço de Arcos, Inner Harbour* ☎ *853/8861–8888* ⊕ *www.ponte16.com.mo.*

TAIPA

Fodor'sChoice
★

Mocha at The Altira Macau. Touting itself as Macau's first "six-star" integrated resort, the Altira Macau is indeed stellar, and its casino—Mocha—is the only classy one on Taipa. Facing the glow of casinos to the north on the peninsula, it offers swank, '70s-style gaming floors decked out in browns and taupes with mod chandeliers. The selection of game play is abundant, from baccarat to straight-up slots to posh VIP gaming rooms. The VIP resort suites, fine-dining, and elegantly discreet 38 Lounge (⇨ *Nightlife*) on the roof add to the overall ambience. ⊠ *Av. de Kwong Tung, Taipa* ☎ *853/2886–8888* ⊕ *www.altiramacau.com.*

COTAI STRIP

City of Dreams. The water theme is immediately apparent here, thanks to giant screens flashing images of mermaids swimming to and fro. Cotai's glitzy entertainment complex boasts a 39,020-square-meter (420,000-square-foot) casino with about 500 gaming tables and around 1,400 gaming machines, plus more than 20 cafés, restaurants, and bars. Kids will love the multimedia show "Dragon's Treasure," as well as the Kids' City playground. "The House of Dancing Water" (⇨ *Nightlife*), an aquatic-based spectacle that cost HK$2 billion to mount, is the main event. Once you're tired out, you can choose to stay at one of its three hotels: the Grand Hyatt, the Hard Rock, or the Crown Towers. ⊠ *Estrada do Istmo, Cotai* ☎ *8868–6688* ⊕ *www.cityofdreamsmacau. com.*

Galaxy Macau Complex. It's impossible to miss the six 24-karat gold cupolas of the Galaxy complex towering over the northwestern end of the Cotai Strip. This 2,200-room palatial resort is home to three hotels—Banyan Tree Macau, Galaxy Hotel, and Hotel Okura Macau—as well as the world's largest wave pool, a 10-screen cinema, and a huge foot reflexology center. Smack in the center is a brightly lit casino floor packed with gaming tables, surrounded by high-end shops and restaurants where you can actually hear yourself think. ⊠ *Estrada da Baia de N. Senhora da Esperanza, Cotai* ☎ *853/2888–0888* ⊕ *www. galaxymacau.com.*

FAMILY **Sands Cotai Central.** This huge hotel, shopping, and casino complex opened across the street from the Venetian Macao in 2012: its jungle-themed shopping center is flanked by the Holiday Inn Macao, the Conrad Macao, and the Sheraton Macao Hotel. The whole thing is perhaps the most child-friendly of the resort complexes, with budget-friendly prices, children's pools, and an array of colorful family suites. The enormous 3,863-room Sheraton—the largest in the world—even offers free popcorn and games near reception. ⊠ *Estrada da Baía de*

8

N. Senhora da Esperança, Downtown ☎ 853/2886–6888 ⊕ www.sands cotaicentral.com.

Fodor'sChoice   **Venetian Macao-Resort-Hotel.** Twice the size of its namesake in Las Vegas,
★   the Venetian Macao-Resort-Hotel offers ample opportunities for gaming, shopping, eating, and sleeping. Expect faux-Renaissance decoration, built-in canals plied by crooning gondoliers, live carnival acts, plenty of sheer spectacle, and more than a touch of pretension. The 35,768 square-meter (385,000-square-foot) gaming floor has some 2,000 slot machines and more than 600 tables of casino favorites. The sprawling property also includes nearly 3,000 suites, plus performance venues like the 1,800-seat Venetian Theatre and 15,000-seat Cotai Arena. It's no wonder the Venetian Macao is the must-see megacomplex that everyone's talking about. ⊠ Estrada da Baía de N. Senhora da Esperança, Cotai ☎ 853/2882–8888 ⊕ www.venetianmacao.com.

WHERE TO EAT

Macau's medley of Portuguese and Cantonese cuisine—spicy and creamy Macanese interpretations of traditional Cantonese dishes such as baked prawns, braised abalone, and seafood stews—has made it one of Asia's top fine-dining destinations for decades.

Now, thanks to the spate of new casino-hotels, Macau has also become an exciting world-class culinary frontier. But local dining isn't all highbrow. Near the Largo do Senado and in the villages of Taipa and Coloane, wander the back alleys to find treats like *zhu-bao-bao* (a slab of fried pork on a toasted bun served with milk tea) or the signature *pasteis de nata* (custard tart): they're simple, delicious, and classic Macau.

Long-renowned restaurants such as Restaurante Fernando and Litoral are staying the course. So, too, are Cantonese eateries such as Fat Siu Lau, particularly well known among Hong Kong residents who travel to Macau just for dim sum, weekend brunches, and seafood feasts at more affordable prices and made from higher-quality ingredients.

PLANNING

Expect to shell out MOP$100 to MOP$250 per person per meal without wine, though you can always go to a hole-in-the-wall noodle shop for MOP$25–MOP$30. Budget at least MOP$500 per person for an unforgettable dinner. A 10% service charge is added automatically, but, depending on the service quality, it's common for customers to round up the total. While major credit cards are accepted at most restaurants, cash is preferred at the smaller spots.

Despite the surge in upscale dining accompanying casino development in Macau, the pace is still siesta style, with serious lunches lasting a few hours. The hotels serve breakfast early, but corner coffee shops start serving ham and cheese on croissants with espresso by around 11 am. Cocktails begin at around 6:30, and dinner at around 8.

DOWNTOWN MACAU

$$$ FRENCH 🍴 **Aux Beaux Arts.** This 1930s-style Parisian brasserie in the MGM Macau is one of the trendiest restaurants around. Chinese diners are particularly fond of its fresh, catch-of-the-day seafood—the lobster is especially choice. So, too, are the French mains, such as beef tartare with french fries. Oysters and caviar are also exclusive, at prices reaching MOP$2,950 for 50 grams. In-house sommeliers are on hand to pair the latest wines with dishes. With tan wood, private booths, and a terrace, the decor is as much old French Concession Shanghai as it is old Paris. Either way, the place has raised the bar for Macau's restaurant scene. [$] *Average main: MOP$205* ✉ *MGM Macau, Av. Dr. Sun Yat-Sen, NAPE, Outer Harbour* ☎ *853/8802–2319* 🌐 *www.mgmmacau.com* 🕒 *Closed Mon.*

$$ PORTUGUESE 🍴 **Clube Militar de Macau** (*Macau Military Club*). Founded in 1870 as a private military club, the stately pink-and-white structure was restored in 1995 and reopened as a restaurant. The languid Old World atmosphere perfectly complements the extensive list of traditional Portuguese dishes, such as *bacalhau dourado* ("golden cod," a specialty of fried cod and potatoes), African chicken, and *arroz de marisco* (flavored rice and seafood). Leave room for dessert—the options include Portuguese sweet rice pudding with mango, warm chestnut tart, and coconut ice cream with caramelized pineapple. [$] *Average main: MOP$150* ✉ *975 Av. da Praia Grande, Downtown* ☎ *853/2871–4000* 🌐 *www.clubemilitardemacau.net.*

$ PORTUGUESE Fodor's Choice ★ 🍴 **Dom Galo.** "Quirky" springs to mind when describing the colorful decor, with plastic monkey puppets and funky chicken toys hanging from the ceilings. A varied clientele includes graphic designers, gambling-compliance lawyers, and 10-year-old Cantonese kids celebrating birthdays. The owner is Portuguese, and the food is usually spot-on, with *insalada de polvo* (octopus salad), king prawns, and steak fries served with a tangy mushroom sauce among the stand-outs. Pitchers of sangria are essential with any meal here. So, too, are reservations, as this place is increasingly popular with tourists. [$] *Average main: MOP$100* ✉ *Av. Sir Andars Ljung Stedt, Downtown* ☎ *853/2875–1383* ✍ *Reservations essential.*

$$$$ CANTONESE 🍴 **The Eight.** Designed by Hong Kong's Alan Chan, The Eight is an opulent-looking restaurant where the food is as impressive as the decor—it was awarded three Michelin stars in 2014. The chefs here prepare fine Cantonese and Huaiyang cuisine; signature dishes include braised abalone with Chinese herbs, steamed Japanese bean curd with dried seafood, and steamed fish-shaped shrimp dumplings. The wine cellar contains more than 14,100 different labels; teetotalers can enjoy teas from an extensive menu that includes a *pu er* that has been aged for 49 years. **■ TIP→ Lunchtime diners can choose from a menu that boasts over 50 types of dim sum.** [$] *Average main: MOP$600* ✉ *2nd fl., Grand Lisboa Hotel, Av. De Lisboa, Downtown* ☎ *853/8803–7788.*

$$ CANTONESE Fodor's Choice ★ 🍴 **Fat Siu Lau.** Well known to both locals and visitors from Hong Kong, Fat Siu Lau has kept its customers coming back since 1903 with delicious Macanese favorites and modern creations. Try ordering whatever you see the chatty Cantonese stuffing themselves with

8

at the surrounding tables, and you won't be disappointed. Your meal might well consist of whole curry crab, grilled prawns in a butter garlic sauce, and the famous roasted pigeon dressed in a secret marinade. Fat Siu Lau 2 is on Macau Lan Kwai Fong Street, and the newer Fat Siu Lau 3 is near the Venetian Macao—both offer the same great food albeit in more modern settings. [$] *Average main: MOP$130* ✉ *64 Rua da Felicidade, Downtown* ☎ *853/2857–3580* 🌐 *www.fatsiulau.com.mo* ✍ *Reservations essential.*

LOVE OF VINHO

Wine lovers should take full advantage of Macau's intimate love of vinho. Some restaurants have wine lists as thick as phone books, and most have at least a couple of bottles of delicious Portuguese wine on hand—usually a hearty red from the Dão region or a slightly sparkling vinho verde from the north.

$$$$ ITALIAN
🍴 **Il Teatro.** With its dedicated view of the Wynn Macau's Performance Lake show and the flashing glows of the Lisboa casinos providing ambience, one of the most romantic restaurants in Macau plays host to Asian celebrities and well-heeled travelers alike. Popular among the impeccable southern Italian delights are tenderloin carpaccio and cioppino starters and sweet potato and pancetta gnocchi, accompanied by chilled wine from an exhaustive list. Desserts range from crispy cannoli to homemade sorbets and ice cream imported straight from Italy. Window seats in particular are at a premium and are best reserved three weeks in advance. The dress code is "casual elegance," which means long pants, closed-toe shoes, and no open shirts for men; this is not the place for children under five. [$] *Average main: MOP$350* ✉ *Wynn Macau, Rua da Sintra, Downtown* ☎ *853/8986–3663* 🌐 *www.wynnmacau.com* 🕒 *No lunch; closed Mon.*

$ MACANESE
🍴 **Pastelaria Koi Kei.** Walking toward the Ruins of St. Paul's, you will likely be accosted by salespeople forcing Macanese snacks into your hands and enticing you to enter one of the street's *pastelarias*—pastry shops that serve traditional almond cakes, ginger candy, beef jerky, and egg rolls. Competition is fierce, but Pastelaria Koi Kei is one of the oldest and best. Hong Kong residents regularly haul the distinctive tan bags, heavy with snacks (in particular, the Portuguese custards), back home for friends and relatives. Other branches are on nearby Rua de São Paulo and on Rua do Cunha in Taipa. Cash is preferred. [$] *Average main: MOP$20* ✉ *70–72 Rua Felicidade, Downtown* ☎ *853/2893–8102* 🌐 *www.koikei.com.*

$$$ SHANGHAINESE
🍴 **Portas do Sol.** Despite the Portuguese name, exquisite dim sum and Chinese haute cuisine are Portas do Sol's specialties. Tiny, sweet Shanghainese pork buns, turnip cakes, and soup dumplings are some of the traditional offerings; there are also innovative new creations that look like miniature jewels on the plate. For dessert you can choose from a wide variety of Chinese sweets, including a fish-shaped chilled mango and coconut pudding, double-boiled papaya with snow fungus (a tasteless mushroom that becomes gelatinous when cooked), and deep-fried sweet milk with longan fruit. Reservations are a good idea on weekends, as this place fills up with Hong Kong and mainland visitors. [$] *Average*

main: MOP$250 ✉ *Hotel Lisboa, Av. da Amizade, Downtown* ☎ *853/8803–3100* 🌐 *www.hotelisboa.com* ✍ *Reservations essential* 🕒 *Mon.–Fri. 11:30 am–2:30 pm; Sat.–Sun. 9:30 am–3 pm; daily 6:30–10:30 pm.*

$$ PORTUGUESE 🍴 **Praia Grande.** Mediterranean beauty is in evidence inside and outside, with a gleaming white facade opening into a dining room with graceful arches, terra-cotta floors, and wrought-iron furniture. The menu is creative, with dishes ranging from African chicken to pork and clams *cataplana* (in a stew of onions, tomatoes, and wine). [$] *Average main: MOP$140* ✉ *10A Praça Lobo d'Avila, Av. da Praia Grande, Downtown* ☎ *853/2897–3022.*

$$$$ FRENCH 🍴 **Robuchon au Dôme.** A slice of Paris overlooking the heart of Macau, this three-Michelin-starred restaurant on the 43rd floor of the Grand Lisboa is a must if you just hit it big in the casino. In the ornate interior, rich velvets, dark woods, and a twinkling crystal chandelier set the tone. Signature dishes are a heavenly mille-feuille of tomato and crabmeat, duck breast with fruit and foie gras, and lamb served with creamy potato puree; however, Robuchon's 12-course tasting menus (complete with two desserts) are the best way to experience his gastronomic delights. The wine list is as thick as an encyclopedia. [$] *Average main: MOP$750* ✉ *Grand Lisboa, Av. de Lisboa, Downtown* ☎ *853/8803–7878* 🌐 *www.grandlisboahotel.com* ✍ *Reservations essential.*

A COLONIAL FEAST

The Macanese like hearty Portuguese fare. Most restaurants serve the beloved bacalhau (salt cod) baked, boiled, grilled, deep-fried with potato, or stewed with onion, garlic, and eggs. Other dishes include sardines, sausages, and *caldo verde* (vegetable soup). Giant prawns in a curry sauce recall the cuisine of Goa, India—another Portuguese colony. Indeed, there are dishes drawn from throughout the colonial empire, including Brazilian *feijoada* (a stew of beans, pork, and vegetables) and Mozambique chicken, baked or grilled and seasoned with piri-piri chili, tangy spices, and coconut.

MACAU OUTER HARBOUR

$ AFRICAN 🍴 **AfriKana.** Macau's historical contacts with Africa, especially Angola and Mozambique, come into sharp focus in one of the few places on the peninsula where you can eat roasted coconut chicken under a thatched roof. Scores of Portuguese-speaking residents who were born in Portugal's African colonies come here for parties or cultural events. The eight thatched pavilions feature resilient colors, from dark blues to mustard yellows to sandy reds. [$] *Average main: MOP$40* ✉ *Fisherman's Wharf, Outer Harbour* ☎ *853/8299–3678* 🕒 *No lunch.*

$$$$ STEAKHOUSE Fodor's Choice ★ 🍴 **Copa Steakhouse.** The first traditional American steak house in Macau serves premium-quality steaks and seafood in a space that evokes 1960s Las Vegas. A large fireplace that pops and crackles during the winter months blends in perfectly with the vintage chandeliers and celebrity photos hanging on the walls. Sip a cocktail at the bar and brace yourself for huge slabs of beef, grilled to juicy perfection before your eyes in the open kitchen. A 20-ounce cowboy Wagyu steak from Australia tops the list at MOP$998. Other dishes include Norwegian salmon fillet and

seared Hokkaido scallops when in season. For dessert, try the sinfully rich crème brûlée. $ *Average main: MOP$310* ✉ *3rd fl., Sands Macao Hotel, 203 Largo de Monte Carlo, Outer Harbour* ☎ *853/8983–8222* ⊕ *www.sandsmacao.com* ☯ *No lunch.*

MACAU INNER HARBOUR

$$ ✕ **A Lorcha.** Vastly popular A Lorcha (the name means "wooden ship") celebrates the heritage of Macau as an important port with a maritime-theme menu. Don't miss the signature dish, Clams Lorcha Style, with tomato, beer, and garlic. Other classics include *feijoada* (Brazilian pork-and-bean stew), seafood paella, and perfect fire-roasted chicken. Save room for serradura (aka Macau sawdust pudding, made from biscuits and vanilla whipped cream). Watch for racers during the Grand Prix, as the Macanese owner Adriano is a fervent Formula fan. $ *Average main: MOP$140* ✉ *289 Rua do Almirante Sérgio, Inner Harbour* ☎ *853/2831–3193* ⌂ *Reservations essential* ☯ *Closed Tues.*

PORTUGUESE
Fodor'sChoice ★

$$ ✕ **Litoral.** In tastefully decorated environs with whitewashed walls and dark-wood beams, one of the most popular local restaurants offers authentic Macanese dishes that are simple, straightforward, and deliciously satisfying. Must-try dishes include the tamarind pork with shrimp paste, as well as codfish baked with potato and garlic, and a Portuguese vegetable cream soup. For dessert, try the *bebinca de leite* (coconut-milk custard) or the *pudim abade de priscos* (traditional egg pudding). Reservations are recommended on weekends. $ *Average main: MOP$180* ✉ *261 Rua do Almirante Sergio, Inner Harbour* ☎ *853/2896–7878* ⊕ *www.restaurante-litoral.com.*

MACANESE

TAIPA

$$ ✕ **O Santos.** A busy little eatery in the heart of Taipa Village, O Santos serves up classic Portuguese fare without frills or fluff. It has a menu similar to many of the diners in Macau, but the personality here is warm and lively. It's not a place for a romantic night out, but the food is great—try the steak and fries, the fried sardines, and, to finish, the *serradura* (a Portuguese dessert containing cookies and cream). ■TIP➜ The house-made sangria is terrific. $ *Average main: MOP$105* ✉ *20 Rua de Cunha, Taipa* ☎ *853/2882–7508* ⊕ *www.osantoscomida portuguesa.com.*

PORTUGUESE

COLOANE

$ ✕ **Lord Stow's Bakery.** Originally a modest, traditional bakery opened by a young Englishman named Andrew Stow in 1989, Lord Stow's Bakery is now a culinary landmark in Coloane, just off the town square. Locals sit on nearby benches munching the signature hot and flaky *pasteis de nata* (custard tarts) straight from the oven. Inside the little shop, breads, muffins, cookies, flapjacks, and other homemade goods are on offer, but be sure to walk out with at least one tart. The neighboring Lord Stow's Café (*853/2888–2174*) has sit-down meals, as does the outpost in the Venetian Macao (*853/2886–6889*). $ *Average main: MOP$40* ✉ *1 Rua da Tassara, Coloane Village Sq., Coloane Island West* ☎ *853/2888–2534* ⊕ *www.lordstow.com.*

PORTUGUESE
Fodor'sChoice ★

$$ ✕ **Restaurante Espaço Lisboa.** Occupying a converted two-story house with a small but pleasant balcony overlooking Coloane Village, this

PORTUGUESE

Make sure to sample one (or more) of Lord Stow's sought-after tarts.

restaurant is Portuguese owned and has a Portuguese chef—so it's no surprise that it is a favorite of Portuguese residents. Menu highlights include codfish cakes, savory duck rice, monkfish rice, boiled bacalhau with cabbage, and smoked ham imported from the motherland. Take your pick from an extensive list of hearty Portuguese wines, and cap the meal by ordering homemade mango ice cream with a cherry flambé. $ *Average main: MOP$180* ⊠ *8 Rua das Gaivotas, Coloane Island West* ☎ *853/2888–2226.*

$$
PORTUGUESE
Fodor'sChoice
★

✕ **Restaurante Fernando.** Everyone in Hong Kong and Macau knows about Fernando's, but the vine-covered entrance close to Hác-Sá Beach is difficult to spot. The open-air dining pavilion and bar have attracted beachgoers for years now, and the enterprising Fernando has built a legendary reputation for his Portuguese fare. The menu focuses on seafood paired with homegrown vegetables, and diners can choose from among the bottles of Portuguese wine on display or opt for the beloved sangria. The informal nature of the restaurant fits in with the satisfying, home-style food such as grilled fish, baked chicken, and huge bowlfuls of spicy clams, all eaten with your fingers. $ *Average main: MOP$150* ⊠ *9 Praia de Hác-Sá Beach, Coloane Island South* ☎ *853/2888–2531* ⊕ *www.fernando-restaurant.com* ✍ *Reservations not accepted* ▬ *No credit cards.*

8

WHERE TO STAY

An influx of luxury hotels has transformed Macau into a posh place to stay. The musty three-stars are still out there, but the five-stars are generally worth the splurge. For a true Macau experience, try staying in *pousadas*, restored historic buildings that have been converted into intimate hotels with limited facilities but lots of character.

PLANNING

When choosing a hotel, consider the surroundings. In pulsating downtown Macau (or in the Outer Harbour, connected to downtown via frequent casino shuttles), historic and cultural sites, casinos, and restaurants are all within walking distance. Hotels in more residential Taipa, just a short bus- or taxi-ride away, often have incomparable sea and bright-lights views. And if you spring for the Altira Macau, you can enjoy the many top-rate facilities within walking distance of Taipa Village. The Cotai Strip offers one-stop sleeping, shopping, eating, and gambling; outside the resorts, however, it's still a construction field, with new, glitzy hotels opening frequently. The peaceful Inner Harbour has excellent sea views, but for true otherworldly quiet, head to Coloane, where you can hit the beach and hiking trails.

For discounted rates in the grand hotels, book a package through a Hong Kong travel agency. If your tastes are more modest, agents at the Macau hydrofoil terminal can get you a room in a three- to four-star property for a reduced price, subject to availability. Macau hotels are busiest during the Grand Prix (mid- to late November) and all official Chinese holidays. Book at least a couple of weeks in advance at these times. Year-round, weekends fill up fast and walk-ins can be prohibitively expensive. Visit on a weekday to avoid crowds and inflated prices.

Hotel reviews have been shortened. For full information, visit Fodors. com.

DOWNTOWN MACAU

$$ ☷ **Hotel Lisboa.** In Macau's infamous landmark, redolent with history
HOTEL and intrigue, labyrinthine hallways and salons display jade and artworks, and an ostentatiously gilded staircase leads to luxurious guestrooms with handcrafted furniture and Jacuzzi baths. **Pros:** historic interior; central location; superior restaurants; linked to the Grand Lisboa. **Cons:** older building; low ceilings; smoky casino. Ⓢ *Rooms from: MOP$1,480* ⊠ *2–4 Av. de Lisboa, Downtown* ☏ *853/2888–3888* ⊕ *www.hotelisboa.com* ⇄ *950 rooms, 50 suites* ⏐⊙⏐*No meals.*

$$ ☷ **Hotel Sintra.** What these business lodgings lack in luxury they make up
HOTEL for with lots of pluses: the location, minutes away from Senado Square, is great; the cozy, carpeted rooms are decorated in soothing brown-and-cream color schemes; and the staff is smartly dressed and helpful. **Pros:** in the heart of downtown; simple but tasteful decor. **Cons:** small rooms; lackluster dining options. Ⓢ *Rooms from: MOP$1,200* ⊠ *Av. de Dom João IV, Downtown* ☏ *853/2871–0111, 800/969–145 in Hong Kong* ⊕ *www.hotelsintra.com* ⇄ *240 rooms, 9 suites* ⏐⊙⏐*No meals.*

$$$ HOTEL **Fodor's Choice** ★ **MGM Macau.** The chic accommodations, with their muted cream, brown, and beige color palette, have everything you'd expect in the way of comfort and elegance from a luxury brand; the striking hotel around them, however, distinguishes these rooms from the rest. **Pros:** tasteful architecture; fine art; refined dining and lounge options. **Cons:** inseparable from the casino, which can get smoky and loud; high-traffic location. [$] *Rooms from: MOP$2,688* ✉ *Av. Dr. Sun Yat-Sen, NAPE, Outer Harbour* ☎ *853/8802–8888* 🌐 *www.mgmmacau.com* 🛏 *468 rooms, 99 suites, 15 villas* 🍴 *No meals.*

$ B&B/INN **Pousada de Mong-Há.** A training hotel run by students of the Institute for Tourism Studies offers exemplary service and spacious rooms nicely decorated with hand-stitched carpets. **Pros:** historic charm; hillside walks and views. **Cons:** half-hour walk north from city center; no pool. [$] *Rooms from: MOP$700* ✉ *Colina de Mong-Há, Downtown* ☎ *853/2851–5222* 🌐 *www.ift.edu.mo/pousada* 🛏 *20 rooms and suites* 🍴 *Breakfast.*

$$$ HOTEL **StarWorld Hotel.** Luminous open-plan suites have high ceilings, Jacuzzi tubs, and panoramic bay windows, and even the deluxe rooms, with their high-quality bedding and dark-wood furniture, make you feel like you're somewhere special. **Pros:** celestially designed suites; live entertainment in the lobby and lounge bar. **Cons:** high energy at all hours; in a heavy-traffic area. [$] *Rooms from: MOP$2,500* ✉ *Av. da Amizade, Downtown* ☎ *853/2838–3838* 🌐 *www.starworldmacau.com* 🛏 *465 rooms, 40 suites* 🍴 *No meals.*

$$$ HOTEL **Wynn Macau.** If you just can't get enough of the Wynn's Performance Lake, all rooms here have floor-to-ceiling windows—many with a plunging view of the fire-and-water spectacle, as well as of the peaceful Nam Van Lake. **Pros:** exclusive VIP club space; Nam Van and Performance Lake views. **Cons:** light pollution from neighboring casinos; lowest rooms on 5th floor. [$] *Rooms from: MOP$2,500* ✉ *Rua Cidade de Sintra, Downtown* ☎ *853/2888–9966, 800/966–963 in Hong Kong* 🌐 *www.wynnmacau.com* 🛏 *460 rooms, 134 suites* 🍴 *No meals.*

MACAU OUTER HARBOUR

$ RESORT FAMILY **Grand Lapa Macau.** With a more understated opulence than many of its neighbors, the Grand Lapa weaves Mediterranean charm throughout the resort. **Pros:** classic luxury facilities; new gym; tennis courts; kid's club. **Cons:** old casino; rooms showing age; high-traffic location. [$] *Rooms from: MOP$1,000* ✉ *956–1110 Av. da Amizade, Outer Harbour* ☎ *853/2856-7888, 2881–1288 in Hong Kong* 🌐 *www.grandlapa.com* 🛏 *389 rooms, 27 suites* 🍴 *No meals.*

$$$ HOTEL **Sands Macao.** The Sands Macao is nothing if not luxurious, with spacious rooms that have deep, soft carpets, large beds, and huge marble bathrooms with Jacuzzis. **Pros:** heated outdoor pool; across the street from Fisherman's Wharf. **Cons:** older property; near lots of traffic. [$] *Rooms from: MOP$2,000* ✉ *203 Largo de Monte Carlo, Outer Harbour* ☎ *853/2888–3388* 🌐 *www.sands.com.mo* 🛏 *238 suites, 51 VIP suites* 🍴 *No meals.*

MACAU INNER HARBOUR

$$$$
B&B/INN
Fodor's Choice
★

Pousada de São Tiago. This romantic lodging's origins as a 17th-century fortress permeate every corner, from the tunnel-like entrance to the 12 modern luxury suites, each boasting a Jacuzzi bathroom and large balcony. **Pros:** all the modern comfort of a luxury hotel; complimentary minibar and Wi-Fi; intimate sunset views of the Inner Harbour. **Cons:** small pool; limited facilities. $ *Rooms from: MOP$3,000 ⊠ Fortaleza de São Tiago da Barra, Av. da República, Inner Harbour ☎ 853/2837–8111 ⊕ www.saotiago.com.mo ⤳ 12 suites ⦿ No meals.*

TAIPA

$$$
HOTEL
Fodor's Choice
★

Altira Macau. Towering over northern Taipa, the Altira provides stunning sea views of the Macau Peninsula from all its suitelike rooms, each of which also comes with a dedicated lounge, walk-in wardrobe, and circular stone bath. **Pros:** eye-popping pool; open-air rooftop bar. **Cons:** may sometimes be noisy from nearby construction; still a taxi ride from the peninsula. $ *Rooms from: MOP$2,500 ⊠ Av. de Kwong Tung, Taipa ☎ 853/2886–8888 ⊕ www.altiramacau.com ⤳ 184 rooms, 24 suites, 8 villas ⦿ No meals.*

COLOANE

$$
RESORT
FAMILY
Fodor's Choice
★

Grand Coloane Beach Resort. This is where you truly get away from it all: built into the side of a cliff, every room faces the ocean, and the vast private terraces are ideal for alfresco dining and afternoon naps. **Pros:** green surroundings on Hác-Sá Beach; golf-club access; free shuttles; fun for kids. **Cons:** isolated location. $ *Rooms from: MOP$1,300 ⊠ 1918 Estrada de Hác Sá, Coloane Island South ☎ 853/2887–1111, 852/2114–4368 in Hong Kong ⊕ www.grandcoloane.com ⤳ 200 rooms, 8 suites ⦿ No meals.*

COTAI STRIP

$$$$
HOTEL

Four Seasons Hotel Macao. With five pools ringed by private cabanas, a restaurant that earned two Michelin stars, and a sensational spa offering the latest treatments, the Four Seasons Hotel Macao conscientiously upholds its brand-name reputation. **Pros:** luxury from start to finish; focus on service; extensive spa treatments. **Cons:** beside a shopping mall. $ *Rooms from: MOP$3,200 ⊠ Estrada da Baía de N. Senhora da Esperança, Cotai ☎ 853/2881–8888 ⊕ www.fourseasons.com/macau ⤳ 276 rooms, 84 suites ⦿ No meals.*

$$$
HOTEL

Grand Hyatt Macau. The Grand Hyatt Macau's two towers were inspired by waves, in keeping with the aquatic City of Dreams theme. **Pros:** stunning pool area; large spa with extensive menu. **Cons:** nearby construction; surrounding neighborhood lacks character. $ *Rooms from: MOP$2,088 ⊠ City of Dreams, Estrada do Istmo, Cotai ☎ 853/8868–1234 ⊕ www.macau.grand.hyatt.com ⤳ 791 rooms, 288 suites ⦿ No meals.*

$$$$
RESORT

Venetian Macao-Resort-Hotel. You either love it or you hate it. **Pros:** living rooms; comprehensive shopping and dining. **Cons:** pretentious decor; gambling and convention crowds; lack of intimacy outside the suite. $ *Rooms from: MOP$4,000 ⊠ Estrada de Baía de N. Senhora da Esperança, Cotai ☎ 853/2882–8888 ⊕ www.venetianmacao.com ⤳ 2,841 suites, 64 Paiza suites ⦿ No meals.*

NIGHTLIFE

Old movies, countless novels, and gossip through the years have portrayed Macau's nightlife as a combustible mix of drugs, wild gambling, violent crime, and ladies of the night. Up until the 1999 handover back to mainland China, this image of Macau was mostly accurate and did much to drive away tourists. But these days you can enjoy live music and cocktails in elegant surroundings at an ever-growing range of hotels and casinos.

DOWNTOWN MACAU

BARS

Bar Cristal. An antique French chandelier from the 19th century is the centerpiece of this opulent spot, designed to look like a life-size jewelry box. Order a cocktail or sample one of the many champagnes in stock. ⊠ *G/F, Encore at Wynn Macau, Rua Cidade de Sintra, Downtown* ☎ *853/8986–3663* ⊕ *www.wynnmacau.com.*

Fodor's Choice ★ **MacauSoul.** Housed in a bright pink building with pine-green shutters, this lively wine bar is just steps away from the Ruins of St. Paul's Cathedral. The two British expats who manage the place have assembled a wine list that includes more than 430 Portuguese varieties, and there's a fine selection of whiskeys available as well. On the food front, look for British cheese plates, charcuterie boards, and many homemade offerings (desserts among them). Live after-dinner music plays on select dates—particularly Fridays, depending on the season. It's best to call ahead for details. ⊠ *31A Rua de Sao Paulo, Travessa da Paixao, Downtown* ☎ *853/2836–5182* ⊕ *www.macausoul.com* ⊘ *Closed Tues. and Wed.*

Whisky Bar. Depending on the time of day or night, this bar on the 16th floor of the StarWorld Hotel provides either upbeat cabaret entertainment or a cool moment of respite from the clinking casinos all around. Happy hour is daily from 5 to 8, and the Star Band starts playing nightly at 10:30. In addition to a full selection of the usual hard stuff, the bar has 100 different kinds of whisky, including the ultra-rare Macallan 1946. ⊠ *StarWorld Hotel, Av. da Amizade, Downtown* ☎ *853/8290–8698* ⊕ *www.starworldmacau.com.*

MACAU OUTER HARBOUR

BARS

Macau's Lan Kwai Fong. A modest collection of bars lines a small stretch of street in NAPE, within sight of the huge golden Guan Yin statue in Macau's Outer Harbour. Although it takes its name from the legendary bar area in Hong Kong, don't expect the wild times and thumping music you might find in the original LKF. In reality, this is a bunch of quiet watering holes where you can meet with friends or watch sports on a big-screen TV. A large number of expats come to relax and drink in the evening. ⊠ *Edifício Vista Magnifica Court, Av. Dr. Sun Yat-Sen, NAPE, Outer Harbour.*

8

TAIPA

BARS

Fodor's Choice
★

38 Lounge. When you're finally done with the casinos and ready to look down on the rest of the world, hop over to Taipa and take the Altira Macau elevator straight up the to this lofty spot. Sip cocktails under the stars on the outdoor terrace, where tapas are served from 2 pm to 2 am. Indoors, a live band plays from 9 pm to 2 am most evenings. ⌧ *38th fl., Altira Macau, Av. De Kwong Tung, Taipa* ☎ *853/2886–8868* ⊕ *www. altiramacau.com* ⊗ *Closed Tues.*

LOUNGES AND PUBS

SHOWS

The House of Dancing Water. Brought to Macau by Franco Dragone, former star director of Cirque du Soleil, The House of Dancing Water aquatic show is the primo attraction at City of Dreams. This 90-minute spectacle harnesses 14 million liters (3.7 million gallons) of water—think five Olympic-sized swimming pools—to weave elaborate stunts, dives, and explosions into a love story. Tickets cost MOP$580, and it's best to book ahead. ⌧ *City of Dreams, Estrada do Istmo, Cotai* ☎ *853/8868–6767* ⊕ *www.thehouseofdancingwater.com.*

SHOPPING

Macau, like Hong Kong, is a free port for most goods, so prices for electronics, jewelry, and clothing are lower here than they are in other international cities. Yet the shopping experience is completely different in Macau than it is in Hong Kong, with a low-key atmosphere, small crowds, and compact areas. It is a hub for traditional Chinese arts, crafts, and even some antiques (but be aware that there are many high-quality reproductions in the mix, too). Macau's major shopping district is along its main street in the downtown area, Avenida Almeida Ribeiro, more commonly known by its Chinese name, **San Ma Lo**; there are also shops downtown on **Rua Dos Mercadores** and its side streets; in **Cinco de Outubro**; and on the **Rua do Campo.**

You can see craftspeople at work making the "new antiques," particularly on the side streets of Tercena and Estalagens and the alleyways in front of the Ruins of St. Paul's. Commonly sold pieces include lacquer screens, Chinese pottery, and huge wooden chests carved from solid mahogany, camphor wood, and redwood.

Major shopping areas for clothes and shoes include the small shops on **Rua do Campo** and around **Rua dos Mercadores** in the downtown area. There are also bustling street markets downtown that sell clothes on **São Domingos** (off Largo do Senado), **Rua Cinco de Outubro**, and **Rua da Palha.**

Jewelry shops across from casinos in the downtown area sell luxury watches, pendants, and rings, some of which have been pawned by desperate gamblers. Prices are generally more reasonable than in Hong Kong. For gold purchases, head to trusted Hong Kong stalwarts **Chow Tai Fook** and **Chow Sang Sang**, which have locations throughout Macau and are known for transparent pricing and knowledgeable staff with good English.

The spa at the Grand Lapa Macau scrubs and rubs customers into relaxation.

Most of Macau's shops operate year-round with a short break for Chinese New Year, and are open from 10 to 8 (later on weekends). While most accept all major credit cards, specialty discount shops usually ask for cash, and street vendors accept only cash. For most street vendors and some smaller stores, some friendly bargaining is expected; ask for the "best price," which ideally produces instant discounts of 10%–20%. The shopping mantra here is "bargain hard, bargain often."

Although Macau is well known for its casinos and restaurants, it's also rapidly gaining a reputation for luxury spa and sauna facilities that offer a huge range of treatments. Almost every posh hotel has its own spa, with special packages and incentives for hotel guests. Macau's independent spas have also become a major force, offering equally exquisite treatments at lower prices. All spas provide services for couples, giving you a great opportunity to relax in a peaceful space with someone special. Treatments begin at around MOP$350 for 60 minutes of service.

DOWNTOWN MACAU

DEPARTMENT STORE

New Yaohan. Originally a Japanese-owned department store, this failing facility was taken over by Macau entrepreneur Stanley Ho several years ago and transformed into a popular shopping destination for locals. "Macau's only department store" offers a good mix of shops selling household goods, clothing, jewelry, and beauty products. It also has an extensive food court, a well-stocked supermarket, and a large bakery. ✉ *Av. Comercial de Macau, Downtown* ☎ *853/2872–5338* ⊕ *www.newyaohan.com.*

OUTER HARBOUR

SPAS

The Spa at the Grand Lapa Macau. The largest and best-known spa in town takes advantage of the Grand Lapa's sumptuous Mediterranean architecture and lets in lots of natural sunlight for a bright and airy spa experience. On offer are numerous Chinese, European, Thai, and Japanese treatments, as well as top-notch heat and sauna facilities. A signature 2½-hour, four-part Macanese Sangría Ritual includes a full body scrub using fresh grapes, a sangria bath in a private outdoor Jacuzzi, and a grape-seed-oil massage for MOP$1,720. Reserve ahead. ⊠ *Grand Lapa, 956–1110 Av. da Amizade, Outer Harbour* ☎ *853/2856-7888* ⊕ *www. grandlapa.com/spa-wellness* ⊗ *Daily 10–10.*

TAIPA

SPAS

Nirvana Spa. In a quiet area of town, Asian-inspired Nirvana has rooms decorated in eastern themes. Therapists from Thailand and the Philippines are trained in deep-tissue, Ayurvedic, herbal, shiatsu, and aromatherapy massages. ⊠ *Third fl., Oceano Plaza, 522-526 Av. dos Jardins do Oceano, Taipa* ☎ *853/2833–1521* ⊕ *www.nirvanaspamacau.com.*

COTAI STRIP

MALLS AND SHOPPING CENTERS

Shoppes at Venetian. The Venetian Macao's vision of a gentrified megamall comes complete with cobblestone walkways, arched bridges, and working canals manned by singing gondoliers (rides are MOP$118). Its 330-plus retailers include all the big-name brands and luxury labels in fashion, accessories, gifts, services, and sporting goods. On-site you'll also find a spa, 30 restaurants, and an international food court. Don't be surprised to see wandering stilt walkers, violinists, and juggling jesters, especially around St. Mark's Square, which hosts two to three daily live performances. The mall connects with the Shoppes at Four Seasons and Shoppes at Cotai Central, further adding to the number of upscale retail options. ⊠ *The Venetian Macao, Estrada da Baía de N. Senhora da Esperança, Cotai* ☎ *853/2882–8888* ⊕ *en.cotaistrip.com/ shopping.html.*

TRAVEL SMART
HONG KONG

GETTING HERE AND AROUND

The many public transportation options in Hong Kong are generally clean, safe, and inexpensive. The first step is to get an Octopus Card from any Mass Transit Railway or Airport Express station. Usable for all public transportation options, the Octopus Card is a good alternative to buying a ticket for each train trip or digging for change on the bus. The initial cost of an Octopus Card is HK$150, and you will have HK$100 available for use right away. The remaining HK$50 is a refundable deposit that provides a buffer in case you go beyond the card's value. You can top off the card at Customer Service Centres or Add Value machines at MTR stations, or at convenience stores, supermarkets, and some fast-food chains. These retail outlets also accept the card as a mode of payment, as do many coffee chains, clothing stores, and vending machines.

When boarding a bus or entering a subway, simply look for the rectangular yellow sensor (on top of the MTR turnstiles or next to the fare box on buses and minibuses) and place the card on it until you hear a beep. The sensors are sensitive enough to scan through wallets and bags, so you don't need to take your card out. Once your card has been read, the remaining balance appears on the sensor screen.

Before you leave Hong Kong, you can cash in your Octopus Card at MTR stations. If your balance is less than HK$500, you will receive that amount plus the HK$50 deposit. There is a refund processing fee of HK$9 for cards that are returned within three months of purchase.

Information Octopus Cards ☎ 2266–2222 ⊕ www.octopus.com.hk.

▌ AIR TRAVEL

Flying time to Hong Kong is around 16 hours nonstop from New York City, 15½ hours nonstop from Los Angeles, or 14 hours nonstop from San Francisco.

Airlines and Airports Airline and Airport Links.com. Airline and Airport Links.com has links to many of the world's airlines and airports. ⊕ www.airlineandairportlinks.com.

Airline Security Issues Transportation Security Agency ⊕ www.tsa.gov/public.

AIRPORTS

Easy to navigate and full of amenities, Hong Kong International Airport (HKG)—also known as Chek Lap Kok, after its location—is a traveler's dream. Terminal 1, one of the largest in the world, handles arrivals and departures for most major airlines. The newer but smaller Terminal 2 handles all other airlines, including budget carriers.

Although the lines usually move quickly at security and immigration checkpoints, it's advisable to arrive at least two hours before departure. Remember that check-in counters are a long distance from the gates. Most major airlines let you use the In-Town Check-In service at the Hong Kong or Kowloon Airport Express stations up to 24 hours before your flight (confirm with your airline first). You can check luggage as well, saving you the bother of lugging bags out to the airport.

Once you're at the airport, there are multiple options for meals, from fast-food outlets to sit-down restaurants. Many open as early as 6 am and close as late as midnight. Beyond immigrations in Terminal 1, you'll find a few places that are open 24 hours, including Café de Coral and McDonald's in the Departures East Hall and the Starbucks at Departures Central Concourse and Departures Check-in Hall. There's also a 7-Eleven convenience store in each terminal, although the one in Terminal 1 is on Level 5 of the Arrivals Hall, making it inaccessible once you've passed through security checkpoints.

Travelex currency-exchange machines in each terminal make it easy to get rid of your leftover Hong Kong dollars. Another way is to take advantage of the wealth of duty-free shopping choices throughout the airport, especially in Terminal 1. If you'd rather relax before or after a flight, you can pay to use one of the 24-hour Plaza Premium Lounges with restrooms, showers, massage services, online access, and hot meals. Packages range from HK$200 to HK$800. Free resting lounges (without showers and other perks) and miniature gardens with comfortable seating are at the Departure Level near Gates 21, 26, 34, 41, and 61.

Most of the airport's public areas have free Wi-Fi access. Otherwise, you can use one of the 62 free computers available throughout Terminal 1 or the 24-hour Internet Zone at the North Satellite Concourse. For local calls, courtesy phones are placed at convenient locations throughout both terminals.

If you have a long layover, catch a movie at the airport's 350-seat IMAX cinema, which is the largest in Hong Kong. You can also wander through one of the frequent art exhibits that pop up throughout the airport.

When arriving in Hong Kong, you'll be asked to fill out an immigrations form. An immigrations officer will collect an arrivals slip and give you a departure slip that you must show when you leave the city. An airport tax is normally included in your ticket price. If it's not, the fee is HK$120. It's levied only on those 12 years and older and is waived for all transit and transfer passengers who arrive and leave on the same day.

Airport Information Hong Kong International Airport ☎ 2181–8888 ⊕ www.hongkongairport.com. **Plaza Premium Lounge** ☎ 2261–0888 ⊕ www.plaza-network.com.

GROUND TRANSPORTATION

The Airport Express train service is the quickest and most convenient way to and from the airport. High-speed trains whisk you to Kowloon in 21 minutes and Central in 24 minutes. Trains run daily every 10 minutes between 5:54 am and 11:28 pm and every 12 minutes between 11:28 pm and 12:58 am. The last train from the airport departs at 12:48 am. The trains have Wi-Fi access, plenty of luggage space, and comfortable seating with video screens showing tourist information and the latest news.

The Airport Express station has stops at the AsiaWorld-Expo, Tsing Yi, Kowloon, and Central stations. Excluding the Asia-World stop, all stations connect to the MTR. One-way or same-day return tickets are HK$90 to Kowloon and HK$100 to Central. Round-trip tickets valid for one month cost HK$160 to Kowloon and HK$180 to Central. Tickets are cheaper if purchased online or through a travel agent. It's the most expensive public transport option, but the speed and dependability justify the extra cost. The Airport Express Travel Pass is a good option if you are planning a very short stay, as it allows you unlimited travel on the MTR for 72 hours; the HK$220 pass includes a single airport journey, and the HK$300 pass includes an airport round-trip.

The Airport Express also provides its customers with free porter service, and free shuttle buses run every 12 or 20 minutes between major hotels and the Hong Kong and Kowloon stations—there are several routes, and a list of stops is displayed prominently at the boarding area. Service begins at 6:12 am and ends at 11:12 pm. To board, you must show your Airport Express ticket and airline ticket or boarding pass.

GROUND TRANSPORTATION TO CENTRAL		
Transport Mode	Time	Cost
Airport Express	24 mins	HK$100
Citybus Line A (Cityflyer)	50 mins	HK$40
Citybus Line E (Regular)	70 mins	HK$21
Coach	45 mins	HK$140
Limo	45 mins	HK$710
Taxi	45 mins	HK$295
Tung Chung (S1 bus) + MTR (train)	10 mins +36 mins	HK$3.50 + HK$24

Citybus runs five buses ("A" precedes the bus number) from the airport to popular destinations. They make fewer stops than regular buses (which have an "E" before their numbers). Two useful routes are the A11, serving Central, Admiralty, Wan Chai, and Causeway Bay and ending in North Point; and the A21, going to Tsim Sha Tsui, Jordan, and Mong Kok. The A11's operating hours are from 6:10 am to 12:30 am, while the A21 runs from 6 am to 12 am. Should you arrive in Hong Kong outside of these hours, you can take the N11 or the N21, which are night buses serving the same routes. The buses are comfortable, have adequate luggage space, and include free Wi-Fi access. The onboard announcements are in Cantonese, Putonghua, and English, so you won't miss your stop.

Several small shuttle buses with an "S" before their numbers run to the nearby Tung Chung MTR station, where you can get the MTR to Central and Kowloon. MTR trains run parallel to the Airport Express route, but they cost much less (HK$27.50 from the airport to Central). However, you won't have the same amenities, and travel time is longer as the trains make more stops.

Taxis from the airport are reliable and plentiful. Trips to Hong Kong Island destinations cost around HK$295, while those to Kowloon are around HK$240. There is also an HK$5 charge per piece of luggage stored in the trunk. Vigor Airport Shuttle Services runs the hotel coach service, which stops at 96 hotels on Hong Kong Island and Kowloon. The coaches depart every 30 minutes for HK$140 to destinations on Hong Kong Island, HK$130 to those in Kowloon. Vigor also offers Mercedes-Benz limousine transfers for HK$650 to HK$860, depending on the destination and type of car. Parklane Limousine and Trans-Island Limousine offer comparable rates.

GROUND TRANSPORTATION TO KOWLOON		
Transport Mode	Time	Cost
Airport Express	19 mins	HK$90
Citybus Line A (Cityflyer)	45 mins	HK$33
Citybus Line E (Regular)	60 mins	HK$14
Coach	35 mins	HK$130
Limo	35 mins	HK$650
Taxi	35 mins	HK$240
Tung Chung (S1 bus) + MTR (train)	10 mins + 38 mins	HK$3.50 + HK$18

Contacts Airport Express ☎ *2881–8888* ⊕ *www.mtr.com.hk.* **Citybus** ☎ *2873–0818* ⊕ *www.nwstbus.com.hk.* **Parklane Limousine** ☎ *2730–0662* ⊕ *www.hongkonglimo. com.* **Trans-Island Limousine Service** ☎ *3193–9332* ⊕ *www.trans-island.com.hk.* **Vigor Airport Shuttle Services** ☎ *2186–6883* ⊕ *www.vigorholding.com.*

FLIGHTS

Cathay Pacific is Hong Kong's flagship carrier. It maintains high standards, with friendly service, good food, an extensive in-flight entertainment system, and an excellent track record for safety. Cathay has nonstop flights from both Los Angeles and San Francisco on the West Coast and from New York–JFK on the East Coast, with connecting services to many other U.S. cities. Singapore Airlines is also another highly rated airline with flights to Hong Kong from multiple American cities, including daily flights from San Francisco.

If you are on a tight budget, Air China and China Airlines offer lower-cost flights between New York and Los Angeles and Hong Kong, although the savings are reflected in the service and amenities. Several other airlines also offer service from the United States to Hong Kong, usually with connections in Asia.

If you're planning to travel to three or four Asian destinations, you might want to consider One World's Visit Asia Pass, which provides travel throughout Southeast Asia via an array of airlines. Cities are grouped into zones, and there's a flat rate for each zone. The pass doesn't cover flights from the United States, Europe, or Australia and New Zealand, however. Inquire through American Airlines, Cathay Pacific, or any other One World member.

Airlines One World ⊕ *www.oneworld.com.*

∎ BOAT AND FERRY TRAVEL

With fabulous views of both sides of Victoria Harbour, the Star Ferry is so much more than just a boat. This icon has been circling the harbor since 1888. Double-bowed, green-and-white vessels connect Central and Wan Chai with Kowloon in less than 10 minutes, daily from 6:30 am to 11:30 pm. A ride on the upper deck costs HK$2.50 on weekdays and HK$3.40 on weekends and public holidays, making it the cheapest scenic harbor tour in town. You can use cash or your Octopus Card to pay the fare. The Star Ferry also offers an hour-long harbor tour for HK$85 during the day and H$160 at night.

There's also regular ferry service to outlying islands, such as Lantau, Lamma, and Cheung Chau. Ordinary ferries are cheap but slow, while fast ferries travel at twice the speed for twice the price. As a general rule, fares are more expensive at night. You can pick up printed copies of the ferry schedules at the Hong Kong Tourist Board information center at the Tsim Sha Tsui Star Ferry Concourse.

FERRY TRAVEL			
Line/ Route	Frequency	Travel Time	Fare
DBTPL Central– Discovery Bay (Lantau)	20–30 mins	25 mins	HK$40– HK$57
NWFF Central– Cheung Chau	30 mins	35–60 mins	HK$13.20– HK$37.20
NWFF Central– Mui Wo (Lantau)	40 mins	35–55 mins	HK$15.20– HK$42.90
Star Ferry Central– Tsim Sha Tsui	6–12 mins	7 mins	HK$2.50– HK$3.40
Star Ferry Wan Chai– Tsim Sha Tsui	10–14 mins	8 mins	HK$2.50– HK$3.40

Information Discovery Bay Transportation Services Limited ☎ *2238–1188* ⊕ *www. discoverybay.com.hk.* **New World First Ferry** ☎ *2131–8181* ⊕ *www.nwff.com.hk.* **Star Ferry** ☎ *2367–7065* ⊕ *www.starferry.com.hk.*

∎ BUS TRAVEL

An efficient network of double-decker buses covers most of Hong Kong, often with stops at locations not accessible via MTR. Figuring out the routes, however, may be a bit daunting for newcomers. Drivers usually don't speak English, and the routes posted at bus stops can be confusing. Your best bet is to look up your destination on the two major bus companies' websites to see whether they serve the route and which bus to take. Citybus and New World First Bus share a common website, as do Kowloon Motor Bus and Long Win Bus Company. Both sites use a map-based route search that allows you check nearby stops. Click on a bus number to pull up information on where the route originates.

More intrepid visitors can take a chance on a minibus. These cream-colored vehicles seat 16 people and rattle through the city at breakneck speeds. Routes and prices are prominently displayed in front. While faster than buses, minibuses are risky if you aren't sure of your destination. There are designated stops, but minibus drivers will also pick up and drop off passengers at other points along the way. To get off, you'll have to shout out to the driver and hold on tight as he screeches to a halt.

FARES

Double-decker bus fares range from HK$2.50 to HK$48; minibus fares from HK$2 to HK$20. The best way to pay is by Octopus Card. Otherwise, you'll need to have exact change. Some minibuses, particularly the overnight ones, accept only cash, but they do give you change.

Bus Information Citybus ☎ 2873–0818 ⊕ www.nwstbus.com.hk. **Kowloon Motor Bus** ☎ 2745–4466 ⊕ www.kmb.com.hk. **Long Win Bus Company** ☎ 2745–4466 ⊕ www.kmb. com.hk. **New World First Bus** ☎ 2136–8888 ⊕ www.nwstbus.com.hk.

▌ CAR TRAVEL

Frankly, you'd be mad to rent a car on Hong Kong Island or in Kowloon. Traffic jams, hard-to-navigate streets, and next to no parking make driving here severely stress inducing. What's more, gasoline costs up to twice what it does in the United States. So why bother, when public transportation is excellent and taxis are inexpensive?

If you must have your own wheels, consider hiring a driver. Most top-end hotels can arrange this; the Peninsula in Kowloon and the Island Shangri-La even have their own fleets of chauffeur-driven Rolls-Royces and Mercedes available for hourly hire. Avis can also provide chauffeur services along with car rentals.

If you're determined to drive yourself, your driver's license must be valid in Hong Kong for up to a year if you're 18 to 70 years old (those over 70 must pass a physical examination before driving). You'll need an International Driver's Permit (HK$80) for stays up to 12 months. Check the AAA and Hong Kong Transport Department websites for more info.

The cheapest option for car rentals is Hawk Rent-a-Car, which has lots of models and prices; there are special rates for weekends and longer-term rentals. Rental rates begin at HK$480 per day and HK$2,550 per week for an economy car with air-conditioning, automatic transmission, and unlimited mileage. Parklane Limousine has a fleet of more than 100 Mercedes-Benzes with hourly rates for chauffeur services.

Information Hawk Rent-a-Car ☎ 2516–9822 ⊕ www.hawkrentacar.com.hk.

PARKING

There's next to no on-street parking in Hong Kong, and the extremely vigilant traffic police hand out copious parking tickets. If you luck out and find a metered space, you'll have to use an Octopus Card to pay.

Most drivers take advantage of parking garages, which cost up to HK$22 per hour in prime locations. However, some mall garages will subsidize parking if you make purchases at their shops or eat in one of their restaurants. Be sure to have the receipt validated by the staff before leaving.

RULES OF THE ROAD

Driving is on the left-hand side of the road in Hong Kong. Wearing a seat belt is mandatory in the front and back of private cars, and the standard speed limit is 50 kph (30 mph) unless signs state otherwise. The police spend a lot of time setting up speed traps and giving out juicy fines. Using handheld cell phones while driving is forbidden. You can't make a right turn on a red light, and you should scrupulously obey lane markings regarding turns.

Drunk driving is taken very seriously: the legal limit is 50 mg of alcohol per 100 ml of blood (or 22 micrograms of alcohol per 100 ml of breath), and there are penalties of up to HK$25,000 and three years in prison for those who disobey. You can get highly detailed information on Hong Kong's road rules on the Transport Department's website.

Road Rules Hong Kong Government Transport Department ☎ *2804–2600* ⊕ *www.td.gov.hk.*

▮ CRUISE TRAVEL

Star Cruises has trips through Southeast Asia that start from, or call at, Hong Kong. The crème de la crème of cruisers, Cunard, docks in Hong Kong on its round-the-world trips. Princess Cruises has a wide variety of packages that call at Hong Kong and many other Asian destinations. Holland America has two-week Asian cruises as well as round-the-world options. Be sure to check out last-minute special offers from all these lines.

Cruise Lines Cunard ☎ *800/728–6273* ⊕ *www.cunard.com.* **Holland America** ☎ *877/932–4259* ⊕ *www.hollandamerica.com.* **Princess Cruises** ☎ *800/774–6237* ⊕ *www.princess.com.* **Star Cruises** ☎ *2317–7711* ⊕ *www.starcruises.com.*

▮ SUBWAY TRAVEL

By far the best way to get around Hong Kong is on the MTR. The network now provides all subway and train services in Hong Kong. The trains are among the cleanest in the world, with hardly any litter to be found. Eating or drinking on the trains or in the paid areas is prohibited, with fines of HK$2,000.

The five major lines are color-coded for convenience. The Island line (blue) runs along the north coast of Hong Kong Island; the Tsuen Wan line (red) goes from Central under the harbor to Tsim Sha Tsui, then up to the western New Territories. Mong Kok links Tsim Sha Tsui to eastern New Kowloon via the Kwun Tong line (green). Also serving this area is the Tseung Kwan O line (purple), which crosses back over the harbor to Quarry Bay and North Point. Finally, the Tung Chung line (yellow) connects Central and West Kowloon to Tung Chung on Lantau, near the airport.

The MTR is extremely safe, even late at night. Glass screens have been installed between the edges of platforms and tracks, preventing falls and other mishaps. Emergency stop buttons and help lines are easy to access and ensure instant response from the staff.

Trains run every two to eight minutes during peak times between 6 am and 1 am daily.

Entrances, platforms, and exits are clearly marked and signposted, and all MTR areas are air-conditioned. Most stations have wheelchair access, and all have convenience stores and other shops or services. All MTR stations have free Wi-Fi, and 13 provide computer terminals with free Internet access. Most stations are situated close to public restrooms, and 11 have station toilets for passenger use.

FARES AND SCHEDULES

You can buy tickets from ticket machines (using coins or notes) or from English-speaking staff behind glass-windowed Customer Service Centres. Fares range from HK$4.20 to HK$47.50, depending how far you travel. Instead of paying cash, consider a rechargeable (and refundable) Octopus Card. It saves time lining up for tickets and fussing for change, gives you a discounted fare on each trip, and can also be used for buses and other forms of transportation.

Another alternative is the Tourist Day Pass. For HK$55, this pass allows you unlimited travel on the MTR, excluding the Airport Express, for one day. However, you cannot use the pass on other public transport or to purchase items.

Information MTR ☎ *2881–8888* ⊕ *www.mtr. com.hk.*

▌ TAXI TRAVEL

Taxis are easy to find in Hong Kong, although heavy rush hour traffic in Central, Causeway Bay, and Tsim Sha Tsui means they aren't always the best option for getting around the city quickly. They're most useful other times of the day, especially after the MTR closes. Drivers usually know the terrain well, but many don't speak English; having your destination written in Chinese is a good idea.

You can hail cabs on the street, provided you're in a stopping area (i.e., not marked by double yellow lines). The white "taxi" sign is lit when the cab is available. Not all taxis will drive from Hong Kong Island to Kowloon (or vice versa). You can usually identify cross-harbor taxis by the red plastic "No Service" sign on their dashboards; you'll find cross-harbor taxi ranks at the Star Ferry terminal and elsewhere around town. It's sometimes hard to find a taxi between 3 and 4 pm, when the drivers switch shifts.

There are three types of taxi: red, green, and blue, with each color representing a geographical area. Red taxis are found throughout most of Hong Kong, and fares start at HK$22 for the first 2 km (1½ miles), then HK$1.60 for each .2 km (.1 mile) or minute of waiting time. (Fares add up fast in bumper-to-bumper traffic.) After the fare reaches HK$78, you're charged HK$1 for each .2 km or minute of waiting time. The Hong Kong

Kowloon Taxi and Lorry Owners Association and the Kowloon Taxi Owners Association operate red taxis.

There's a surcharge of HK$5 for each piece of luggage you put in the trunk. The Cross-Harbour Tunnel, Eastern Harbour Crossing, and Western Harbour Crossing all incur surcharges of the toll plus HK$10 or HK$15 return toll. The surcharge for crossing the Tsing Ma Bridge over to Lantau is HK$30. Passengers must pay the toll amount for other tunnels and roads.

In the New Territories, taxis are green; on Lantau Island they're blue. Fares are lower than in urban areas, but while red urban taxis may travel into rural zones, rural green and blue taxis can't cross into urban zones. Call the Lantau Taxi Call Station for blue taxis, and the NT Taxi-call Service Centre for green taxis.

Passengers are required by law to wear a seat belt when available. Most locals don't tip; however, if you round up the fare by a few Hong Kong dollars you're sure to earn yourself a winning smile from your underpaid and overworked driver. Taxis are usually reliable, but if you have a problem, note the taxi's registration number and the driver's name, which are usually prominently displayed on the dashboard, and call the Transport Complaints Unit. If you've left an item behind in your taxi, you can call the Road Co-op Lost and Found hotline.

In urban areas it's as easy and safe to hail a cab on the street as it is to call one. There are hundreds of taxi companies, so it's usually best to get your hotel or restaurant to call a company it works with. Note that there's a HK$5 surcharge for phone bookings.

Contacts Hong Kong Kowloon Taxi and Lorry Owners Association ☎ *2574–7311.* **Kowloon Taxi Owners Association** ☎ *2760–0411.* **Lantau Taxi Call Station** ☎ *2984–1328.* **NT Taxi-call Service Centre** ☎ *2382–0168.*

Contacts Road Co-op Lost and Found Hotline ☎ *1872–920.* **Transport Complaints Unit Hotline** ☎ *2889–9999.*

▌ TRAIN TRAVEL

The ultra-efficient MTR train network connects Kowloon to the eastern and western New Territories. Trains run every five to eight minutes, and connections to the subway are relatively quick. This is a commuter service and, like the subway, has sparkling-clean trains and stations—smoking, eating, and drinking are strictly forbidden.

The train network has three main lines. The East Rail line begins at Hung Hom, with notable stops at Mong Kok, Kowloon Tong, Sha Tin, Racecourse, Chinese University, and Tai Po on its way to Lo Wu at the mainland Chinese border. East Rail is the fastest way to get to Shenzhen—it's a 40-minute trip from Hung Hom to Lo Wu. The Hung Hom train station terminus connects via a series of walkways with East Tsim Sha Tsui; you can also transfer to the MTR at Kowloon Tong.

The short Ma On Shan Rail service starts at Tai Wai and has eight stops in the northeastern New Territories.

West Rail starts at East Tsim Sha Tsui, moves on to Tsim Sha Tsui for a possible connection to the subway, then extends westward through 10 more stops to Tuen Mun, in the New Territories. Here West Rail connects with the local Light Rail Transit, an aboveground train serving mainly residential and industrial areas in the western New Territories.

The regular fare from Central to Lo Wu is HK$47.50, while a first-class ticket will set you back HK$85. You can pay by Octopus Card or buy tickets from the Customer Service Centres or ticket machines inside MTR stations.

Trains have television screens that constantly barrage you with news and advertisements. To avoid this, avail yourself of the cars marked "Quiet."

▌ TRAM TRAVEL

PEAK TRAM

It's Hong Kong's greatest misnomer—the Peak Tram is actually a funicular railway. Since 1888 it's been rattling the 1,365 feet up the hill from Mid-Levels to the Victoria Peak tram terminus. As well as a sizable adrenaline rush due to the steepness of the ascent, on a clear day the trip offers fabulous panoramas. Most passengers board at the Lower Terminus between Garden Road and Cotton Tree Drive. (The tram has five stations.) The fare is HK$28 one way, HK$40 round-trip, and the tram runs every 10 to 15 minutes between 7 am and midnight daily. You can walk up to the Lower Terminus or take Bus 15C, which shuttles passengers from the Star Ferry.

STREET TRAMS

Old-fashioned double-decker trams have been running along the northern shore of Hong Kong Island since 1904. Most routes start in Kennedy Town or Western Market, and go eastward all the way through Central, Wan Chai, Causeway Bay, North Point, and Quarry Bay to Shau Kei Wan. A branch line turns off in Wan Chai toward Happy Valley, where horse races are held in season.

Destinations are marked on the front of each tram and route maps are displayed at the stops; you board at the back and get off at the front, paying a flat rate of HK$2.30 (by Octopus or with exact change) as you leave. Avoid trams at rush hours, which are generally weekdays from 7:30 to 9:30 am and 5 to 7:30 pm. Although trams move slowly, for short hops between Central and Western or Admiralty they can be quicker than going underground to take the MTR. A leisurely top-deck ride from Western to Causeway Bay is a great city tour. There is no air-conditioning on trams.

Tram Information Hong Kong Tramways
☎ *2548–7102* ⊕ *www.hktramways.com.* **Peak Tram** ☎ *2522–0922* ⊕ *www.thepeak.com.hk.*

ESSENTIALS

■ BUSINESS AND TRADE SERVICES

BUSINESS CENTERS

Hong Kong has many business centers located outside the major hotels, and some are considerably cheaper. You can arrange for everything from a private desk (from HK$250 per hour) to a serviced office (upward of HK$8,000). Amenities include phone-answering and forwarding services. Many centers are affiliated with accountants and lawyers who can expedite company registration. Some will even process visas and wrap gifts for you.

Harbour International Business Centre provides secretarial support and office rentals. Reservations aren't required. Jumpstart Business Centre, Regus, and the Executive Centre are international business services companies with several locations in Hong Kong. They provide similar services, along with meeting and conference facilities. You can also rent space at the American Chamber of Commerce.

For translation services, try Polyglot Translation and Venture Language Training.

Information American Chamber of Commerce ⊠ *Bank of America Tower, 12 Harcourt Rd., Room 1904, Central* ☎ *2530–6900* ⊕ *www.amcham.org.hk.* **The Executive Centre** ⊠ *Two Exchange Square, 8 Connaught Place, Levels 5, 7, and 8, Central* ☎ *2297–2297* ⊕ *www.executivecentre.com.* **Harbour International Business Centre** ⊠ *Admiralty Centre Tower One, 18 Harcourt Rd., Admiralty, Central* ☎ *3748–3748* ⊕ *www.hibc.com.* **Jumpstart Business Centre** ⊠ *Wheelock House 17/F, 20 Pedder St., Central* ☎ *2961–4888* ⊕ *www.jumpstartoffices.com.* **Polyglot Translations** ☎ *2851–7232* ⊕ *www.polyglot.hk.* **Regus** ☎ *2166–8000* ⊕ *www.regus.hk.* **Translation Business** ☎ *2893–5000* ⊕ *www.translationbusiness.com.hk.*

CONVENTION CENTER

The five-level Hong Kong Convention and Exhibition Centre is a state-of-the-art complex on the Wan Chai waterfront. The HKCEC houses six exhibition halls, two convention halls, two theaters, and 52 meeting rooms. The center is adjacent to the Convention Plaza, which includes the 825-room Renaissance Hong Kong Harbour View Hotel, the 549-room Grand Hyatt, a shopping arcade, and an underground parking garage. The Hong Kong Trade Development Council regularly uses the space for trade fairs, some of which are among Asia's largest.

Information Hong Kong Convention and Exhibition Centre ⊠ *1 Expo Dr., Wan Chai* ☎ *2582–8888* ⊕ *www.hkcec.com.hk.* **Hong Kong General Chamber of Commerce** ☎ *2529–9229* ⊕ *www.chamber.org.hk.* **Hong Kong Trade Development Council** ☎ *1830–668* ⊕ *www.hktdc.com.* **Hong Kong Trade and Industry Department** ☎ *2392–2922* ⊕ *www.tid.gov.hk.* **Hong Kong Innovation and Technology Commission** ☎ *3655–5856* ⊕ *www.itc.gov.hk.*

MESSENGERS

Most business centers offer delivery service, and you can sometimes arrange a delivery through your hotel concierge. Courier services such as City-Link International will pick up from your hotel, as will FedEx and DHL, which also have drop-off points all over Hong Kong. Price is based on weight and distance. Hong Kong Post also has a dependable and speedy courier service. You can drop off your package at a post office or at any one of the local courier post boxes in the city.

Information City-Link Express ☎ *2382–8289* ⊕ *www.citylinkexpress.com.*

▮ COMMUNICATIONS

INTERNET

Going online has never been easier in Hong Kong. Free public Wi-Fi is available at multiple locations, including public libraries, major museums, public parks, indoor markets, MTR stations, ferry terminals, and popular tourist spots. Some buses, including those to and from the airport, also provide free onboard Wi-Fi—look for the Webus sticker by the door. Many fast-food outlets, cafés, and shopping malls also offer free Wi-Fi service.

PCCW, a Hong Kong–based communications company, has more than 12,000 Wi-Fi hotspots scattered around the city, including areas near universities, convenience stores, and shopping malls. You can access these hotspots via a prepaid Discover Hong Kong Tourist Card. A five-day pass costs HK$69 and includes free local calls and other perks. The cards can be purchased at convenience stores, PCCW locations, and the Hong Kong Tourism Board's Kowloon Visitor Centre.

Internet cafés can be found tucked away in small, hard-to-find corners of Wan Chai, Mong Kok, and Tsim Sha Tsui. Public libraries and some MTR stations provide free access to computer terminals.

Contacts Hong Kong Public Libraries
☎ 2921–0208 ⊕ www.hkpl.gov.hk. **PCCW-HKT Discover Hong Kong Tourist Card**
☎ 183–3803 ⊕ www.pccw-hkt.com/en/Prepaid.

PHONES

Hong Kong was the first city in the world with a fully digitized local phone network, and the service is efficient and cheap. Even international calls are inexpensive relative to those in the United States. You can expect clear connections and helpful directory assistance. Don't hang up if you hear Cantonese when calling automated and prerecorded hotlines; English is usually the second or third language option. The country code for Hong Kong is 852; there are no local area codes.

CALLING WITHIN HONG KONG

Hong Kong phone numbers have eight digits: landline numbers usually start with a 2 or 3; cell phones with a 9, 6, or 5.

If you're old enough to talk in Hong Kong, you're old enough for a cell phone. This means public phones can be difficult to find, although you'll find a few tucked away in MTR stations. Local calls to both land and cell lines cost HK$1 per five minutes. If you're planning to call abroad from a pay phone, remember that convenience stores like 7-Eleven sell international phone cards. You may need to specify the country you're calling to get the right type of card. Some pay phones also accept credit cards.

Some hotels may charge as much as HK$5 for a local call, while a few others include them for free in your room rate. In a pinch, restaurants and shops will often let you use their phones for free.

Dial 1081 for directory assistance from English-speaking operators; 10013 for international inquiries and for assistance with direct dialing; 10010 for collect and operator-assisted calls to most countries, including the United States; and 10011 for credit-card, collect, and international conference calls.

CALLING OUTSIDE HONG KONG

International rates from Hong Kong are reasonable, even more so between 9 pm and 8 am. The international dial code is 001, followed by the country code.

The country code for the United States is 1, so you must dial 0011 before the area code and number. You can dial direct from many hotel and business centers, but always with a hefty surcharge.

MOBILE PHONES

Most GSM-compatible mobile phones work in Hong Kong. Roaming fees can be steep, however—99¢ a minute is considered reasonable—and overseas you normally pay the toll charges for incoming calls. It's almost always cheaper to send a text message than to make a call, since text messages have a very low set fee (often less than 5¢).

If you can unlock your phone, buying a SIM card locally is the cheapest and easiest way to make calls. PCCW's prepaid Discover Hong Kong Tourist Card can be found at convenience stores, PCCW outlets, and the Hong Kong Tourism Board's Kowloon Visitor Centre. A standard five-day pass costs HK$69.

Cellular Abroad rents and sells GSM phones and sells SIM cards that work in many countries. Mobal and PlanetFone rent and lease GSM phones (starting at $21) that will operate in countries around the world, though per-call rates can be expensive.

Once you're in Hong Kong, mobile phones can be rented at the airport through Handy, which charges HK$88 per day for unlimited Internet access and local calls, as well as free international calls to 17 countries.

Contacts Cellular Abroad ☎ *310/862–7100 international service line* ⊕ *www.cellularabroad.com.* **Handy Hong Kong** ☎ *8120–2233* ⊕ *www.handy.travel.* **Mobal** ☎ *888/888–9162 in U.S.* ⊕ *www.mobal.com.* **PlanetFone** ☎ *888/988–4777 in U.S.* ⊕ *www.planetfone.com.*

▮ CUSTOMS AND DUTIES

You're allowed to bring goods of a certain value back home without having to pay duty or import tax. But there's a limit on the amount of tobacco and liquor you can bring back duty-free, and some countries have separate limits for perfumes; for exact figures, check with your customs department. When you shop abroad, save all your receipts, as customs inspectors may ask to see them along with the items you purchased. If the total value of your goods is more than the duty-free limit, you'll have to pay a tax (most often a flat percentage) on the value of everything beyond that limit.

Except for the usual prohibitions against endangered species, narcotics, explosives, firearms, and ammunition, and limits on alcohol, tobacco products, and perfume, you can bring anything you want into Hong Kong, including an unlimited amount of money. Visitors may bring in, duty-free, 19 cigarettes or 1 cigar or 25 grams of tobacco, and 1 liter of alcohol.

Information in Hong Kong Hong Kong Customs and Excise Department ☎ *2545–6182 24-hour hotline* ⊕ *www.customs.gov.hk.*

U.S. Information U.S. Customs and Border Protection ☎ *877/227–5511* ⊕ *www.cbp.gov.*

▮ ELECTRICITY

The current in Hong Kong is 220 volts, 50 cycles alternating current (AC), so most American appliances can't be used without a transformer. Exceptions are most laptops and mobile phone chargers, which are dual voltage (i.e., they operate equally well on 110 and 220 volts), and thus require only an adapter. The same may be true of some hair dryers and other small appliances. Always check labels and manufacturer instructions to be sure. Don't use 110-volt outlets marked "for shavers only" for high-wattage appliances such as hair dryers.

Most plugs have three square prongs, like British plugs, but you can buy adapters in just about every supermarket and at electronics stalls in street markets. If you travel frequently, consider making a small investment in a universal adapter, which has several types of plugs in one lightweight, compact unit.

Walkabout Travel Gear has a good coverage of electricity under "adapters."

Contacts Walkabout Travel Gear ☎ *800/852–7085 in U.S.* ⊕ *www.walkabouttravelgear.com.*

LOCAL DOS AND TABOOS

CUSTOMS OF THE COUNTRY

By and large Hong Kongers are a rule-abiding bunch. Avoid jaywalking, eating on public transport, and feeding birds. Legislation has banned smoking in restaurants, most bars, workplaces, schools, and even public areas such as beaches, sport grounds, and parks. A whopping fine of HK$1,500 should deter even the most diehard smoker. Littering is also frowned upon, and it's not unusual to see police handing fines (also HK$1,500) out to litterbugs. Hong Kong is *crowded*; most people walk quite fast on the street. When on escalators, make sure you stand on the right side, leaving the left side for those who are in a hurry.

Saving face is ever important in Hong Kong. Never say anything that will make people look incompetent or bad, especially in front of superiors. However, you'll find that locals are comfortable commenting on things like weight and appearance that Westerners may balk at. Take it in stride; it's not meant maliciously. Hong Kongers like to talk about money—salaries, stocks, insurance, and real estate—so don't be surprised to be asked about these things.

Hong Kongers aren't touchy-feely. Be discreet. Stick to handshakes and low-key greetings.

DOING BUSINESS

Make appointments well in advance and be punctual. Hong Kongers have a keen sense of hierarchy in the office. Let the tea lady get the tea and coffee—that's what she's there for. If you're visiting in a group, let the senior member lead proceedings.

Suits are the norm, regardless of the outside temperature. While flashiness may suit local pop stars and teens, err on the side of discretion with your appearance when doing business. A well-fitting pair of trousers and jacket will suffice for both men and women.

When entertaining, locals may insist on paying: after a slight protest, accept, as this lets them gain face. Conversely, you can insist on paying for drinks or a meal to signal your gratitude for the hospitality you've received.

Business cards are a big deal: not having one is like not having a personality. If possible, have yours printed in English on one side and Chinese on the other. Proffer your card with both hands, and receive one in the same way, handling it with respect.

OUT ON THE TOWN

Meals are a communal event, so food in a Chinese restaurant is always shared. You usually have a small bowl or plate in which to transfer food from the center platters. Although cutlery is common in Hong Kong, chopsticks are ubiquitous. Be sure not to mistake the communal serving chopsticks (usually black or a different color) with your own.

It's fine to hold the bowl close to your mouth and shovel in the contents with your chopsticks. Slurping up soup and noodles is acceptable. Avoid leaving your chopsticks standing up in a bowl of rice—they look like the two incense sticks burned at funerals.

▌EMERGENCIES

Locals and police are usually very helpful in emergencies. Most police officers speak some English or will contact someone who does. For police, fire, and ambulance emergency services, dial 999.

There are 24-hour accident and emergency services at Caritas Medical Centre, Pamela Youde Nethersole Eastern Hospital, Prince of Wales Hospital, Queen Elizabeth Hospital, Queen Mary Hospital, Ruttonjee, and Tseung Kwan O Hospital. Nonresidents will always be treated immediately, although they are usually charged a set fee of HK$990 for each use of the public health-care system.

The following hospitals also have 24-hour pharmacies: Pamela Youde Nethersole Eastern Hospital, Prince of Wales Hospital, Queen Elizabeth Hospital, and Queen Mary Hospital. Local drugstore chains Watsons and Mannings have shops throughout the city; closing times generally vary between 7:30 pm and 10:30 pm.

Consulate U.S. Consulate General ✉ *26 Garden Rd., Central* ☎ *2523–9011* ⊕ *hongkong. usconsulate.gov.*

General Emergency Contacts Police, Fire, and Ambulance Emergency Services ☎ *999.* **Hong Kong Police Hotline** ☎ *2527–7177.*

Hospitals and Clinics Caritas Medical Centre ✉ *111 Wing Hong St., Sham Shui Po, Kowloon* ☎ *3408–7911* ⊕ *www.ha.org.hk.* **Pamela Youde Nethersole Eastern Hospital** ✉ *3 Lok Man Rd., Chai Wan* ☎ *2595–6111* ⊕ *www.ha.org.hk/pyneh.* **Prince of Wales Hospital** ✉ *30–32 Ngan Shing St., Sha Tin, New Territories* ☎ *2632–2211* ⊕ *www.ha.org. hk/pwh.* **Queen Elizabeth Hospital** ✉ *30 Gascoigne Rd., Yau Ma Tei, Kowloon* ☎ *2958–8888* ⊕ *www.ha.org.hk/qeh.* **Queen Mary Hospital** ✉ *102 Pok Fu Lam Rd., Pok Fu Lam, Western* ☎ *2255–3838* ⊕ *www3.ha.org.hk/ qmh.* **Ruttonjee Hospital** ✉ *266 Queen's Road E., Wan Chai* ☎ *2291–2000* ⊕ *www.ha.org. hk.* **Tseung Kwan O Hospital** ✉ *2 Po Ning La., Tseung Kwan O, Kowloon* ☎ *2208–0111* ⊕ *www.ha.org.hk.*

Pharmacies Mannings ☎ *2299–3381* ⊕ *www.mannings.com.hk/eng.* **Watsons** ☎ *2608–8383* ⊕ *www.watsons.com.hk.*

GOVERNMENT ADVISORIES

As different countries have different worldviews, look at travel advisories from a range of governments to get a sense of what's going on out there. Be sure to parse the language carefully. For example, a warning to "avoid all travel" carries more weight than one urging you to "avoid nonessential travel," and both are much stronger than a plea to "exercise caution." A U.S.-government travel warning is more permanent (though not necessarily more serious) than a so-called public announcement, which carries an expiration date.

The U.S. Department of State's website posts travel warnings and advisories, as well as consular information sheets issued for every country that contain general safety tips, entry requirements (though be sure to verify these with the country's embassy), and other useful details.

■**TIP**➔ Consider registering online with the State Department (https://travelregistration.state.gov), so the government will know to look for you should a crisis occur in the country you're visiting.

Contacts U.S. Department of State ☎ *888/407–4747 in U.S., 202/501–4444 from outside U.S.* ⊕ *www.travel.state.gov.*

▌HEALTH

When visiting Hong Kong, it's a good idea to be immunized against typhoid and hepatitis A and B, and in winter, a flu vaccination is also advisable, especially if you're infection-prone or are a senior citizen. Speak with your physician and check the Centers for Disease Control and Prevention (CDC) or World Health Organization (WHO) websites for health alerts, particularly if you're pregnant, traveling with children, or have a chronic illness.

Water from government mains satisfies WHO standards, but most locals don't drink water straight from the tap. Expect to pay HK$10 to HK$20 for a 1½-liter bottle of distilled or mineral water, or drink boiled tap water.

Condoms can help prevent most sexually transmitted diseases, but they aren't absolutely reliable, and their quality varies from country to country. However, most major brands, such as Durex, are easily available in Hong Kong and can be purchased at convenience stores and pharmacies.

Health Warnings Centers for Disease Control and Prevention (*CDC*). ☎ *800/232–4636 24-hour hotline in U.S.* ⊕ *www.cdc.gov/travel.* **World Health Organization** ⊕ *www.who.int.*

HONG KONG–SPECIFIC ISSUES
Avian influenza, commonly known as bird flu, is a form of influenza that affects birds (including poultry) but can be passed to humans. It causes initial flu symptoms, followed by respiratory and organ failure. Although rare, it's often lethal. The Hong Kong government now exercises strict control over poultry farms and markets, and there are signs warning against contact with birds. Pay heed to warnings, and make sure that any poultry or eggs you consume are well cooked.

Local Health Information Hong Kong Department of Health Hotline ☎ *2961–8989* ⊕ *www.dh.gov.hk.* **Hong Kong Travel Health Service** ☎ *2961–8840 on Hong Kong Island, 2150–7235 in Kowloon* ⊕ *www.travelhealth.gov.hk.*

OVER-THE-COUNTER REMEDIES
You can easily find most familiar over-the-counter medications (like aspirin and ibuprofen) in pharmacy chains like Watsons or Mannings, and usually in supermarkets and convenience stores. Acetaminophen— or Tylenol—is known as paracetamol and is sold under the brand name Panadol. Oral contraceptives are available without a prescription at pharmacies.

▮ HOURS OF OPERATION

Banks are open weekdays from 9 to 4:30 or 5 and Saturday from 9 to 1. Office hours are generally from 9 to 5 or 6, although working longer hours is common. Some offices are open from 9 to noon on Saturday. Lunch hour is usually 1 pm to 2 pm; don't be surprised if offices close during lunchtime. Museums and tourists attractions are usually open weekdays 9 to 6, a bit longer on weekends and public holidays. Most are closed one day a week, usually Monday or Tuesday. Pharmacies are generally open from 10 am until about 9 or 10 pm. Many 24-hour pharmacies are located in local hospitals.

HOLIDAYS
Public holidays in Hong Kong are: New Year's (January 1), Chinese New Year (three days in late January or early February), Ching Ming (April 4 or 5), Good Friday and Easter Monday (April), Labor Day (May 1), Buddha's Birthday (May), Dragon Boat Festival (late May or early June), Hong Kong SAR Establishment Day (July 1), Mid-Autumn Festival (late September or early October), National Day (October 1), Chung Yeung (October), and Christmas and Boxing Day (December 25 and 26).

▮ MAIL

Hong Kong's postal system is efficient and inexpensive. Airmail letters to anywhere in the world should take three to eight days. The Kowloon Central Post Office in Yau Ma Tei is open weekdays 9:30 to 6 and Saturday 9:30 to 1. The General Post Office in Central is open Monday to Saturday 8 to 6 and Sunday and holidays 9 to 5. All other post offices are open weekdays 9:30 to 5 and Saturday 9:30 to 1.

Airmail sent from Hong Kong is classified by destination into one of two zones. Zone 1 covers all of Asia except Japan. Zone 2 is everywhere else. International airmail costs HK$2.90 (Zone 1) or HK$3.70 (Zone 2) for a letter or postcard weighing 20 grams or less. To send a letter within Hong Kong, the cost is HK$1.70. The post office also has a dependable overnight international courier service called Speedpost.

Main Postal Branches Hong Kong General Post Office ⊠ *2 Connaught Rd., Central* ☎ *2921–2222* ⊕ *www.hongkongpost.hk.* **Kowloon Central Post Office** ⊠ *405 Nathan Rd., Yau Ma Tei, Kowloon* ☎ *2928–6247* ⊕ *www.hongkongpost.hk.*

SHIPPING PACKAGES

Packages sent via airmail to the United States can take up to two weeks. Airmail shipments to the United Kingdom—both packages and letters—arrive within three to five days, while mail to Australia often arrives in as little as three days.

You are probably best off shipping your own parcels instead of letting shop owners do this for you, both to save money and to ensure that you are actually shipping what you purchased and not a quick substitute—though most shop owners are honest and won't try to cheat you in this way. The workers at Hong Kong Post are extremely friendly and will sell you all the packaging equipment you need at unbelievably reasonable prices. Large international couriers in Hong Kong include DHL, Federal Express, and S.F. Express, which also has an international forwarding service.

Express Services DHL ☎ *2400–3388* ⊕ *www. dhl.com.hk.* **Federal Express** ☎ *2730–3333* ⊕ *www.fedex.com/hk_english.* **S.F. Express** ⊠ *Kowloon* ☎ *2730–0273* ⊕ *www.sf-express. com.*

∎ MONEY

Very few shops or restaurants accept U.S. dollars, so either exchange your cash or withdraw Hong Kong dollars direct from an ATM. Traveler's checks aren't accepted in most shops, and can be a pain to cash—avoid them, if possible. Getting change for large bills isn't usually a problem, although you will find that some shops will refuse to accept HK$1,000 bills for fear they might be counterfeit.

SAMPLE PRICES	
Cup of Coffee/Tea	HK$25–HK$30
Glass of Wine	HK$50–HK$80
Glass of Beer	HK$40–HK$60
Sandwich	HK$25–HK$40
Fresh Juice from a Stall	HK$20
Bowl of Noodle Soup	HK$20

▨ TIP➔ Banks never have every foreign currency on hand, and it may take as long as a week to order. If you're planning to exchange funds before leaving home, don't wait until the last minute.

ATMS AND BANKS

Your own bank will probably charge a fee for using ATMs abroad; the foreign bank you use may also charge a fee. Nevertheless, you'll usually get a better rate of exchange at an ATM than you will at a currency-exchange office or when changing money in a bank. And withdrawing funds as you need them is a safer option than carrying around a large amount of cash.

Reliable, safe ATMs are widely available throughout Hong Kong. In a pinch, MTR stations usually have at least one Hang Seng Bank ATM. If your card was issued from a bank in an English-speaking country, the instructions on the ATM machine will appear in English.

▨ TIP➔ PINs with more than four digits are not recognized at ATMs in many countries. If yours has five or more, remember to change it before you leave.

CREDIT CARDS

Major credit cards are widely accepted in Hong Kong, but be sure to ask first at small shops and restaurants. You may also get better rates paying in cash. When adding tips to restaurant bills, be sure to write "HK$" and not just "$."

It's a good idea to inform your credit-card company before you travel, especially if you're going abroad. Otherwise, the company might put a hold on your card owing to unusual activity—not a good thing at the beginning of your trip. Record all your credit-card numbers—as well as the phone numbers to call if your cards are lost or stolen—in a safe place, so you're prepared should something go wrong. Both MasterCard and Visa have general numbers you can call (collect if you're abroad) if your card is lost, but you're better off calling the number of your issuing bank, as MasterCard and Visa usually just transfer you to your bank; your bank's number is usually printed on your card.

Although it's often cheaper (and safer) to use a credit card rather than cash for large purchases you make abroad (so you can cancel payments or be reimbursed if there's a problem), note that some credit-card companies *and* the banks that issue them add substantial percentages to all foreign transactions, whether they're in a foreign currency or not. Check on these fees before leaving home, so there won't be any surprises when you get the bill. If you plan to use your credit card for cash advances, you'll need to apply for a PIN at least two weeks before your trip—but remember, most banks charge heavily for issuing cash advances.

■TIP➜ **Before you charge something, ask the merchant whether he or she plans to do a dynamic currency conversion (DCC). In such a transaction the credit-card *processor* (shop, restaurant, or hotel, not Visa or MasterCard) converts the currency and charges you in U.S. dollars. In most cases you'll pay the merchant a 3% fee for this service in addition to any credit-card company and issuing-bank foreign-transaction surcharges. Plus, the exchange rate is often less favorable than that offered by the credit-card company.**

Dynamic currency conversion programs are becoming increasingly widespread. Merchants who participate in them are supposed to ask whether you want to be charged in dollars or the local currency, but they don't always do so. And even if they do offer you a choice, they may well avoid mentioning the additional surcharges. The good news is that you *do* have a choice. You can avoid the potentially costly practice altogether thanks to American Express; with its cards, DCC simply isn't an option.

Reporting Lost Cards American Express ☎ *800/333–2639 in U.S., 715/343–7977 collect from abroad* ⊕ *www.americanexpress. com.* **Diners Club** ☎ *800/234–6377 in U.S., 2860–1888 in Hong Kong* ⊕ *www.dinersclub. com.* **MasterCard** ☎ *800/627–8372 in U.S., 636/722–7111 collect from abroad, 800/966-677 in Hong Kong* ⊕ *www.mastercard.com.* **Visa** ☎ *800/847–2911 in U.S., 800/967–025 in Hong Kong* ⊕ *www.visa.com.*

CURRENCY AND EXCHANGE

The only currency used is the Hong Kong dollar, divided into 100 cents. There are bronze-color coins for 10, 20, and 50 cents; silver-color ones for 1, 2, and 5 dollars; and chunky bimetallic 10-dollar pieces. Bills can be confusing, as there are a range of designs and issuing banks. There are new purple and a few remaining older green $HK10 bills in circulation, as well as bills for HK$20 (blue-green), HK$50 (purple), HK$100 (red), HK$500 (brown), and HK$1,000 (yellow). Don't be surprised if two bills of the same value look different: three local banks (HSBC, Standard Chartered, and Bank of China) all issue bills, and each has its own design. Although the image of Queen Elizabeth II doesn't appear on new coins, old ones bearing her image are still valid.

The Hong Kong dollar has been pegged to the U.S. dollar at an exchange rate of HK$7.8 to US$1 since 1983. You can exchange currency at the airport, in hotels, in banks, and through private money changers scattered through the tourist areas. Banks usually have the best rates, but as they charge a fee of up to HK$100 for non-account holders, it's best to change large sums. Money changers do not charge fees, and they are open at conveniently late hours, but the rate of exchange is usually less favorable than it is at banks.

▮ PACKING

Appearances in Hong Kong are important. This is a city where suits are still de rigueur for meetings and business functions, and many residents care about looking stylish. Slop around in flip-flops and baggy shorts and you *will* feel there's a neon "tourist" sign over your head. Pack your nicer pairs of jeans, slacks, or skirts, especially if you're planning on going to a nice restaurant or out on the town.

From May through September conditions are seriously hot and sticky, but air-conditioning in hotels, restaurants, museums, and movie theaters can be arctic—keep a crushproof sweater or shawl in your bag. Don't forget your swimsuit and sunscreen; many large hotels have pools, and you may want to spend some time on one of Hong Kong's many beaches. In October, November, March, and April a jacket or sweater should suffice, but from December through February bring a light overcoat, preferably waterproof. Compact folding umbrellas can come in handy to protect against either rain or sun, but hotels will also lend you larger ones for the day.

▮ PASSPORTS AND VISAS

Citizens of the United States need only a valid passport to enter Hong Kong for stays of up to three months. Your passport must be valid for at least six more months. All minors regardless of age, including newborns and infants, must also have their own passports. Upon arrival, you'll have to fill in an immigrations form. Keep the departure portion of the form safe—you'll be asked to present it again for your return trip home. If you're planning to pop over the border into mainland China, you must first get a visa, although it's not necessary for Macau.

INSPIRATION

Get in the mood for your trip with some great reads. **Epic Novels:** Timothy Mo's *An Insular Possession* and James Clavell's *Noble House.* **History 101:** *A History of Hong Kong* by Frank Welsh. **Classic Cultural Primer:** *Hong Kong* by Jan Morris. **Reminiscence:** *Gweilo* by Martin Booth.

PASSPORTS

U.S. passports are valid for 10 years for adults, five years for minors under 16. You must apply in person if you're getting a passport for the first time; if your previous passport was lost, stolen, or damaged; if your previous passport has expired and was issued more than 15 years ago; or if your previous passport was issued when you were under 16. All children under 18 must appear in person to apply for or renew a passport. Both parents must accompany any child under 16 and provide proof of their relationship to the child.

The cost to apply for a new passport is $165 for adults, $130 for children under 16; adults (over 16) may renew passports for $140. Allow four to six weeks for processing, both for first-time passports and renewals. For a fee of $60 you can reduce this time to two to three weeks. If your trip is less than two weeks away, you can get a passport even more rapidly by going to a passport office with the necessary documentation. Private expediters can get things done in as little as 24 hours, but charge hefty fees.

▮**TIP**→ Before your trip, make two copies of your passport's data page (one for someone at home and another for you to carry separately). Or scan the page and email it to someone at home and/or yourself.

U.S. Passport Information U.S. Department of State ☎ 877/487–2778 ⊕ *www.travel.state. gov.*

U.S. Passport and Visa Expediters A. Briggs Passport & Visa Expediters

☎ *800/806–0581, 202/338–0111* ⊕ *www. abriggs.com.* **American Passport Express** ☎ *800/455–5166* ⊕ *www.americanpassport. com.* **Travel Document Systems** ☎ *800/874– 5100 in Washington D.C., 877/874–5104 in New York, 888/874–5100 in San Francisco* ⊕ *www.traveldocs.com.* **Travel the World Visas** ☎ *866/886–8472* ⊕ *www.world-visa. com.*

VISAS

A visa is essentially formal permission to enter a country. Visas allow countries to keep track of you and other visitors—and generate revenue (from application fees). You *always* need a visa to enter a foreign country; however, many countries routinely issue tourist visas on arrival, particularly to U.S. citizens. When your passport is stamped or scanned in the immigration line, you're actually being issued a visa. Sometimes you have to stand in a separate line and pay a small fee to get your stamp before going through immigration, but you can still do this at the airport on arrival. Getting a visa isn't always that easy. Some countries require that you arrange for one in advance of your trip. There's usually—but not always—a fee involved, and said fee may be nominal ($10 or less) or substantial ($100 or more).

If you must apply for a visa in advance, you can usually do it in person or by mail. When you apply by mail, you send your passport to a designated consulate, where your passport will be examined and the visa issued. Expediters—usually the same ones who handle expedited passport applications—can do all the work of obtaining your visa for you; however, there's always an additional cost (often more than $50 per visa).

Most visas limit you to a single trip—basically during the actual dates of your planned vacation. Other visas allow you to visit as many times as you wish for a specific period of time. Remember that requirements change, sometimes at the drop of a hat, and the burden is on you to make sure that you have the appropriate visas. Otherwise, you'll be turned away at the airport or, worse, deported after you arrive in the country. No company or travel insurer gives refunds if your travel plans are disrupted because you didn't have the correct visa.

Travel agents in Hong Kong can issue visas to visit mainland China. If you have time, it's less hassle to let a company like China Travel Service handle this for you. It has more than 20 branches all over Hong Kong and can generally get you a visa between two to five business days starting at $60. If you prefer to apply for a China visa before leaving home, the wait time is usually four to five days and the fee is $130.

China Visa Information Chinese Consulate ☎ *212/868–2078* ⊕ *www.nyconsulate.prchina. org/eng.* **Chinese Embassy Visa Office.** ☎ *202/337–1956* ⊕ *www.china-embassy.org/ eng.*

Hong Kong General Information Hong Kong Immigration Department ☎ *2824– 6111* ⊕ *www.immd.gov.hk.*

Hong Kong Travel Agents China Travel Service ☎ *2998–7888* ⊕ *www.ctshk.com.*

▌RESTROOMS

Big shopping malls, especially high-end ones, are your best bet for clean, well-stocked restrooms. If there isn't one nearby, you will likely find public toilets near indoor markets, public parks, and MTR stations. (There's a handy guide on the MTR website.) It's best to carry bathroom tissue with you, and don't expect to find tampon or sanitary napkin dispensers in Hong Kong toilets.

▌SAFETY

Hong Kong is an incredibly safe place—day and night. The police do a good job maintaining law and order, but there are still a few pickpockets about, especially in

Tsim Sha Tsui and Mong Kok. Exercise the same caution you would in any large city: be aware of your surroundings, avoid crowded areas, and don't carry large amounts of cash or valuables with you.

Nearly all consumer dissatisfaction in Hong Kong stems from the electronics retailers in Tsim Sha Tsui. Get some reference prices online before buying, and always check the contents of boxed items before you leave the shop. Have a good idea of what you're looking for before you shop, and keep all receipts.

■ TIP➜ **Distribute your cash, credit cards, IDs, and other valuables between a deep front pocket, an inside jacket or vest pocket, and a hidden money pouch. Don't reach for the money pouch once you're in public.**

▌TAXES

Hong Kong levies a 10% service charge and a 3% government tax on hotel rooms. There's no other sales tax or V.A.T. Many restaurants also include a 10% service charge.

▌TIME

Hong Kong is 12 hours ahead of Eastern Standard Time and eight hours ahead of Greenwich Mean Time. There is no daylight savings time in Hong Kong, so remember to add an hour to the time difference between the United States or other countries that observe it.

Time Zones Timeanddate.com ⊕ *www. timeanddate.com/worldclock.*

▌TIPPING

Tipping isn't a big part of Hong Kong culture. Hotels and restaurants usually add a 10% service charge; however, in almost all cases this money does not go to the waiters and waitresses. In restaurants, add up to 10% more for good service, or simply round up the tab. In hotels, tip bellhops and other helpful staff members.

Tipping restroom attendants is common, but it is generally not the custom to tip taxi drivers.

TIPPING GUIDELINES FOR HONG KONG	
Bartender	HK$10–HK$20 per round of drinks, depending on the number of drinks
Bellhop	HK$10–HK$20 per bag, depending on the level of the hotel
Hotel Concierge	HK$20–HK$50, more if he or she performs a service for you
Hotel Doorman	HK$10 if he helps you get a cab
Hotel Maid	HK$10 a day
Restroom Attendants	HK$5
Porter at Airport or Train Station	HK$10–HK$15 per bag
Waiter	5%–10% if service was good

▌VISITOR INFORMATION

The *Standard* is a free English-language tabloid that you can pick up at MTR stations, and the *South China Morning Post* is Hong Kong's leading local English-language daily. *Time Out Hong Kong* is the local edition of the well-known city guide magazine, and the free weekly *HK Magazine* can be found all over the city.

ONLINE TRAVEL TOOLS

For a guide to what's happening in Hong Kong, check out the Hong Kong Tourist Board's excellent site. The government portal Hong Kong Leisure and Cultural Services Department is a useful resource that provides access to the websites of all of Hong Kong's museums and parks, as well as information on special events and festivals. You can also book tickets on the website.

For up-to-date weather information, check out the website maintained by Hong Kong Observatory. Centamap provides online Hong Kong street maps so detailed they give street numbers and building names.

To discover bars and restaurants, try the online guide Eat Drink Hong Kong or Open Rice, a popular site where locals rate and discuss restaurants. Both AsiaX-PAT and Geoexpat collect wisdom from Hong Kong's large expat community. Hong Kong Outdoors is the authority on hiking, camping, and all things wild in Hong Kong. Love HK Film reviews the latest Hong Kong and mainland releases.

For currency conversion, go to Google and type in the amount and currencies to be converted (e.g., "600 HKD to USD"). XE.com also provides quick and straight-forward currency conversion. Oanda.com offers comprehensive currency exchange rates and money transfers.

All About Hong Kong Centamap ⊕ *www. centamap.com.* **Hong Kong Leisure and**

Cultural Services Department ⊕ *www.lcsd. gov.hk/en/home.php.* **Hong Kong Observatory** ⊕ *www.weather.gov.hk.* **Hong Kong Tourism Board** ⊕ *www.discoverhongkong.com.*

Currency Conversion Google ⊕ *www. google.com.* **Oanda.com** ⊕ *www.oanda.com.* **XE.com** ⊕ *www.xe.com.*

Local Insight AsiaXPAT ⊠ *Central* ⊕ *www. hongkong.asiaxpat.com.* **Eat Drink Hong Kong** ⊕ *www.eatdrinkhongkong.com.* **Geoexpat** ⊕ *www.geoexpat.com.* **Hong Kong Outdoors** ⊕ *www.hkoutdoors.com.* **Love HK Film.com** ⊕ *www.lovehkfilm.com.* **Open Rice** ⊠ *Central* ⊕ *www.openrice.com/english/restaurant/index. htm.*

Publications HK Magazine ⊕ *www. hk-magazine.com.* **South China Morning Post** ⊕ *www.scmp.com.* **The Standard** ⊕ *www. thestandard.com.hk.* **Time Out Hong Kong** ⊕ *www.timeout.com.hk.*

INDEX

PHOTO CREDITS

Cover credit: Steve Hamblin/age fotostock [Description: Nathan Road]. 1, Jose Fuste Raga / age fotostock. 2, LeeYiuTung/iStockphoto. Chapter 1: Experience Hong Kong: 8-9, Walter Bibikow / age fotostock. 10, Li Wa/Shutterstock. 11 (left), Sze Kit Poon/iStockphoto. 11 (right), Khoroshunova Olga/Shutterstock. 12, Hong Kong Tourism Board. 13 (left), Ian Muttoo/Flickr. 13 (right), Ella Hanochi/iStockphoto. 16 (left), mary416/Shutterstock. 16 (top center), HU-JUN/iStockphoto. 16 (bottom center), K.C. Tang/wikipedia.org. 16 (top right), Hong Kong Tourism Board. 16 (bottom right), maveric2003/Flickr. 17 (left), karendotcom127/Flickr. 17 (top center), James Cridland/Flickr. 17 (top right), amybbb/Shutterstock. 17 (bottom right), Hong Kong Tourism Board. 18, oksana.perkins/Shutterstock. 19, Hong Kong Tourism Board. 20, John Leung/Shutterstock. 21, Hong Kong Tourism Board. 22, leungchopan/Shutterstock. 23 (left), winhorse/iStockphoto. 23 (right), Jess Yu/Shutterstock. 24, Hong Kong Tourism Board. Chapter 2: Central Hong Kong and Kowloon: 25, Hemis / Alamy. 26, Laoshi/iStockphoto. 29, Hong Kong Tourism Board. 31, Hong Kong Tourism Board. 33, Hong Kong Tourism Board. 36, Dallas & John Heaton / age fotostock. 39, Hemis / Alamy. 41, MAISANT Ludovic / age fotostock. 42, Hippo Studio/iStockphoto. 45, claudio zaccherini/Shutterstock. 47, Gavin Hellier / age fotostock. 49, LungSanLau/wikipedia.org. 50, James Montgomery / age fotostock. 53, Hong Kong Tourism Board. 54, Ian Muttoo/Flickr. 59, cozyta/Shutterstock. 60, Iain Masterton / Alamy. Chapter 3: Day Trips: 61, Pat Behnke / Alamy. 62, Hong Kong Tourism Board. 65, Let Ideas Compete/Flickr. 66, David Ewing / age fotostock. 67, Oksana Perkins/iStockphoto. 68, Hong Kong Tourism Board. 71, AngMoKio/wikipedia.org. 72, Hong Kong Heritage Museum. 73, wikipedia.org. 75, Ella Hanochi/iStockphoto. 76, Doug Houghton / Alamy. 79, Ian Trower / age fotostock. Chapter 4: Shopping: 81, Ian Cumming / age fotostock. 82, Grotto Fine Art. 89, Amanda Hall / age fotostock. 93, VH / age fotostock. 95, Doco Dalfiano/age fotostock. 104, Sylvain Grandadam / age fotostock. 122, Hong Kong Tourism Board. 125, Gavin Hellier / age fotostock. 128, Douglas LeMoine/Flickr. 133, Jochen Tack / age fotostock. Chapter 5: Where to Eat: 135, Hong Kong Tourism Board. 136, The Pawn. 141, JTB Photo / Alamy. 146, Hong Kong Tourism Board. 159, Florian/Flickr. 166, BrokenSphere/wikipedia.org. 175, InterContinental Hong Kong. Chapter 6: Where to Stay: 189, Worldhotels. 190, flowerego/Flickr. Chapter 7: Nightlife: 209, Mrallen I Dreamstime.com. 210, Hong Kong Tourism Board. 215, Fumio Okada / age fotostock. 224, K. Koroda / age fotostock. Chapter 8: Side Trip to Macau: 227, Steve Vidler / age fotostock. 228 (top), Lance Lee I AsiaPhoto.com/iStockphoto. 228 (bottom), Cloodlebing and Great Kindness/Flickr. 229 (top), Roger Price/Flickr. 229 (bottom), Lauri Silvennoinen/wikipedia.org. 230, leungchopan/Shutterstock. 242, Tito Wong/Shutterstock. 248 and 250, Christian Goupi / age fotostock. 252, dadokit, INC. 259, dbimages / Alamy. 265, George Apostolidis. Back cover (from left to right): Roger Price/Flickr [Attribution License]; estherpoon / Shutterstock; Hong Kong Tourism Board. Spine: sutsaiy/Shutterstock.

About Our Writers: All photos are courtesy of the writers.

NOTES

NOTES

NOTES

NOTES

NOTES

NOTES

NOTES

ABOUT OUR WRITERS

 Charley Lanyon is an American journalist based in Hong Kong. He reports on anything and everything from current events to nightlife, but has a special fondness for food, especially Chinese. His work has appeared in *Fodor's*, the *South China Morning Post*, *Vice*, and the *Washington Post*. When not writing he eats geese and dances on boats.

 Maloy Luakian moved to Hong Kong after watching *Chungking Express* in 1999 and, aside from a few years in Italy, has lived there ever since. She has written travel articles for both print and online newspapers and magazines, focusing mostly on food, subculture, architecture, and alternative activities for travelers, such as ghost hunting in Manila or visiting abandoned parks and cities in China.

Dorothy So studied in Los Angeles where she developed a passion for exploring different food cultures. Honing in on her interest in food, she moved back to her home city of Hong Kong in 2009 to work as a dining journalist. Her writing has appeared in many publications, including *HK* magazine, *Time Out*, and the *South China Morning Post*. Dorothy updated the Where to Eat chapter of this edition of *Fodor's Hong Kong*.

 Kate Springer is an American journalist based in Hong Kong. As the features editor at weekly lifestyle publication *HK Magazine*, she focuses on travel, dining, and cultural reporting. Her freelance work has appeared in *Fodor's*, *Time*, and *Forbes Travel Guide*. When she's not ambling around Asia, you'll find her teaching English, dabbling in photography, and devouring dumplings. Kate updated the Where to Stay, Shopping, Exploring, and Side Trip to Macau chapters of *Fodor's Hong Kong*.